Brief Contents

Contents

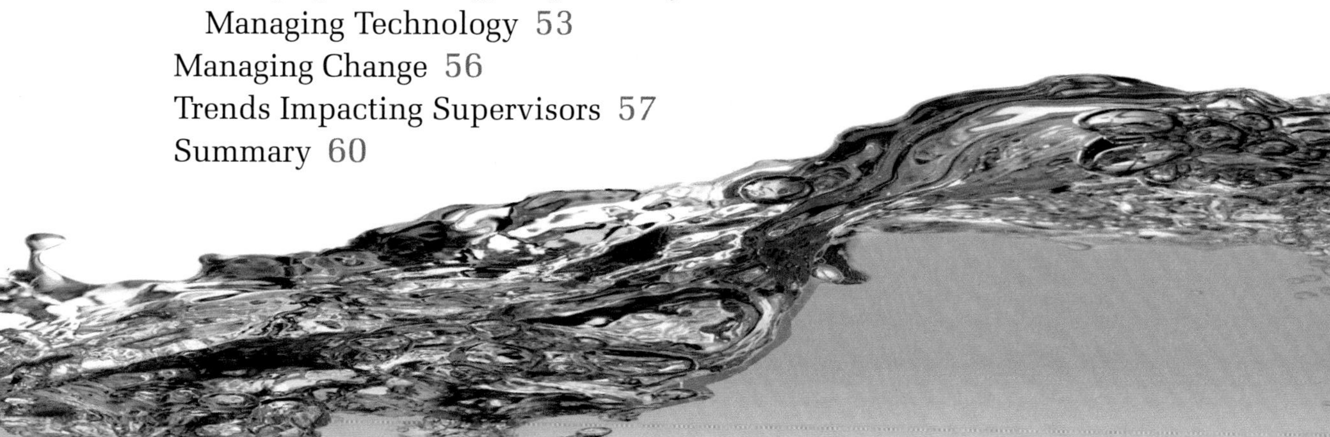

© iStockphoto.com/artJazz

> "Using [an interview] as an example was a great way to begin the chapter. I also like that you referred to [the interviewee] again in the chapter."
>
> – Kathleen Locke
> *Spartanburg Community College*

Straight Talk From the Field

Vickie Sokol Evans is CEO and president of The Red Cape Company, a technology and productivity training company. She is a Microsoft Certified Trainer and launched her technology career in the early 1990s, when colleagues came to her for help on databases and other software applications.

Printed by permission from Vickie Sokol Evans

Photo courtesy V. Evans

What is your greatest training challenge?

Time. It is becoming increasingly challenging for business users to get away from their desk or the office to attend training.

When I first began teaching desktop technology classes in 1997, they were full-day sessions. Employees would leave work for an entire day for technology training. That's nearly impossible for business users to do today. Yet, the pace at which technology changes has increased.

Time away from a busy manager's desk means lost revenue opportunities. The assistant to the executive who supports the revenue-generating employee, and who might even support multiple managers, also finds it challenging to get away for training. Time away from the desk means lower productivity for the organization.

One of the many solutions to meet the challenge is by teaching smaller, bite-sized topics that are relevant to the audience. However, motivating employees to take the time to attend the smaller classes is still difficult.

This is why a half-hour tips and tricks session or webinar is effective for bringing many employees through the learning funnel. Business users can immediately see the time-saving tricks, one after the other, in a room filled with their peers. The session also identifies training needs.

How do you handle new-hire training?

To shorten the learning curve, training new employees has to be a process rather than a one-time experience. Additionally, training must include subject matter that experts within the organization have identified as crucial for new hires to know the first day, week, month, or three months of their employment. Training is best when it is phased in over time as opposed to overwhelming new employees with a flood of new information.

On the first day, only teach what is critical to know that day to get started, and then follow up when it is appropriate to do so.

How do you handle the rollout of new technology?

Organizations vary on how they deploy a new version of software, such as Microsoft Office. Some organizations do so with virtually no training. Others might develop a training process. In my experience, the ideal rollout would be a phased approached which is recommended by Microsoft.

1. The first phase begins with an affinity or awareness campaign with brief introductions to what's new and to get employees excited about what is coming. Some enterprise companies offer a home-use program, giving employees an incentive to purchase the new software to use at home so they can get comfortable with it before they use it at work.

158

Straight Talk From the Field
Offers real-world insights from "guest speakers" who provide candid personal examples from their own supervisory experience

They Said It Best
Provides students with inspiring and informative quotes from highly respected contemporary and historical figures

Emotional intelligence seems to be largely learned, and it continues to develop as we go through life and learn from our experiences—our competence in it can keep growing.

—Daniel Goleman

Source: Goleman, *Working with Emotional Intelligence*, 7.

LEVERAGING TECHNOLOGY

LARGE-GROUP COMMUNICATION

Most leaders believe face-to-face communication and interaction is the most effective way to communicate important information to the entire organization. In small businesses, leaders often have that luxury. In large enterprises that are geographically dispersed, it may not be possible. Today's technology provides a workable alternative.

Assume you are a manager in a company that has ten offices with 250 employees in the United States, Canada, and South America. Your team has developed a new product, and the CEO has asked you to participate in an announcement about the product to the entire company. Your team includes a representative from each office. It is not feasible to bring in all the employees for a live presentation.

The first step in using technology effectively is to determine the barriers to communication enabled by technology:

- *One-way versus two-way communication*. Will information be provided without feedback, or will employees be able to comment and ask questions?
- *Time and language differences*. Can all employees be reached at the same time during the workday, and can they all speak English?
- *Individual or group reception*. Will employees listen to the announcement streamed on their own computers or in groups in the various office locations?

In this scenario, overcoming the barriers is much easier with one-way communication than with two-way communication. One effective method is video. Another is a presentation in the main office with a live audience, streamed to all computers via a webinar or webcast with slides in the appropriate language. A follow-up discussion period with local leaders in the remote offices would allow for feedback.

Leveraging Technology
Introduces emerging and useful technologies that will help students succeed

Applying Your Skills for Success

Questions for Reflection
Bring topics from the chapter up for discussion and review

Questions for Reflection

1. Which path to management would you be most likely to pursue? Would you prefer a small or large organization, and why?
2. Will you be qualified for any of the three levels of management when you graduate?
   a. Which one? If none, go to item c.
   b. What skills do you currently have to be successful in this role?
   c. What skills do you need to develop to be successful for the level you identified in item a or for first-line management if you are not qualified for any level now?
3. How can technology enable you to be more productive and effective in the job you aspire to obtain?
   a. What areas of technology do you think present major challenges for managers?
   b. Provide five tips you would offer to help managers leverage technology.
4. Why is a personal plan for development of soft skills important for you?
   a. What five skills would you include in your plan?
   b. Why did you select these five skills?
5. Identify and describe five skills or attributes you possess that would make you an effective team member.
6. Do you belong to a professional organization?
   a. If so, what value does it provide?
   b. If not, identify a professional organization you think would be of value to you.
   c. Explain why you selected this organization.

"These activities are appropriate and practical. They involve analysis and critical thinking of the concepts learned in the chapter."
– Ed Thompson
Jefferson Community College

Hands-On Activities

Form a Team

1. Form a diverse team of three or four people. No leader will be appointed. You will work with teams throughout this textbook. If you are taking the course online, you will be working with virtual teams (all members will be online).
2. Communicate with your team members about completing this exercise. Use whatever communication options are available to you—face-to-face, email, telephone, Skype, etc.
   a. Get acquainted with your team members.
   b. Get organized. Discuss how the team will operate and prepare a project plan including tasks with due dates. See Chapter 5 to learn about teamwork.

Interview Managers

1. Select three managers from any business to interview (one by each team member): a first-line manager, a middle manager, and an executive or senior manager. If the team has four members, include a nonmanagerial employee. The interviewees may be from the same company or different companies. Try to select local companies so interviews can be face-to-face.
2. Determine who will conduct each interview.
3. Prepare for the interview. Begin with the sample questions on page 19. Brainstorm with your teammates to develop additional questions and to make modifications to those provided.

Hands-On Activities
Bring concepts to life and give students the opportunity to practice what they've learned

You Decide | Case Study

Responsible Blogging and Social Networking for Work

Mimi is the supervisor for a local electronics store that also sells and installs home theaters. The store has a loyal following and an excellent reputation. The business recently expanded, which required hiring three new people.

Eldrick, one of the new employees, has outstanding skills and expertise with all the store's products. He is also a regular Internet user, blogger, and social networker. Eldrick is very enthusiastic about his new job. In fact, he placed a lengthy posting on his social networking page describing the store, his coworkers, and a few of

the store know whom he was talking about. One of his comments describes his boss as "really nice and pretty hot." Mimi learned about the posting from a customer.

Questions

1. If you were Mimi, how would you handle this situation?
2. What are the potential consequences if Mimi ignores Eldrick's actions?
3. How can Mimi take advantage of Eldrick's interest in Internet resources to benefit the store?
4. Does Eldrick's blog pose any security risk

End-of-Chapter Applications
Provide critical thinking and analysis of management concepts

MANAGER'S TOOLKIT

As manager of a real estate company, you want to make your company as efficient and effective as you can. You have decided to use a systems management approach. You have three work groups within your organization: a sales group responsible for soliciting real estate listings and selling real estate; a property management group responsible for managing rental properties for clients, including collecting deposits and rent and handling maintenance; and an administrative and accounting group responsible for daily and financial operations.

The sales and property management groups operate fairly independently of each other. However, both groups interact extensively with the administrative and accounting group.

Diagram or describe how an open systems management process would work for the sales and property management groups. Be sure to include feedback from sellers and buyers in the sales group and from clients and renters in the property management group.

Soft Skills for Success

Work Ethic

Many employers specify on job descriptions that a strong work ethic is a required quality for applicants. A good way to analyze your own work ethic is to list characteristics a good work ethic requires and barriers to a good work ethic. Next, rate yourself, being very objective and honest on both the positives and the negatives. Then develop a plan with the goal of improving your work ethic.

Work Ethic Attributes	Work Ethic Barriers
• Good work habits • Self-motivation and initiative • Commitment to get the job done • Self-discipline • Willpower • High energy • Willingness to do your share plus a little more	• Procrastination • Lack of sleep • Lack of focus • Distractions such as Internet surfing, texting, and attention to personal activities • Lack of persistence • Not managing time effectively and not working smart

Put It to Work

1. Rate yourself on each attribute on a scale of 1 to 10 with 10 being *outstanding* and 1 being *very poor.*
   ___ Good work habits
   ___ Self-motivation and initiative
   ___ Commitment to get the job done
   ___ Self-discipline
   ___ Willpower
   ___ High energy
   ___ Willingness to do your share plus a little more
2. Rate yourself on each barrier on a scale of 1 to 10 with 1 being *a major problem* and 10 being *does not apply to me.*
   ___ Procrastination
   ___ Lack of sleep
   ___ Lack of focus
   ___ Distractions
   ___ Lack of persistence
   ___ Not managing time effectively and not working smart
3. Select the two attributes and the two barriers with the lowest scores.
4. Find at least two credible articles on the Internet on how to develop the two attributes selected and two on how to prevent or remove the two barriers selected.
5. Use the information to develop a written professional development plan on how to improve your work ethic. List the articles you used with appropriate citations.

Soft Skills for Success
Emphasize the most critical abilities in business today, such as work ethic, decision making, responsibility, and self-management.

VALUE ADDED RESOURCES

Make the grade with CourseMate! This interactive website helps you make the most of your study time by providing everything you need to succeed online in one convenient place. CourseMate for ***Administrative Management*** provides an interactive eBook that allows you to take notes, highlight, bookmark, and search the text and reference in-context glossary definitions. Numerous interactive learning tools such as quizzes, flashcards, videos, and more help you master the concepts.

Administrative Management offers plentiful resources with tools and activities to enhance learning.

Instructor Resources available on the instructor's companion site or Instructor's Resource CD offer complete and customizable content, including the Instructor's Manual and PowerPoint® presentations.

Cengage Learning Testing Powered by Cognero is a flexible, online system that allows you to:

- author, edit, and manage test bank content from multiple Cengage Learning solutions
- create multiple test versions in an instant
- deliver tests from your LMS, your classroom or wherever you want

Student Resources only available at CengageBrain.com

On CengageBrain.com students will be able to save up to 60% on their course materials through our full spectrum of options. Students will have the option to rent their textbooks, purchase print textbooks, e-textbooks, or individual e-chapters and audio books all for substantial savings over average retail prices. CengageBrain .com also includes access to Cengage Learning's broad range of homework and study tools, and features a selection of free content.

CourseMate **Engaging. Trackable. Affordable.**

REVIEWERS

Edward Kufuor
ASA College
Brooklyn, New York

Kathleen E. Locke
Spartanburg Community College
Spartanburg, South Carolina

Ivan Lowe
York Technical College
Rock Hill, South Carolina

Anne M. Matthew
Valencia College
Orlando, Florida

Sandra Metcalf
Grayson County College
Denison, Texas

Tatyana Pashnyak
Bainbridge College
Bainbridge, Georgia

Cynthia N. Robertson
Remington College
Shreveport, Louisiana

Dr. Michelle Taylor
East Mississippi Community College
Scooba, Mississippi

Edwin G. Thompson
Jefferson Community College
Watertown, New York

CHAPTER 1

Management Career Paths

Learning Outcomes

1. Explain why you should study management regardless of your career goals.
2. Discuss two common paths to a management position.
3. Identify the three broad categories of management skills common to virtually all management positions.
4. Explain the importance of each category for each managerial level.
5. Identify and describe the four Cs required for success at every organizational level.
6. List and describe at least three ways to develop conceptual skills.

Straight Talk From the Field

Cathy B. Novinger is president and chief executive officer of Novinger QTR, Inc., a consulting company in Columbia, South Carolina. She was formerly a senior vice president at SCANA, a *Fortune* 500 public utility company also located in Columbia.

Photo courtesy of Hart Photography

Tell us about your career path.

SCANA provided me with an exciting and challenging career path that began with a file clerk position and culminated in a group executive senior vice president position. As executive senior vice president, I oversaw human resources, safety, procurement, strategic planning, governmental affairs, economic development, and a variety of administrative functions. My career path was a series of moves to stenographer, to several levels of secretarial positions, to administrative assistant, to assistant to the president, to vice president of human resources, to my final position as senior executive vice president.

What are the most important steps an employee can take to be successful at any company?

As I moved up the organization hierarchy, two things occurred to me. The first was that you need to understand the culture and what is most important to the company. The culture of every company is different—the culture of MTV or Disney is very different from the culture of a bank. Make sure you have the skills to do the job effectively and then focus on fitting in with the culture—be able to communicate appropriately, look the part, and act the part. In my first job, the company was most concerned about increasing productivity. At SCANA, quality was far more important than quantity. In other companies, the bottom line may be most important.

The second thing that occurred to me was that people who moved up in the organization were the ones who focused on excelling in their present job—no matter what the level of the job was—rather than those who focused on trying to get ahead. When I was vice president of human resources, I always compared the personnel records of the person who got the job with those who did not. Invariably, those who complained about not getting the job had average performance or did not have a good performance record in their current job.

How can students prepare for success in the job market?

In my human resources position, we participated in a survey of *Fortune* 500 companies that dealt with factors that were most important in hiring new employees. The results made a lasting impression on me. The first thing recruiters did was to ensure that potential employees had the knowledge and technical skills required to do the job effectively. Then 60 percent of the time and effort was focused on the way they communicated, and 40 percent was spent on trying to determine how the employee would fit in with others who had similar jobs and with the total company. Much was based on how they looked, how they presented themselves, and how they would represent the company.

As vice president of human resources, did you develop any insights into the types of skills needed for advancement?

Often I noted that both men and women who were hard-charging, aggressive, and focused and who performed very well at the upper ranks of middle management had a very difficult time moving to the executive level. Women often blamed the lack of progress on the "glass ceiling," which I did not believe existed. What I observed was that the things that made them successful in getting to their current position were actually detrimental in getting to the executive level. They could not make the transition from letting go of the technical skills that made them successful and focusing on the conceptual skills that are critical at the top level. At the top level, your success comes through the success of those who report to you. You have to move from doing to focusing on the big-picture conceptual skills of putting everything together for the success of the whole organization.

> The things that made them successful in getting to their current position were detrimental in getting to the executive level.

What advice would you share with young people about being successful in supervisory positions?

- Build trust with your colleagues.
- Never take credit for the work of your subordinates; recognize them for what they do.
- Focus on excelling in the job you have, not on the job you want.
- If you disagree with the team or department, state your position carefully and explain. However, if the decision made by the team differs from your position, support the decision.
- Recognize that you may not like some people in your work group; however, you have to learn how to work effectively with them.
- Know how to use your staff effectively; learn how to delegate.
- Assure your own security; do not depend on the company to do it for you. Keep your skills up-to-date, and prepare for your own health care, retirement, and other benefits that many companies are no longer providing.
- Recognize when you need assistants and use them effectively.

Visit *www.cengagebrain.com* to read the complete profile.

Chapter Outline

Why should you study **management**? Your current career goal may or may not be to obtain a managerial position. Regardless of the position you obtain, you will likely report to a manager and work with one or more managers. The more you know about management, the more effective you can be in working with managers and meeting their expectations as well as satisfying your own career ambitions. Another important reason for studying management is that much of what you will learn is transferable to any position. In this text, you will acquire the basic knowledge and skills needed to be an effective entry-level manager (or employee). Equally important, you will learn how to package your strengths and demonstrate to employers that you can meet and exceed their job requirements.

If your initial or near-future career goal is to obtain a management position, you will obviously need to study management in more depth than this initial course. Many options are available for additional management study while in college or after securing a position.

Paths to a Management Career

Most employees enter the workforce in a nonmanagerial position and remain in nonmanagerial positions. For those wanting to become managers, several different paths to achieve their goals are available. These employees normally fit in two groups: those who aspire to managerial careers directly from an educational institution and those who are employed in nonmanagerial positions and seek to move into management.

Education

Community colleges offering associate degrees, four-year colleges offering baccalaureate degrees, and universities with graduate programs generally offer programs designed to prepare students for management careers. Many programs are tailored for specific areas, such as sales, professional office, hospitality, and medical office management. Many excellent management programs are located in business administration departments at colleges or universities. However, employers frequently seek employees who major in areas outside business, such as arts and science, believing these areas may place more emphasis on critical thinking, decision making, communication, creativity, and innovation rather than primarily on business skills.

One of the challenges in obtaining a management position directly from an educational program is that most positions require relevant work experience. The experience full-time students have ranges from none, to part-time experience in either a related area or a non-related area, to full-time experience in either a related area or a non-related area prior to entering the education program.

management
the process of leading and working with people to accomplish organizational goals and objectives using available resources efficiently and effectively

Most management positions require relevant work experience.

Often, students are more likely to be hired and placed in management development programs offered by the employer rather than being placed directly into a management position. These programs vary in length and type, with successful completion generally resulting in placement in a regular management position.

Nonmanagerial Positions

The most frequently used path to a management position begins with employment in a nonmanagerial position. Employees with outstanding job performance records who have demonstrated the ability to work effectively with other employees are the most likely to be moved into supervisory, team leader, and other **first-line management** positions.

Size, Type of Organization, and Industry

Paths to management positions vary widely depending on the size and type of **organization** and the industry or field. Generally, small organizations employ individuals with a broad range of knowledge and skills who can perform a variety of roles. For example, an office manager for a small real estate, insurance, or retail company may be expected to handle a wide range of responsibilities such as scheduling employees, organizing tasks and projects, handling employee benefits, managing customer service, coordinating training, maintaining company records, managing internal meetings and meetings with clients and customers, preparing proposals, and managing accounts.

In contrast, large organizations are far more likely to employ individuals with specific knowledge and skills for a particular department or area. In a large insurance, real estate, or retail company, the responsibilities and duties listed above might be handled by separate departments or divisions. For example, employee benefits would likely be managed in a department within human resources.

Many of these responsibilities may also be performed by individuals who are not managers. Employees can develop excellent management skills while employed in a wide variety of positions.

first-line management
the operational team that manages day-to-day operations and ensures goals and objectives are achieved

organization
any type of business (small, large, entrepreneurial, or professional), nonprofit entity, or governmental office

Skills Required for Success

The specific package of knowledge and skills required to be a successful manager (or employee) varies from one organization or level of management to another. However, in virtually all organizations, a core of common knowledge and skills exists. These common elements are often grouped into three broad categories: technical skills, soft skills, and conceptual skills. The concept of the three basic types of skills was developed by Robert Katz in 1955[1] and has been updated over the years.

Technical Skills

Technical skills are the knowledge, expertise, and ability required to do the job. The terms *hard skills* and *tangible skills* are sometimes used to describe technical skills. An easy way to think of technical skills is to ask yourself two basic questions about the various tasks you would have to do in your job:

- What information do I need to know?
- What things must I be able to do in order to perform this task accurately and efficiently?

Your answer may include, among many other things, basic knowledge, an understanding of policies and procedures, the tools or software needed to do the job, and the ability to use them. Basically, technical skills enable you to perform the various tasks required in your job effectively and efficiently using the resources available to you.

Soft Skills

Soft skills are often referred to as 21st Century Skills,[2] human skills, personal attributes, and interpersonal skills, although technical differences exist among these terms. Soft skills relate to how you interact and work with others. Soft skills frequently listed as job requirements are communication skills, critical thinking, **work ethic**, integrity and honesty, teamwork and collaboration skills, problem-solving skills, creativity, trust, and multicultural skills.

technical skills
the knowledge, expertise, and ability required to do the job

soft skills
skills that relate to how you interact and work with others

work ethic
the willingness and ability to get things done effectively and efficiently

conceptual skills
the ability to view the organization as a whole and to understand the relationships among its components

executives
the senior leadership team that takes the lead in casting the organization's vision and strategic mission

Conceptual Skills

Conceptual skills are the ability to view isolated or abstract ideas as they relate to the whole organization. They are often described as the ability to see the big picture. From an organizational perspective, conceptual skills require **executives** to have the vision to design and implement plans, systems, and programs that impact the entire organization. From your own career perspective, you can think of conceptual skills as the ability to understand how your job fits into the overall business strategy of the organization.

Managerial Skills Development

As you think about the three types of skills just described, you can see that some are required more than others at different levels of management.

TECHNOLOGY TIPS

LEVERAGING TECHNOLOGY

The following list provides a quick overview of some of the challenges and opportunities managers face as they try to embrace, manage, and leverage technology for the benefit of the entire organization. They will be covered in more depth in later chapters.

- Having access to technology does not ensure it will be used effectively.
- The technology you use today will be outdated quickly.
- Learning how to learn new technology is an important skill for all employees to master.
- Training is an important part of the investment in technology.
- Abuse or misuse of technology can create tremendous problems for employees and their organizations.
- Privacy and security are key issues that require constant attention.
- Information obtained from the Internet may or may not be reliable or valid.
- The use of technology does not eliminate the need for or negate the effectiveness of face-to-face contact.
- You should not post anything on social media that you would not want your manager or subordinates to see.
- Language used in email and text messages, which frequently includes abbreviations and symbols, often has to be translated to be acceptable for business purposes.

Figure 1.1 illustrates a typical way of viewing the hierarchy or levels of employees and their responsibilities in an organization. Later chapters focus on the responsibilities of managers at the various levels in more depth. Keep in mind that every organization is different; therefore, you can expect to discover many variations of this pyramid.

Notice in Figure 1.1 that the top levels have fewer people than the lower levels. The **middle management** level is "flattened," or not as tall as the two levels below it. This flattening represents the current trend toward reducing the numbers of middle managers while empowering and expecting greater leadership from first-line managers (often team leaders) and those actually doing the job.

middle management
the management team that translates strategies into operational plans and oversees first-line management

Small, entrepreneurial businesses tend to have much flatter organizations than large enterprises. They often have positions that do not require substantial experience.

FIGURE 1.1
General organizational structure

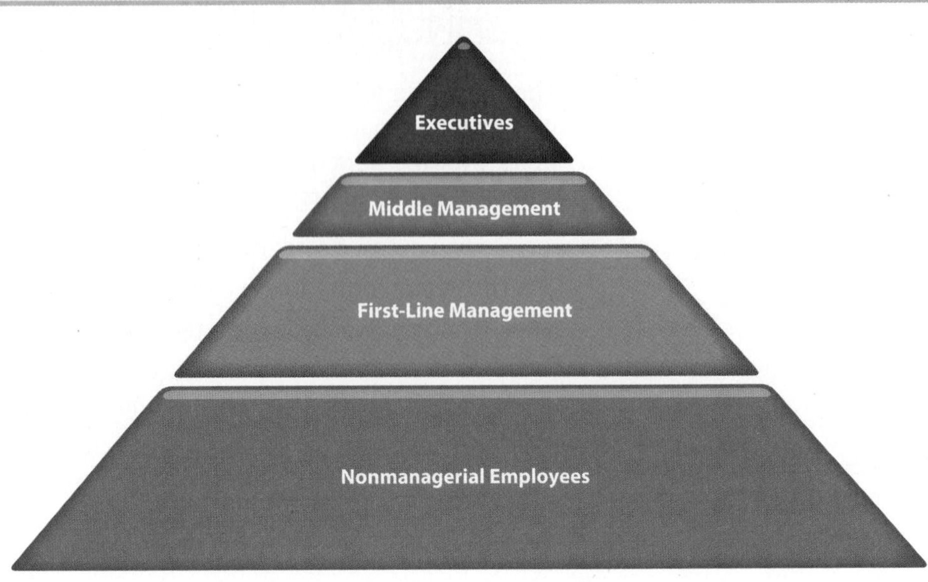

Figure 1.2 illustrates the kinds of skills most needed at each managerial level. All employees need technical skills, soft skills, and conceptual skills, but the level and depth of skill development needed is different at each level. As you can see, substantially more technical skills are required for nonmanagerial employees and first-line managers, and substantially fewer technical skills are required for middle managers and executives. On the other hand, conceptual skills are highly important for senior managers and less important for first-line and middle managers. Soft skills are not shown because they are required at every level.

FIGURE 1.2
Skills required by organization level

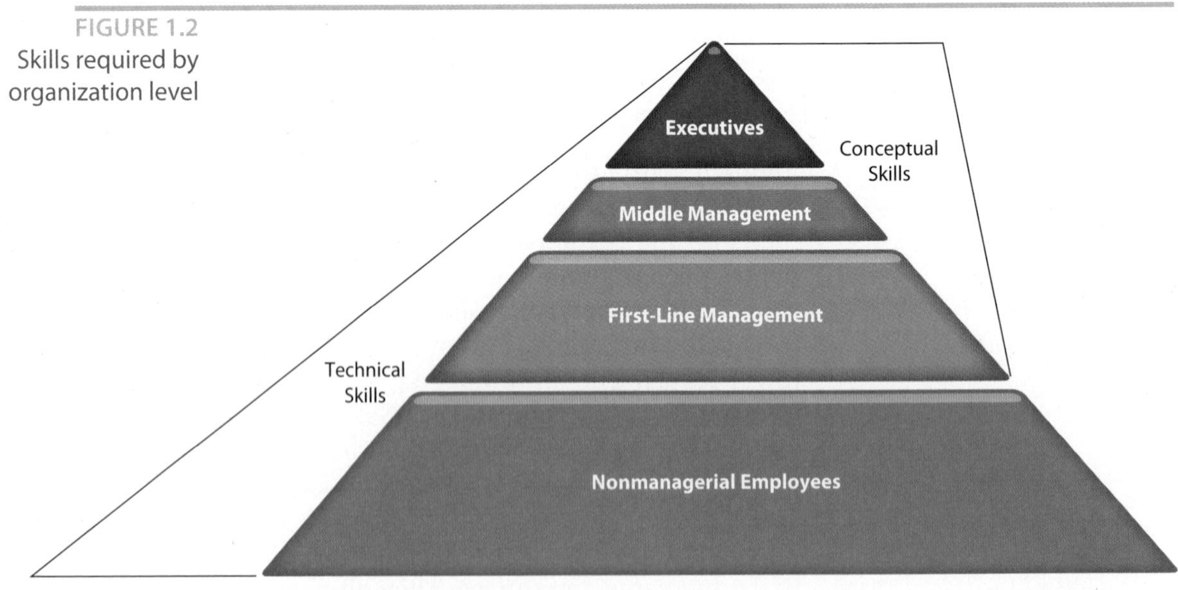

As you think about your career, remember that you will need to develop conceptual skills for advancement. Conceptual skills replace technical skills as one moves up in the organization.

1. Why are first-line managers important to organizations and their management structure?

   ____

2. Why do so many organizations make soft skills a high priority in their job descriptions when they are recruiting and training new employees?

   ____

Technical Skills Development

Much of the technical skills training required for management is accomplished in a classroom setting, generally at technical colleges, community colleges, four-year colleges, and universities. Specialized courses and training programs are also offered by private consultants and vendors. Internships and apprenticeships provide excellent alternatives for developing skills. In addition, many companies provide on-the-job training and specialized skill training programs. Computer and software skills are among the most requested technical skills for virtually all types of positions.

Soft Skills Development

Soft skills are not as easy to identify and develop as technical skills. Figure 1.3 lists important soft skills for managers that appear in many job

FIGURE 1.3
Soft skills for managers

Adaptability/flexibility	Honesty/integrity	Problem solving/decision making
Analytical skills	Influencing skills	Responsibility
Communication—speaking, writing, listening	Interpersonal/people skills	Self-management/ self-motivation
Conflict management/ negotiation skills	Leadership/"followership"	Teamwork/collaboration
Creativity/innovation	Multicultural skills	Trust/respect
Critical thinking	Personal effectiveness	Visualization/futuristic thinking
Emotional intelligence	Positive attitude	Work ethic/high energy

descriptions and articles regarding management skills. Many of these skills are covered extensively in this textbook.

Generally, soft skills are up to you to develop. School, work, and personal activities provide opportunities for practicing these skills. Once you have identified the soft skills you need to improve, begin observing how others apply these skills. You can learn from their experience. Instructors and trainers often videotape situations in which you have to apply the skills and then critique yourself. They also have students or employees critique each other and provide feedback.

An emphasis on soft skills is not new; employers have requested soft skills for many years. Beginning in the early 1990s, three significant reports were published identifying skills needed for success in the workforce at all levels. All three reports provide instructive insights about the importance of soft skills.

SCANS

In 1991, the U.S. Department of Labor released a major report documenting skills required for success in the workplace. It was produced by the Secretary's Commission on Achieving Necessary Skills (SCANS), a group of government, business, and educational representatives. SCANS was based on a year-long survey of public and private employers, union officials, and employees. The report placed the skills in two categories: competencies and foundation skills that underlie them.[3] Figure 1.4 lists and describes the SCANS skills.

FIGURE 1.4
SCANS competency and foundation skills

Competencies

Effective workers can productively use:

- **Resources**—allocating time, money, materials, space, and staff
- **Interpersonal skills**—working on teams, teaching others, serving customers, leading, negotiating, and working well with people from culturally diverse backgrounds
- **Information**—acquiring and evaluating data, organizing and maintaining files, interpreting and communicating, and using computers to process information
- **Systems**—understanding systems, monitoring and correcting performance, and designing or improving systems
- **Technology**—selecting equipment and tools, applying technology to specific tasks, and maintaining and troubleshooting technologies

FIGURE 1.4
SCANS competency and foundation skills (Continued)

Foundation

Competence requires:

- **Basic skills**—reading, writing, arithmetic and mathematics, speaking, and listening
- **Thinking skills**—thinking creatively, making decisions, solving problems, seeing things in the mind's eye, knowing how to learn, and reasoning
- **Personal qualities**—individual responsibility, self-esteem, sociability, self-management, and integrity

Source: Adapted from "What Work Requires of Schools: A SCANS Report for America 2000" (1991), iii.

Partnership for 21st Century Skills

In 2009, the Partnership for 21st Century Skills published a framework defining skills needed for success in the workforce. Partnership members include education groups, professional organizations, publishers, *Fortune* 500 corporations, and other public and private organizations. Figure 1.5 lists these skills.

FIGURE 1.5
21st Century Skills

Learning and Innovation Skills

- Creativity and innovation
- Critical thinking and problem solving
- Communication and collaboration

Information, Media, and Technology Skills

- Information literacy
- Media literacy
- ICT (information, communications, and technology) literacy

Life and Career Skills

- Flexibility and adaptability
- Initiative and self-direction
- Social and cross-cultural skills
- Productivity and accountability
- Leadership and responsibility

Source: "Framework for 21st Century Learning," Partnership for 21st Century Skills, March 2011, http://www.p21.org/storage/documents/1.__p21_framework_2-pager.pdf.

AMA 2010 Critical Skills Survey

In 2010, the American Management Association (AMA) surveyed 2,115 of its member and customer managers and executives about the importance of the three Rs and the four Cs in their organizations. Responses indicated that the three Rs—reading, writing, and arithmetic—are necessary but insufficient by themselves. The four Cs are required at every level in the organization, and more than 75 percent of those surveyed said they would be even more important in the next three to five years.[4]

Four Cs

The four Cs are required at every level in the organization.

- Critical thinking and problem solving
- Communication
- Collaboration
- Creativity and innovation

Figure 1.6 shows the percentage of organizations whose executives said they assess both their current employees and job applicants for the four Cs.

FIGURE 1.6
Organizations that assess employees and applicants' skills

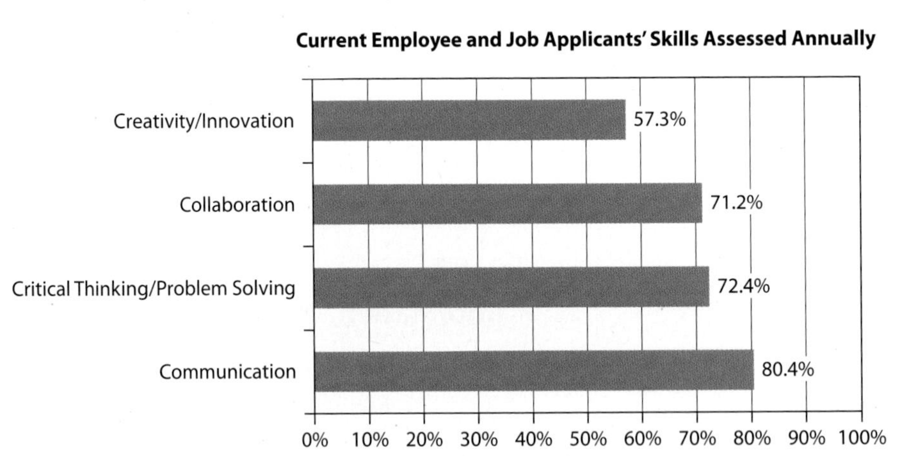

Source: Data from "AMA 2010 Critical Skills Survey."

Executives were also asked to rate their current employees on the four Cs. Figure 1.7 on page 13 shows their ratings.

FIGURE 1.7
Employee ratings on the four Cs

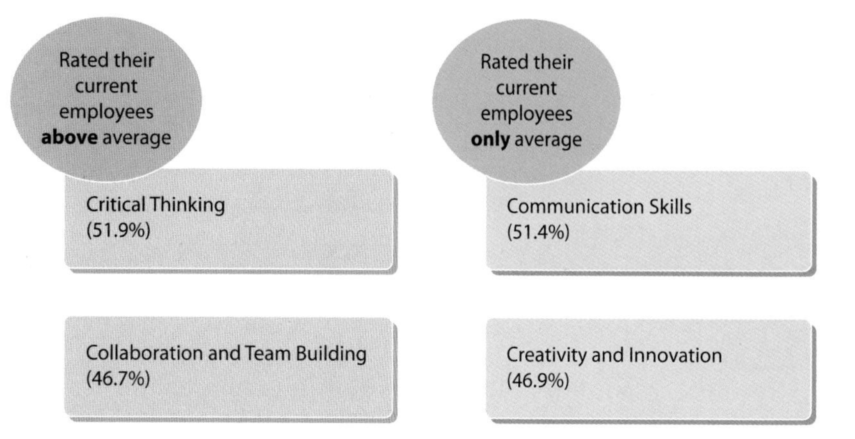

Source: Data from "AMA 2010 Critical Skills Survey."

Finally, executives were asked why these skills have taken on critical importance in the business environment. They provided the following reasons:

- The pace of change in business today (91 percent)
- Global competitiveness (86.5 percent)
- How work is accomplished today (77.5 percent)
- How organizations are structured (66.3 percent)

As you compare the results from the three major reports, note that the soft skills they cite are

- very consistent, even though the time frames and originators of the reports vary;
- appropriate for all levels in the organizational structure; and
- required for both team members and team leaders to be successful.

The skills identified in these reports provide an excellent blueprint for management development programs and for your own personal development plan.

Executives said these skills and competencies have been articulated within their organizations as priorities for employee development, talent management, and succession planning.

—AMA 2010 Critical Skills Survey

Conceptual Skills Development

The first step to developing conceptual skills is to learn as much as you can about your organization. Beyond this initial step, many organizations offer their employees conceptual skill development programs, sometimes as part of a skills or career development program. These programs typically focus on two areas:

- Executives work with, coach, and mentor managers or selected employees who have the potential to move up in the organization.
- Managers or selected employees with potential are placed in programs in which they are assigned to work in the various departments and divisions of the organization on a rotating basis. This gives trainees a closer look at the operations of each area, while enabling them to establish valuable contacts with managers in each area.

Many additional opportunities exist in organizations to develop conceptual skills. Employees in certain positions can also take advantage of their situation to learn these skills.

Executive and Administrative Assistants

As top-level administrative and executive assistants gain experience within either a large or a small company, they have a unique opportunity to develop excellent conceptual skills. They typically work closely with executives and have almost unlimited opportunities to observe how the executives handle a variety of situations, often in many different areas of the organization. They also make contacts with managers throughout the organization, and they gain an understanding of the basic operation of most areas within the organization. In addition, executive and administrative assistants are privy to information the average employee cannot access.

The conceptual knowledge and skills executive and administrative assistants gain are transferable to many different departments and organizations. In small businesses, executive and administrative assistants frequently assume responsibilities often considered senior management responsibilities.

Cross-functional teams offer excellent opportunities to develop conceptual skills.

Team Leaders and Members

As you will learn in Chapter 5, organizations place a great deal of emphasis on developing high-performance teams. Many of these teams are very diverse and are cross-functional—that is, the team members represent different levels and specialties within the organization, such as finance, legal, senior management, marketing, production, and human resources. For team leaders and members, exposure both to different areas of the organization and to the employees representing them provides excellent opportunities to develop conceptual skills.

Small Business Opportunities

Many young people find greater opportunities to move into responsible management positions in small businesses than in large businesses. Small businesses normally cannot afford the luxury of layers of management, nor can they afford highly specialized employees. Job responsibilities are much broader, giving the individual an opportunity to view how the entire organization functions. A person with excellent organizational skills often is the logical choice to manage the small business office. The same is true of a person with excellent sales skills; he or she is very likely to manage the sales and marketing area of the company.

1. List the ten soft skills you think are most important.

   ____

2. Select the three soft skills from your list that you think are your weakest. What could you do to improve those skills?

   ____

Management Development Alternatives

As mentioned earlier, many companies provide management development programs for qualified employees. The programs may be developed and presented internally, or the organization may hire consultants or other vendors to conduct company-specific programs.

Numerous external programs are also available. Many business schools offer management and executive development programs for experienced managers. They tend to spread the content over a period of weeks, months, or even a year. The programs are usually expensive, but the participant's employer typically pays all costs. A host of commercial groups also provides management development programs.

An alternative that should always be considered is to create your own professional development plan. Professional development is important to all employees, regardless of whether their career goal is to become managers or simply to continue to grow in their chosen profession. Belonging to a professional organization and reading the literature related to your areas of specialization are excellent ways to develop your skills and enhance your value to the organization. You may be surprised at how self-fulfilling professional development can be.

Professional Organizations

In many cases, industry groups and professional organizations associated with specific industries provide management development or leadership programs. Professional associations typically provide a wide range of information including best practices (discussed in Chapter 2), job and career information, salary information, educational programs, and articles about the industry. They also provide great networking opportunities.

The following list provides examples of professional organizations for administrative management. Your college may also have professional organizations or chapters of national organizations in areas that might interest you.

- American Association of Dental Office Managers
- American Bankers Association
- American Management Association
- ARMA International (association for records and information managers)
- Association of Executive and Administrative Professionals
- Association of Professional Office Managers
- Hospitality Sales and Marketing Association International
- International Association of Administrative Professionals
- The Law Office Management Association
- Medical Group Management Association
- National Association of Legal Assistants
- National Office Managers Association of America
- Physician Office Managers Association of America
- Professional Association of Health Care Office Management
- Sales & Marketing Executives International

Professional Literature

One way to keep up with trends and best practices in your area of specialization is to read the relevant literature. The Internet contains a vast amount of information that will help you grow and develop. Always remember to ensure the source is reliable. Check to see who is providing the information and what credentials the provider possesses. Also check to see if reference information is supplied and if the provider is affiliated with respected professional groups.

Think of professional development as an investment in yourself; it may be one of the very best investments you will ever make. You can have a greater impact on your future success than anyone else. Your own development is too important to entrust to anyone else.

1. Investigate and determine if your college has an organization that is related to the area you are studying or to your career goals. If not, locate a professional organization on the Internet that is closely related to your career goals. What is the name of the organization?

   ____

2. What would be the advantages of belonging to this organization?

   ____

SUMMARY

1. Studying management is beneficial regardless of whether you plan to be a manager because everyone needs to know how organizations operate.
2. Paths to management include moving from an educational institution directly into management or being promoted from a nonmanagerial position.
3. A successful manager needs technical, soft, and conceptual skills.
4. Technical skills are most important at the first-line level of management. Soft skills are needed at every level. Conceptual skills are essential at the senior or executive level.
5. The AMA Critical Skills Survey considers reading, writing, and arithmetic essential entry-level skills. The four Cs—critical thinking and problem solving, communication, collaboration, and creativity and innovation—are required at every level.
6. Technical skills are generally developed in an educational environment. Many soft skills are up to the individual to develop. Conceptual skills are generally developed by mentoring from senior management or in management development programs.
7. Professional development, including participating in professional associations and reading professional literature, is an excellent way to develop managerial skills.

Terms

conceptual skills, 6
executives, 6
first-line management, 5
management, 4
middle management, 7
organization, 5
soft skills, 6
technical skills, 6
work ethic, 6

Located at www.cengagebrain.com

- Chapter Outlines
- Flashcards
- Interactive Quizzes
- Tech Tools
- Video Segments

and More!

Questions for Reflection

1. Which path to management would you be most likely to pursue? Would you prefer a small or large organization, and why?
2. Will you be qualified for any of the three levels of management when you graduate?
   a. Which one? If none, go to item c.
   b. What skills do you currently have to be successful in this role?
   c. What skills do you need to develop to be successful for the level you identified in item a or for first-line management if you are not qualified for any level now?
3. How can technology enable you to be more productive and effective in the job you aspire to obtain?
   a. What areas of technology do you think present major challenges for managers?
   b. Provide five tips you would offer to help managers leverage technology.
4. Why is a personal plan for development of soft skills important for you?
   a. What five skills would you include in your plan?
   b. Why did you select these five skills?
5. Identify and describe five skills or attributes you possess that would make you an effective team member.
6. Do you belong to a professional organization?
   a. If so, what value does it provide?
   b. If not, identify a professional organization you think would be of value to you.
   c. Explain why you selected this organization.

Hands-On Activities

Form a Team

1. Form a diverse team of three or four people. No leader will be appointed. You will work with teams throughout this textbook. If you are taking the course online, you will be working with virtual teams (all members will be online).
2. Communicate with your team members about completing this exercise. Use whatever communication options are available to you—face-to-face, email, telephone, Skype, etc.
   a. Get acquainted with your team members.
   b. Get organized. Discuss how the team will operate and prepare a project plan including tasks with due dates. See Chapter 5 to learn about teamwork.

Interview Managers

1. Select three managers from any business to interview (one by each team member): a first-line manager, a middle manager, and an executive or senior manager. If the team has four members, include a nonmanagerial employee. The interviewees may be from the same company or different companies. Try to select local companies so interviews can be face-to-face.
2. Determine who will conduct each interview.
3. Prepare for the interview. Begin with the sample questions on page 19. Brainstorm with your teammates to develop additional questions and to make modifications to those provided.

4. Conduct the interviews. Make sure you get the contact name, title, company name, telephone number, email address, and mailing address of each interviewee.
5. Remember to send a follow-up thank-you note to each interviewee.

Prepare and Deliver a Presentation

1. Develop a 15- to 20-minute presentation using presentation software or another delivery format such as video. All members of the team must participate in preparing the presentation.
   a. The team should agree on the design and content of the presentation. Use a consistent style for all slides.
   b. Use the sample presentation guide below; modify it as appropriate for the presentation.
2. Deliver the presentation; all team members must participate. If technology for online students is not available for delivering the presentation, prepare extensive notes that could be used for delivering it. Use the notes feature of the software.

Sample Questions

1. Describe the nature of the business and why you chose this company.
2. What background and skills are required to do your job?
3. Describe a typical workday.
4. What are the main challenges in your job?
5. Do you use teams to accomplish work? If yes, how frequently are teams used? Describe why you use teams and how they are organized.
6. To move up in your organization, what additional skills would you have to develop?
7. How does your job differ from that of the person to whom you report?
8. What are the strengths of your manager?
9. What would you do differently if you were in that role?
10. What advice would you give to someone preparing for a career in management?
11. May I have your permission to take your picture for inclusion in our class presentation?

Sample Presentation Guide

1. Introduce the team members. Prepare a slide for each member with information about the member and a picture if available.
2. Describe the company and each person interviewed, with a picture of each if available. The team member who interviewed the individual should prepare and deliver all slides pertaining to that interview.
3. Use several slides to summarize the information each manager or employee provided.
4. Conclude the description of each interview by stating the most important points you learned from it.
5. End the presentation by describing the experience of working as a team to complete this project.
6. Conduct a question-and-answer session.

Assess Your Career Progress

1. Think about the courses you have taken that have helped you develop the technical, conceptual, and soft skills needed to meet your career objectives. List three

major skills in each category that you believe you will need to develop at a higher level to be successful in meeting your career objectives.

2. Review the description of the remaining courses for the completion of your academic program. Determine which courses will help you develop the nine skills listed in step 1. Note on your list the course that will help develop each skill.
3. Check to see if each of the nine skills has a course listed next to it. If any skills do not have a corresponding course to help you, prepare your own professional development plan by listing ways you can go about improving these skills.

You Decide | Case Study

Overcoming Lack of Relevant Work Experience

Matt, a recent graduate, is extremely frustrated, having been turned down on numerous job applications for a first-line managerial position because he "did not have relevant work experience." He was an outstanding student and has only applied for positions for which he met all requirements except the one for work experience.

The only experience listed on Matt's résumé is *part-time bartender.* He chose a bartending job at an upscale restaurant near campus because the schedule allowed him to be a full-time student and his earnings were better than he could get in any other job. For the past year, Matt was the head bartender, worked five nights a week, and had total responsibility for managing the bar, the other bartenders (hiring, scheduling, etc.), and all beverage services for the restaurant and bar, including preparing the bar for opening and closing.

Questions

1. What responsibilities did Matt have at his bartending job that are similar to those of any first-line manager?
2. What soft skills did Matt have the opportunity to develop while working as head bartender?
3. What general responsibilities are likely to be required for a position as a first-line manager in any company?
4. What skills did Matt develop in fulfilling his responsibilities as lead bartender that are transferable to other management positions? Explain.
5. What soft skills did Matt develop in dealing with clients, customers, and employees that are transferable to other positions? Explain.
6. How can Matt present his bartending experience to demonstrate that he has developed many managerial skills that can be transferred to a variety of management positions?

MANAGER'S TOOLKIT

A small insurance company with approximately 50 employees wants to hire an office manager. Technical insurance knowledge is not required. The company is looking for someone with good organizational skills, managerial and supervisory skills, the ability to manage budgets and schedules, the ability to coordinate meetings, and excellent communication, interpersonal, and computer skills. Work experience is preferred.

1. Analyze your knowledge and skills to determine if you have the qualifications to apply for this position.
   a. List your technical skills that are strengths and the ones you need to develop.
   b. List your soft skills that are strengths and the ones you need to develop.
   c. List your conceptual skills that are strengths and the ones you need to develop.
2. Analyze your work experience, if you have any. If not, consider your volunteer work.
   a. List the skills you developed through your work experience that are transferable to this position.
   b. What alternative experiences (internships, projects, service learning, simulations, or team experiences) can you cite that helped you develop workforce skills?
3. Are you qualified for this position?
4. If you have a year left prior to graduation, what steps can you take that will improve your qualifications for this position or a similar one?

Soft Skills for Success

Work Ethic

Many employers specify on job descriptions that a strong work ethic is a required quality for applicants. A good way to analyze your own work ethic is to list characteristics a good work ethic requires and barriers to a good work ethic. Next, rate yourself, being very objective and honest on both the positives and the negatives. Then develop a plan with the goal of improving your work ethic.

Work Ethic Attributes	Work Ethic Barriers
• Good work habits • Self-motivation and initiative • Commitment to get the job done • Self-discipline • Willpower • High energy • Willingness to do your share plus a little more	• Procrastination • Lack of sleep • Lack of focus • Distractions such as Internet surfing, texting, and attention to personal activities • Lack of persistence • Not managing time effectively and not working smart

Put It to Work

1. Rate yourself on each attribute on a scale of 1 to 10 with 10 being *outstanding* and 1 being *very poor*.

   ____ Good work habits
   ____ Self-motivation and initiative
   ____ Commitment to get the job done
   ____ Self-discipline
   ____ Willpower
   ____ High energy
   ____ Willingness to do your share plus a little more

2. Rate yourself on each barrier on a scale of 1 to 10 with 1 being *a major problem* and 10 being *does not apply to me*.

   ____ Procrastination
   ____ Lack of sleep
   ____ Lack of focus
   ____ Distractions
   ____ Lack of persistence
   ____ Not managing time effectively and not working smart

3. Select the two attributes and the two barriers with the lowest scores.

4. Find at least two credible articles on the Internet on how to develop the two attributes selected and two on how to prevent or remove the two barriers selected.

5. Use the information to develop a written professional development plan on how to improve your work ethic. List the articles you used with appropriate citations.

CHAPTER
2

Basic Management—Functions, Theories, and Best Practices

Learning Outcomes

1. List and describe the four functions of management.
2. Explain the key elements and significance of three historical management theories.
3. Analyze and determine which of Fayol's principles of management are appropriate in today's environment.
4. Describe two categories of contemporary management theories.
5. Define best practices and explain why managers should keep abreast of them.

Straight Talk From the Field

Thomas E. Suggs is president and CEO of Keenan Suggs Insurance Company in Columbia, South Carolina. Prior to that, he worked as a bank executive. A former University of South Carolina quarterback, Suggs also serves as a broadcaster for the South Carolina Gamecocks football team.

Printed by permission from Thomas E. Suggs

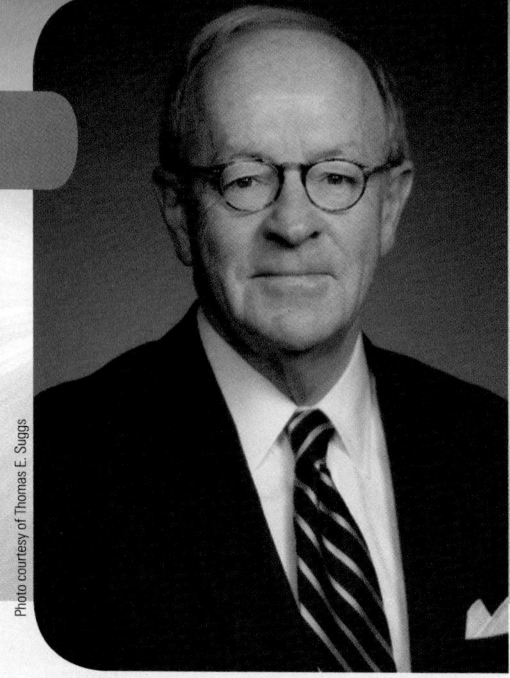

Photo courtesy of Thomas E. Suggs

How has your company enabled you to be successful in establishing strategic partnerships with clients?

Our first steps (when starting the company) were to set up an offsite strategic planning session devoted to establishing the vision, mission, and key values we wanted to build the company upon. Then we involved all seven employees and gave them a form to be returned to us a couple of days later requesting suggestions that would become actions and later commitments of the company. The suggestions were focused on increasing growth and improving service quality, productivity, operational efficiencies, and the work environment for our employees. The owners/managers then took the suggestions, put them into categories, and set priorities. We accepted every suggestion because we wanted every employee to buy into what we were doing and take some responsibility for the things we were trying to accomplish.

How did your initial steps impact your company on a long-term basis?

Our company was established with good strategic planning and strong employee engagement; the rest is history. We continue to do strategic planning every year and still involve all employees in the process. We want every employee to feel a part of the company and to have an opportunity to provide input into ways to improve the company. Management takes the input provided during the planning session, reviews it carefully, assigns priorities, and establishes a task force to work on the suggestions and provide feedback to the employees. The process takes a lot of time and involves a number of meetings, but effective face-to-face communication is a critical part of the success that results from the process.

Your company has been recognized several times as a best place to work and for your use of best practices. To what do you attribute this recognition?

Our philosophy is to hire the best people we can get, bring them into our culture, and create a work environment that makes our organization a desirable place to work. We believe the environment is critical in team building. We want the workplace to be light, airy, friendly, and viewed by all employees as a comfortable, productive place to work with each other.

Our primary focus is on revenue growth—obtained by retaining our current clients and attracting new clients. What we make our employees understand is that when revenue is increased, we have both the flexibility and capability of enhancing their positions. We promote internally, and additional growth provides new opportunities for employees. We have created a culture that includes paying employees a little more than the market, but we also expect a little more. We treat them fairly and hold them accountable for reaching goals. Our focus is on team building, quality service for clients, accountability, and motivating with appropriate incentives for all employees. The result is that we have very little turnover, and normally that results from terminating a few individuals who cannot meet our standards and goals.

How do you measure and improve employee engagement?

We use the Gallup Q[12®] survey that measures employee engagement and best predicts employee and workgroup performance. An employee committee handles the survey each year and provides us with results and suggestions for improvement. We review the results with employees and take action. For example, one question on the survey was "I have a best friend at work." To correct the problem that the item was addressing, we set up a company-paid dinner without any managers present once every quarter for any employee who wants to attend. Employees select the date and place. It has provided an excellent way to get to know and develop friendships and relationships with other employees.

We believe that employee engagement with accountability is one of the reasons that we have been named several times as one of the best places to work in South Carolina. Employees are the ones who participate in these surveys, and they would not rate us well if they did not believe we were a great place to work. The best practices recognition comes from objective company data that are provided to a firm that manages these awards in our industry. It is a way of benchmarking that stems from producing outstanding results.

> We believe employee engagement with accountability is one of the reasons we have been named several times as one of the best places to work in South Carolina.

Another thing that is important to our company and our employees is that our mission statement includes giving back to our community. Our employees work together on a number of projects to benefit the community, such as the Harvest Hope Food Bank.

Visit *www.cengagebrain.com* to read the complete profile.

Chapter Outline

Chapter 1 focused on the skills required to be a successful manager. This chapter focuses on the process of management, which is critical to organizational success, rather than on the managers themselves. We present a brief overview of basic functions of management and explore several alternative theories of management. You will note as you review the theories how they have changed over time. Most organizations today apply a practical combination of lessons from the past in the form of best practices to ensure continuous improvement. In the chapter opening interview, Thomas Suggs provides insight into how he manages his company for continuous improvement and the emphasis he places on the vitally important element of employee engagement.

Functions of Management

The functional approach to management was developed in the early 1900s by Henri Fayol, an engineer and manager of a French mining company.[1] You will learn more about his work in the "Historical Management Theories" section of the chapter. Fayol's basic functions are still relevant today, but current literature describes them using slightly different terminology and condenses his five functions into four categories: planning, organizing, leading, and controlling.

The functional view of management has been popular for nearly a century because it divides the management process into distinct activities and duties that can be taught and learned. **Management functions** are general administrative duties that need to be carried out in virtually all productive organizations.

management functions
general administrative duties that need to be carried out in virtually all productive organizations

planning
determining the mission and goals of an organization and specifying what it will take to achieve those goals

organizing
creating the structure of an organization

organization chart
a diagram of an organization's official positions and formal lines of authority

vertical hierarchy
chain of command

Planning

Planning is the process of determining the mission and goals of an organization and specifying what it will take to achieve those goals. Chapter 6 discusses in depth the processes of planning and achieving results. Note the weight Thomas Suggs gives to planning and establishing the organization's vision, values, mission, and goals.

Organizing

Organizing is the process of creating the structure of an organization. An organization chart is typically used to depict the structure. An **organization chart** is a diagram of an organization's official positions and formal lines of authority. Organization charts are common in both profit and nonprofit organizations.

Every organization has two dimensions, one representing vertical hierarchy and one representing horizontal specialization. **Vertical hierarchy** establishes the chain of command, or who reports to whom.

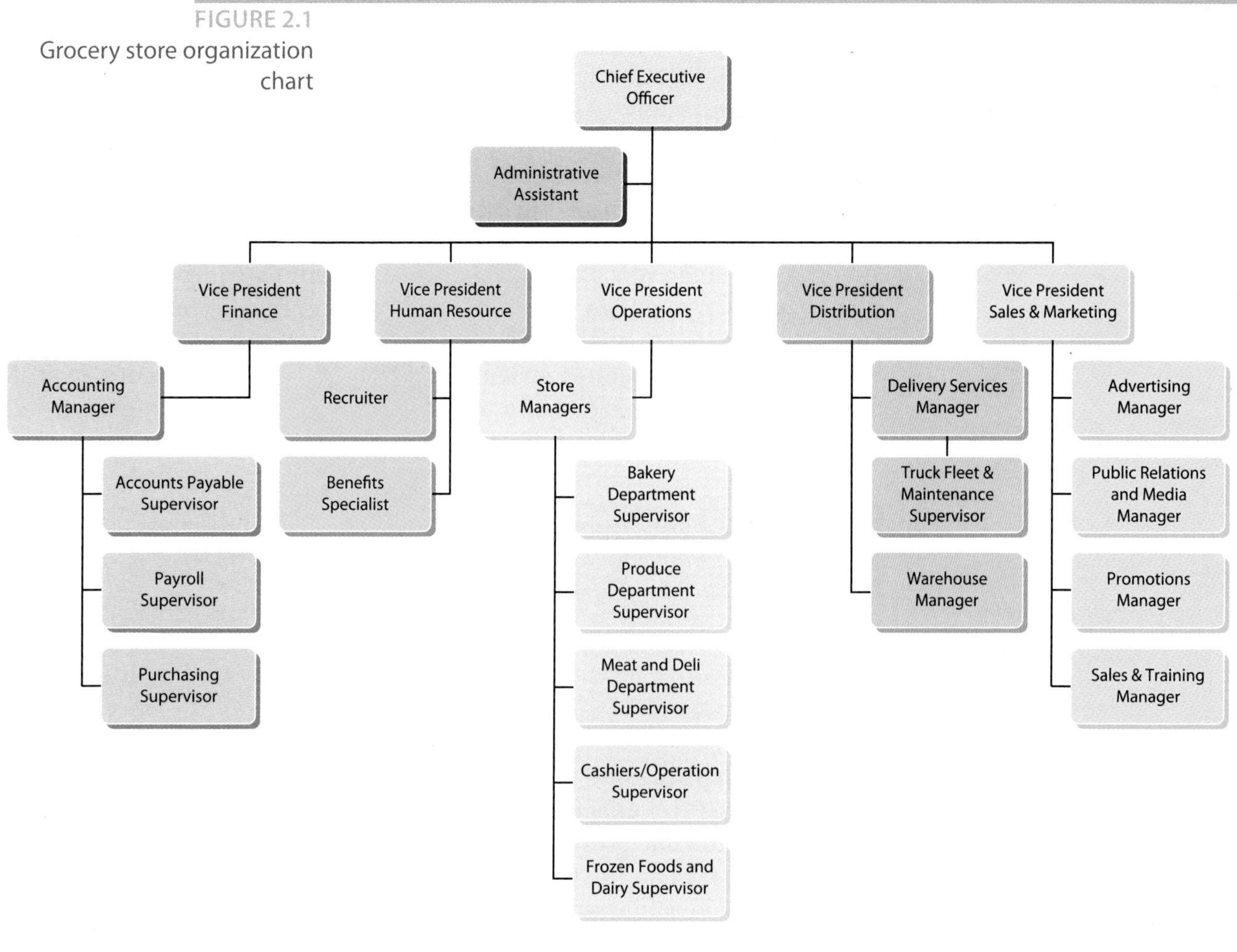

FIGURE 2.1
Grocery store organization chart

Horizontal specialization shows the various divisions of labor across an organization. The organization chart in Figure 2.1 provides a typical visual tool to describe hierarchy and specialization. The chart lets everyone in the company know who reports to whom and who does what, both of which represent important information for managers and their employees.

What about small organizations lacking multiple levels of hierarchy and lots of specialized jobs? Entrepreneurs and small businesses make up a significant portion of our economy. Just like large *Fortune* 500 corporations, **entrepreneurial ventures** need to establish a formal organizational structure for long-term success. In addition, someone in the company needs to accept the supervisory role. Typically, the business owner assumes these responsibilities.

horizontal specialization
the various divisions of labor across an organization

entrepreneurial ventures
a new or emerging start-up business

What may be different with a new venture is fewer resources and greater personal responsibility. For example, when Doris Christopher started The Pampered Chef in the basement of her home in the Chicago suburb of

River Forest, she had to do it all. Twenty-five years later, The Pampered Chef had 1,000 employees and 70,000 independent "Kitchen Consultants" to accomplish the same tasks—but on a much larger scale in a much more complex organization.[2]

During the start-up phase, companies often rely on the founders to handle multiple roles. In small companies, communication is typically more frequent and informal because there are fewer people to reach and feedback is often immediate. In addition, smaller organizations can usually adapt and change more quickly because decisions can be made on the spot rather than requiring committee or board approval. Therefore, smaller organizations are often more flexible than larger organizations.

Many large companies strive to benefit from the economies of scale that come with their size, while maintaining the small company style and corporate culture, which is typically more creative and nimble.

In my one-woman show, I did everything from answering the phone to emptying wastepaper baskets.

—Doris Christopher describing the early days of The Pampered Chef

Source: Doris Christopher, The Pampered Chef

Leading

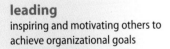

leading
inspiring and motivating others to achieve organizational goals

Leading is inspiring and motivating employees to achieve organizational goals. Successful managers employ a wide range of leadership skills in taking the vision and goals established by executives and higher-level management and translating them into reality. Chapter 3 briefly outlines the leadership responsibilities of managers, and Chapter 4 introduces leadership theories, models, and styles.

Leading can occur in a variety of settings, at any level of the organization, and with a variety of leadership styles. The photo on the left is typical of a large sales meeting with an animated approach to motivating a sales team. On the right, an informal team meeting is common in all types of organizations.

Controlling

Controlling is ensuring that performance meets the goals of the organization. It involves setting standards to achieve goals, monitoring performance by comparing it against the standards, detecting any deviations, and making changes to correct for them. In *Effective Management*, Chuck Williams provides the following example:

> Needing to cut costs (the standard) to restore profitability (the goal), major airlines began paying Pratt and Whitney to power-wash the grime from inside their jet engines two to three times a year at a cost of $3,000 per wash. Why? Cleaner engines consume less fuel and can go 18 months longer without having to be rebuilt for regular maintenance—at a high cost.[3]

1. Assume you are taking over a family-owned business with 20 employees and no formal organizational structure. Would it be important to develop a formal structure? Why or why not?

___

2. Would it also be important to develop an organization chart and provide copies to all employees? Why or why not?

___

Historical Management Theories

The discussions of key management theories in this section and the next are an overview to acquaint you with the science on which management is based. Both historical (sometimes called classical) and contemporary theories are included because many of the historical theories served as stepping-stones for the development of contemporary theories.

The historical theories were developed during the 19th and early 20th centuries. They go by a variety of names and generally are associated with specific individuals.

controlling
ensuring that performance meets the goals of the organziation

scientific management
an approach to management that emphasizes scientifically determined jobs and management practices as the way to improve efficiency and labor productivity

Scientific Management

Frederick Taylor is often referred to as the father of **scientific management**.[4] Taylor was a worker, supervisor, and ultimately chief engineer at a steel company. His focus was on improving the productivity of factory workers by simplifying jobs and optimizing the way tasks were performed.[5] Taylor proposed four principles of scientific management:

1. Conduct a scientific study of workers' tasks, and replace old rule-of-thumb methods with improved ones.
2. Scientifically select, train, and develop each employee rather than leaving workers to teach themselves.
3. Cooperate with employees to ensure they do their work according to the scientifically developed principles.
4. Divide work nearly equally between managers and workers, with managers doing the planning and workers the execution.[6]

Because Taylor's principles were intended for industrial and factory settings, some question their usefulness in today's service-dominated economy. But his emphasis on systematic procedures and efficiency is as relevant as ever.

Industrial engineers Frank and Lillian Gilbreth were part of the scientific management movement. Working as consultants, they focused on **motion studies** designed to simplify work, improve productivity, and reduce the level of effort required to perform a job safely. Frank Gilbreth's early experiences as an apprentice bricklayer provide a good example of motion study. After carefully observing his fellow workers on the job, Gilbreth designed a stand for bricks so workers wouldn't have to bend down to pick up each one. Another idea was to have lower-paid workers arrange the bricks with the best-looking side up so the higher-paid bricklayers wouldn't have to spend time turning each brick over to find that side. Taken together, Gilbreth's improvements increased productivity from 120 to 350 bricks per hour and from 1,000 to 2,700 bricks per day.[7]

Bureaucratic Management

German sociologist Max Weber developed many of the main concepts of bureaucratic management. He regarded with dismay the unproductive favoritism and hiring of unqualified family members he observed in pre-World War I Germany. Weber envisaged a system focused on hierarchical lines of a chain of command and control. As he conceived of it, **bureaucracy** is the exercise of organizational control on the basis of knowledge, expertise, or experience.[8]

From Weber's perspective, bureaucratic management ensured that the organizational structure established a hierarchy in which employees had the proper skills and training to perform the job effectively and moved up in the organization based on their knowledge, experience, and performance. Thus, bureaucratic management theory differs from scientific management theory, which focuses on determining the most efficient way to do work.

Curiously, Weber's term *bureaucracy* has come full circle and is now an unflattering label for inefficiency, waste, and red tape in large businesses and

motion studies
the process of breaking each task or job into separate motions and then eliminating those that are unnecessary or repetitive

bureaucracy
the exercise of control on the basis of knowledge, expertise, or experience

government agencies. Thus, in moderation, bureaucratic elements promote efficiency. Taken to extremes, bureaucracy becomes unwieldy and self-defeating.

Figure 2.2 shows Weber's elements of bureaucratic organizations. At face value, and not taken to extremes, these elements remain relevant and instructive today.

FIGURE 2.2
Elements of bureaucratic organizations

Qualification-based hiring	Employees are hired on the basis of their technical training or educational background.
Merit-based promotion	Promotion is based on experience or achievement. Managers, not organizational owners, decide who is promoted.
Chain of command	Each job occurs within a hierarchy, the chain of command, in which each position reports and is accountable to a higher position. A grievance procedure and a right to appeal protect people in lower positions.
Division of labor	Tasks, responsibilities, and authority are clearly divided and defined.
Impartial application of rules and procedures	Rules and procedures apply to all members of the organization and will be applied in an impartial manner, regardless of one's position or status.
Recorded in writing	All administrative decisions, acts, rules, or procedures will be recorded in writing.
Managers separate from owners	The owners of an organization should not manage or supervise the organization.

Source: http://www.management1e.nelson.com/pdf/history.pdf. Reproduced by permission from Williams, MGMT (2012, Exhibit 2.4).

Administrative Management

Administrative management emphasizes the ability of managers to lead and the actions they take to get things done. As noted earlier, scientific management theories focus on performing work efficiently, and bureaucratic management establishes a hierarchy to ensure employees have the skills and knowledge to do the job and are promoted based on knowledge, experience, and performance.

administrative management
an approach to management that emphasizes managers' ability to lead and to use effective management practices in accomplishing the organization's goals

Administrative management focuses on managers' having the ability to lead and using effective management practices in accomplishing the goals of the organization. These practices are categorized as major functions, and management principles are established to put the practices into effect.

As mentioned earlier, Henri Fayol developed the functions of management. He also established 14 principles to expand upon the functions. As you review the 14 principles listed in Figure 2.3 on page 32, note that most still apply in today's management environment.

FIGURE 2.3
Fayol's 14 Principles of Management

1. **Division of work**
Increase production by dividing work so that each worker completes smaller tasks or job elements.
2. **Authority and responsibility**
A manager's authority, which is the "right to give orders," should be commensurate with the manager's responsibility. However, organizations should enact controls to prevent managers from abusing their authority.
3. **Discipline**
Clearly defined rules and procedures are needed at all organizational levels to ensure order and proper behavior.
4. **Unity of command**
To avoid confusion and conflict, each employee should report to and receive orders from just one boss.
5. **Unity of direction**
One person and one plan should be used in deciding the activities to be carried out to accomplish each organizational objective.
6. **Subordination of individual interests to the general interest**
Employees must put the organization's interests and goals before their own.
7. **Remuneration**
Compensation should be fair and satisfactory to both the employees and the organization; that is, don't overpay or underpay employees.
8. **Centralization**
Avoid too much centralization or decentralization. Strike a balance depending on the circumstances and employees involved.
9. **Scalar chain**
From the top to the bottom of an organization, each position is part of a vertical chain of authority in which each worker reports to just one boss. For the sake of simplicity, communication outside normal work groups or departments should follow the vertical chain of authority.
10. **Order**
To avoid conflicts and confusion, order can be obtained by having a place for everyone and having everyone in his or her place; in other words, there should be no overlapping responsibilities.
11. **Equity**
Kind, fair, and just treatment for all will develop devotion and loyalty. This does not exclude discipline, if warranted, and consideration of the broader general interest of the organization.
12. **Stability of tenure of personnel**
Low turnover, meaning a stable workforce with high tenure, benefits an organization by improving performance, lowering costs, and giving employees, especially managers, time to learn their jobs.
13. **Initiative**
Because it is a "great source of strength for business," managers should encourage the development of initiative, or the ability to develop and implement a plan, in others.
14. **Esprit de corps**
Develop a strong sense of morale and unity among workers that encourages coordination of efforts.

Source: Henri Fayol, *General and Industrial Management* (London: Pittman and Sons, 1949)

Behavioral or Human Relations Management

Australian Elton Mayo, a Harvard professor, was best known for directing the Hawthorne Studies at the Western Electric plant near Chicago. Initially, the Hawthorne researchers were simply trying to determine the effect of light on productivity in groups of workers. They measured the workers' productivity and then in stages brightened the lighting. Each time the level of light was increased, productivity increased. Surprisingly, when they *lowered* the level of light, productivity still increased. They concluded that the amount of light did not affect productivity.

Mayo then did additional experiments to determine whether other factors, such as wages or workday length, influenced productivity. Ultimately, he concluded that workers became more productive when they received more attention, worked together as a group, and were made to feel their contributions were important to the organization's success.

Recent reexaminations of the Hawthorne studies show that money and other factors did in fact affect the performance of some employees.[9] Nevertheless, the studies retain their historical importance: They recognized and brought to the attention of employers that the social interaction of a group and other human relations factors greatly impact individual and group performance. Recall how, in the chapter opening interview, Thomas Suggs focuses on the work environment and how it impacts teamwork. You will learn more about the importance of teams in Chapter 5.

Contemporary Management Theories

This section briefly highlights several theories from more recent studies. They will be covered in more detail in the various chapters that relate to them. Note that these theories are called contemporary because early work on them began in the 1960s, and researchers continue to work on them.

system
a set of parts that work together to accomplish a common purpose or goal

systems management theory
an approach to management that focuses on managing all parts of a system to ensure that they are working together and that synergies occur

synergy
the increased effectiveness that results from combined action or cooperation

Systems Management Theory

In general terms, a **system** is a set of parts that work together to accomplish a common purpose or goal. Systems have inputs, processes, and outputs. They also often have feedback, in which information from the output (e.g., letters of complaint from customers) generates changes in input (e.g., an adjustment in customer service practices). **Systems management theory** focuses on managing all parts of a system to ensure that they are working together and that synergies occur. **Synergy** is the increased effectiveness that results from combined action or cooperation.[10]

In the 1960s, theorists Daniel Katz, Robert Kahn, and James Thompson applied their "open systems" view to organizations. Systems that use feedback are called open systems; those that are self-sufficient and do not rely on feedback are called closed systems. Most organizations are open systems because customer comments, complaints, and suggestions provide essential feedback.

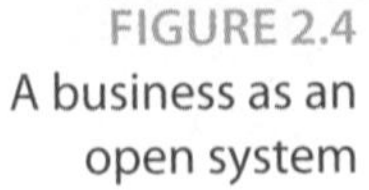

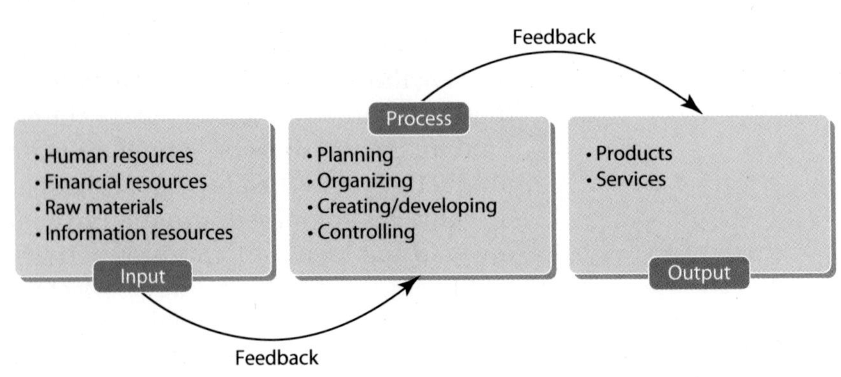

FIGURE 2.4
A business as an open system

Figure 2.4 illustrates an open system. It shows how input with appropriate feedback can be processed by a business and, with additional feedback, developed into marketable products and services. Customer feedback is the lifeblood of modern organizations.

A good way to think about how an open system works is to examine the system used to create this textbook (a new product):

Input

- *Human resources.* An acquisitions editor saw a need for the textbook. She hired the authors and a consulting editor to work with them. The publisher assigned a developmental editor, designer, and production manager.
- *Financial resources.* The acquisitions editor created a budget.
- *Raw materials.* Various editors and managers determined the raw materials needed, such as the design and quantity of paper.
- *Information resources.* The authors and editors used the publisher's information resources, such as a conference call service and an FTP site for sharing and transferring materials.

Feedback

- Reviewers (instructors) read (1) the text upon which this text was based and (2) the proposed outline for the new text and made suggestions.

Process

- *Planning.* The editors and authors planned the text, timeline, and process.
- *Organizing.* The editors organized and assigned tasks to appropriate individuals to complete.
- *Creating/developing.* The authors prepared the first draft of the chapters, working from an approved outline.
- *Controlling.* The consulting editor edited the chapters to meet the publisher's standards.

Feedback

- As each chapter was written, it went to instructors for review and suggestions for improvement.

Output

- The authors and consulting editor finalized the chapters and, along with the developmental editor, checked accuracy of page proofs.
- The product was printed.

For the book to be successful, the system and all its subparts had to work together and meet the budget, deadlines, and quality control standards.

Situational or Contingency Theories

Situational or contingency theories are generally applied to leadership styles. Therefore, they will be briefly highlighted in this chapter and discussed in more detail in Chapter 4, "Leadership Essentials." Situational or contingency theories hold that, to be effective, leaders must use different leadership styles as situations change.

Situational leadership is the concept that successful leadership occurs when the leader's style matches the situation. Ken Blanchard and Paul Hersey developed one widely known model of situational leadership.

Fred Fiedler's contingency theory is similar to Blanchard and Hersey's situational leadership theory. However, Fiedler asserts that a leader's performance depends, or is *contingent* on, the likelihood that he or she can successfully do the job and the person's basic motivation. Fiedler thinks leaders must be matched with situations that fit their personalities.

A third situational leadership theory is the path-goal theory. This theory suggests leaders can improve employee satisfaction and performance by clarifying how workers can achieve organizational goals, clearing the path to the goals (removing obstacles, for example), and adding more and different kinds of rewards to motivate workers to attain the goals. This theory assumes leaders can change and adapt their leadership styles.[11]

situational leadership
the concept that successful leadership occurs when the leader's style matches the situation

1. Are all of Fayol's 14 principles of management still valid in the current work environment? If not, which ones are not valid and why?

2. Would applying Fayol's principles in a small entrepreneurial organization be different from applying them in a large, well-established company? Explain.

LEVERAGING TECHNOLOGY

INFORMATION SECURITY RISKS

A key responsibility for managers at all levels is the safety and security of company information. Adopting new technologies is essential for business success, but at the same time, it creates risks to vital proprietary data. People typically assume that information technology (IT) specialists take care of data security. However, a company's employees may be the weakest link in its efforts to protect its data.

In the *Wall Street Journal* article "What's a Company's Biggest Security Risk? You," Geoffrey Fowler points out ways in which your perspective as an employee may be different from a hacker's perspective and may make it easy for a hacker to access key data (Figure 2.5 on page 37). An important point to remember is that employees have good intentions in taking the actions described in the figure. However, they are being outsmarted by hackers. If it is that easy for well-meaning employees to create major security problems, think how easy it is for rogue or dishonest employees.

In most organizations, the IT group handles the technical tools used to protect data. Managers need to focus on reducing risks caused by end users in their departments or divisions. Here are four steps you, as a manager, can take to reduce the risks created by end users:

1. Be a good role model in how you use technology.
2. Use company-wide policies and procedures, and add any specific policies and procedures that apply to your area.
3. Make employees aware of the causes of security breaches, and train them repeatedly on how to prevent breaches.
4. Observe and monitor employees as they use technology.

The security gap is end users.

—Kevin Mandia, chief executive of security, MANDIANT

Source: Quoted by Geoffrey Fowler in *The Wall Street Journal*

FIGURE 2.5
Security risks created by end users

Opening an unexpected email attachment from a colleague	Adding a new personal gadget to the work network
HOW YOU SEE IT Being a good coworker **HOW HACKERS SEE IT** An opportunity to inject a virus inside the corporate network, bypassing the firewall	**HOW YOU SEE IT** An opportunity to keep up with the latest technology **HOW HACKERS SEE IT** A new route for viruses and spyware to make their way into corporate systems
Posting job details on an online professional network	**Using personal web email for work**
HOW YOU SEE IT Creating a professional presence and finding another potential job **HOW HACKERS SEE IT** Reconnaissance data to map out company hierarchies and target specific users with computer attacks	**HOW YOU SEE IT** Making it easier to work from home or to move files between computers **HOW HACKERS SEE IT** A path to access critical data from relatively unprotected services

Source: Data from Geoffrey A. Fowler, "What's a Company's Biggest Security Risk? You," *The Wall Street Journal*, September 26, 2011, R1.

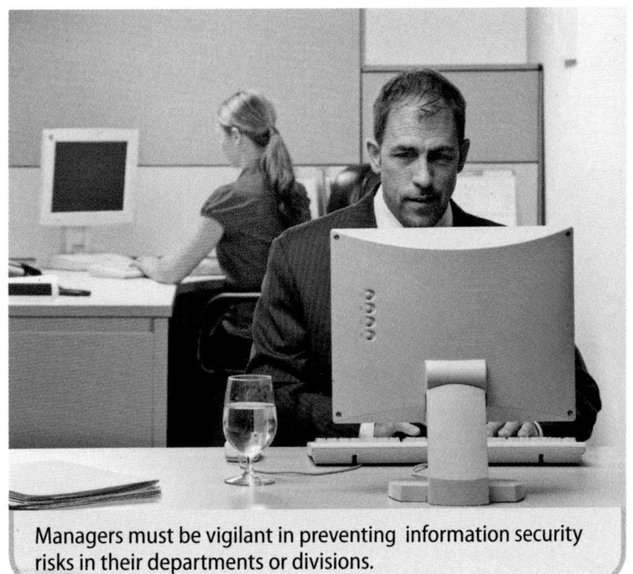

Managers must be vigilant in preventing information security risks in their departments or divisions.

Best Practices

Continuous improvement means you should never accept the status quo. You continue to search for ways to be more productive or to provide better service.

This section introduces the concept of **best practices**, broad standards, policies, procedures, and guides used by the most successful businesses and nonprofit organizations. They are an excellent way to achieve continuous improvement. Best practices focus on role model behavior in specific areas or industries. For example, what are the best practices for customer service in a bank or an insurance agency? What you are really asking is, What procedures, policies, practices, and standards relating to excellent customer service do the most successful banks or insurances agencies follow? Perhaps the professional associations to which bankers or real estate professionals belong have accumulated information about those standards or practices. Their lists of best practices may come from the professional literature, surveys, discussions at meetings, and years of accumulated practical experience.

However, that does not necessarily mean your company should automatically *adopt* them as is. Each company has its own unique situations, and some best practices may not be appropriate for your particular circumstances. Therefore, you may have to *adapt* the practices to meet your needs.

Another factor to consider is how today's best practices can quickly become obsolete because of economic, political, legal, and technological changes. The key to continuous improvement is to stay well informed about the policies, practices, and standards of successful companies in your field. Then examine what your company is doing, get as much input as you can from the people who are actually doing the task or job, and work with them to incorporate all the information to improve the way the task or job is being done. Continuous improvement means you should never accept the status quo. You continue to search for ways to be more productive or to provide better service.

best practices
broad standards, policies, procedures, and guides used by the most successful businesses and nonprofit organizations

SUMMARY

1. The four functions of management are planning, organizing, leading, and controlling.
2. Historical management theories include scientific management, bureaucratic management, and administrative management.
3. Contemporary management theories include systems management theory and situational or contingency theories.
4. Best practices are standards, policies, procedures, and guides used by the most successful businesses and nonprofit organizations. They are an excellent way of achieving continuous improvement.

Terms

administrative management, 31
best practices, 38
bureaucracy, 30
controlling, 29
critical thinking, 43
entrepreneurial venture, 27
horizontal specialization, 27
leading, 28
management functions, 26
motion study, 30
organization chart, 26
organizing, 26
planning, 26
scientific management, 29
situational leadership, 35
synergy, 33
system, 33
systems management theory, 33
vertical hierarchy, 26

Located at www.cengagebrain.com

- Chapter Outlines
- Flashcards
- Interactive Quizzes
- Tech Tools
- Video Segments

and More!

Questions for Reflection

1. Are the four functions of management important in very small businesses (under 25 employees)? Why or why not?
2. Why are both dimensions of an organization chart—vertical hierarchy and horizontal specialization—important?
3. What are some differences between Frederick Taylor's ideas about scientific management and Max Weber's concepts of bureaucratic management?
4. What do you think are the key advantages and disadvantages of businesses using social media, such as Facebook, YouTube, LinkedIn, or Twitter?
5. Review the three situational or contingency theories described in the chapter. Do you think they can be applied effectively in today's business environment? Explain.
6. Do you think it is important to keep up with best practices in your career field? Explain. How would you go about keeping abreast of best practices in your career field?

Hands-On Activities

Work With Your Team

You have been approached by Karen Spencer, the administrative manager of a local nonprofit organization with 15 employees. Ms. Spencer graduated three years ago from the program you are pursuing. She would like your help in identifying technology risks her organization faces and developing a plan to manage them. Currently, the organization has no policies or procedures for using technology and reducing the risk to proprietary information. Ms. Spencer provided the following information:

- The organization has a network with a large database containing information about donors and supporters. Safeguarding this database is critical.
- Many of the donors are affluent and influential in the community.
- The organization uses social media extensively for marketing, public relations, and communication with supporters.
- Employees use computers and handheld devices provided by the organization as well as personal handheld devices to connect to the organization's computer network.
- The network is protected by a firewall and a virus checker.
- The organization outsources its IT technical support. Lynn, a technology-savvy employee, coordinates all support requests.

1. Each member of the team should read the feature on critical thinking on page 43.
2. Identify the organization's technology risks and discuss how to minimize them. A list of suggested resources appears on page 41. Use a balanced approach so you do not rule out using social media and other technology tools advantageously.
3. Prepare a report to Ms. Spencer in memo format with the following information:
   a. A comprehensive summary of the technology risks the team believes the organization must address.
   b. A plan for managing the risks. Explain how to implement the plan and what managers can do to ensure employees take the appropriate actions to protect the database. Apply critical thinking to each step of developing the plan.

Resources

- Review the "Leveraging Technology" feature on page 36. It discusses the role of the manager in protecting company data and many of the end-user (employee) risks that exist in this organization.
- Ask your instructor or lab manager what policies your school has established to protect its IT labs.
- If you have a job, ask a company IT resource to explain the plan and policies used to safeguard company data.
- Search the Internet for helpful articles using the keywords *protect company data* and *information technology policies.*
- Remember to include the outsourced IT specialists in your plans.

Apply Management Principles

You have been named the general manager of a small telecommunication services company. You want to establish a good management team that will apply effective management principles to supervise the work of approximately 50 employees.

1. Review Fayol's 14 principles of management.
2. Determine which of the 14 principles you would use in your management approach.
3. Provide a brief description explaining how you will implement the principles you select.

You Decide | Case Study

Responsible Blogging and Social Networking for Work

Mimi is the supervisor for a local electronics store that also sells and installs home theaters. The store has a loyal following and an excellent reputation. The business recently expanded, which required hiring three new people.

Eldrick, one of the new employees, has outstanding skills and expertise with all the store's products. He is also a regular Internet user, blogger, and social networker. Eldrick is very enthusiastic about his new job. In fact, he placed a lengthy posting on his social networking page describing the store, his coworkers, and a few of the customers. He did not use anyone's name, but he used enough details that people familiar with the store know whom he was talking about. One of his comments describes his boss as "really nice and pretty hot." Mimi learned about the posting from a customer.

Questions

1. If you were Mimi, how would you handle this situation?
2. What are the potential consequences if Mimi ignores Eldrick's actions?
3. How can Mimi take advantage of Eldrick's interest in Internet resources to benefit the store?
4. Does Eldrick's blog pose any security risk to the company? Why or why not?

MANAGER'S TOOLKIT

As manager of a real estate company, you want to make your company as efficient and effective as you can. You have decided to use a systems management approach. You have three work groups within your organization: a sales group responsible for soliciting real estate listings and selling real estate; a property management group responsible for managing rental properties for clients, including collecting deposits and rent and handling maintenance; and an administrative and accounting group responsible for daily and financial operations.

The sales and property management groups operate fairly independently of each other. However, both groups interact extensively with the administrative and accounting group.

Diagram or describe how an open systems management process would work for the sales and property management groups. Be sure to include feedback from sellers and buyers in the sales group and from clients and renters in the property management group.

Soft Skills for Success

Critical Thinking

The ability to think critically is among the primary skills required for success in the workplace. **Critical thinking** is the use of logical thinking, reasoning, and evidence to question assumptions and evaluate ideas before determining an outcome or reaching a conclusion.

Critical Thinking Attributes	
• Use of inductive (from specific to general) and deductive (from general to specific) logic • Research from credible sources to collect appropriate information • Objective thinking • Separating opinions from facts • Recognition of biases • Avoiding emotional appeals and faulty logic	• Seeking alternative explanations • Asking questions to clarify information • Challenging the validity of statements including one's own • Knowledge of historical context—what may have been true in the past may not be true now • Questioning generalizations from facts to ensure they are accurate

Put It to Work

1. Read at least two credible articles on inductive and deductive reasoning. To ensure you understand these concepts, write two examples of inductive reasoning and two of deductive reasoning.
2. Read at least two credible articles on critical thinking.
3. Prepare a list of the articles you read; include complete documentation of sources.
4. As a team, discuss how you can use critical thinking to be effective in the project you are doing for the nonprofit organization.
5. After the team report is in rough-draft form, the team should review everything in it using the critical thinking attributes described above and the information in the articles each member read to evaluate the validity of the information and judgments in the report.

CHAPTER

3

Effective Supervision: Path to Success for New Managers

Learning Outcomes

1. Describe the supervisor's position in a typical organizational pyramid.
2. Identify and briefly explain common supervisor roles and responsibilities.
3. List skills needed for a supervisor to be successful.
4. Explain why a supervisor should understand transformational change as well as changes within the supervisor's area.
5. Identify key trends impacting supervisors.

Photo courtesy of Charles N. Bass

Straight Talk From the Field

Charles N. Bass is Florida area manager for The Fishel Company, a utilities construction company headquartered in Columbus, Ohio. He is based in Plant City/Tampa, Florida. The company is branded as Team Fishel and refers to all employees as teammates.

Printed by permission from Charles N. Bass

What is your most important responsibility as a manager and supervisor?

My first responsibility is to ensure we have profitable work to keep our teammates fully employed. To do this requires a tremendous amount of time and effort spent developing relationships with a variety of customers. As a result of the recent downturn in the economy, our clients look for the lowest price quotes. If a company is to survive, it must understand costs in order to ensure the quotes provided to a customer will allow it to be profitable while providing the best possible pricing for the work. It has also become even more imperative to build these relationships among a diverse client base to help offset the economic impact in the different market segments.

What other important roles and responsibilities do you have?

As an area manager, I have to be willing to make a decision and possibly say no to a request. Always providing a positive outcome is the easy way out. As a manager, I have to evaluate each request as to how it affects not only the requestor but also the other teammates and our company as a whole.

Another key element of my job is to be a listener and create a culture that promotes an atmosphere for teammates and customers to feel comfortable approaching me with suggestions, problems, or successes. Creating this type of environment will hopefully lead to creativity and increased opportunities for teammates, customers, and ultimately our company.

What are your major challenges and how do you deal with them?

One challenge I face that affects nearly every facet of our business is controlling and understanding our costs. Costs impact all aspects of our work and include but are not limited to things like payroll, office supplies, equipment, fuel, overtime, etc. Having costs under control allows me to forecast our financial performance accurately, which in turn allows me to be ahead of any surprises. An added benefit to understanding costs is to put our company in a better position when pricing work to ensure we do not lose money on our work.

Another challenge is the ability to consistently obtain and retain qualified teammates. Due to the economic situation, many of our competitors have downsized and retain only the cream-of-the-crop employees. We have to be diligent with our hiring practices to ensure we do not lower our expectations just to fill a slot. For example, we require a written and practical test for one of our highest-paying positions. About 20 to 25 percent of the applicants either won't take or do not pass the test. As a result, we will not hire them, even though they may have been doing the same type of work for one of our competitors. We have to ensure we have teammates that allow us to know we can put our company name on their work at the end of the day and be proud of that.

Possibly the most difficult challenge is trying to stay ahead of the next economic change that could affect our business. This really comes in two forms, one being a change that could adversely affect us such as being financially exposed to a customer facing bankruptcy or in a market that is about to suffer. The other is being prepared for opportunities in an emerging market or with customers in a new market that would allow us to position ourselves in the market or with the customer before our competitors.

Visit *www.cengagebrain.com* to read the complete profile.

Chapter Outline

Supervisors are essential to any organization that depends on people to achieve success. Chapter 1 introduced the field of management and the organizational pyramid. This chapter focuses on supervisory roles and responsibilities. In every organization, at least one person must take the role of supervisor. Most organizations have many supervisors. It is important to understand how the supervisor fits into the organizational pyramid and what skills a successful supervisor needs.

Supervisors and the Organizational Pyramid

You learned in Chapter 1 that management is the process of leading and working with people to accomplish organizational goals and objectives using available resources efficiently and effectively. Supervisors are an integral part of the management team and process. The legal definition of **supervisor**

> is any individual having authority, in the interest of the employer, to hire, transfer, suspend, lay off, recall, promote, discharge, assign, reward, or discipline other employees, or responsibly to direct them, or to adjust their grievances, or effectively to recommend such action, if in connection with the foregoing the exercise of such authority is not of a merely routine or clerical nature, but requires the use of independent judgment.[1]

Supervisors are an integral part of the management team and process.

In the workplace, it is common to hear the words *manager* and *supervisor* used interchangeably. Supervisors are typically considered part of first-line management. Figure 1.1 on page 8 shows nonmanagerial employees at the base of the organizational pyramid and first-line management in the tier above. However, it should be noted that generally managers at all levels have some supervisory responsibilities.

The following list contains typical job titles for first-line managers. Many more could be added as titles vary widely from one organization to another.

- Office manager
- Administrative manager
- Unit manager
- Branch manager
- Department supervisor
- First-line supervisor (or manager)
- Shift manager or supervisor
- Team leader
- Project manager

supervisor
an individual who typically has the authority to hire, direct, promote, discharge, assign, reward, or discipline other employees

First-line managerial positions often include a wide range of responsibilities, such as the following:

- Operational planning (one week to one year)
- Meeting production goals/quotas

- Customer service
- Coordinating staffing and work schedules
- Personnel and job assignment decisions
- Organizing training, orientation, and team-building activities
- Unit-level facilities/resource planning and purchasing
- Day-to-day and local crisis management
- Enforcing job safety regulations and accident reporting
- Coordinating and managing a team

First-line managers or supervisors have regular contact with employees and, in many situations, customers. They have responsibility for day-to-day operations, which are essential to organizational success. In addition, supervisors interact regularly with middle managers, providing them with status reports and performance updates while also receiving guidance and direction regarding organizational goals and operational plans. In organizations where participative management is practiced, supervisors may also interact with top management. Participative management, discussed more fully in the next chapter, welcomes employees' ideas and includes input into decision making by employees at all levels.

1. Why do you think first-line supervisors are important to organizations and their management structure?

____

2. Assume you work in the office of a large retail store such as Best Buy or Home Depot and the company decides to eliminate all first-line management positions. What do you think will be the impact on employees and customers?

____

Supervisory Roles

The roles supervisors play vary by the size and type of organization, the industry, and the philosophy of senior executives. However, many roles are common to most supervisory positions. Brief explanations of the more common supervisory roles and responsibilities follow.

trainer
a person who teaches employees and coworkers new information and skills

Trainer

As a **trainer**, a supervisor teaches employees and coworkers new information and skills. One of the keys to any new employee's success is being prepared to do his or her job. This requires proper orientation and training.

Effective supervisors realize that training is an ongoing process. Although it is emphasized for new employees, all employees benefit from periodic training and professional development opportunities. Chapter 8, "Setting Up Employees for Success," discusses new-employee orientation and training for new and current employees.

Planner

A **planner** evaluates goals, objectives, and future needs to prepare plans that provide the necessary resources and action items to achieve success. In most organizations, senior management is primarily responsible for broad strategic planning, and middle managers and first-line supervisors implement those plans. A key to success is to have plans for achieving department-level goals and objectives. This includes planning for training, staffing, purchasing, advertising, evaluation, and more. Important components of planning include setting goals, defining critical success factors, and developing tactics for getting your employees involved. Chapter 6 focuses on planning.

planner
a person who evaluates goals, objectives, and future needs to prepare plans that provide the necessary resources and action items to achieve success

scheduler
a person who prepares the schedule to ensure proper staffing and resources are available to meet production or customer needs

motivator
a person who inspires people to perform at their best and achieve a common goal

Scheduler

As a **scheduler**, a supervisor prepares the schedule to ensure proper staffing and resources are available to meet production or customer needs. In organizations both large and small, supervisors need to arrange human, material, and informational resources productively. In addition, supervisors are responsible for scheduling facilities, inventory, and equipment to maximize efficiency and provide exceptional quality and/or service. Several chapters discuss different types of scheduling.

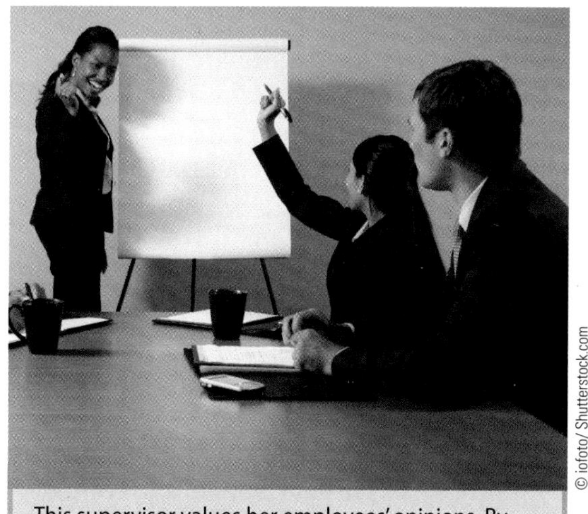

© iofoto/ Shutterstock.com

This supervisor values her employees' opinions. By being involved in planning sessions, they are more likely to achieve desired team results. Meaningful participation can be a powerful motivator in today's complex and fast-paced workplaces.

Motivator

Supervisors also serve as **motivators** who inspire their employees to perform at their best and achieve a common goal. One of the most difficult but important roles for a supervisor is that of motivator. To inspire their teams to work together, managers and supervisors need to recognize that each person is unique and that everyone is not motivated by the same incentives and rewards. For example, some people thrive on praise and recognition. For others, a salary increase or promotion is a strong incentive. Frequent feedback may encourage some employees but may be a disincentive to others. A number of chapters focus on different aspects of motivation, and Chapter 11 describes it in detail.

Coach

A **coach** is a person who guides employees with instruction, feedback, and encouragement. Effective supervisors coach their employees. Coaching goes beyond motivation by helping employees focus on their "high-payoff" activities, providing positive feedback, allowing them to learn from their mistakes, and celebrating successes. In addition, it is important for supervisors to spend time coaching all their employees—the top performers as well as the underachievers. Chapter 8 offers proven coaching strategies.

Supervisors should spend time coaching all their employees.

Controller

As a **controller**, a supervisor measures quality and performance. Control does not have to be negative or unpleasant. In fact, positive and proactive supervisors realize their job is to focus on controlling quality and keeping things headed toward organizational goals and objectives. Success needs to be measured so deviations can be corrected. Effective supervisors involve their employees in developing tools to assess quality and performance. By involving employees, supervisors share the responsibility for control with their team. Ultimately, supervisors are responsible for the performance of their units. However, involving team members makes assessing quality and performance a much more open and positive experience. Chapter 9 provides techniques for evaluating performance.

Leader

A **leader** sets the tone for the organization, creates vision, and inspires others to achieve. Supervisors set the tone for their employees. This includes everything from attitude to behavior. We have all heard the advice "lead by example." This is essential for supervisors because their employees will look to them to establish moral and ethical values; create a positive, pleasant work environment; communicate in a professional manner; and use technology appropriately—all the while staying focused on organizational goals, production standards, and customers' needs. Chapter 4, "Leadership Essentials," describes strategies, skills, styles, and qualities of successful leaders.

Recruiter

A **recruiter** assists in identifying potential job candidates, screening applications, interviewing, and hiring new employees. Supervisors are involved in many aspects of recruitment. In a small business, the supervisor may handle all elements. In larger organizations, supervisors generally work with the human resources department to accomplish these tasks. Chapter 7 presents recruiting strategies and considerations.

coach
a person who guides employees with instruction, feedback, and encouragement

controller
a person who measures quality and performance

leader
one who sets the tone for the organization, creates the vision, and inspires other to achieve

recruiter
one who assists in identifying potential job candidates

Essential Skills for Successful Supervisors

Supervisors need to be passionate about their jobs, with a strong desire to do the work, help other people succeed, and accept additional responsibility. Individuals who apply for supervisory positions simply because they want to earn more money are usually not successful. This section provides an overview of essential skills for supervisors. Future chapters will place additional emphasis on many of these skills.

Supervisors need to be passionate about their jobs, with a strong desire to do the work, help other people succeed, and accept additional responsibility.

Communication

In Chapter 1, you learned soft skills are needed at all levels of management. Communication skills are among the most important soft skills. Depending on the circumstances, supervisors may communicate with a variety of groups, including their employees, customers, suppliers, managers, government agency representatives, banks, labor unions, the media, consumer advocacy groups, and the public. Every day, supervisors encounter opportunities to exchange information with others. To be effective, they need to understand their audience, be clear about the message they wish to convey, and seek feedback. The following communication capabilities are essential:

- Listening
- Interpreting nonverbal communication
- Articulating their point, both orally and in writing
- Projecting a positive demeanor

Communication skills for supervisors and managers are so important that Chapter 13, "Effective Workplace Communication," is devoted solely to this topic.

© EDHAR/Shutterstock.com

© Robert Kneschke/Shutterstock.com

© Geo Martinez/Shutterstock.com

Nonverbal communication can occur through eye contact, facial expression, gestures, body position, and other means. These three businesspeople are communicating different nonverbal messages. How do you interpret them?

Entrepreneurial Thinking

Organizations move at a rapid pace, and change is the norm rather than the exception. This type of environment requires supervisors to be quick on their feet. Entrepreneurial thinkers tend to stand out as supervisors.

Entrepreneurial thinkers are employees who have learned to think and act like owners of an entrepreneurial or start-up business. When supervisors in any type of organization take ownership of their areas of responsibility, they tend to make the same types of decisions the business owners would make. Entrepreneurial thinkers adapt quickly, are creative problem solvers, and develop new ideas to increase productivity, enhance quality, increase profits, and/or expand market share. They are opportunistic, meaning they know when the time is right to make a change or try something new.

Decision Making

Supervisors make decisions every day. Some are routine and others more complex, with significant short-term and longer-term consequences. Regardless of the type of decision, supervisors need the ability to gather information, validate facts, identify consequences, analyze data, and stay focused on the goal. In addition, their decisions need to be ethical ones that are in the best interests of the organization and society.

In the chapter opening interview, Charles Bass cites making decisions as one of the most important responsibilities of his job. When making a hard decision on a teammate's request, Bass considers the effect not only on the teammate but also on other teammates and the entire company. The "Soft Skills for Success" activity at the end of the chapter focuses on decision making.

Technical Skills

You learned about technical skills in Chapter 1. Remember that they involve the entire package of skills required to do a job effectively. For example, if you plan to become an executive chef, you need all the culinary and kitchen management skills to handle this responsibility, train your employees, and solve problems as they arise. Recall, too, that first-line managers need significantly more technical skills than middle managers or executives.

Computer information systems are commonplace in both small and large organizations. As mentioned earlier, nearly every position requires computer and software skills. Supervisors should understand computer technology and information systems and how these tools can be used to benefit both individuals and the organization.

Team Building and Leadership

Doris Christopher, founder of The Pampered Chef, attributes much of her success to the team of people who work for her company.[2] Recruiting, training, and motivating a group of individuals to work together to achieve a common goal requires careful planning based on proven approaches. In addition, a team needs a leader like Doris Christopher who can inspire, motivate, and adapt quickly. Chapter 4 introduces qualities, styles, and other factors in effective leadership, while Chapter 5 provides established strategies for developing and leading both traditional and virtual teams.

LEVERAGING TECHNOLOGY

SUPERVISORY ROLES IN MANAGING TECHNOLOGY

Supervisors play many roles in managing technology in their areas. The primary technology roles are as follows:

- Ensure employees are aware of, understand, and follow all company technology policies. Many companies have policies regarding protection of company information; social media, email, and Internet use; use of mobile devices to access company data; and a host of other areas.
- Provide appropriate technology for employees to perform their jobs effectively and efficiently.
- Balance the need for upgrading technology with budgetary constraints.
- Ensure employees are trained properly and know how to use new technology appropriately.
- Monitor the use of technology to avoid abuse, particularly in Internet sites visited, information posted on social media sites, and email use.
- Ensure productivity is not hindered by time spent on personal activities such as following sports, shopping, visiting social media sites, or texting friends.
- Ensure the quality of electronic communications—especially external communication such as email and posts to Internet sites—meets business standards and conveys a positive image of the company.
- Use technology to improve working conditions for employees, appropriately based on company policies such as flexible scheduling and working from remote locations.
- Provide employees who work outside the office or travel for business purposes with suitable technology to do their work.

Delegation

Delegation is the process of sharing authority and responsibility with others. Supervisors need others to get things done. This requires delegating appropriate tasks and authority to the right employees. It also requires preparing employees to succeed with delegated tasks. Chapter 5 discusses delegation.

Political Skills

When you see or hear the word *political*, do you immediately think of elected officials in public office? In the workplace, political skills focus on positive attributes including the ability to build long-term relationships of trust with others. Just as good politicians understand the needs of their constituents, politically savvy supervisors understand the needs of their employees, boss, organization, and internal and external customers.

With this knowledge, supervisors are better prepared to make good decisions, to be responsible, and to be accountable. Effective supervisors are diplomatic. They know how to get things done through support, cooperation, and effort from others. Managers and supervisors who are politically naive can get shortchanged. Consider this situation, for example:

You attend an important meeting in which managers will vote on a plan to reorganize the support staff. You make a carefully prepared speech in support of the plan, only to find that other managers who oppose it got together earlier and "decided" the outcome. You're defeated without having the chance to make your case. If you had acted as they did, talking to other managers beforehand and building support, the outcome might have been different.

Emotional Intelligence and Self-Awareness

Research has shown that academic intelligence, represented by items such as test scores, grades, and intelligence quotient (IQ), is not always a reliable predictor of success in work and life. Social skills play a very important role. While others had previously studied this topic, a series of books by psychologist and journalist Daniel Goleman presenting his concept of social or emotional intelligence have had a profound impact on the business world.

As Goleman defines it, **emotional intelligence** means "managing feelings so that they are expressed appropriately and effectively, enabling people to work together smoothly toward their common goals."[3] For instance, the manager who never loses his or her cool and is known for the ability to calm a heated exchange or achieve a consensus among sharply divided parties is using emotional intelligence.

Increasing your self-awareness is an important aspect of developing emotional intelligence. With emotional intelligence, supervisors are able to position themselves and their employees in situations that reduce negative emotional responses and increase the likelihood of positive interactions. Chapter 15 discusses self-awareness, emotional intelligence, and personal discovery.

emotional intelligence
the ability to manage feelings so they are expressed appropriately and effectively, enabling people to work together smoothly toward common goals

Emotional intelligence seems to be largely learned, and it continues to develop as we go through life and learn from our experiences—our competence in it can keep growing.

—Daniel Goleman

Source: Goleman, *Working with Emotional Intelligence*, 7.

Administrative Skills

Supervisors spend a lot of time organizing, scheduling, planning, preparing and managing budgets, conducting performance appraisals, monitoring quality and key indicators, and processing paperwork or online forms. All these activities require an understanding of basic business functions and the related legal issues as well as the ability to execute effectively in each of these areas. Several chapters focus on key administrative skills.

Time Management

Time is valuable to the individual and the organization alike. Supervisors need excellent time management skills, including the ability to say no and manage an ever-changing schedule. The following tips can be useful in time management:

- Remember that an online personal information management (PIM) system, such as *Microsoft® Outlook®* messaging software, facilitates sharing materials and assignments. It is also more efficient and effective than a paper-based system. If you do not have access to a PIM, use a paper-based planner.
- Don't underestimate the value of organization. An organized workspace and files, including electronic files, will save you substantial amounts of time.
- Converting paper-based files to electronic files makes storing information and accessing it quickly much easier.
- Use your PIM to create a realistic "to-do" task list each day. Set priorities, and group like tasks together.
- Try to handle each document only once.
- Read email at set intervals rather than interrupting your work when it arrives. If possible, act on email as soon as you read it and then store it if necessary.
- Streamline tasks. Constantly look for ways to apply the productivity tools in your software or to do tasks more efficiently.
- Tackle your toughest assignments when you are freshest.

A PIM enables you to share and sync your calendar, contacts, tasks, and notes easily with your work unit or team.

- When you slow down or stall on a task, take a break or switch to something else. Even a short break can help you regain your momentum.
- Find graceful ways to control interruptions. For example, if you're working and a coworker stops by to chat, talk for a few minutes and then politely excuse yourself, explaining you have an assignment to do. Offer to continue the conversation later.

Managing Change

Change is a constant in business and nonprofit organizations, and it occurs at every level of an organization. Technology plays a major role in accelerating the pace of change. Change that affects an entire organization is often called **transformational change**. The following are common examples of transformational change:

- Acquiring or being acquired by another organization
- Expanding from a local to a regional, national, or international organization
- A new or current executive team decides to make a major change in the company's vision or management, such as moving from a hierarchical approach to a participative style of management or to extensive use of teams.

John Kotter: Leadership and Change

Transformational change is usually led by visionary senior leaders. John Kotter, an international expert on leadership and change, notes that the failure rate in organizations that try to make transformational change is very high. Kotter says that four sets of obstacles typically keep change from succeeding: structures, skills, supervisors, and systems.

Four sets of obstacles typically keep change from succeeding: structures, skills, supervisors, and systems.

In an interview with John Kotter he explains, "In many organizations, silos and fragments in authority and resources can make it difficult to take actions that support the change effort. [Silos are departments or work units that function independently and communicate little.] In others, workers may lack the skills necessary to carry out the new vision.... In some cases, supervisors are unenthusiastic or fearful of change, and actively work to undermine it. And oftentimes, the systems an organization has in place—say, for performance evaluation or sales—are subjective or outdated."[4]

Supervisors have a critical role in helping to implement major changes in an organization. Supervisors must also be able to work with employees they supervise in implementing changes in their area that are necessary for the area's success.

transformational change
change that affects an entire organization

Kurt Lewin: Stages of Change

Organizations frequently turn to a system or model for implementing change. In the early 1950s, social psychologist Kurt Lewin developed a three-step system for changing people's behavior, skills, and attitudes that organizations still use today:

1. *Unfreezing* usually involves reducing the forces that are maintaining things the way they are. Organizations sometimes accomplish this step by introducing information that shows discrepancies between desired and actual performance.
2. *Moving* is the change process in which employees learn new, desirable behaviors, values, and attitudes.
3. *Refreezing* makes the desired performance the permanent way of doing things. It often takes place through reinforcement and support for the new behavior.[5]

Supervisors can play an important role in helping employees accept change. They should recognize that change, especially technological change, is not easy. Employees often fear change because it is outside their control and has unknown consequences. Coaching and training are key elements in helping employees adapt to change.

Trends Impacting Supervisors

Trends in the workforce, business, and society frequently have a profound effect on organizations and supervisors. One trend described earlier is the increasing tendency of businesses to reduce the numbers of middle managers and to empower and expect greater leadership from first-line managers. Three other prominent trends impacting today's business, governmental, and nonprofit organizations are an increasingly diverse workforce, globalization, and changing technology.

Diverse Workforce

The U.S. Bureau of Labor Statistics (BLS) has documented the increasing diversity of the U.S. workforce over time. It reports that "compared with the labor force of the past decades, today's labor force is older, more racially and ethnically diverse, and composed of more women."[6] Here are two examples of this change:

- In 1990, 11.9 percent of the civilian workforce was age 55 or older. By 2010, that share had nearly doubled to 19.5 percent. And by 2020, the BLS predicts that these older workers will compose 25.2 percent, or more than a quarter, of the workforce.[7]
- The BLS projects that by 2020, Hispanics, blacks, Asians, and members of other traditional minority groups will make up nearly 40 percent of the civilian workforce.[8]

© EDHAR/Shutterstock.com

Supervisors need to recognize, respect, and work with people as unique individuals.

Many people think of **diversity** strictly in terms of race, gender, and ethnicity. However, our definition is much broader, with a wide range of variables. These variables include attitudes, perspectives, opinions, gender, age, race, ethnic background, language skills, education, work experience, socioeconomic status, religion, sexual orientation, disabilities, and alternative family structures (for example, single parents or caregivers for children and parents).

Age diversity provides an example of how workforce diversity can affect supervisors. The increasing proportion of older workers reflects the aging baby-boomer generation. Many boomers are staying on the job longer than they anticipated, while others are reentering the job market and ultimately working side by side with the Generation X and Y populations. Figure 3.1 shows a breakdown of these generations by birth years. Except for baby boomers, the span of birth years differs slightly according to different sources.

These groups differ in more than just age or physical appearance. For example, their work ethic may be different, their perceptions of quality may vary, and the ways they learn and work often are not the same. Supervisors need to be aware of such differences in training, inspiring, motivating, and retaining employees, in order to facilitate their working together.

As you can see, the increased diversity of our workforce creates opportunities and challenges for supervisors. Successful organizations have learned how to integrate diversity into their corporate culture by leveraging individual strengths and talents to develop a more innovative, creative, and effective workforce.

FIGURE 3.1
What generation are you, and how does it impact your work life?

Generation	Birth Years
Baby Boomers	1946 – 1964
Generation X	1965 – 1980
Generation Y (Millennials)	1981 – 2000

Source: Based on discussions in Linda G. Keidrowski, "Whose Generation Is It, Anyway?" *Small Business Times* (February 2, 2008), http://www.biztimes.com/news/2008/2/8/whose-generation-is-it-anyway, (accessed on October 16, 2011); and Anne Houlihan, "The New Melting Pot: How to Effectively Lead Different Generations in the Workplace," *Supervision 68* (September 2007): 10–11.

diversity
a wide range of individual characteristics

outsourcing
the use of outside organizations to complete work that was previously done internally

off-shoring
the outsourcing of business activities and processes to foreign countries

Globalization

The increasingly global nature of the world economy has changed the way many organizations do business. Many companies have had to seek new and wider markets for their goods and services just to survive. Globalization affects nearly every industry and small organizations as well as large ones.

One outcome of globalization has been a change in how and where work gets done. **Outsourcing** is the use of outside organizations to complete work that was previously done internally. **Off-shoring** is the outsourcing of business

© Purestock/ Jupiter Images

Outsourcing creates opportunities for employees to monitor the performance of contractors or to work with them in external teams. Supervisors must assist employees in serving customers in different cultures and nations.

activities and processes to foreign countries. Both activities have increased as companies contract different aspects of their operations to outside firms to streamline costs, remain competitive, improve services, and increase profitability.

Business functions such as manufacturing, payroll processing, bookkeeping, technology services, human resources management, supply chain management, and marketing and public relations are just a few of many functions being outsourced. In some instances, companies may outsource certain business functions to competitors. This trend is not limited to private industry. Federal, state, and local governments also contract out certain functions to outside vendors.

Globalization creates both challenges and opportunities for supervisors. An obvious challenge is the difficulties created when outsourcing results in staff reductions. Managing the work of contractors remotely is another; implementing changes to cut costs is a third. However, outsourcing may result in the creation of new jobs as employees shift from performing certain tasks to monitoring the work of the contractors hired to do them. External teams may be formed in which house staff and contractors work together. Supervisors may also assist employees in better serving customers in different cultures and nations.

Technology

Technology is changing constantly, rapidly, and in major ways. This key trend makes technology a permanent and important part of every supervisor's job. The "Leveraging Technology" feature on page 53 lists responsibilities of supervisors in managing technology, which fall generally into three categories:

- Providing technology for employees to do their work and to improve working conditions for them within budgetary constraints
- Keeping employees informed about company policies and trained on new and changing technologies
- Monitoring employee use

The tips on page 55 provide an overview of technology issues affecting supervisors. Future chapters will discuss handling flexible scheduling and telecommuting, building virtual teams, managing meetings electronically, enhancing productivity, and a variety of other technology topics.

The justification many companies give for off-shoring is that it increases productivity and decreases costs. Assume you are a manager in a company that wants to increase productivity without off-shoring. What are some things that you think might help to increase productivity with current staffing levels?

Terms

coach, 50
controller, 50
diversity, 58
emotional intelligence, 54
leader, 50
motivator, 49
off-shoring, 58
outsourcing, 58
planner, 49
recruiter, 50
scheduler, 49
supervisor, 47
trainer, 48
transformational change, 56

SUMMARY

1. Supervisors are typically considered part of first-line management and are vital to daily operations and organization success.
2. Supervisors have a wide variety of roles including trainer, planner, scheduler, motivator, coach, controller, leader, and recruiter.
3. For success, supervisors need skills in communication, entrepreneurial thinking, and decision making. They also need technical, team-building, and leadership skills, as well as skills in delegation, politics, emotional intelligence, self-awareness, administration, and time management.
4. Supervisors must help executive management implement major organizational changes and must manage change effectively in the areas they supervise.
5. Three trends impacting supervisors are workforce diversity, globalization, and changing technology.

Located at www.cengagebrain.com

- Chapter Outlines
- Flashcards
- Interactive Quizzes
- Tech Tools
- Video Segments

and More!

Questions for Reflection

1. At what level does the supervisor fit in the organizational pyramid? Describe a major trend that is changing the role of the supervisor at that level.
2. Which of the supervisory roles described in this chapter is most appealing to you?
   a. Explain why.
   b. What skills do you have that will enable you to perform this role successfully?
   c. What skills do you need to develop to succeed in this role?
3. Name six of the essential skills for supervisors described in this chapter.
4. Pick three of the skills you identified in question 3. Give an example of how supervisors use them to be effective in their jobs.
5. Provide two examples of how technology may be making supervisors' jobs easier or more efficient.
6. Provide two examples of how technology may be creating new challenges for supervisors.
7. Supervisors were listed as one of the obstacles to change. What are some things that you could do as a supervisor to work with employees in getting them to accept needed change?
8. Describe three trends impacting businesses and supervisors.

Hands-On Activities

Work With Your Team

1. As a team, discuss the following questions:
   a. How has globalization impacted your local community?
   b. Who on your team is wearing an article of clothing made outside the United States?
   c. Who has electronic equipment made outside the United States?
   d. How does the shift in manufacturing overseas impact each of you as a consumer?
   e. How does it impact you as a future supervisor or manager?
2. Prepare a brief written summary of your team's responses to the questions.
   a. Discuss the ideas you will include.
   b. Draft the summary.
   c. Have the team edit and finalize it.

You Decide | Case Study

Hiring a New Day Care Center Director

Katie has decided to expand her day care business. She has one location licensed to accommodate 12 children between 6 months and 5 years old. It is open from 8:00 a.m. to 5:30 p.m. Monday through Friday. Many of her customers have been asking for Saturday and extended hours. In addition, she has a waiting list of seven children. Finally, the local military base is about to add 5,000 new jobs, so Katie believes there will be even greater demand for her services.

Katie's expansion plans include tripling the size of her current space and extending the hours. The center will be open from 7:00 a.m. to 9:00 p.m.

Monday through Friday and from 8:00 a.m. to 4:00 p.m. Saturday. Katie will also open another location across town, near the military base, that will accommodate up to 36 children.

Katie will continue to run the main location. She is getting ready to hire a director for the new center. She has identified two finalists for the position. Both meet all the local legal requirements for working at a day care center.

- Shawn has a bachelor's degree in early childhood development as well as extensive experience working in a day care center. He has never been a supervisor.
- Elizabeth has a degree in elementary education with a teaching certificate that includes pre-K, which qualifies her to work at a day care center. She has been a supervisor at a local restaurant that caters to children for five years, but she has never worked in a day care center.

Questions

1. What will be some of the new director's responsibilities?
2. What are the most important skills for the applicant to have?
3. Describe the type of person Katie should hire.
4. What interview questions should Katie ask to help her determine which is the better candidate?
5. Whom would you hire: Shawn or Elizabeth? Why?
6. In what areas will Katie need to provide training for this new person?

MANAGER'S TOOLKIT

Political skills are an important part of the conceptual skills need to move up in management. Locate at least two credible articles describing the political skills needed by managers and explaining how to develop effective political skills.

1. Compose a paragraph explaining what the term *political skills* means.
2. Create a checklist of the political skills you need to develop to be an effective manager.
3. Prepare a professional development action plan for improving your political skills.

Soft Skills for Success

Decision Making

Decision making involves selecting a solution from among alternatives. Making good decisions is critical to effective management and leadership. As Charles Bass pointed out in the chapter opening interview, effective managers must make hard decisions and turn down requests when it is appropriate to do so. Managers should use a proven process to make decisions, and they should communicate the results appropriately.

Many decision-making models are available. Generally, they consist of the following steps:

1. Understand the problem and related issues clearly. Identify what is involved and what is not involved. Understand the issues. Clarifying the problem will help you determine whether you should make the decision yourself or seek others' input.
2. What are the alternatives? To make the best choice, consider all the alternatives. Often you may need to obtain additional information. This process may require more time than requesters expect. A good tip for supervisors who are pressed by employees to make a decision before adequate information is available is to respond: *If I have to make the decision now, the answer is no. However, if I have time to research the alternatives, we may be able to work out a suitable alternative.* Rarely will anyone select the "no" answer rather than waiting for the decision.
3. Evaluate the alternatives carefully.
4. Select the alternative that is best for all concerned. Then implement the decision.
5. After a period of time, reevaluate your decision. This will help you determine how effective it was, whether changes need to be made, and how you might improve your decision making in the future.

Once you have made a decision, you should communicate both the process you used and the final result. This is especially important if the decision was negative. Most people do not question positive decisions. However, they do tend to question negative decisions.

Put It to Work

You are an office manager for a public relations firm whose primary clients are small- to medium-sized banks, law offices, insurance companies, and accounting firms, as well as a variety of financial firms. Several employees have requested that you revise the company dress policy to include casual dress Fridays. You tell them the final decision must be approved by Linda West, the senior partner who is your manager, but you will research the issue and make a recommendation.

1. Using the Internet or other sources, do research to determine the advantages and disadvantages of a dress policy that includes casual dress on Fridays. Use recent sources (preferably no more than two years old).
2. Try to find companies similar to that of your client to determine their position on casual Friday dress policies. Then think about people likely to visit your office on Fridays. How do you think they will be dressed?
3. Analyze the advantages and disadvantages of casual Friday dress policies.
4. Determine whether your recommendation will be positive or negative.
5. Prepare a memo to the senior partners.
   a. Explain the request you have had from employees.
   b. Summarize the results of your research.
   c. Communicate your recommendation.
   d. Ask Ms. West to let you know what course of action she prefers you to take.

CHAPTER

4

Leadership Essentials

Learning Outcomes

1. Define leadership and list characteristics of an inspiring leader.
2. Describe what developing your people means.
3. Identify and discuss basic leadership theories and models.
4. Describe transformational and servant leadership.

Straight Talk From the Field

During his 18 years at Motorola, then a single telecommunications company, Michael Mallette held an array of managerial and executive positions in personnel, sales, and marketing. Previously, he was a customer service manager, production control manager, and teacher.

Reprinted by permission from Michael Mallette

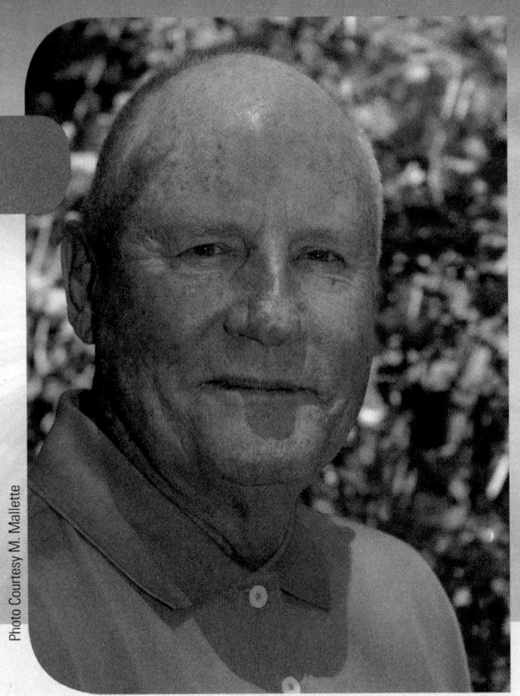

Photo Courtesy M. Mallette

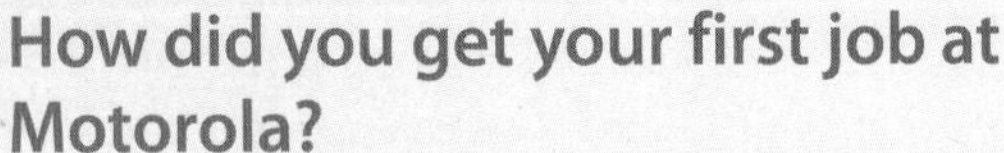

How did you get your first job at Motorola?

Early one morning, I was correcting some papers in the faculty office and came to the conclusion that I could very well be reviewing these very same papers 40 years from now! Later that day I called a good friend of mine who was an executive at Motorola. I asked if he knew of anyone in the employment office who might grant me a courtesy interview. He agreed to meet and told me to bring a résumé. I will always be grateful to him for taking it and arranging my first interview with Don.

Don and I shared an immediate affinity for each other. Don had been a recruiter for Motorola for many years. He later told me he had agreed to interview me only as a favor to my friend; he had no positions for which he was actively recruiting. In the course of our conversation, we determined that, based on my experience, there were many areas for which I might qualify. All of a sudden, Don said, "What would you think about doing what I do?" I was so naive that I immediately thought to myself, can this really be a full-time job? But I was smart enough to skip that question and simply respond, "That sounds exciting. What can you tell me about it?"

Don said he was about to get a new boss, a former peer who had just been promoted. The new boss would be looking to hire a replacement for his previous position. Would that hold any appeal for me? I immediately said, "Yes!"

About eight weeks later, after many interviews and my constant follow-up, I was offered the job and immediately accepted it.

What can you tell us about the importance of leaders knowing their own strengths and limitations?

Don and I became close friends, now working as peers on the same staff. As I did throughout my career, I used to get to work around 5:30 in the morning, well before most other employees. This made the two to three hours before the start of the actual workday my most productive. Don used to arrive early as well, usually about 7:00 a.m. He would wander over to my office, and we would have coffee and talk.

Don had one character flaw that I always found amusing: He always saw the glass as being significantly less than half full. His first reaction to any idea was always negative. "That was tried before—it failed." "That would never work." "Ha! You'll never be able to sell that."

One morning Don arrived at my door, leaned his head around the corner, and said with a big grin, "You son of a gun!"

I flinched and asked, "What did I do?"

"I was driving in this morning and was thinking of all the changes that have occurred around here since you came—and all of them have been successful. I got to thinking ... with every one of those ideas, I told you they would never work. Then I realized, you've been pumping me for information every morning! I believe I've been pretty important in all of this."

I looked at [him] and said, "Don, I can't begin to tell you how important! You've been invaluable. When you were telling me all the things we couldn't do, you were actually telling me about all the things we could do! You provided the solutions by telling me where all the land mines were, the history of any previous attempts, and where all the pitfalls were. I would never have been able to do all this without you, and I will always be grateful."

> "When you were telling me all the things we couldn't do, you were actually telling me about all the things we could do!"

The lessons I learned from this experience remained with me for the rest of my career:

- Naïveté is never a weakness, but a major strength. What is required is but a modicum of intelligence and a creative mind. Bolster that with the ability to work with others so as to capitalize on and learn from their knowledge and experience. To gain the support of your associates, you must be willing to admit your own lack of knowledge and experience. This will require a certain measure of self-confidence and humility. But if you are comfortable with this, you then can provide a vision of where you wish to go and garner their support in the achievement of significant goals.
- True diversity goes far beyond race or gender. It is the ability to capture all the strengths of our fellow employees by valuing their opinions, capitalizing on their intelligence and experience, focusing their strengths, and supporting them in achieving the vision you've provided.

Visit *www.cengagebrain.com* to read the complete profile.

Chapter Outline

This chapter introduces you to leadership as a concept, common characteristics of leaders, leadership theories, and leadership styles. Leadership is not an exact science, and leadership traits and styles are simply examples identified by leadership scholars. Many great leaders possess some but not all the attributes you will learn about. The purpose of this chapter is to have you think about your own theories and preferences as you begin to develop a personal leadership style that will work for you.

Leadership

Leadership is the process of inspiring, influencing, directing, and guiding others to participate in a common effort.[1] To encourage participation, leaders supplement the authority and power they possess with their personal attributes, vision, and social skills. Many leadership theories and expert opinions argue about what is (and is not) most effective. There is no perfect definition or theory. Developing leadership takes time, commitment, and the ability to learn from your mistakes.

As you reflect on your own leadership qualities, remember that each leader is unique. You may have some, but not all, of the leadership qualities mentioned. The fact that you do not have all the qualities does not mean you do not have the potential to be a great leader. Think about people you know in leadership positions: parents, past and present bosses, friends, coaches, deans, or the president of your college, for example. Do they all have the same qualities? Are they effective leaders just because they are in leadership positions? Often, people who are not in traditional leadership positions are effective leaders.

Developing your own leadership style and honing your leadership skills will take time and focused effort. Find ways to practice leadership skills both on and off the job. For example, serving in campus, community, or religious organizations will give you opportunities to experiment with different leadership styles. Leading effectively is learned by doing.

Leadership Versus Management

Before we proceed, it is important to think about the difference between leadership and management. Warren Bennis, a leadership author, speaker, and business professor at the University of Southern California, described the difference as follows:

> There is a profound difference between management and leadership. "To manage" means "to bring about, to accomplish, to have charge of or responsibility for, to conduct." "Leading" is "influencing, guiding in direction, and action."[2]

leadership
the process of inspiring, influencing, directing, and guiding others to participate in a common effort

Managers and supervisors are not necessarily the organization's formal leaders. However, they use an array of qualities and skills, including leadership qualities and skills, in managing and working with people to accomplish organizational goals. Recall the description of a supervisor's leadership role and responsibilities on page 28 of Chapter 2. Managers set the tone for their employees; they lead by example. At the same time, they stay focused on organizational goals, production standards, and customer needs.

Characteristics of Inspiring or Charismatic Leaders

Figure 4.1 provides two lists of qualities and skills of inspirational leaders. The first list is from the leader's perspective. This list was developed from a series of interviews of high-performing leaders. The second list, the follower's perspective, was compiled from a survey of followers.[3]

jargon
informal terminology unique to a business or industry, often not understood by new employees, customers, and other people outside the organization

Clearly, both leaders and followers value effective communication and interpersonal skills. These include the ability to articulate their vision using storytelling and other techniques to bring an idea to life, the ability to listen effectively and not do all the talking, and an effort to minimize the use of jargon. **Jargon** is informal terminology unique to a business or

FIGURE 4.1
Characteristics of inspiring leaders

From the Leader's Perspective
• Strong communication—storytelling and listening
• Passion for learning and intense curiosity
• Focus on developing people
• Having fun and very energized
• Strong self-belief, coupled with humanity and humility
• Committed to giving something back and to making a significant difference
• Clarity of vision and ability to share it with their people
• Dogged determination and often "relentless"
• Very strong focus on priorities
• Not afraid to show some vulnerability
• Regular use of reflective periods
• Almost universal dislike of jargon
• Passion for and pride in what they do
From the Follower's Perspective
• Genuine shared vision
• Real confidence and trust in their teams
• Respect for employees and customers
• Commitment to developing people
• Clear standards of ethics and integrity
• Willingness to take risks

Source: Adapted from U.K. Department of Trade and Industry, "Inspired Leadership," 5.

Managers will frequently assess employee skills and prepare an action or professional development plan for the annual performance evaluation.

industry that is often not understood by new employees, customers, and other people outside the organization.

Notice that the two lists include personal attributes. *Respectful*, *ethical*, *passionate*, *determined*, *energetic*, *confident*, and *humble* are among the characteristics of inspirational leaders. Another item that appears on both lists is the idea of developing people, which is essential for managers. One of the primary roles of managers is to get work accomplished through other people. To set people up for individual success in their jobs, a manager should be committed to helping each person develop and grow.

What Does "Developing People" Mean?

The first step involves learning about your employees and their skills, knowledge, education, goals, and dreams. The next step is to meet with your employees individually to create a development plan that is consistent with their personal goals and that will help the organization.[4]

© Konstantin Chagin/ Shutterstock.com

One of the keys to success in any organization is trust. When managers are trying to develop their staff, it is important that they provide the necessary training and resources. As trust grows among team members, managers no longer need to work side by side with their employees. However, they should routinely meet to solicit feedback and provide guidance and coaching when necessary.

Managers will frequently assess employee skills and prepare an action plan or professional development plan as part of the employee's annual performance evaluation. The plan may include action items such as the employee's enrolling in training classes, taking some college courses, job shadowing, sitting in on meetings, working on special projects, cross-training, and/or accepting more responsibility.

As a manager, you must be patient as you work to develop your people into more effective employees and potentially future managers and leaders. Learning new skills and taking on new assignments are processes that take time and commitment. Plan to develop your people to the point where they can have confidence and trust in their ability to do their jobs without constant supervision.

Basic Leadership Theories and Models

Scholars have spent decades studying various leadership theories and examining the traits, behaviors, and approaches used to lead people effectively. We will explore some basic leadership theories.

trait theory
a leadership theory that contends effective leaders have similar personality or behavioral characteristics that ineffective leaders lack

Trait Theory

Perhaps no leadership theory has been more controversial than trait theory, which originated in the early twentieth century. **Trait theory** contends that effective leaders have similar personality or behavioral characteristics that

Traits such as height, age, and education do not distinguish effective from ineffective leaders.

ineffective leaders lack. Initial research focused on physiological factors (height, weight, etc.), particularly in military leaders, and on demographics (age, education, affluence, etc.). Subsequent studies showed these traits did not distinguish effective from ineffective leaders.

In later research, Shelley Kirkpatrick and Edwin Locke of the University of Maryland provided evidence that effective leaders differ from other people in certain respects. They identified six key leadership traits:

- Drive—a broad term that includes achievement, motivation, ambition, energy, tenacity, and initiative
- Leadership motivation—the desire to lead but not to seek power for its own sake
- Honesty and integrity—essential qualities for building credibility and trust
- Self-confidence—believing in yourself and controlling your emotions
- Cognitive ability—good judgment and strong analytical abilities
- Knowledge of the business—a high level of knowledge that also encompasses the industry and technical matters[5]

Certain leadership traits help leaders acquire skills, form a vision and plan, and make the vision a reality.

Kirkpatrick and Locke believe these traits help leaders acquire the necessary skills for leadership, formulate an organizational vision and an effective plan for pursuing it, and take the necessary steps to make the vision a reality.[6]

Behavioral Styles Theories

This perspective of leadership is probably the most widely recognized. Rather than focusing on individual traits, behavioral leadership theorists examine patterns of leadership behavior, called **behavioral leadership styles**. The three classic styles of leadership behavior are authoritarian, democratic, and laissez-faire (or hands-off). Each has strengths and limitations.

Authoritarian

Authoritarian leaders retain all authority and responsibility. They assign people to clearly defined tasks, and there is primarily a downward flow of communication. This leadership style tends to stress prompt, orderly, and predictable performance. However, it can also stifle individual initiative and breed resentment.

behavioral leadership styles
patterns of leadership behavior

authoritarian leader
one who retains all authority and responsibility

democratic leader
one who delegates authority while retaining ultimate responsibility

Democratic

Democratic leaders delegate a great deal of authority while retaining ultimate responsibility. Work is divided and assigned on the basis of participatory decision making. An active, two-way flow of upward and downward communication is common. Democratic leaders typically enhance personal commitment through participation. However, this approach can be very time-consuming.

Laissez-Faire

Laissez-faire leaders grant responsibility and authority to a group of individuals. Group members are told to work problems and challenges out themselves and to do the best they can. Communication is primarily horizontal among peers. This approach permits self-starters to do what they think is appropriate without interference or direction from their leader. However, in the absence of direction and guidance from their leader, groups may become unfocused and drift aimlessly.

laissez-faire leader
one who grants responsibility and authority to a group of individuals, who are told to work problems out themselves

Comparing the Three Styles

For a number of years, theorists and managers hailed democratic leadership as the key to productive and happy employees. Eventually, however, their enthusiasm was dampened when critics noted that the original study relied on children as subjects and virtually ignored productivity. Although there is a general agreement that these basic styles exist, debate has been vigorous over their relative value and appropriateness. Practical experience has shown, for example, that the democratic style does not always stimulate better performance. Some employees prefer to be told what to do rather than to participate in decision making. This can be the result of cultural differences. For instance, in some cultures, publicly disagreeing with a leader is considered disrespectful, even if you think the leader is wrong.

Figure 4.2 provides an overview of each of these leadership styles along with their strengths, their weaknesses, and examples of situations where each approach may be used in the workplace.

FIGURE 4.2
Behavioral leadership styles

Characteristics	Authoritarian	Democratic	Laissez-Faire
Authority	Leader retains all authority and responsibility.	Leader delegates a great deal of authority while retaining ultimate responsibility.	Leader grants responsibility and authority to group.
Work Assignments	Leader assigns people to clearly defined tasks.	Work is divided and assigned on the basis of participatory decision making.	Group members are told to work things out themselves and do the best they can.
Communication	Primarily a downard flow of communication	Active, two-way flow of upward and downward communication	Primarily horizontal communication between peers
Primary Strengths	Stresses prompt, orderly, and predictable performance	Enhances personal commitment through participation	Permits self-starters to do things as they see fit without leader interference
Primary Weaknesses	Tends to stifle individual initiative	Democratic process is time-consuming.	Group may drift aimlessly without leader direction.
Examples	Urgent/emergency situation such as a team of firefighters responding to a call. The leader takes control and assigns others specific tasks and responsibilities.	Planned change such as extending a restaurant's hours to provide lunch as well as dinner sevice. Employees are involved in menu planning and promotional ideas.	Routine staffing such as a team of home-care nurses responsible for round-the-clock, on-call scheduling. The nurses negotiate among themselves to accommodate personal preferences and vacation days.

Imagine you are the office manager of an internal medicine group. The building loses power during a sudden storm, and you do not have a full-building generator. A leading expert in your field is conducting a seminar for physicians on the latest treatments available in your specialty, and a number of patients are in the building.

1. Which behavioral leadership style would be best for this situation? Explain your answer.

2. After the crisis is resolved, the partners ask that you create an emergency plan to address a power outage. Which behavioral leadership style will you use when preparing the plan? Explain why.

Blake/Mouton Leadership Grid

Many attempts have been made to categorize different patterns of behavior and to promote them as styles. One of the most popular and best-known schemes for developing behavioral styles in the workplace is the Blake/Mouton Managerial Grid (1964), which later became the Blake/Mouton Leadership Grid (1991). This grid has been used extensively in management development programs. It blends concern for people and concern for production or the task to create five alternative styles as shown in Figure 4.3.

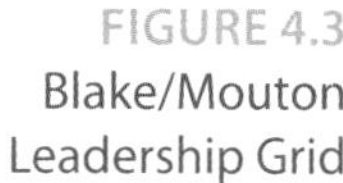
FIGURE 4.3
Blake/Mouton Leadership Grid

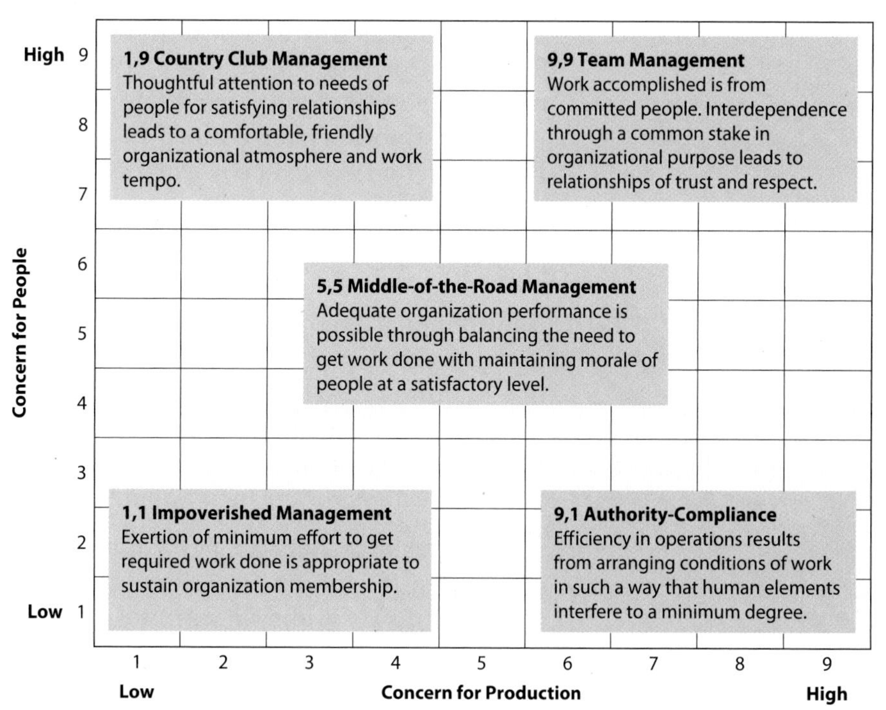

Source: R. R. Blake and A. A. McCanse, *The Leadership Grid®," Leadership Dilemmas—Grid Solutions* (Houston: Gulf Publishing Company), 21. Copyright © 1991, by Scientific Methods, Inc. Reproduced by permission of the owners.

Advocates of the Blake/Mouton Leadership Grid believe the 9,9 Team Management style is the preferred style. It emphasizes appropriately balanced concern both for people and for the work to be done. However, they recognize that one style may not always work or be effective in every work environment. For example, in a crisis situation, a 9,1 Authority-Compliance style may produce the best results. The limitations of the Blake/Mouton Leadership Grid are that it is based on only two dimensions—concern for production and concern for people—and that generally one style of leadership is recommended as the best to use. These limitations led to the development of situational leadership models.

1. As a general style (knowing you may have to alter your style depending on the situation), which of the five styles in the Blake/Mouton Leadership Grid would you prefer to use? Why?

___

2. Which style would you be least comfortable with as a general style? Why?

___

Situational Theories and Models

Convinced that no one best style of leadership exists, some management experts have identified situational or contingency thinking as a more effective approach. **Situational leadership** occurs when the leader's style matches the situation. Three different approaches to situational leadership, which were briefly introduced in Chapter 2, are discussed here: (1) Ken Blanchard and Paul Hersey's model, (2) Fred E. Fiedler's contingency theory, and (3) the path-goal theory.

Blanchard and Hersey Model

Ken Blanchard and Paul Hersey have been called the pioneers of situational leadership.[7] The framework for **Blanchard and Hersey's situational leadership model** is based on four different leadership styles or characteristics: (1) directing, (2) coaching, (3) supporting, and (4) delegating.[8] Blanchard and Hersey emphasize that "no single ... leadership style is universally successful."[9] They provide this overview of situational leadership:

> Successful leaders can adapt their behavior to meet followers' needs and the particular situation. Effectiveness depends on the leader, the followers, and situational elements. Leaders must be able to diagnose their own behavior in light of their environments.[10]

situational leadership
the concept that successful leadership occurs when the leader's style matches the situation

Blanchard and Hersey's situational leadership model
a model based on four different leadership styles or characteristics: directing, coaching, supporting, and delegating

To be successful using the Blanchard and Hersey model, managers need to shift styles to handle the situation and accommodate the needs of their employees. For example, imagine you are the manager of a bank branch. When you hire a new employee and he or she is scheduled to open the bank for the first time, your leadership style needs to be directive. As you build trust in the employee and the employee's confidence and level of readiness increase, you can shift to coaching, supporting, or delegating leadership styles. In other words, your leadership style accommodates the individual's personal growth and development.

Fiedler's Contingency Theory

Fiedler's contingency theory is based on the notion that a leader's performance depends on the likelihood that he or she can successfully accomplish the job and the leader's basic motivation. Although it is closely aligned with Blanchard and Hersey's situational leadership model, there are unique aspects and distinct differences that are worth exploring. Among the leadership theories discussed so far, Fiedler's is the most thoroughly tested. It is the product of more than 30 years of research by Fred E. Fiedler and his associates. Fiedler's contingency theory gets its name from the following assumptions:

> The performance of a leader depends on two interrelated factors: (1) the degree to which the situation gives the leader control and influence—that is, the likelihood that [the leader] can successfully accomplish the job; and (2) the leader's basic motivation—that is, whether [the leader's] self-esteem depends primarily on accomplishing the task or on having close supportive relations with others.[11]

Regarding the second factor, the leader's basic motivation, Fiedler believes leaders are either task-motivated or relationship-motivated. These two motivational profiles are roughly equivalent to managers' being primarily concerned about production (task-motivated) or about people (relationship-motivated).

As illustrated in Figure 4.4, task-motivated leaders seem to be effective in extreme situations when they have either very little control or a great deal of control over situational variables. In moderately favorable situations, however, relationship-motivated leaders tend to be more effective. Consequently, Fiedler and one of his colleagues summed up their findings by noting that "everything points to the conclusion that there is no such thing as an ideal leader."[12] Instead, there are leaders, and there are situations. The challenge, according to Fiedler, is to analyze a leader's basic motivation and then match that leader with a suitable situation to form a productive combination. He believes it is more efficient to move leaders to a suitable situation than to tamper with their personalities by trying to get task-motivated leaders to become relationship-motivated, or vice versa.

Fiedler's contingency theory
a model based on the notion that a leader's performance depends on the likelihood that he or she can successfully accomplish the job and the leader's basic motivation

path-goal theory
a model that suggests leaders motivate their followers by providing clear goals and meaningful incentives for reaching them

Path-Goal Theory

Another situational leadership theory is the **path-goal theory**. This theory gets its name from the assumption that effective leaders can enhance

FIGURE 4.4
Fiedler's contingency theory of leadership

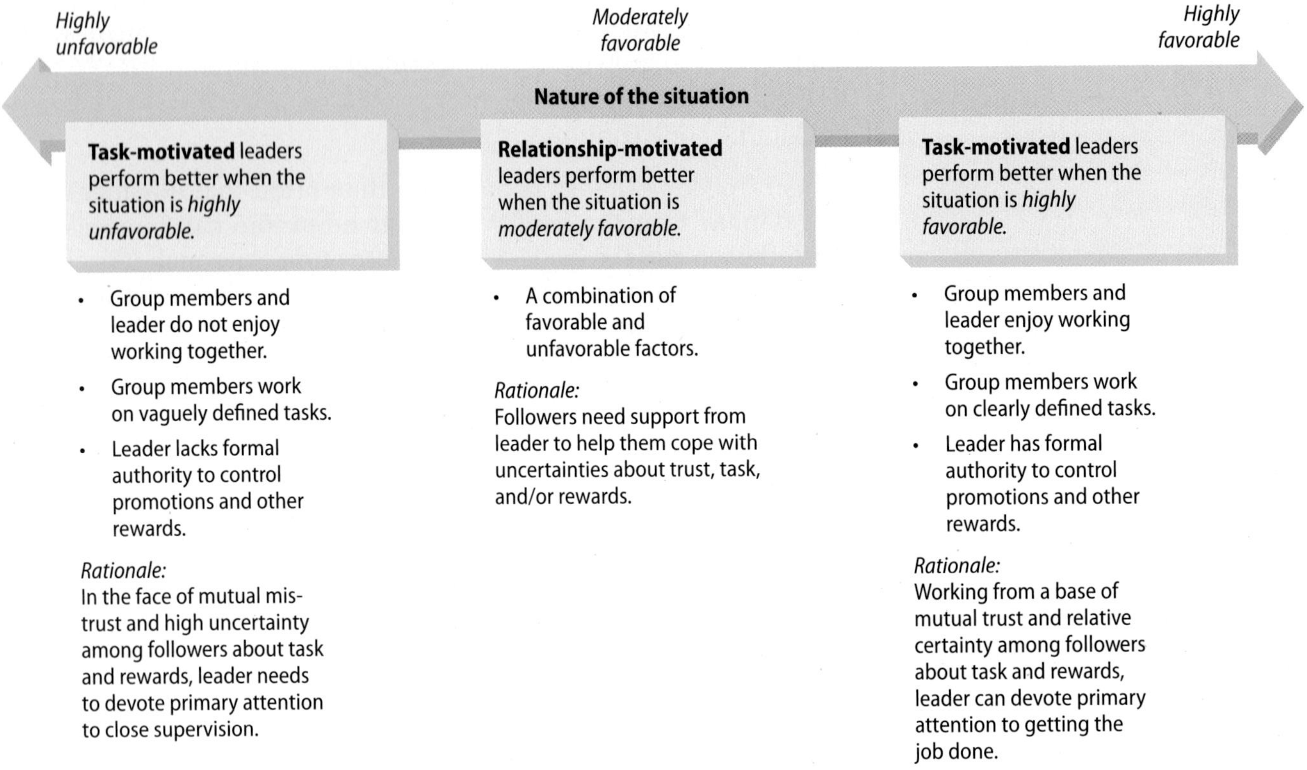

Highly unfavorable — *Moderately favorable* — *Highly favorable*

Nature of the situation

Task-motivated leaders perform better when the situation is *highly unfavorable.*

- Group members and leader do not enjoy working together.
- Group members work on vaguely defined tasks.
- Leader lacks formal authority to control promotions and other rewards.

Rationale:
In the face of mutual mistrust and high uncertainty among followers about task and rewards, leader needs to devote primary attention to close supervision.

Relationship-motivated leaders perform better when the situation is *moderately favorable.*

- A combination of favorable and unfavorable factors.

Rationale:
Followers need support from leader to help them cope with uncertainties about trust, task, and/or rewards.

Task-motivated leaders perform better when the situation is *highly favorable.*

- Group members and leader enjoy working together.
- Group members work on clearly defined tasks.
- Leader has formal authority to control promotions and other rewards.

Rationale:
Working from a base of mutual trust and relative certainty among followers about task and rewards, leader can devote primary attention to getting the job done.

Motivation is essential for successful supervision.

employee motivation by (1) clarifying the individual's perception of work goals, (2) linking meaningful rewards with goal attainment, and (3) explaining how goals and desired rewards can be achieved. In short, leaders need to motivate their followers by providing clear goals and meaningful incentives for reaching them. Motivation is essential for successful supervision in the path-goal model.

According to path-goal theorists, leaders can enhance motivation by increasing the number of opportunities for their employees to earn personal rewards for goal attainment. This level of achievement will increase personal satisfaction on the job as well. To set up their employees for success, leaders should provide a clear path to goal attainment, make necessary resources available, and eliminate potential barriers.[13]

Path-goal proponents believe managers need to rely on four different leadership styles, choosing the one that is best suited to the situation. These four leadership styles are (1) directive, (2) supportive, (3) participative, and (4) achievement-oriented.

1. Under the **directive leadership style**, managers tell employees exactly what is expected of them. They provide specific guidance for performing tasks, set schedules and performance standards, and ensure employees follow rules and regulations.[14] This leadership style is often used when employees are new, lack experience, and need direction. It is also common in situations that require quick decisions and have a sense of urgency, such as a team of firefighters responding to an emergency call.
2. Under the **supportive leadership style**, managers treat employees as equals in a friendly manner while striving to improve their well-being. This style may be appropriate, for example, in a professional office setting such as an accounting firm where knowledgeable employees perform the majority of the work. They typically do not need much direction or guidance. However, they want to be treated with respect and to know they are valued.
3. Under the **participative leadership style**, managers consult with employees to seek their suggestions and then seriously consider those suggestions when making decisions. This style of leadership is often used in organizations where the employees understand the organization and can contribute creative ideas that will help the company grow and succeed.
4. Under the **achievement-oriented leadership style**, managers set challenging goals, emphasize excellence, and seek continuous improvement while maintaining a high degree of confidence that employees will meet difficult challenges in a responsible manner.[15] Supervisors with talented and goal-oriented people are likely to use this leadership style at some time.

directive leadership style
a leadership style in which managers tell people what is expected of them and provide specific guidance, schedules, rules, regulations, and standards

supportive leadership style
a leadership style in which managers treat employees as equals in a friendly manner while striving to improve their well-being

participative leadership style
a leadership style in which managers consult with employees to seek their suggestions and then seriously consider those suggestions when making decisions

achievement-oriented leadership style
a leadership style in which managers set challenging goals, emphasize excellence, and seek continuous improvement

Comparing Fielder's Contingency Theory With Path-Goal Theory

The assumption that managers can and do shift their style of management clearly sets path-goal theory apart from Fiedler's model. Recall that Fiedler claims managers cannot and do not change their basic leadership styles. Another valuable contribution of path-goal theory is its identification of the achievement-oriented leadership style. As managers and supervisors deal with an increasing number of highly educated and self-motivated employees, particularly in advanced technology industries, they will need to become skilled facilitators rather than just order-givers or hand-holders.

Select a situation from your job or an extracurricular group you are involved with. Choose a situation that will ultimately lead to change, such as a new sales campaign, a fundraiser, or a recruitment drive.

1. Describe the situation.

   ____

2. Which situational leadership style do you think would be most effective in the scenario you described above? Explain why.

   ____

3. What variables did you consider when selecting a leadership style?

   ____

Transformational and Servant Leadership

Researchers have continued to study leadership from a variety of different perspectives. Transformational leadership and servant leadership are somewhat similar to charismatic leadership (see Figure 4.1 on page 69), but they also have significant differences. A concern about charismatic leadership is that it has been used to inspire, manipulate, or brainwash and to lead followers to death and destruction as well as to great things. If you think about history, the following examples might come to mind: Alexander the Great, Adolf Hitler, and Jim Jones. All were charismatic leaders who used and exploited their followers to their peril. Transformational leadership is used to motivate employees to reach a shared organizational vision and goals.

Transformational Leadership

Researchers including James MacGregor Burns and Bernard M. Bass defined transformational leadership theory. Burns's philosophy was that leadership was either transactional or transformational. Transactional leadership is based on transactions between managers and employees with rewards given when performance is good and punishment when it is not. **Transformational leadership** is based on relationships between managers and employees that result in a higher level of motivation and achieving shared goals. Transformational leaders inspire followers to share a vision, motivate and empower them to achieve it, and provide the coaching and support needed to develop their personal potential.[16] Bass extended Burns's work and identified four behavior characteristics of transformational leadership. Transformational leaders:

transformational leadership
leadership that inspires followers to share a vision, motivates and empowers them to achieve the vision, and provides coaching and support to develop their potential

1. Influence their employees in a positive way so that employees trust them and consider them role models. When employees trust and emulate their leaders, they share the vision and believe it can be achieved.
2. Motivate and inspire their employees to understand the importance of their jobs and to work together to achieve the vision and goals of the organization, not just their own goals.

3. Encourage their employees to use their intellectual abilities to solve problems in creative ways and to explore new ways to do things.
4. Coach and develop individual employees to help them reach their potential for personal growth as well as for the benefit of the organization.[17]

Servant Leadership

Servant leadership differs from transformational leadership in that transformational leadership focuses on leaders who inspire employees to achieve a shared vision. The leader's ability to inspire and empower employees is a key part of the theory. Servant leaders focus on employees and meeting their needs first rather than the organization's needs. Ethics is a key component of servant leadership.

Robert F. Greenleaf, founder of the Greenleaf Center for Servant Leadership, is known for defining the concept of servant leadership in 1970. This approach to leadership reflects a philosophy that leaders should think of their employees first and be concerned about serving their needs rather than their own needs or their organization's needs.[18] In a practical sense, this approach views leaders and employees as being on the same level of the organizational pyramid. The goal is to develop the employees so that they all become servant leaders and everybody in the work group serves and is responsible for each other. Many of the behavioral characteristics of the servant leader are similar to those of charismatic leaders listed in Figure 4.1 and to those of transformational leaders. A strong commitment to honesty, integrity, ethics, and building trust is important to servant leadership.

Many researchers are critical of servant leadership because of its strong tie to religion or spirituality and label it as a philosophy rather than a theory subjected to extensive empirical testing. They also point out that it is not practical as a leadership theory because it does not place primary emphasis on achieving organizational objectives. Most of the support for servant leadership comes in the form of anecdotal evidence from companies who have implemented some of the tenets of servant leadership. Concepts of servant leadership having been implemented in a number of companies both large and small, particularly those classified as service organizations.

1. The foundation of effective leadership is thinking through the organization's mission, defining it and establishing it, clearly and visibly.
2. The second requirement is that the leader sees leadership as responsibility rather than as rank and privilege.
3. The final requirement ... is to earn trust. Otherwise there won't be any followers— and the only definition of a leader is someone who has followers.

—Peter F. Drucker (known as the father of modern management)

Source: Peter F. Drucker, "Drucker on Management: Leadership: More Doing Than Dash," *The Wall Street Journal*, January 6, 1988, 1.

servant leadership
ethical leadership that focuses on employees and meeting their needs first rather than the organization's needs

In the past two decades, a number of researchers have tested different assumptions of servant leadership and have also compared transformational and servant leadership. Some conclude that transformational leadership is better suited to a competitive organization, whereas servant leadership is better suited to a public, religious, educational, or nonprofit organization.[19]

LEVERAGING TECHNOLOGY

LARGE-GROUP COMMUNICATION

Most leaders believe face-to-face communication and interaction is the most effective way to communicate important information to the entire organization. In small businesses, leaders often have that luxury. In large enterprises that are geographically dispersed, it may not be possible. Today's technology provides a workable alternative.

Assume you are a manager in a company that has ten offices with 250 employees in the United States, Canada, and South America. Your team has developed a new product, and the CEO has asked you to participate in an announcement about the product to the entire company. Your team includes a representative from each office. It is not feasible to bring in all the employees for a live presentation.

The first step in using technology effectively is to determine the barriers to communication enabled by technology:

- *One-way versus two-way communication.* Will information be provided without feedback, or will employees be able to comment and ask questions?
- *Time and language differences.* Can all employees be reached at the same time during the workday, and can they all speak English?
- *Individual or group reception.* Will employees listen to the announcement streamed on their own computers or in groups in the various office locations?

In this scenario, overcoming the barriers is much easier with one-way communication than with two-way communication. One effective method is video. Another is a presentation in the main office with a live audience, streamed to all computers via a webinar or webcast with slides in the appropriate language. A follow-up discussion period with local leaders in the remote offices would allow for feedback.

1. Assume you are the manager in the scenario described above, and the CEO made a one-way presentation that all employees watched together in a large training room. How would you follow up the CEO's presentation?

    ____

2. What types of questions and comments would you expect from your employees? Think about how you might respond.

    ____

3. What would you expect to accomplish in your follow-up session?

    ____

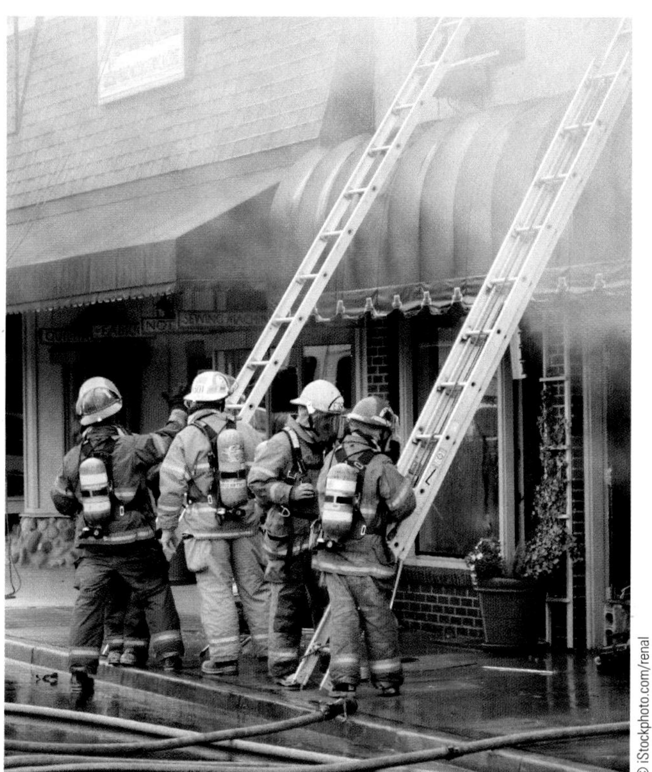

Supervisors should adapt their leadership style to the situation. What is the ideal leadership style for a supervisor of firefighters during and after the fire?

What Is the Ideal Leadership Style?

You have learned about several leadership behaviors, theories, models, and styles. With the wide variety of options, it can be somewhat overwhelming to try to figure out which style is best. Put your mind at ease because there is no such thing as the ideal leadership style. In fact, the best answer to this question is, "It depends." Choosing the appropriate leadership style depends on many variables, including the following:

- Your personal leadership style and experience
- The level of readiness of your followers
- The organizational culture
- The situation

SUMMARY

1. Leadership is the process of inspiring, influencing, directing, and guiding others to participate in a common effort. Some characteristics of inspiring leaders are strong communication skills; personal attributes such as respect, ethics, and passion; and a commitment to developing people.
2. Trait theory contends that effective leaders share certain personality or behavioral characteristics.
3. Behavioral leadership theory examines patterns of leadership behavior. Three well-known behavioral leadership styles are authoritarian, democratic, and laissez-faire.
4. Situational leadership occurs when the leader's style matches the situation. Three approaches to situational leadership are Ken Blanchard and Paul Hersey's model, Fred Fiedler's contingency theory, and the path-goal theory.
5. Transformational leadership calls for leaders to inspire employees to achieve a shared vision.
6. Servant leadership focuses on employees and meeting their needs first rather than those of the organization.
7. No ideal leadership style exists. The best style depends on many variables, including your personal style, the level of readiness of your followers, the organization, and the situation.

Terms

achievement-oriented leadership style, 77
authoritarian leader, 71
behavioral leadership styles, 71
Blanchard and Hersey's situational leadership model, 74
democratic leader, 71
directive leadership style, 77
Fiedler's contingency theory, 75
jargon, 69
laissez-faire leader, 72
leadership, 68
participative leadership style, 77
path-goal theory, 75
servant leadership, 79
situational leadership, 74
supportive leadership style, 77
trait theory, 70
transformational leadership, 78

Study Tools
CourseMate
Located at www.cengagebrain.com

- Chapter Outlines
- Flashcards
- Interactive Quizzes
- Tech Tools
- Video Segments

and More!

Questions for Reflection

1. There are many different leadership theories and no ideal leadership style. Explain what "It depends" means to you in the context of choosing the best leadership style.
2. Which of the primary traits identified by Kirkpatrick and Locke that distinguish effective from ineffective leaders do you possess?
3. Could you develop the traits you do not possess? How would you go about it?
4. What are some differences between the three behavioral styles of leadership? Provide examples to illustrate when it would be appropriate to use each behavioral style.
5. How does transformational leadership differ from servant leadership?

Hands-On Activities

Leadership Styles

1. Carefully reread the interview with Thomas E. Suggs on pages 24–25 in Chapter 2.
2. Referring to the Blake/Mouton Leadership Grid on page 73, answer the following questions:
   a. Which of the five leadership styles do you think Suggs uses?
   b. On what factors did you base your response?
3. Carefully reread the interview with Charles N. Bass on pages 45–46 in Chapter 3. Note that Bass describes his major roles and responsibilities. Referring to the four path-goal situational styles described on pages 76–77, answer the following questions:
   a. Which style or styles do you think Bass uses for the situations he describes?
   b. Would you use the same styles? Why or why not?

You Decide | Case Study

Selecting an Appropriate Leadership Style

You are the office manager for a real estate branch office that includes an accountant, two office assistants, ten sales associates (agents), and two rental property managers. The main office is in a different city about twenty miles away. The sales associates report to the vice president for sales in the main office, but you coordinate their work, and your assistants provide office support for them. The accountant, office assistants, and property managers report to you. You and your staff are responsible for preparing all listing and sales contracts, reports, and financial documents; ordering and having signs installed; coordinating open house showings and other events; and all general office work.

Over the past couple of weeks, several sales associates have been making a number of last-minute demands on the accountant and office assistants. These associates have also insisted the staff do their work immediately even though staff members were doing projects for other sales associates. You have been waiting to see how the staff would handle the situation, but it has worsened, so you have decided you need to work with everyone to resolve the issues.

Questions

1. Would your leadership style be the same for working with your staff and the sales associates?
2. If you answered yes, explain what style you would use and why. If you answered no, explain what style you would use with each party and why.

MANAGER'S TOOLKIT

Complete this survey of your skills, interests, goals, and motivators. With this knowledge, you can be more focused on your career planning and academic goals. In addition, you should have all your employees complete this inventory. This will allow you to learn more about them. The results can be used as a tool to work with each person to prepare a professional development plan. You can list specific knowledge or skills that are unique to your workplace and add or edit questions to meet your needs.

1. What are your goals and expectations for work?
2. What skills do you have, and how would you rate your level of proficiency in each (beginner, intermediate, or advanced)?
3. What do you like doing the most? Why?
4. In what areas would you like to improve?
5. Would you like more or less responsibility? Explain.
6. What motivates you?
7. What do you want to get out of this job (e.g., social interaction, new skills, money)?
8. Identify three work-related performance rewards that are meaningful to you.

Soft Skills for Success

Responsibility

Many employers seek employees that can assume responsibility. In the "They Said It Best" quote from Peter Drucker on page 79, responsibility was the second of the three leadership basics. One way of looking at responsibility is that it means doing what you are expected to do in the time frame allocated and producing the results expected. In a business setting, responsibility extends to yourself, your organization, and your community.

In the "Straight Talk From the Field" interview in Chapter 1, Cathy Novinger provided insight into how she and companies in general view responsibility to yourself. When you accept a job, you accept the roles and responsibilities attached to that job. Moving to a higher level is dependent on an excellent performance record in your current job. You are accountable for your own results. This means accepting responsibility for your mistakes and not blaming others. It also means learning from mistakes and bad decisions.

When you are in a leadership role in an organization, you are responsible not only for yourself but also for those you lead. Former President Harry Truman said it this way: "The buck stops here!" A good leader accepts responsibility for the mistakes of those he or she leads and takes appropriate action to prevent mistakes from recurring.

Leaders also have a responsibility to their communities, often called social responsibility. It means ensuring their organizations are being good citizens. Examples of good corporate citizenship are protecting the environment, conserving energy, and giving back by working with nonprofit organizations.

Put It to Work

1. Review the Knowledge to Action scenario on page 73.
2. Describe your responsibilities to the patients in the building.
3. Describe your responsibilities to the visiting consultant and to your organization that is paying for the services provided.
4. Describe your responsibilities for devising a plan to prevent the problems caused by the power outage. Look at this question from the perspective of being able to take care of the people in your building, the temporary loss of your computer and medical information systems you experienced, and preventing the loss of power in a storm.

CHAPTER

5

High-Performance Teams—Key to Productivity

Learning Outcomes

1. Identify and discuss characteristics of high-performance teams.
2. Describe the stages of developing work groups into effective teams.
3. Name three special types of teams.
4. Explain how to build effective face-to-face and virtual teams.
5. Describe empowerment and explain how it differs from delegation.
6. Explain delegation and list steps to delegate effectively.

Photo courtesy of B. Huffman

Straight Talk From the Field

Barbara Schwenger-Huffman is a leadership training consultant for BAE Systems in Washington, DC. BAE Systems is a global company that develops, delivers, and supports advanced defense, security, and aerospace systems.

How did your approach to leadership change as a result of leading virtual teams?

Thus far in my career, and even earlier in school, I have fallen into leadership roles quite naturally. I was fortunate to have early leadership learning experiences to gather skills and to begin building my leadership repertoire. Coupled with a strong sense of responsibility and passion for each job, I thought I had the basics of leadership figured out. Of course, I would need to make adjustments to my style, depending on the organization and the people I was working with, but I found that my general skills adapted easily enough from place to place.

However, once I started leading remote teams, I found that what got me there would not keep me there. My skills and practices from the traditional work setting needed to evolve. Virtual leadership situations place greater demands on planning and staged executions, defining objectives and expectations, communicating, and your ability to flex supervisory styles for the unique abilities of each team member.

In the past, I have had the good fortune of leading virtual teams. Striving for successful and productive teams while leading from a distance, via the phone, email, and occasional visits, required a change in my leadership behaviors and style. No longer could I rely on micromanager habits, leading by popping in, or managing the environment by keeping abreast of water-cooler chatter. Instead, more thoughtful communication and planning skills were required.

What does it take to be an effective leader of in-person and virtual teams?

Here are my five tips:

1. Be flexible with your leadership style. For some, daily coaching and planning calls filled with guidance and support are necessary. Others may require only weekly meetings to report their progress and respond better to being challenged with additional tasks.
2. Long-distance leadership means it is often impossible to be that hero-leader who jumps in and saves the day. Instead, ask questions about and explore what a team needs to move forward and then challenge the team to take the appropriate action. Often I find that teams much prefer operating this way. What team doesn't want to own the success of solving its own problem?
3. In the past, I enjoyed reading a situation in the moment and relying on my ability to react correctly no matter what came my way. I may have missed opportunities in terms of planning, predicting, and establishing desired results. With a virtual team, it is imperative to give definition to everything from next steps in a project to satisfactory performance criteria.

4. Plan and choose words and actions that make your intentions clear to team members. Without mutual eye contact to read how your message is being received, the ability to shift and clarify in the moment may be lost. As I learn more about and then consider each team member's preferences and needs, I find the potential barriers of long-distance communication dropping away.
5. Leadership requires strong listening skills. Listen for meaning, not just words. During conference calls, take time to listen fully and understand each participant prior to responding. This may require asking clarifying questions or possibly asking team members to repeat themselves. You may have to wait until others have finished speaking and revisit a topic from earlier in the conversation before getting clarification. Interestingly enough, this forced waiting and revisiting often creates new and better solutions and does not allow a leader to shut down productive peer discussion inadvertently.

Interestingly enough, this forced waiting and revisiting often creates new and better solutions.

Although my goals are still the same—productive teams that contribute to the bottom line while working in a healthy environment—being a virtual team leader makes me ask myself, Why am I here? How can I be helpful to my team? Once I began approaching leadership in the "helpful mode" and literally started asking, "How can I help?" (versus telling), I found that team results and relationships improved.

Visit *www.cengagebrain.com* to read the complete profile.

Chapter Outline

What is a team, and why is teamwork emphasized so much? In *The Wisdom of Teams*, Jon R. Katzenbach and Douglas K. Smith define a **team** as a small group of people ... with complementary skills committed to a common purpose and set of specific performance goals. Its members are committed to working with each other to achieve the team's purpose and hold each other fully and jointly accountable for the team's results.[1]

Organizations use teamwork extensively because they believe effective teams improve the organization. Teams make better decisions, are better problem solvers, and generally feel empowered, which leads to employee satisfaction. Effective teams create synergies. *Effective* is the operative word; however, not all teams are effective or successful. Huge differences exist between ordinary work groups and **high-performance teams**, those whose performance consistently exceeds that of competent individuals in the organization. The emphasis in this chapter is on building high-performance teams.

Organizations use teamwork extensively because they believe effective teams improve the organization.

Characteristics of High-Performance Teams

Katzenbach and Smith suggest that groups can forge themselves into effective teams through a disciplined approach to the following actions:

- Shaping a common purpose
- Agreeing on performance goals
- Defining a common working approach
- Developing high levels of complementary skills
- Holding themselves mutually accountable for results[2]

They also propose eight approaches to build team performance:

1. Establish the urgency of the team's purposes and clear direction.
2. Choose members for skills and the ability to develop them, not personalities.
3. Pay special attention to first meetings and actions.
4. Set clear rules of behavior.
5. Set and focus on a few immediate performance-oriented tasks and goals.
6. Challenge the team regularly with new facts and information.
7. Spend a lot of time together.
8. Use positive feedback, recognition, and reward.[3]

Literature about high-performance teams is packed with dozens of lists of their characteristics. The following list includes ten characteristics that represent the common factors:

1. Team members have shared goals and objectives. The team should have input into the purpose or goals it is expected to achieve within an appropriate time frame.

team
a small group of people with complementary skills committed to a common purpose and specific performance goals

high-performance team
a team that consistently outperforms competent individuals in the organization

2. Each member has the knowledge and skills necessary to contribute to the team, but all members should not have the same knowledge and skills.
3. Each member focuses on attaining the team goals and puts them ahead of his or her own goals.
4. Each member is empowered, controls his or her own responsibilities, and is held accountable for them. Each member is also accountable to the team.
5. Each member is committed to the work of the team, to the way the team chooses to accomplish it, and to doing his or her fair share.
6. Each member is given and accepts the opportunity to make decisions that affect the team and participates in team decisions.
7. Team members are receptive to other members' ideas, share their own, and communicate openly and effectively with each other.
8. Each member respects and trusts the others.
9. Each member supports team decisions once they have been made.
10. Evaluation and rewards are based on team performance, not on individual performance.

Work Group Versus High-Performing Team

work group
two or more employees who work together to complete a task or achieve a common goal

synergy
the idea that the whole exceeds the sum of the parts

A **work group** consists of two or more employees working together to complete a task or achieve a common goal. Many work groups and teams in various stages of development are used in industry. It should be obvious from the list above, however, that most work groups could not meet the standards of high-performance teams, nor would they be given the autonomy that high-performing teams need to be effective. It should also be obvious that high-performance teams are not easy to build, lead, or manage. However, the synergy they create makes it worth the time and effort. **Synergy** is the idea that the whole exceeds the sum of the parts.

If you think about teams on a continuum of development, work groups would be at the beginning stage of development with high-performance teams at the opposite end (Figure 5.1):

FIGURE 5.1
Team development continuum

Stages of Team Development

In 1965, educational psychologist Bruce W. Tuckman proposed a four-stage model of team development based on research and a literature review. This model is still widely accepted today. Tuckman later revisited his work with associate Mary Ann Jensen and added a fifth stage.[4] Many researchers have analyzed these stages and have developed methods of managing them.

Stage 1: Forming

The forming stage occurs when the individuals begin to work together as a group. They are eager to learn about each other and their assignment. They may also have some anxiety about being part of a new team. At this stage, managers should focus on helping members get to know each other and explaining the team's task clearly but not in too much detail.

Stage 2: Storming

The storming stage occurs as individuals begin work and start to question and argue about their roles and any unclear issues or assignments. Managers should apply their skills in resolving any conflicts that arise and should clarify information as needed to prevent conflict.

Stage 3: Norming

The norming stage occurs when roles and conflicts are settled. Members accept one another and come together as a group, focusing their energies on the task. At this stage, managers should divide their focus between team members and the group's task.

Stage 4: Performing

The performing stage occurs when the team works together effectively to accomplish the task. The group is now a high-performance team. Managers can concentrate primarily on the team's assignment while continuing to monitor people issues. Not all teams can sustain this level of work or become high-performing teams.

Getting to know each other is part of the first stage in team development.

Stage 5: Adjourning

The adjourning stage occurs when the work has been completed and the group begins to dissolve. Managers should work to help individuals cope with the change and prepare for new endeavors.[5]

Misperceptions About Teamwork

In 2011, J. Richard Hackman, a professor of social and organizational psychology at Harvard University, posted a number of misperceptions about teamwork on the HBR (*Harvard Business Review*) Blog Network (Figure 5.2, page 92). He confirmed them through his research in the U.S. intelligence community.[6]

FIGURE 5.2
Misperceptions about teamwork

Misperceptions	Actual Research Shows
1. The best teams work together harmoniously. They collaborate rather than create conflicts and waste time debating how to get things done.	Teams that experience conflict focused on the objectives and the work to be accomplished are more likely to be creative problem solvers than teams that are conflict-free. Disagreements that are not about the work itself can be harmful.
2. Rotating team members produces better results because new members energize the team with a fresh perspective.	Teams produce better results when the same members of the team work together for a long period of time.
3. Large teams produce better results than teams with fewer members because they have access to more resources.	Small teams are easier to manage, collaborate better, and are more likely to produce better results.
4. Today's technology facilitates communication and coordination and enables teams to work effectively and efficiently thereby eliminating the need for face-to-face meetings.	Face-to-face communication is far more effective than electronic meetings. Working electronically solves distance and time problems, but does not provide the necessary nonverbal communication.
5. The success of a team depends on the leader. Compare teams that you have led or others have led that have been successful and those that have been unsuccessful.	The leader is important, but what makes the difference is creating a collaborative environment that helps team members become effective self-managers. Also, getting the project off to a good start and following up with coaching and teaching as needed lead to team success.
6. Putting talented people on a team, describing the desired outcomes, and letting the team determine what to do is all that is needed for a successful outcome.	Teams must be prepared for success. Successful results are the product of clear, specific objectives that must be accomplished and having the resources and support needed to accomplish the objectives.

Source: J. Richard Hackman, "Six Common Misperceptions about Teamwork," HBR Blog Network, June 7, 2011.

Special Types of Teams

You will encounter many different types of teams in the workplace. Three important types are cross-functional teams, virtual teams, and project teams.

Cross-Functional Teams

A **cross-functional team** consists of employees from different functional areas of the organization who are focused on a specific objective. The purpose of using cross-functional teams is to have individuals with different perspectives collaborate on common goals to achieve greater synergy. A cross-functional team with a strong leader and with members selected because they have the expertise or potential to help solve complex problems or to reach complex goals is likely to be a high-performing team.

cross-functional team
a team consisting of employees from different functional areas of the organization

Cross-functional teams have exciting potential. But they present management with the immense challenge of getting technical specialists to cooperate and work effectively together.

Virtual Teams

A **virtual team** consists of employees who use electronic technology for their primary interactions. Corporate use of virtual teams continues to increase because they save time and money and enable employees who otherwise would not be able to participate in key projects to do so. Shared proprietary servers and secure cloud-based services are the most-used tools for team participation. They are typically used in conjunction with web conferencing, email, text messages, and conference calls for team interaction.

While virtual teams have many benefits, they also pose challenges for team leaders. One of the most common is communication problems. As Figure 5.2 notes, research shows "teams working remotely are at a considerable disadvantage. There really are benefits to sizing up your teammates face-to-face."[7] Special considerations for leading virtual teams are discussed later in the chapter.

Project Teams

Project teams are teams that work on a specific project until it is completed. Members are selected for their knowledge and expertise about the project. A project team requires a strong leader to focus on the project and to complete it on schedule. Project teams may begin as work groups, mature into teams, and then be assigned to various projects. In some organizations, project teams do most of the work, completing one project and then moving to the next. Project teams are often high-performing teams and may also be virtual teams. Chapter 12, "Project Management," discusses project teams in more depth.

Developing Effective Teams

Leaders should consider each of the following areas when developing their team: (1) set up the team properly, (2) build trust and credibility, (3) value diversity, and (4) leverage individual strengths.

virtual team
a team of employees who use electronic technology for their primary interactions

project team
a team that works on a specific project until it is completed

Set Up the Team Properly

The initial step is the selection of team members. You will not always have the opportunity to choose your team members, but when you do, look for people with complementary skills and diverse backgrounds who have the ability and willingness to contribute.

The next steps are to clarify the team's purpose and to establish operating procedures. Before the team meets, develop a mission statement along with teamwork expectations and norms. In establishing ground rules, keep in mind that every team has unique personalities, goals, resources, and timelines. Kick off the first meeting with an explanation of the mission statement and a discussion of ground rules that are relevant and meaningful for the situation. Figure 5.3 offers a few practical tips.

FIGURE 5.3
Tips for expectations and norms

Team Ground Rules

- Keep an open mind.
- Give constructive feedback directly and openly.
- Stay focused on clear objectives, directions, and project plans.
- Acknowledge problems and deal with them.

Agree on project goals, deadlines, and ways of communicating. Team members need a clear purpose, goal(s), an awareness of available resources, and background information such as budgets and deadlines. They also need to understand expectations. In addition, team members need to know how to communicate with one another and with the team leader. Managers should foster open lines of communication where channels for feedback and suggestions are easy and clear. Frequent updates and verification that everyone has the same understanding are important.

Cultural differences, gender, age, educational level, and work experience are just a few variables that can lead to misunderstandings and unnecessary conflict. As the team leader, take the extra time to be sure everyone is on the same page. Clarifying expectations up front can reduce wasting time later.

Team up with your classmates to brainstorm about ground rules you can establish for your project team or for the entire class. Your goal is to come up with at least five rules on which everyone agrees.

Build Trust and Credibility

trust
a belief in the integrity, character, or ability of others

One of the keys to successful teamwork is team chemistry. When individuals respect and trust one another, they will work better as a team. **Trust** is a belief in the integrity, character, or ability of others, and it is essential if people are to achieve anything together in the long run.

Sadly, trust is not one of the hallmarks of the current U.S. business scene. In a recent national survey by the Ethics Resource Center, 34 percent of employees reported that their direct supervisor does not show ethical behavior, a 10 percent increase since the last survey two years before and the highest percentage ever.[8] To a greater extent than they may initially suspect, leaders heavily influence the level of trust in their work groups and teams.

Trust is a fragile thing. As most of us know from personal experience, trust grows at a painfully slow pace, yet it can be destroyed in an instant with a thoughtless remark. Mistrust can erode the effectiveness of work teams and organizations. Figure 5.4 suggests ways for team leaders to develop relationships of trust both among team members and between themselves and their teams.

The team leader's role is to facilitate the team-building process in an effort to develop a cohesive group. The following additional steps can help:

- Make sure everyone is involved (during meetings and overall).
- Arrange team-building exercises and leisure activities.
- Encourage collaboration between and among team members on subtasks.

FIGURE 5.4
Trust within teams

Ways to Build Trust

Establish a good team climate.	As leader, you have a major responsibility for setting the tone and establishing a climate that reflects commitment to the team and support of all the members.
Set a good example.	In terms of specific group behaviors, the leader serves as a role model. If he or she shows respect, appreciation, and trust toward other members, the other members are more likely to adopt those behaviors.
Promote a healthy approach to controversy and conflict.	You should encourage the expression of differing opinions while maintaining an atmosphere of trust and mutual acceptance.
Be honest.	Always be honest with your team. If they catch you in a lie, they are unlikely ever to trust you again.
Be competent.	If people do not think you know what you are doing, they will not trust you or the work you do.
Follow through on promises.	If you tell a team member you will do something by a certain day, plan to deliver a day or two earlier than promised. That way, you can still deliver on time even if something unexpected happens (e.g., you get sick or your computer crashes).
Foster frequent, open, and honest communication.	This is one of the best ways to build and reinforce trust.

Source (items 1–3): Adapted from Career Solutions Training Group, *Quick Skills*, 2nd edition (Mason, OH: Cengage Learning, 2010).

As a team leader, you must build trust with your employees and coworkers. Consider and discuss five specific action items you can do in the next week to help build trusting relationships with your team.

Credibility means being believable and worthy of trust. Team leaders can enhance their relationships with team members by building and demonstrating credibility. Figure 5.5 lists four requirements for building credibility.

FIGURE 5.5
Credibility requirements

Building Credibility With Your Team

Expertise	Demonstrate that you know what you are doing. You can demonstrate credibility by subtly referencing experience doing similar tasks, your background, and any relevant special training.
Trust	Be honest and open. Use empathy and build rapport with your team; show things you have in common.
Consistency	Be predictable so team members know what to expect from you.
Commitment	Do what you say you will do, show that you work hard, and persevere.

Value Diversity

In addition to cultural differences, team members may have different levels of experience and education. These differences require you to communicate everything in a format that everyone can easily understand. The people on your team who are more advanced may get bored if too much time is spent providing basic information. Consider conducting a separate orientation meeting for individuals who need more time or a more lengthy explanation.

A difficult task for team leaders is to get all team members to value diversity rather than create biases, stereotypes, or negative energy. Begin by sharing how and why each person's unique qualities and characteristics are valued. Launching meetings with a brief activity allows members to get to know one another in a fun and educational way. As the team leader, it will be your job to make sure everyone knows his or her ideas, opinions, and suggestions are valued.

credibility
the quality of being believable and worthy of trust

A difficult task for team leaders is to get all team members to value diversity rather than create biases, stereotypes, or negative energy.

A great example of this is a story told by a sales associate working at a local bookstore where all the other employees were at least fifteen years older. At a team meeting, the group was brainstorming ideas for expanding the store's video, gaming, and DVD offerings. When he shared his idea for a section featuring *anime* (Japanese or Japanese-style animated entertainment), many of his colleagues did not know what he was talking about; however, his supervisor encouraged them to listen and learn.

The young man explained and concluded with a recommendation to advertise the bookstore's new anime holdings in local high school and college newspapers. The supervisor supported his recommendation. Had his supervisor not created an environment where everyone was valued and treated with respect, this young man may not have felt safe making this suggestion, and ultimately the store would have lost out on what turned out to be a profitable idea.

Leverage Individual Strengths

Most of the time, team leaders focus on getting their teams to execute and achieve results. Therefore, the team leader needs to know each team member's skills, knowledge, talents, interests, goals, dreams, values, and motivations (Figure 5.6). In addition, he or she needs to know if each employee is properly trained, is ready to take on the task, and understands the value and importance of the job.

Every member of a team is unique—each person's strengths, interests, values, and motivators will be different. To set your employees up for success, know their abilities and where they excel. Then assign individuals to tasks and roles that take advantage of their strengths. Team leaders who assign tasks based on skills and abilities benefit the organization by leveraging individual strengths to create an efficient and effective team.

One of the keys to team leadership is to know your employees' abilities.

FIGURE 5.6
Look for ways to motivate your team

Tips for Team Motivation

To keep your team focused and inspired, consider the following:

- Post a scoreboard to mark team progress toward goals.
- Celebrate team accomplishments.
- Begin each meeting with praise and recognition for outstanding individual contributions.
- Keep team members' line managers informed of their accomplishments and progress.

Considerations for Virtual Teams

As noted earlier, the principles that apply to face-to-face teams also apply to virtual teams. However, virtual teams operate in a unique environment

© Golden Pixels LLC/ Shutterstock.com

On a high-performance team, members are far more likely to rely on internal motivation than external motivation. Members of high-performance teams tend to be self-motivated and thrive on being creative and meeting challenges.

and generally require more resources and support. The following additional guidelines will help you develop effective virtual teams:

- If you are recruiting the members, make sure they are willing and able to contribute in a virtual environment.
- On the company intranet or project web page, post a biographical sketch, contact information, and "local time" matrix to familiarize members with one another and their geographic dispersion.
- Choose technology for communicating and collaborating on documents that is appropriate for the task and that all team members will have and can use comfortably. Your organization may provide some or all of the technology.
- Be prepared for the different demands of leading a virtual team. In the chapter opening interview, Barbara Schwenger-Huffman recalls her discovery that leading virtual teams requires more flexibility in leadership style and different skills, practices, and priorities.
- Be sensitive to potential communication problems.

In her article "Leading Virtual Teams: Five Essential Skills Will Help You Lead Any Project—No Matter How Distant," Joyce A. Thompsen describes five categories of effective leadership skills for virtual project team or distance-management situations:

- Communicating effectively and using technology that fits the situation
- Building community, based on mutual trust, respect, fairness, and affiliation, among project team members
- Establishing clear and inspiring shared goals, expectations, purpose, and vision
- Leading by example with a focus on visible, measurable results
- Coordinating/collaborating across organizational boundaries[9]

While some of these skills are unique to virtual teams, most can be applied to leading any type of team.

Empowering Your Team

As you have read before, managers are responsible for getting work done through other people. When you achieve a high level of trust and confidence in your team members, you should be able to empower them to achieve goals and objectives without constant supervision. People generally resent having "micromanagers" looking over their shoulder and telling them every move to make.

What Is Empowerment?

empowerment
the process of making employees full partners in decision making and giving them the necessary tools and rewards

Empowerment occurs when employees are adequately trained, provided with all relevant information and the best possible tools, fully involved in key decisions, and fairly rewarded for results.[10] Those who endorse this key building block of progressive management view power as an unlimited resource. The challenge for today's managers is to understand how and why to empower their employees.

COLLABORATION AND COMMUNICATION

Many tools are available to facilitate work for both face-to-face and virtual teams. They are typically used to collaborate on documents, to communicate, or to do both.

Collaborating on Documents

Two types of tools ease the work involved in preparing documents as a team: (1) collaborative software features and (2) secure proprietary servers such as *SharePoint*® or cloud-based services where members can post, access, and work on documents simultaneously. Software such as the *Microsoft Office* suite of applications, the iCloud® online service, and Google Docs offer features for making comments and revisions in a document that enable members to edit and review each other's work. Coauthoring capabilities in *Word*, *Excel*, and Google Docs software allow team members to work on a document online at the same time. Documents posted on a secure shared server or in the cloud (using a service such as Dropbox or SkyDrive®) are available at any time and from any location.

Communicating With Team Members

Communication may be *synchronous* (at the same time) or *asynchronous* (at different times). Instant messaging, web conferencing using software such as *WebEx*®, Internet calls with pictures and video using *Skype—Business Version* or similar software, chat, and digital whiteboards are examples of tools for synchronous communication. Email, podcasts, blogs, and wikis and other collaborative websites are examples of tools for asynchronous communications.

The more power you give away, the more you have.

—Frances Hesselbein, former head of Girl Scouts of the USA

Source: Laurel Shaper Walters, "A Leader Redefines Management," *Christian Science Monitor*, September 22, 1992, p. 14.

Why Empower Team Members?

Empowerment is a characteristic of high-performance teams. They are given the autonomy required for empowerment because they consistently outperform competent employees in the organization.

Empowering your team achieves a variety of positive results. It enables employees to serve customers and users quickly, and it frees managers from some responsibilities so they can focus better on more important matters.[11]

Many see an empowered corporate culture as a place where all employees, regardless of their position or title, accept responsibility for their own and the organization's performance.[12] The essence of empowerment is to train your employees so they understand the organization's values, policies, and procedures and their role in achieving the desired outcomes.

One goal of empowerment is to allow employees to make decisions without checking in with their supervisor. Retail giant L.L. Bean provides an excellent example. If a customer has a product that has failed (for example, a broken zipper), every employee at L.L. Bean has been empowered to handle the situation. Every employee has been trained in L.L. Bean's mission, values, policies, and procedures, and employees have been empowered to take action to support each of these. The employee who is presented with the failed zipper knows that he or she can either offer to have it repaired or allow the customer to choose a replacement. The employee does not need to check with a supervisor. It is at his or her discretion to do what is necessary to make sure the customer leaves satisfied and remains loyal to L.L. Bean.

1. Why do you think L.L. Bean has empowered its employees to make independent decisions that ultimately have financial consequences?

   ____

2. What steps do you think L.L. Bean took in the process of empowering its employees and setting them up for success?

   ____

Steps Toward Empowering a Team

Empowering your team takes time, training, desire, commitment, vision, and trust. In 2004, Martin Tillman, then an instructor of program management and leadership with the Defense Acquisition University at Fort

Belvoir, Virginia, identified seven key considerations related to empowering a team:

- Not everyone wants to be empowered.
- There must be a common vision/strategic direction.
- Convey the strategic direction in a manner that inspires and helps people to see their role in its accomplishment.
- Gain your subordinates' trust.
- Build on shared values.
- Strive for complete business process/vision alignment.
- Don't forget to use the right tools.[13]

You have already learned about developing a common vision that appeals to everyone. Part of this process is letting people on your team know how their skills and knowledge contribute to the success of the team. Gaining coworkers' trust (and learning to trust your team) takes time. The suggestions in Figure 5.4 on page 95 will help you to gain and keep trust.

All [the triumphant moments in my career] involve collaborative successes, where you realize the effectiveness of teamwork and working with really smart people who deliver really amazing results.

—Ursula Burns, CEO, Xerox Corporation

Source: Xerox Corporation, "Entrepreneurial Spirit: Ursula Burns, Chief Executive Officer," http://outputlinks.com/html/people/xerox_Ursula_Burns_CEO_083109.aspx.

Delegation

Delegation is the process of assigning duties and responsibilities to another individual and giving that person the necessary decision-making authority to be successful in the completion of assigned tasks.[14] Although the individual completing the work is accountable to the manager, the manager has ultimate accountability for the quality of the work and overall performance of the team.

Many people use the terms *empowerment* and *delegation* interchangeably. There is certainly overlap, and the steps to implementation are fairly similar. However, empowerment is more broadly focused on a philosophy, a culture, and an overall thread running through an organization. Delegation involves sharing direct authority and responsibility for specific work with your employee(s). Delegation is a vital basic step toward empowering them.

delegation
the process of assigning duties and responsibilities to others

The delegation process is not a quick fix for a manager's time management dilemmas. Although authority may be passed to people at lower levels, *ultimate* responsibility cannot. Delegation is the sharing of authority, not the abdication of responsibility.

Why Delegate?

As you learned in Chapter 3, managers and supervisors wear many hats and have a wide variety of responsibilities. Most successful managers choose to delegate authority and responsibility to their employees. Delegation can provide two major benefits: (1) it allows you to train and develop your employees and (2) it increases the efficiency and effectiveness of the entire team.[15]

It can be a challenge for supervisors to motivate and inspire their employees when they practice delegation. Employees sometimes perceive delegation as simply having more work dumped on them. However, if done properly, delegation is an effective way to make more time available for supervisors to plan, train, coach, and motivate. In addition, employees who desire more challenge generally become more committed and satisfied when they are given the opportunity to take on more responsibility or tackle significant problems.

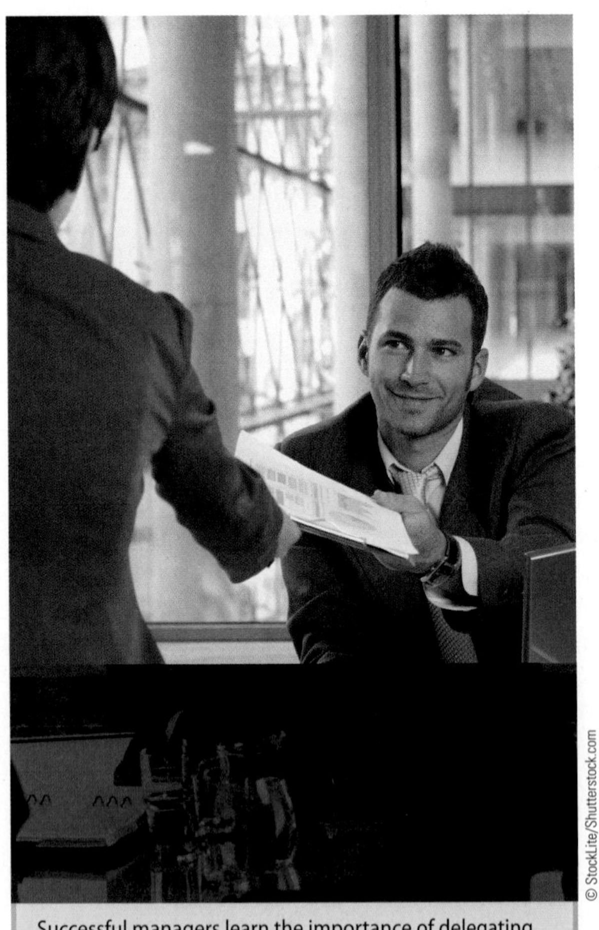
© StockLite/Shutterstock.com

Successful managers learn the importance of delegating tasks that can be accomplished by others.

Conversely, a lack of delegation can stifle initiative among employees and can negatively affect managers as well. Supervisors who are perfectionists have a tendency to micromanage and avoid delegation. As a result, they have problems in the long run when they become overwhelmed by minute details.

There are a number of reasons why managers generally do not delegate as much as they should. Here are some common ones:

- The belief that by delegating, they lose power and authority
- A lack of trust in others
- Fear that employees will make mistakes (because the managers are accountable for results)
- Fear of competition from employees[16]

Steps to Effective Delegation

Managers can go a long way toward delegating effectively by recognizing and correcting such tendencies both in themselves and in their fellow supervisors. Since successful delegation is habit-forming, the first step is usually the hardest. Properly trained and motivated people who know how to take initiative in challenging situations often reward a delegator's trust with a job well done.

Delegation takes time, planning, patience, and frequent communication. Therefore, it is important to be thoughtful and purposeful in your approach to delegation. Consider following these steps:

1. **Assess employees' readiness.** Assess the level of readiness of your employees before you decide to delegate.
2. **Choose what to delegate.** Identify a specific task, job, or responsibility that can be delegated. Choose something that is relatively straightforward, fairly simple to teach, and easily measured or monitored. Imagine you manage a customer service call center. Your shift ends at 10 p.m. Each evening you follow a closing procedure that includes transferring the telephones to a remote operator, printing a call summary report for the shift, setting the alarm system, and locking up. Rather than delegating all your responsibilities at once, you may choose to delegate them one at a time. First, train someone on a simple task such as transferring the phones. Let this individual try it for a few nights. Then make sure proper procedures are being followed simply by placing a test call.
3. **Prepare training materials.** Once the task is identified, prepare a document that explains it in detail. Include any guidelines, forms, contracts, limitations, or parameters. For example, you may choose to delegate office supplies purchasing to one of your employees. However, you decide to create a limitation that any purchase over $500 requires your signature. After a trial period, you may choose to increase the dollar amount based on performance, trust, and confidence.
4. **Identify performance measures.** Determine how you will measure success. Remember, delegating does not mean you are no longer accountable for the end result. Therefore, you need to identify a method to verify that the work is being completed and continues to meet the usual quality standards. Determine when and how you will monitor progress.
5. **Train employees.** Meet with employees when there is plenty of time to train them, let them practice while you are there to assist, and give them ample opportunity to ask questions.
6. **Let employees, customers, and vendors know.** Communicate with everyone connected with the task to let them know you have delegated authority to someone new. Explain how training will take place and how they should communicate any concerns or questions. The entire team needs to be on board and supportive of the person to whom the work has been delegated.
7. **Give it meaning.** When communicating with team members, take a few extra minutes to explain why you are choosing to delegate and how this continues to support the vision, mission, and goals of the organization.

8. **Set your person up for success.** Set the proper tone—realize your employees will probably make mistakes. Let them know it is okay to ask questions. You also want them to report any problems to you right away. It is far better to be made aware of a potential problem than to hear about it weeks later from an irate customer or concerned boss. This requires that you make it "safe" for employees to report issues to you. The first time you yell at them or discipline them will likely be the last time they are forthcoming with bad news. Find the proper balance and be patient.
9. **Follow up.** Check in with your employees, review their work and reports, and go over the performance measures discussed in step 4.
10. **Celebrate success and give credit.** Give credit where credit is due. Successful leaders and managers get satisfaction from seeing their people succeed. Employees always appreciate being recognized and thanked. Be sure to acknowledge your employees' contributions and achievements. It can be a great investment of your valuable time.

Project Delegation

The previous section focused on delegating to individual employees. Major projects from a work unit or relating to the entire company are often delegated to high-performance teams because they have shown they can accept the responsibilities and make the decisions necessary to complete the project successfully. In fact, high-performance teams are often project teams. As soon as they complete a project, they are assigned a new one.

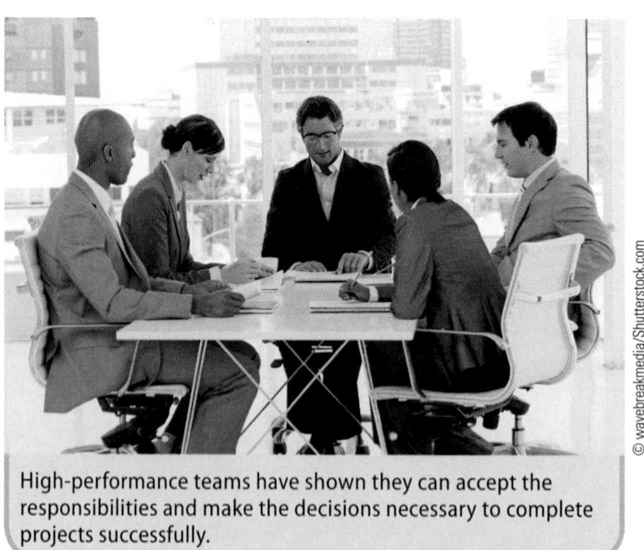

High-performance teams have shown they can accept the responsibilities and make the decisions necessary to complete projects successfully.

SUMMARY

1. Organizations use teamwork extensively because they believe effective teams improve both individual and organizational performance.
2. High-performance teams share certain characteristics. Not all work groups qualify as high-performing teams.
3. The five stages of developing work groups into effective teams are forming, storming, norming, performing, and adjourning.
4. Three special types of teams are cross-functional, virtual, and project teams.
5. To develop an effective team, team leaders should (1) set up the team properly, (2) build trust and credibility, (3) value diversity, and (4) leverage individual strengths.
6. Empowerment occurs when employees are adequately trained, provided with all relevant information and the best possible tools, fully involved in key decisions, and fairly rewarded for results.
7. Delegation is the process of assigning duties and responsibilities to another individual and giving that person the necessary decision-making authority to be successful in the completion of assigned tasks.

Terms

Located at www.cengagebrain.com

- Chapter Outlines
- Flashcards
- Interactive Quizzes
- Tech Tools
- Video Segments

and More!

Questions for Reflection

1. Describe a synergistic team you have observed or been a part of.
   a. Why was it synergistic?
   b. What were some of the benefits?
   c. What were some of the challenges?
2. What would be some advantages and disadvantages of working on a cross-functional team rather than a team from your work unit?
3. Describe some of the misperceptions about teams and why it is important to avoid them.
4. Why are team ground rules necessary? What are some of the most important ground rules to consider?
5. Why is empowerment especially important for high-performance teams?
6. What are the major benefits of delegation for managers and employees?

Hands-On Activities

Diversity at Google

Work in a team of four or five for this activity.

1. Read the following statement from Google's 2010 report on diversity and teams:

   At Google we understand that diverse teams create diversity of thought which leads to creativity and innovation. Creating teams with individuals from different backgrounds, cultures and ideas is the foundation of Google's success. Diversity is a key element of our strategy—it is not only essential to the development of innovative products but also supports and strengthens Google's unique culture and reinforces our reputation as the employer of choice in our industry.[17]

2. Read the following statement on diversity from Google's website:

   At Google, we don't just accept difference—we thrive on it. We celebrate it. And we support it, for the benefit of our employees, our users, our culture and students interested in the technology industry.[18]

3. Determine which of the following groups each team member will explore on Google's website to gain a better understanding of how Google supports that group.
   a. Employees
   b. Users
   c. Culture
   d. Students
4. Each member will report back to the team about the group investigated.
5. If the team has five members, the fifth member should review the 2010 diversity report to determine how supporting diversity benefits Google. If it does not, the entire team should focus on that topic in addition to those outlined in step 3.

Technology for Teams

1. Review the Leveraging Technology feature on page 99.
2. Select one or two tools for document collaboration you are not familiar with, and search for articles about them on the Internet.

3. Read at least two articles.
4. Repeat these steps for one or two tools for communicating with team members.
5. Key the documentation for the articles, and name the document "Technology Tools: Sources of Information."

You Decide | Case Study

Delegation

Connor is the housekeeping manager at a five-star hotel. His company is committed to a corporate culture of empowerment. The company is completing construction on a conference center adjacent to the hotel. Connor has been asked to take responsibility for recruiting, hiring, and training the housekeeping staff for the conference center while maintaining his current job as housekeeping manager.

Connor realizes he cannot do everything himself, so he plans to delegate some responsibilities and authority to one of his employees, Christopher. Christopher has been with the hotel for 12 years. He is a reliable, high-performing member of the housekeeping department. In fact, he was selected as employee of the year for two of the last three years. Although he has never been responsible for supervision or training, Christopher has taken a supervision class at the local community college and has expressed an interest in taking on more responsibility.

Questions

1. How would you recommend Connor begin the process of delegating?
2. What are some potential barriers?
3. What can Connor do to set Christopher up for success?
4. What responsibility, if any, will Connor have for the hotel housekeeping department once he has delegated responsibility and authority for day-to-day operations to Christopher?

MANAGER'S TOOLKIT

As a manager, you are thinking about trying to create an environment that is conducive to developing high-performance teams with the potential to becoming more self-managed. Read the Soft Skills for Success feature on the next page before completing this activity.

1. Analyze your preferred management style. Consider the "Organizational Conditions Conducive to Self-Management" in the Soft Skills feature as necessary for self-management to be successful.
2. List the conditions you would be comfortable creating for your employees.
3. List the conditions that would require a considerable change in your management style.
4. Describe how you would go about determining if your employees are good candidates to be empowered.

Soft Skills for Success

Self-Management

Collaboration is the essence of teamwork—which requires many soft skills. This chapter focuses on building effective, synergistic teams. The Leveraging Technology feature describes tools to enhance collaboration. In Figure 5.2, J. Richard Hackman's research shows that "the most powerful thing a leader can do to foster effective collaboration is to create conditions that help members competently manage themselves."[19]

Organizational Conditions Conducive to Self-Management

For self-management to be successful, the organization (and its managers) must be willing to:

- Create a high-involvement culture and environment where employees are expected to participate in decisions affecting their work and employee initiative is accepted.
- Give up control and be willing to empower employees.
- Articulate goals and desired results effectively.
- Accept mistakes as long as employees learn from them.
- Provide effective coaching, training, and teaching.

Requirements of Team Members for Self-Management

Not all team members can manage themselves effectively. To be an effective self-manager, a team member must be:

- Willing to be accountable for his or her decisions and work.
- Able to use initiative, prioritize, and manage time effectively.
- Able to identify and evaluate his or her own skills accurately.
- Trustworthy and credible.
- Willing to embrace change and deal with stress and competing pressures.
- Willing to seek support when needed.

Put It to Work

1. Would you like to work in a team environment that is conducive to self-management? Why or why not?
2. Rate yourself on each requirement to be an effective self-manager on a scale of 1 to 10 with 10 being outstanding and 1 being poor.

   ____ Willing to be accountable for your decisions and work
   ____ Able to use initiative, prioritize, and manage time effectively
   ____ Able to identify and evaluate your skills accurately
   ____ Trustworthy and credible
   ____ Willing to embrace change and deal with stress and competing pressures
   ____ Willing to seek support when needed
3. Select the two requirements on which you rated yourself the lowest. If you would like to work in a team environment that is conducive to self-management, think about how you could develop the skills and attributes needed to be an effective self-manager.
4. Find and read two credible articles on the attributes on which you rated yourself the lowest.

company and ensure that their values are aligned with the company's. For individuals searching for a new job, one of the most important things to do is to read the VMV statements of potential companies and ensure that their values are compatible.

How can managers engage employees effectively in the planning process at each level?

In most companies, the planning process is a broadly shared development process. At the strategic level, the final plan is completed by senior leaders, but the initial development is done by many. Most companies have large meetings in a Town Hall setting where they lay out the strategic plans and talk about the strategic goals with employees in a forum that includes opportunities to ask questions. When employees have that context to understand the "why" of their jobs, they are more engaged in working to implement the strategic plans successfully.

Is contingency planning important?

In my experience, contingency planning is more critical today than ever before. Most companies are global, and we live in a global economy. Things that happen in one country often affect stock prices, prices we pay for supplies, and prices that we can charge for our products; they also may delay the production process. What happens across the world impacts our strategic plan. Many things that happen in a global economy are out of our control; therefore, you have to have a contingency plan in place if you want to meet your strategic goals and keep your stakeholders happy. Publicly traded companies are particularly affected by the global economy.

Most of the companies I have worked with do not separate contingency and crisis planning, but we worked on contingency planning continually. Many companies do not plan adequately for employee contingencies in a variety of areas. Employee contingencies are not limited to senior leadership. Loss of employees who have specialized knowledge, sales expertise in a particular market, or a number of other talents and skills that are not easily replaced can result in costly losses that impact revenue. Recruiters always try to recruit the top talent from other organizations, and succession and contingency planning is critical.

How is planning and goal setting linked to accountability?

Planning and goal setting is the basis for accountability. When a department or division plan is put into place, the department or division leader is held accountable to make the plan. Employees receive their assignments from this plan and are held accountable to deliver. For each project, standards for quality, budget, and time are used to measure results.

How can you increase the accountability of employees you manage?

I believe accountability comes with engagement, and engagement comes from a number of things:

- Motivation—both leader and employee have ownership.
- Stretch assignments—challenge employees to handle difficult things to enhance their growth.
- A say about their job—projects can be done in different ways, and employees should have freedom to do things their way.
- Owning the process—leads to being accountable for the results.
- Being held accountable for the quality, budget, and time for each project or task.
- Recognition and rewarding a project of high quality, on time, and on budget.
- Inspect what you expect—the manager needs to pay attention to what is going on.

Visit *www.cengagebrain.com* to read the complete profile.

Chapter Outline

Planning is an essential component of the manager's role. In this chapter, you will be introduced to various types of planning and strategies for achieving desired results. **Planning** refers to the process of determining the mission and goals of an organization and specifying what it will take to achieve the goals. To ensure that plans and strategies at all levels are clear, consistent, and focused on the overall corporate direction, most organizations provide clear, written statements of the vision, mission, and values of the organization.

Vision, Mission, and Values

A common characteristic of successful organizations is that the vision, mission, and values are understood and shared by all stakeholders. A **stakeholder** is anyone who has a vested interest in the success of an organization. Stakeholders include but are not limited to owners, employees, clients, customers, investors, partners, vendors, suppliers, and often the communities in which the organization does business.

planning
the process of determining the mission and goals of an organization and specifying what it will take to achieve the goals

stakeholder
anyone who has a vested interest in the success of an organization

vision
the future direction of the organization; what it wants to become

Vision

Vision refers to the future direction of the organization. The leadership role of the CEO includes creating a shared, compelling vision that all stakeholders can embrace. A vision is typically designed to inspire stakeholders to think or dream of what the organization wants to become in the future.

Samsung provides a good example of a corporate vision statement (Figure 6.1 on page 113). Developed in 2010 for the next decade, the statement explains how the company intends to implement its vision and derive strategic plans from it:

> As part of this vision, Samsung has mapped out a specific plan of reaching $400 billion in revenue and becoming one of the world's top five brands by 2020. To this end, Samsung has also established three strategic approaches in its management: "Creativity," "Partnership," and "Talent."[1]

FIGURE 6.1
Samsung vision statement

Vision 2020

Samsung Electronics' vision for the new decade is, "Inspire the World, Create the Future."

This new vision reflects Samsung Electronics' commitr[illegible]ient to inspiring its communities by leveraging Samsung's th[illegible]e key strengths: "New Technology," "Innovative Products," and [illegible]reative Solutions"—and to promoting new value for Samsung[illegible]ore networks—Industry, Partners, and Employees. Through t[illegible]e efforts, Samsung hopes to contribute to a better world and [illegible]ner experience for all.

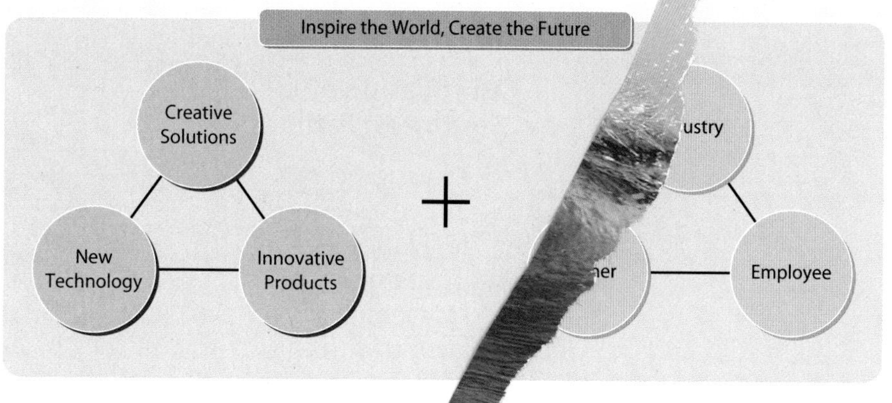

Source: "Vision—Corporate Profile—About Sams[illegible]w.samsung.com/us/aboutsamsung/corporateprofile/vision.html.

mission
a formal statement of the core purpose of an organization that defines its objectives and focus

Mission

A clear, formally written, and well-publicized statement of an organization's mission is the cornerstone of any planning system.

The **mission** is a form[illegible]tement of the core purpose of an organization that defines [illegible]ectives and focus. A good mission statement generates a [illegible] image for all stakeholders and provides a focal point for t[illegible]e planning process. A clear, formally written, and well-[illegible]d statement of an organization's mission is the cornersto[illegible]y planning system that will effectively guide the organiz[illegible]ough uncertain times.

© Erik S. Lesser/EPA/Landov

Gary Kelly is the CEO of Southwest Airlines. When explaining how his company distinguishes itself from the competition, he said, "One of Southwest's rituals is finding and developing people who are 'built to serve.' That allows us to provide a personal, warm level of service that is unmatched in the airline industry."

Southwest Airlines provides a good example of a mission statement (Figure 6.2). The statement was crafted in 1988 and has not changed over the years.

A well-written mission statement:

- Defines the organization for its key stakeholders.
- Creates an inspiring vision of what the organization can be and can do.
- Outlines how the vision is to be accomplished.
- Establishes key priorities.
- States a common goal and fosters a sense of togetherness.
- Creates a philosophical anchor for all organizational activities.

FIGURE 6.2
Southwest Airlines mission statement

The Mission of Southwest Airlines

The mission of Southwest Airlines is dedication to the highest quality of Customer Service delivered with a sense of warmth, friendliness, individual pride, and Company Spirit.

To Our Employees

We are committed to provide our Employees a stable work environment with equal opportunity for learning and personal growth. Creativity and innovation are encouraged for improving the effectiveness of Southwest Airlines. Above and caring attitude within the organization that they are expected to share externally with every Southwest Customer.

Source: Southwest Airlines, www.southwest.com/html/about-southwest/index.html?int=GFOOTER-ABOUT-ABOUT.

- Generates enthusiasm and a "can do" attitude.
- Empowers present and future organization members to believe that every individual is the key to success.[2]

Values

values
the core beliefs of the organization and the principles that guide behavior

Values are the core beliefs of the organization and the principles that guide behavior. Organizations know their stakeholders expect high standards of integrity and conduct from them. Therefore, they usually publish their values on their website to emphasize to current and potential stakeholders that they plan to meet and exceed their expectations for ethical conduct. They also publish the values statement in their employee manual to establish the foundation for the proper conduct expected of all employees. Microsoft Corporation has published the values statement in Figure 6.3 on its website.

FIGURE 6.3
Microsoft Corporation values statement

Our Values

As a company, and as individuals, we value integrity, honesty, openness, personal excellence, constructive self-criticism, continual self-improvement, and mutual respect. We are committed to our customers and partners and have a passion for technology. We take on big challenges, and pride ourselves on seeing them through. We hold ourselves accountable to our customers, shareholders, partners, and employees by honoring our commitments, providing results, and striving for the highest quality.

Source: Microsoft, www.microsoft.com/about/en/us/default.aspx?navindex=0.

Read the Samsung vision statement, the Southwest Airlines mission statement, and the Microsoft values statement.

1. Does the Samsung vision statement map out the company's direction for 2020 clearly? Why or why not?

   ____

2. Does the Southwest Airlines mission statement define the primary purpose of the organization? Why or why not?

   ____

3. Does the Microsoft values statement define values for employees as well as the company clearly? Why or why not?

   ____

Planning Essentials

As you learned in Chapter 2, planning is one of the functions of management that managers are frequently responsible for, or at least involved in. The planning process involves many people at many levels. Successful organizations view planning as an ongoing process rather than a one-time event.

Virtually everyone is a planner, at least in the informal sense. We plan leisure activities after school or work; we plan what to cook for dinner; we make career plans. Personal or informal plans give purpose and direction to our lives. In a similar fashion, more formalized plans enable managers to organize their resources to achieve organizational purposes.

A **plan** consists of a goal and one or more action statements. The goal is the end result or desired outcome, and the action statement(s) represent the means to that end. In other words, the goal gives managers the primary target to shoot at, whereas action statements provide the *objectives*, or the arrows for hitting the target. Properly developed plans tell *what, when*, and *how* something is to be done.

Properly developed plans tell what, when, and how something is to be done.

Although many managers use the terms *goals* and *objectives* interchangeably, technically they are different. The goal is a broad, general statement of what is expected to be achieved. The objectives are specific statements of what must be achieved if the goal is to be reached.

Managers may encounter a wide variety of formal planning systems on the job. Regardless of the various tools that are available, sound planning involves certain essential characteristics. Among these common denominators are three types of plans, the mission, goals and objectives, priorities, and the implementation and control cycle.

Types of Plans

Five types of plans are discussed in this section, beginning with three essential types: strategic, tactical, and operational plans. These three types of plans are developed by different levels of management and are intertwined—each level of planning depends on the support of the other two levels. Figure 6.4, on page 117, provides a brief comparison of the three types of plans. Because of rapidly changing circumstances, organizations must assess their strategic, tactical, and operational plans regularly to make sure they are still relevant.

plan
a goal and one or more action statements

strategic plan
a document that specifies the overall direction, long-term goals, and decision-making process for resource allocation and describes how the organization will position itself to achieve its goals

Strategic Plan

A **strategic plan** is a formal document that specifies the overall direction, long-term goals, and decision-making process for resource allocation and describes how the organization will position itself to achieve its goals. A well-conceived strategic plan communicates much more than general intentions about profit and growth. It specifies *how* the organization will achieve a competitive advantage, with profit and growth as necessary by-products.

FIGURE 6.4
Three types of plans

Type	Description	Prepared By	Time Frame
Strategic	Provides overall direction, goals, and how to reach them	Senior executives	Two to five years
Tactical	Gives steps needed to reach goals of strategic plan	Middle managers	Six months to two years
Operational	Explains how a work unit's specific objectives will be accomplished	First-line managers and team leaders	30 days to six months

Nonprofit organizations need strategic plans every bit as much as for-profit organizations. However, the objective may be slightly different. Rather than focusing on earnings, nonprofit groups may focus on how to achieve their goals and also sustain or increase financial and human resources while continuing to serve.

Strategic plans typically cover a period of two to five years, but may range up to ten years. Because of this extended outlook, strategic plans tend to be more general in nature.

Executive-level management is usually responsible for strategic planning. This is the first stage of planning. Goals developed during the strategic planning process are further refined and put into action in the next two levels of planning. In other words, strategic plans need to be translated into shorter-term and more specific actions.

Tactical Plan

The second stage is tactical planning. A **tactical plan** is a plan created and implemented by middle managers that specifies how the company will use resources, budgets, and people over the next six months to two years to accomplish specific goals within its mission.[3] It is sometimes called an intermediate plan. Tactical plans contain very specific steps required to implement the strategic plan.

Operational Plan

The third stage is operational planning. An **operational plan** is a plan specifying how the work will be done to accomplish the objectives of a work unit over a 30-day to six-month period. Operational plans include everything from preparing staffing schedules to business processes to budget planning. First-line managers and team leaders are frequently responsible for preparing these detailed plans. Operational plans are essential to implementing the strategies defined in the strategic and tactical plans successfully.

The three types of plans just discussed are a high priority for most organizations because they are essential for accomplishing the organization's overall goals. The next two plans are quite different. They come into play only when something goes wrong. Managers often procrastinate in preparing contingency and crisis management plans because they think other tasks are more important. Too often something adverse happens before the plans have been created.

tactical plan
a plan that specifies how the company will use resources, budgets, and people over the next six months to two years to accomplish specific goals within its mission

operational plan
a plan specifying how the work will be done to accomplish a work unit's objectives over a 30-day to six-month period

Contingency Plan

As we learned from Kathy Shields in the chapter opening interview, having a contingency plan is an important part of effective operational planning. **Contingency plans** are often referred to as *Plan B*. In other words, a contingency plan is a backup plan that is prepared just in case a situation does not turn out as expected. Preparing a contingency plan begins by anticipating what could go wrong (e.g., a busy student doesn't hear the alarm and misses a big exam). Asking your team for input during this process can reveal scenarios and/or variables you may not have considered. You can then identify potential solutions to each item identified.

Contingency plans prepare for things that are likely to happen. They are designed to take care of problems that may occur but are not likely to be a disaster to the organization. Contingencies are a normal part of budgeting. A project that is budgeted over a six-month period may experience delays that are out of the organization's control, or prices may increase unexpectedly. To cover these contingencies, a good planner may add a 10 or 15 percent reserve to the budget.

© Denise Kappa/Shutterstock.com

Many businesses, especially small businesses, do not survive after a major crisis because of a lack of crisis planning.

Crisis Management Plan

A **crisis management plan**—the often forgotten plan—outlines steps the company should take if some type of crisis causes a serious threat to or disruption of business. The plan may not be precise because you may not know what the exact steps are in a crisis. It describes scenarios and the options you should take, but it also accounts for scenarios you did not envision and how you would go about making decisions. Crisis management plans are similar to contingency plans but are designed to handle serious situations that could impact the entire organization. They are usually prepared by a high-level team with input from all areas.

Many different types of crises can affect businesses. Some are caused by natural disasters, such as floods, fires, hurricanes, or tornadoes. Others result from a product or service defect that harms customers or clients and disrupts production and sales. Employee actions such as fraud, bribery, or assault can precipitate a crisis. With today's instant communications, one negative comment by a customer or inappropriate comment by an employee on social media can spread rapidly and widely, causing a major disruption of business.

Most crisis management plans focus on mobilizing a competent team to analyze the situation as quickly as possible, determine the real cause of the problem, and decide how to solve it. Often, deciding among alternative solutions is difficult, and the choices are expensive. The CEO as spokesperson conveys the information with an honest and open statement that puts the public or customer first and places emphasis on how the problem will be solved. Public relations are critically important in the recovery strategy.

contingency plans
a backup plan prepared in case a situation does not turn out as expected

crisis management plan
a plan that outlines steps the company should take if a crisis causes a serious threat to or disruption of business

Assume you are the office manager of a family-owned pizza business. An influential individual in the community with a large social media following recently posted a complaint about being treated badly at your restaurant and wrote, "Never to return." The comment spread and has caused a significant decline in business. Your family is away and you have been left in charge.

1. How would you handle the situation?

 ____

2. If your company had previously developed a crisis management plan, would it have been helpful? How?

 ____

Employee Involvement

Successful execution of any plan—strategic, tactical, operational, contingency, or crisis management—requires the understanding and commitment of those directly involved. One of the best ways of securing employees' understanding and commitment is to include them in the planning process. One by-product of their participation is a more thorough understanding of how their tasks support the execution of the strategic plan. In addition, the plan will be stronger thanks to suggestions and ideas from those who are usually closest to customers and/or products. Ideas that percolate up from the bottom frequently yield the best results. Finally, including employees from all levels of the organization makes the planning process part of the culture. This makes it less threatening and more inclusive. Employee morale is better, and outcomes tend to be positive.

Our company was established with good strategic planning and strong employee engagement; the rest is history. We continue to do strategic planning every year and still involve all employees in the process. We want every employee to feel a part of the company and to have an opportunity to provide input into ways to improve the company.

—Thomas E. Suggs, president and CEO, Keenan Suggs Insurance Company

Goals

As noted earlier in this chapter, goals and objectives are different, but managers often use the terms interchangeably. For the purpose of simplifying the discussion in the remainder of this chapter, the term **goal** is used to represent both terms and is defined as a specific commitment to achieve a measurable result within a given time frame. Many experts view goals as the single most important feature of the planning process. They help managers, supervisors, and entrepreneurs build a bridge between their dreams, aspirations, and visions and an achievable reality.

goal
a specific commitment to achieve a measurable result within a given time frame

The Importance of Written Goals

From the standpoint of planning, carefully prepared written goals have several benefits for employees, managers, and senior managers. They serve as targets and measuring sticks, thus fostering commitment and enhancing motivation.[4] Goals must be written so they can be documented, shared across the company, and referenced and tracked over time. Written goals command more attention, are less subject to different interpretations, and are more readily accepted than goals presented orally.

Carefully prepared written goals benefit employees, managers, and senior managers.

Targets

Goals function as targets, focusing the activities of managers across the organization. Without goals, managers at all levels would find it difficult to make coordinated decisions. People quite naturally tend to pursue their own ends in the absence of formal organizational goals.

Measuring Sticks

Goals are useful for measuring how well a team or an individual has performed. When appraising employee performance, supervisors and managers need an established standard against which they can measure. Well-defined, measurable goals enable supervisors to weigh performance objectively on the basis of accomplishment, rather than subjectively on the basis of personality or prejudice.

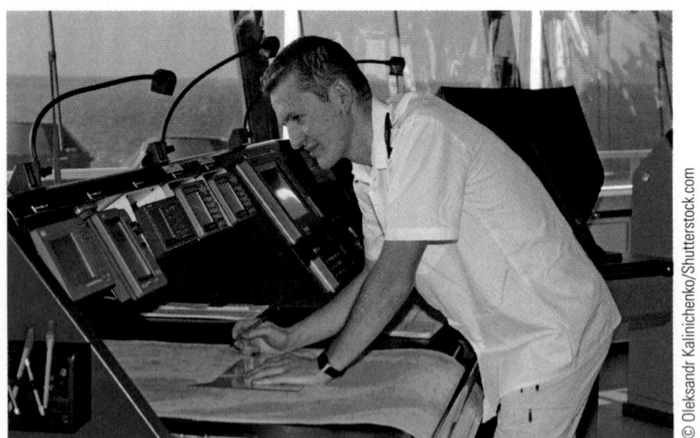

This navigation officer would never enter difficult waters without charting a course. He knows the final destination and charts a path to arrive there safely. Supervisors in organizations of all types and sizes face a similar challenge. They need to work with their employees to define measurable goals and identify the best pathways to success.

Commitment

The process of getting an employee to agree to pursue a specific goal gives that individual a personal stake in the success of the enterprise. Without individual commitment, even well-intentioned and carefully conceived strategies are doomed to failure.

Motivation

Goals represent a challenge—something to reach for. As such, they provide motivation. People usually feel good about themselves and what they do when they successfully achieve a challenging objective. Moreover, goals give managers a rational basis for rewarding performance. Employees who believe they will be equitably rewarded for achieving a given goal will be motivated to perform well.

Setting Goals

A common approach to goal setting is developing SMART goals. SMART is an acronym standing for *specific, measurable, attainable, relevant*, and *time-bound*. Figure 6.5 explains each element.

FIGURE 6.5
SMART goals

SMART Goals

- Specific—clearly defined; answer *what*, *why*, and *how*
- Measurable—contain concrete criteria for measuring progress toward the goal
- Attainable—challenging, yet realistic (you are capable and have the resources)
- Relevant—is important to you and to the organization
- Time-bound—specify the time frame for accomplishing the goal

Compare the following examples of poorly written goals to effective goals written using the SMART goals guidelines:

WEAK: Get to work early.

EFFECTIVE: Be at my desk ten minutes before workday start time (9:00) each morning.

WEAK: Prepare my project reports on time.

EFFECTIVE: Complete a draft of my weekly project report on Thursday each week. Review, finalize, and submit to project team leader on Friday by noon (due 4 p.m.).

WEAK: Get approval for the marketing project our team is proposing.

EFFECTIVE: Complete the budget on Friday for the proposed marketing team project, including a strong justification for the project; present the budget Monday morning to the marketing director for approval.

Much of the leading research on goal setting has been done by Professors Edwin Locke of the University of Maryland and Gary Latham of the University of Toronto. In addition to endorsing most of the SMART goals elements in Figure 6.5, they have cited ways managers can encourage employees to work hard toward goals. Three of the most important are the following:

- Managers can stoke commitment by explaining the reasons for the goal rather than simply stating it or by allowing employees to participate in setting it. Meaningful incentives, support, and recognition also encourage commitment.
- Employees need feedback on their progress toward the goal.
- When goal-related tasks are complex, managers should be ready to help employees develop strategies to complete them, provide a reasonable time frame for learning, and coach employees along the way.[5]

1. Rewrite the following bad examples of SMART goals:
   Prepare my résumé.

   ____

   Improve my sales.

   ____

   Increase my budget.

   ____

2. Review the goals you have written. Analyze them to determine if they meet the SMART goal guidelines. If not, revise them.

   ____

Achieving Goals

Many people are excellent at setting goals but fail to prepare a written plan for achieving them. The following process can help. The Manager's Toolkit on page 133 also provides a useful goal development tool.

1. **Write down your goals**. Each goal should meet the SMART goal guidelines. Ask yourself these questions:
   - Is the goal clear and specific?
   - Can I measure progress toward it?
   - Is it challenging, but realistic? Do I have what I need to achieve it?
   - Is it important to me and/or the organization?
   - Have I set a specific time frame for accomplishing it?
2. **Visualize the end result**. You often hear athletes such as professional basketball players describe how they use visualization to prepare themselves. For example, they picture the shot in their mind before they step up to take a free throw. The same technique can help you achieve your goals. Imagine that one of your goals is to graduate from college. A visual image representing achievement of this goal might be you walking across the stage to receive your diploma dressed in your cap and gown, with your family and friends cheering. Write down a few *affirmations*, sentences or phrases that reinforce your visual image (e.g., *I am smart. I work very hard. I enjoy tough challenges.*).
3. **Give it meaning**. Identify why achieving the goal is useful and important. How does it support the mission and strategic plan of the organization? What are the benefits of attaining this goal to you and/or the company?
4. **Prepare a detailed action plan**. Identify incremental steps toward achieving the goal. Write action statements listing the specific tasks along with target dates for completion. Also note the resources you will require and opportunities to obtain feedback as needed.
5. **Prepare contingency plans for potential obstacles or threats**. Identify any likely barriers to completing each task. Develop contingency plans so you can stay on track.

6. **Define measures**. Identify how and when you will measure progress to be sure you achieve your goals.
7. **Assess results**. If there are deviations, put corrective action plans in place. If you are achieving the desired results, celebrate incremental success.

You can have unbelievable intelligence, you can have connections, you can have opportunities fall out of the sky. But In the end, hard work is the true, enduring characteristic of successful people.

—Marsha Evans, former national executive director, Girl Scouts of the USA

Source: Lorraine A. DarConte, ed., *Pride Matters: Quotes to Inspire Your Personal Best* (Kansas City, MO: Andrews McMeel, 2001), 89.

Operational Planning

The seven-step process outlined above is intended for individuals, to help them set effective goals and prepare a plan to achieve them. This section of the chapter focuses on operational planning for a work unit or team because that is the level at which most supervisors, first-line managers, and team leaders are heavily involved. The characteristics of a plan like the one developed above and an operational plan are basically the same. An operational plan applies to a work group or team that must work collaboratively to achieve goals. These detailed plans answer the questions *who, how,* and *when* for day-to-day operations. They must also focus on the resources available to accomplish the results. Many different approaches can be used for operational planning. The following are basic steps to help you get started.

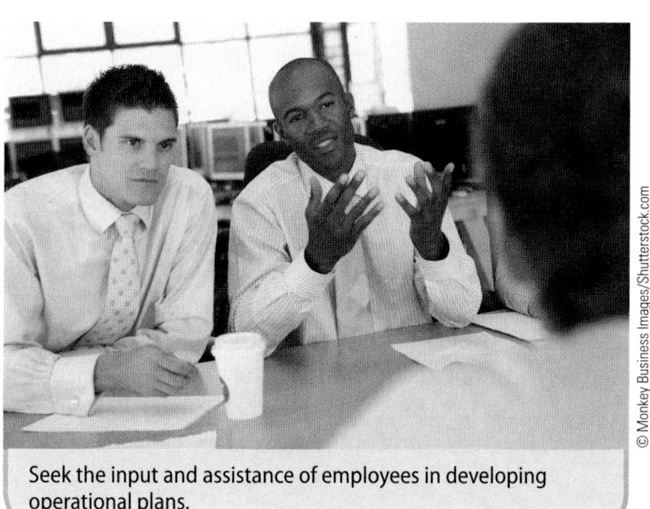

Seek the input and assistance of employees in developing operational plans.

Involve Your Employees

You learned earlier about the benefits of involving employees in planning. Provide them with as much detail as possible. Let them know how important their contributions are to the planning process. Getting them involved from the beginning will increase the likelihood of success. Use brainstorming techniques, surveys, and other tools to get your employees' input, ideas, and suggestions.

Review Your Mission and Purpose

Everyone on the team must understand the organizational mission as well as the business unit's mission and purpose. In addition, as team leader or manager, you can help members realize how your team contributes to the overall success of the organization. Everyone on the team should be able to answer the question "Why does the work I do make a difference?" There is an old story

Everyone on the team should be able to answer the question, "Why does the work I do make a difference?"

about two men who were digging a trench. When asked what they were doing, the first replied, "I'm digging a trench." The other man leaned on his shovel for a moment and said, "I'm helping to build the foundation for a hospital that will make sick people better."

Understand the Strategic and Tactical Plans

Everyone on the team must understand these plans and know what is expected. One way to emphasize the value and importance of the team is to invite a senior executive to your team's kick-off meeting. Ask this person to provide an overview of the strategic plan and to reiterate the contributions your team makes to the overall success of the business.

Develop SMART Goals

Developing SMART goals takes time. Give your team members ample time to brainstorm, research, and analyze alternatives. This step can take anywhere from a few days to several weeks.

Identify Necessary Resources

Determine necessary resources to achieve your agreed-upon goals. Resources include facilities, equipment, materials, labor, and any other items necessary to get the job done.[6]

Prepare a Task List and Timeline

List each step in the process to achieve the agreed-upon goals. Estimate how many hours it will take and over what period of time. It is also important to identify any related or dependent tasks.

Establish Plans to Measure Progress

Define how you will measure progress and completion. This includes establishing due dates, deadlines, and milestones. This step also requires the team to determine how and when they will compare their progress to the original plan. If this is left to chance and not scheduled ahead of time, it will often be forgotten or put at the bottom of the priority list. When you finally get around to measuring progress, it may be too late.

Develop an Action Plan

This stage is critical to the success of the operational plan. Recall that the operational plan is the overall plan for the work unit or team, whereas the action plan relates to each individual member. At this point, the team decides who will handle each task, when the task will start, and when it must be finished. Each person on the team should know his or her roles and responsibilities. Team members should also know by now if additional resources will be needed. Remember, a major aspect of setting your people up for success is making sure they have the right tools to get the job done.

Celebrate Success

One of the steps many new supervisors forget is to stop and celebrate success. Don't wait until the entire plan is achieved. Celebrate incremental achievement. It may be as simple as buying pizza for the team when the first milestone is accomplished. Recognizing progress and performance will reenergize the team and keep members motivated. One excellent strategy is to ask team members for their ideas and suggestions for rewards (both incremental and upon final completion). Be sure to establish some parameters (budget, time, etc.).

Assess and Measure Performance Outcomes

Imagine studying hard all semester and never getting a grade until the end. Progress needs to be measured. On the job, this requires managers to determine how the organization will assess and measure performance. The variables that should be defined should answer the questions *what, when,* and *how*. This means that you and your team will decide *what* to measure (remember, measures need to be specific and quantifiable), *when* to measure (for example, daily, weekly, monthly, or when specified milestones have been met), and *how* to measure progress. This may include measuring quality using sampling techniques or comparing actual progress with target due dates. Deciding how you will measure depends on what you are measuring.

Case Example

To bring this all together, let's look at the case of two restaurant owners and one of their managers:

Brooke and Robert own four restaurants in the Dallas area. In their strategic plan, one goal is to double the number of restaurants they own over the next five years. Another goal is to increase revenue in existing locations by 15 percent per year.

Grahame manages one of the restaurants, a Japanese steakhouse and sushi bar that serves only dinner. Included in his tactical plan is a goal to open the restaurant for lunch six days a week. He links this goal to the strategic plan based on the assumption that expanding operating hours should contribute to increased revenue.

Grahame's next step is to develop an operational plan to achieve the goal of opening for lunch. He pulls together his team for a kick-off meeting. He invites Brooke and Robert to attend the meeting for the first 30 minutes. Their role is to review the company mission and go over the strategic and tactical plans. Brooke and Robert also use this opportunity to thank all employees for their efforts, to compliment Grahame's leadership, and to reinforce how valuable each person is to the overall success of the restaurant.

Grahame uses the second half of the meeting to review the team's mission and purpose and begin developing the operational plan. He then begins the process of developing the overarching goal. Over the next three weeks, the team brainstorms, researches, and analyzes the opportunity to open for lunch. Here is the SMART goal they write: "By July 1, we will be open for

Converting a restaurant from dinner service only to lunch and dinner service requires extensive operational planning.

lunch Monday to Saturday from 11 a.m. to 2 p.m., serving at least fifteen entrees on our lunch menu." Note that this goal has several parts or subgoals (objectives)—to serve lunch, the opening date, days and time open for lunch, and the number of entrees on the menu.

Their next step is to outline all the tasks involved in achieving this goal, along with a timeline and the necessary resources. In addition, team members agree to track their performance in reaching this goal by meeting weekly to review the original plan and compare their actual progress to the activities and milestones outlined previously. Finally, they discuss each person's role, responsibilities, and due dates.

As you can see, this approach follows a logical, sequential order of events. However, this type of comprehensive planning requires excellent communication and frequent updates. If members of your team are not in the same location, it is essential that you use information technology and other methods to keep your virtual team members engaged and involved in the planning process.

Compare the case example you just read to the operational planning steps in the previous section. Identify the paragraph of the case example in which each operational planning step takes place.

a. Involve your employees.
b. Review your mission and purpose.
c. Understand the strategic and tactical plans.
d. Develop SMART goals.
e. Identify necessary resources.
f. Prepare a task list and timeline.
g. Establish plans to measure progress.
h. Develop an action plan.

______ "Grahame's next step ..."
______ "Grahame uses the second ..."
______ "Their next step is to outline ..."

Controlling

controlling
ensuring performance does not deviate from standards

In Chapter 2, you learned that another key function of management is **controlling**, or ensuring performance does not deviate from standards. To put the planning process into perspective, you must understand how it is connected with the control function. They are a package deal; one cannot succeed without the other. Figure 6.6 illustrates the cyclical relationship

LEVERAGING TECHNOLOGY

FINANCIAL AND BUDGETING SOFTWARE

The types of technology used for financial control vary widely depending on the size and type of business and the industry. In a large business, budgeting software generally is a component of a total financial management system. The financial planning and budget aspects are linked to the total planning process. In a small business, the software may be as basic as a spreadsheet, *Quick Books*® or *Quicken*® software, or specially designed budget software that integrates other functions, such as paying bills, tracking income and expenses, and creating a variety of financial reports.

Financial and budgeting software that has been customized to fit the needs of a particular type of organization or industry is widely available. The budget needs of a nonprofit organization are different from those of a service-based organization; a professional office such as a legal, medical, or accounting office; or a manufacturing organization.

Software simplifies not only the creation of the budget, but also the monitoring and reporting processes. Most programs offer a wide range of templates to produce reports quickly and accurately.

SUMMARY

1. All stakeholders must understand and share the vision, mission, and values of the organization.
2. Planning is a major function of management. Most organizations prepare strategic, tactical, and operational plans. Many also prepare contingency and crisis management plans.
3. Carefully prepared written goals and objectives benefit employees, managers, and senior management. Effective goals and objectives meet SMART goal guidelines.
4. Controlling is another major function of management. The steps of the ongoing planning and control cycle are plan, execute, assess, and correct.
5. Accountability is extremely important for achieving results. Quality control is an essential part of accountability.

Terms

budget, 127
contingency plan, 118
controlling, 126
crisis management plan, 118
goal, 119
mission, 113
operational plan, 117
plan, 116
planning, 112
stakeholder, 112
strategic plan, 116
tactical plan, 117
values, 115
vision, 112

Study Tools

CourseMate

Located at www.cengagebrain.com

- Chapter Outlines
- Flashcards
- Interactive Quizzes
- Tech Tools
- Video Segments

and More!

Questions for Reflection

1. Explain the difference between an organization's vision, mission, and values.
2. Describe the three types of plans most organizations develop.
   a. As a new manager, which type would you be most likely to prepare?
   b. What do you think would happen to an organization that prepared only one of these types of plans?
3. How do contingency and crisis management plans differ?
4. Do you think it is important to prepare both types of plans? Why or why not?
5. What distinguishes a SMART goal from other goals?
6. How are planning and control linked and form an ongoing cycle?
7. What is meant by a culture of accountability, and why is it important?

Hands-On Activities

Vision, Mission, and Values Statements

1. Assign three team members to find vision, mission, and values statements for three different types of companies for the team to analyze:
   - A professional group, such as a medical, hospital, or legal group or an accounting practice
   - A nonprofit, such as a community organization, United Way, or the Red Cross
   - A retail, sales, or hospitality-related business, such as a hotel, restaurant, or conference center
2. What do the statements have in common, and what is different?
3. Select the best vision, mission, and values statements. What about each statement led the team to select it?

Crisis Management Plan

1. Assign one member of the team to obtain a summary of the 1982 Johnson & Johnson Tylenol crisis for the team to analyze.
2. As a team, discuss the following questions:
   a. Why is this case considered a landmark example of public relations management of a major crisis?
   b. What did the company do that was so effective?
   c. What could your team learn about writing a crisis management plan from the Johnson & Johnson situation?

You Decide | Case Study

Goal Setting

Doug is the general manager of a regional painting and home improvement contractor business. He has been working hard to create a goal-oriented environment. He is meeting with his painting-crew team leaders. One of the problems they are experiencing is a high number of complaints that require crews to return to the customer's home or office for additional work or cleaning. Currently, crews are returning to 37 percent of job sites to respond to complaints.

Doug's team leaders have identified a goal: "Improve customer service and reduce customer complaints." Doug takes the time to explain SMART goals and asks the team leaders to go back and reword their goal so it meets the SMART criteria. They return with the following: "Our goal is to reduce customer complaints to 15 percent."

The next step is to identify specific tasks that will help them achieve this goal. The team leaders make a lengthy list that includes everything from better up-front communication with customers to increased training for painters. One of the items they are implementing is a customer satisfaction checklist. Each painting crew will go over the checklist in detail with customers to be sure they are satisfied before the crew leaves the work site. The expectation is that this will get potential problems resolved so customers will not need to call to complain.

The team leaders agree to monitor the use of the checklist on a weekly basis with their crews. Doug will monitor the number of complaints on a monthly basis to see if they begin to decline.

After the first month, Doug reviews the number of customer complaints. He discovers that the percentage of complaints has actually increased.

Questions

1. Does the revised goal meet the SMART criteria? If yes, explain why. If not, revise it so it does meet the criteria.
2. How would you recommend Doug handle the situation of complaints increasing after steps were implemented to reduce complaints? Explain in detail the steps he should take.
3. What can Doug do now to help his crew leaders be successful?

MANAGER'S TOOLKIT

Review the goal-setting section of the chapter, and then develop three personal SMART goals. These goals can be related to your work, school, or your life. Develop a list of action statements to achieve your goals, and remember to schedule time to complete each item. In addition, schedule time for follow-up to be sure you are on track to achieve your goals.

This technique should be added to your manager's toolkit. It can be used with individual employees to help them develop personal goals. It can also be an effective approach when you work with teams to develop team goals. Remember to ask yourself the following:

1. Is the goal clear and specific?
2. Can I measure progress toward it?
3. Is it challenging, but realistic? Do I have what I need to achieve it?
4. Is it important to me and/or the organization?
5. Have I set a time frame to accomplish it?

Soft Skills for Success

Honesty and Integrity

Honesty and integrity are important character traits. Many organizations include these qualities in their values statement, emphasizing their significance in the actions of the company and the behavior of all employees. The Microsoft Corporation values statement in Figure 6.3 cites both qualities.

If you have ever observed or participated in a court case, you have heard the common legal definition of honesty. Each person swears to tell the truth, the whole truth, and nothing but the truth. *Integrity* is adhering to ethical principles or a code of conduct. A person with integrity is often described as someone who is honest and who does the right thing regardless of the circumstances. For example, assume someone saw a person getting off an elevator drop something valuable, such as money or jewelry, and leave the building. No one else saw this happen. A person with integrity would make every effort to find the rightful owner instead of keeping the item.

Honesty and integrity are essential if you wish to be known as trustworthy and credible. A good question to ask yourself is, Would you trust someone who was not honest with you about a situation? Would you trust a leader at your company who was not honest or does not adhere to a personal code of ethical conduct? Leaders with integrity lead by example.

Put It to Work

1. Think of an individual you know in a workplace setting whom you believe is honest and has integrity. Write five words or phrases to describe the person that show why you made that assessment.
2. Think of an individual you know in a workplace setting whom you believe is dishonest and does not have integrity. Write five words or phrases to describe the person that show why you made that assessment.
3. If the members of your team were asked if they thought you were honest and had integrity, how do you think they would respond? Be objective—this is a self-assessment that only you will see.
4. Write five words or phrases you think they might use to describe you regarding honesty and integrity.
5. What five words or phrases would you like them to use when they describe you regarding honesty and integrity?

CHAPTER
7

Staffing Essentials

Learning Outcomes

1. Explain why effective recruitment is important.
2. Describe the basic process of doing a job analysis, job specification, and job description.
3. Explain why both internal and external recruiting are important.
4. Describe several strategies for external recruiting.
5. Identify five sources of data used to make selection decisions.

Straight Talk From the Field

Photo courtesy of Martha Scott Smith

Martha Scott Smith is director of public affairs/foundations at AT&T-SOUTHEAST. AT&T has received many awards for workforce diversity.

Printed by permission from Martha Scott Smith

What sets companies with strong commitments to diversity apart from others?

Today, companies with serious commitments to true diversity have expanded, though not abandoned, the boundaries of the traditional tenets of race (black/white) and gender (male/female). These visionary, astute companies aggressively recruit, embrace, and incentivize those individuals who, by their varied talents, ultimately enrich the company's portfolio in the workplace, marketplace, and community.

Why do you consider a diverse workforce (or workforce inclusion) critical for success?

A diverse workforce allows a company to attract and retain the best and brightest in order to develop the most innovative products and services needed to meet the competitive demands of the marketplace.

What approach do you recommend to attract and retain a talented, diversified workforce?

Clearly, commitment to diversity must start at the top. Management must assume accountability for leading diversity initiatives as part of an inclusive workforce. Leaders themselves must understand and internalize the value of inclusiveness—train their managers to understand a simple philosophy: they better serve their customers when diversity is an innate part of everything that is done. Ultimately, that positively impacts the bottom line.

Leaders themselves must understand and internalize the value of inclusiveness.

Many companies, such as AT&T, have created employee resource groups (ERGs) that are open to all employees and reflect the diversity of the company's employee and customer base. These ERGs support the company's commitment to diversity and inclusion through their efforts in the communities where they live and work.

What other advice would you offer companies regarding diversity?

Companies must help people grow and develop in their careers by encouraging management and non-management employees to improve themselves through job-based training, tuition aid, and various training and retraining programs. Companies must also strategically use their philanthropic resources to enrich and strengthen diverse communities and support organizations and projects that increase inclusion and create opportunities for diverse populations. In short, they must set both the example and the pace.

As consumers, we have a plethora of choices in almost every aspect of our lives. Companies, too, have choices. Those companies that wisely choose to invest in individuals with varied social, cultural, and professional backgrounds are ensuring their continued success in an ever-changing, competitive landscape.

Visit *www.cengagebrain.com* to read the complete profile.

Chapter Outline

Staffing is the heart of human resources management. Recruiting, selecting, hiring, orienting, training, and retaining talented employees are key components of managing human resources effectively. This chapter focuses on recruiting and selecting employees. Chapter 8 covers orienting, training, and retaining, and Chapter 9 discusses appraising and rewarding performance. In large organizations, staffing is handled by a separate human resources department or division with input from the various departments or units. In small or medium-size organizations, staffing is often handled by office managers or managers of various units.

staffing
the process of recruiting, selecting, hiring, orienting, training, and retaining employees

Forecasting Staffing Needs

In many organizations, much of the budget is spent on employee salaries and benefits. Therefore, "right-sizing" an organization is critical. Right-sizing refers to having no more or no fewer than the number of employees needed to get the job done effectively. Increasing productivity and reducing costs are major objectives of most organizations. Providing the technology or tools for employees to do the job effectively and training them to use the tools are key ways of enhancing productivity without adding more employees.

Right-sizing an organization is critical.

Many factors influence staffing such as seasonal needs, economic conditions, availability of the labor pool, and special needs of the organization. In small organizations, facilities are often a factor if the staff is increased. Alternative scheduling (Chapter 8), outsourcing (Chapter 3), and temporary employees are often used to balance staffing needs.

First-line or office managers are usually in the best position to analyze the needs of their units and to estimate the resources required to accomplish work cost-effectively. Well-developed operational plans including the unit budget should provide much of the information required to determine staffing needs. Remember that operational plans are derived from the organization's strategic and tactical plans.

Recruitment

The high cost of employee turnover is a key reason why recruitment and retention are so important.

Recruitment refers to efforts by an organization to find and hire qualified employees. Major efforts are made to select employees who will remain with the company for a long time. The high cost of **employee turnover** is a key reason why recruitment and **retention** are so important. The cost varies depending on the organization and the type of labor involved. *Thinking Leaders*, a blog for small business owners, provides an idea. It reports that losing one hourly employee to turnover can cost a company from 30 to 150 percent of yearly salary, with a conservative estimate of one year's salary.[1]

recruitment
efforts by an organization to find and hire qualified employees

employee turnover
the process of employees' leaving a company voluntarily or because they were asked to leave

retention
efforts by an organization to keep employees; the opposite of turnover

The expenses associated with an employee's leaving and the process to replace that employee include both direct and hidden costs. Direct costs include the time of everybody involved in recruiting, selecting, hiring, orienting, and training the new employee. Other direct costs include advertising, candidate travel expenses, testing, orientation, and training. Indirect or hidden costs often include but are not limited to the cost of getting the work done while the position is vacant, declining productivity during the vacancy and transition to a new employee, and increased costs for supervision and management.

Why Recruit?

A company normally recruits for the following reasons:

- To replace an employee who has left the company. When employees leave, normally the job description exists and can be used or may require only minor updating.
- To add staff to existing job categories. This situation occurs when an organization is growing or expanding hours of operation. Again the job description exists, and typically managers have prior experience recruiting for these positions.
- To fill new jobs as a result of organizational growth and expansion. A job analysis, job description, and job specification must be completed for each new job.

It is important to distinguish between a job analysis, job description, and job specification.

Job Analysis

A **job analysis** identifies the task and skill requirements for a specific job, determined by studying superior performers in related jobs. A job analysis should be done for all new positions. In addition, it is important to review job analysis data periodically for existing positions to be sure they are current. Figure 7.1 lists questions to ask when conducting a job analysis.[2]

Job Description

A **job description** is a document that outlines expectations, tasks, and responsibilities—as well as education and skill requirements—for a specific job. Preparing a job description involves a variety of activities, such as defining the job duties; identifying the necessary skills, knowledge, personal attributes, education, and experience; deciding on the compensation level; and determining the work schedule.

A job description should be done for all new positions. Descriptions for existing jobs should be reviewed and updated, if necessary, before using them in the recruitment process.

job analysis
the process of identifying the task and skill requirements for a specific job, determined by studying superior performers in related jobs

job description
a document that outlines expectations, tasks, responsibilities, education, and skill requirements for a specific job

job specification
a written summary of the qualifications needed to successfully perform a particular job

Job Specification

A **job specification** is a written summary of the qualifications needed to successfully perform a particular job.[3] It is developed during the job analysis and is sometimes referred to as the *core abilities* required to be successful in a position. Some organizations combine the job description and job specification in one document. Others believe keeping them separate is more effective because one relates to tasks and the other to the employee performing those tasks.

FIGURE 7.1
Job analysis questions

Sample Job Analysis Questions

1. What is the purpose of the job?
2. What are the main duties and responsibilities?
3. How does the job fit into the structure of the organization?
4. What is the content of the job; what tasks make up the job on a day-to-day basis?
5. How long do they take?
6. What skills or qualifications are needed to carry out the job?
7. What training is required?
8. What (if any) personal attributes are needed to carry out the job?
9. What experience is required to carry out the job?
10. What knowledge is required to perform the job?
11. What tools and equipment are needed?
12. What is the level of accountability, and to whom are you accountable?
13. Are you responsible for any confidential material? If so, describe how you handle it.
14. Do you feel the compensation for this job is fair? Why or why not?

Sources: "Job Analysis: Asking Questions"; David Ngo, "Job Analysis Interview Questions"; "Job Analysis: Overview" (note 2 in chapter references).

Preparing the Job Analysis, Specification, and Description

This section describes the process of completing the job analysis and writing the job specification and description.

Job Analysis and Specification

In a job analysis, you identify the job tasks and the skills required to do them. You must also specify the knowledge, technical skills, behavioral skills, and personal attributes required to do the job successfully. This information can be used to help potential candidates know from the beginning exactly what is expected. It is also helpful in developing the job description and interview questions.

Begin by identifying the physical and mental tasks required and outlining how the job will get done. This may include listing specific equipment used and standards or methods.[4]

Next, draft a list of the core abilities you think are necessary for the position. You can break them down into three categories: (1) technical skills, (2) behavioral skills, and (3) personal attributes. You are preparing a competency-based document that should include a list of specific and measurable skills.[5]

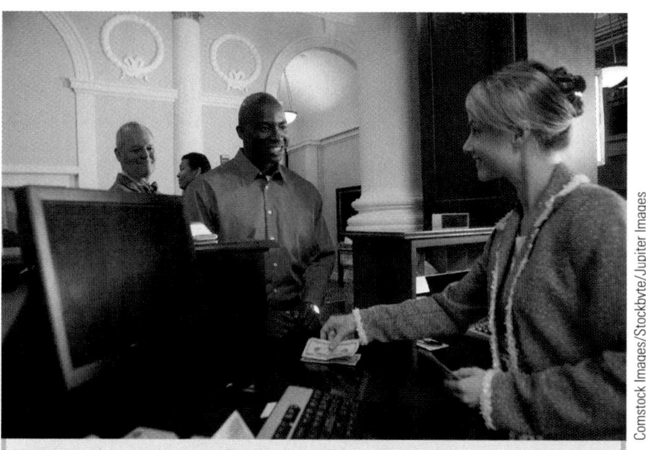

Comstock Images/Stockbyte/Jupiter Images

This bank teller is demonstrating many of the skills and attributes on her list of core abilities. She is serving her customer in a pleasant fashion during the course of the entire transaction. That's service her employer and customers can bank on!

Technical Skills

List all specific technical skills required for the job. For example, let's say you are preparing a job specification for a bank teller. Technical skills may include the following:

- Knowledge of bank products and services, such as investment products (e.g., savings/checking accounts), lending services (e.g., mortgages), safe deposit boxes, and vault operations
- Basic math skills, such as the ability to add, subtract, calculate percentages, and understand compounding and amortization
- Computer skills, such as basic keyboarding, word processing, and spreadsheets

Behavioral Skills

List all the desired behaviors for a person in this position. Continuing with the bank teller example, behavioral skills may include the following:

- Demonstrating professionalism, such as dressing and appearing comfortable in appropriate business attire
- Conducting oneself in a confident and professional manner, such as making eye contact, listening without interrupting, always remaining calm, and treating people with respect

- Responding in a timely and appropriate fashion by being punctual and meeting deadlines
- Working with customers and coworkers quickly, efficiently, and accurately
- Learning quickly and having the desire to acquire new knowledge and skills
- Demonstrating effective problem-solving and dispute resolution skills
- Thinking critically and analytically

Personal Attributes

List the qualities and characteristics necessary for the person in the position to be successful. Again, using the bank teller example, personal attributes may include the following:

- Being friendly and helpful
- Demonstrating integrity and honesty and understanding the need to maintain customer confidentiality
- Being respectful and valuing diversity (e.g., treating everyone the same regardless of education, age, gender, disability, sexual orientation, religion, ethnic background, and other personal characteristics)

It is important to look at the position from two perspectives: the employee's and the customers', including both internal and external customers. Once you have drafted the list, ask for feedback from various people who will work with the person you hire. Invite suggestions for additions, edits, and perhaps deletions. Ask for assistance in defining methods for measuring each item. The final version becomes the job specification, which can be added to the job description.

Job Description

As noted previously, a job description provides specific information about the responsibilities and duties for the position. It also includes essential skills and desired qualifications, along with information about the organization and its culture. Again, it can be helpful to involve others, such as employees and customers, in preparing the job description.

One of the benefits of a written job description is that it allows both the supervisor and the employee to clearly understand what the individual will be doing on a regular basis. In addition, a job description is an excellent resource during the recruitment process because it allows candidates to learn about the position and know ahead of time what will be expected of them. Clear expectations from the beginning can boost job satisfaction and, ultimately, employee retention. In this section, we will discuss components that should be included in every job description.

Job Title

A good job title is concise and descriptive. It should reflect the organization's culture and values and should give others a clear idea of what the employee does. For example, in a retail clothing store, the person responsible for working the floor and answering customers' questions is commonly referred to as a salesperson, customer associate, or fashion consultant. The title should fit the circumstances. Calling someone with little or no experience in the business a fashion consultant could be misleading. However, that title could be perfect for someone at a high-end store who has years of fashion-related experience.

Position Description

This section provides a brief narrative description of the position, the employee's goals and responsibilities, and major job functions.[6]

Reporting and Organizational Structure

The question answered by this section is, where does the person filling this position fit in the organizational hierarchy? For a supervisory or managerial role, those positions reporting directly to the individual should be listed.

Organizational Values and Culture

In this section, unique characteristics of the organization and expected behavior, attitudes, and values are specified.[7] They may include value-oriented items such as honesty, integrity, respect, creativity, and diversity and product/service-oriented items such as quality, customer loyalty, and safety.

Desired Qualifications

Here, specific qualifications for performing the job well are listed, such as number of years of experience, education, specialized skills, certifications, licenses, knowledge, and personal attributes. The ideal candidate will have these qualifications, but lacking one or more of them will not necessarily disqualify an applicant.[8]

Requirements

What are the physical and mental requirements for the job? This important information helps interviewers ask precisely the right questions. Physical requirements might include the ability to lift a certain amount or stand for an extended period of time. Mental requirements may include items such as working in a high-stress environment, handling customer complaints on a regular basis, working alone, or working in a fast-paced environment.

Recruitment Strategies

In his best-seller *Good to Great: Why Some Companies Make the Leap … and Others Don't*, business researcher and writer Jim Collins uses the metaphor of a bus when referring to an organization and its employees.[9] He believes that a busload of great people can go just about anywhere it wants. But a bus filled with confused and unruly passengers is destined for the ditch. It is also important to have the right people on the right bus at the right time moving in the right direction. In other words, supervisors need to match employees' talents with tasks and responsibilities, as well as organizational goals, in an efficient and effective manner.

Match employees' talents with tasks and responsibilities.

Recruiting employees with the necessary talent or potential to be productive is essential. A recent annual survey of CEOs reinforces the importance of getting the right people on the bus and keeping them there. The CEOs viewed skills shortages as the biggest threat to business expansion. Two-thirds said they wanted to spend more time developing a "leadership and talent pipeline"—recruiting, developing, and retaining the right employees for the job. And among the types of change they anticipated at their company, strategies for managing talent were the top priority.[10]

The job analysis, description, and specification provide the necessary information about the type of employee that would be successful in the position. The next step is to determine how to locate candidates with the potential to be successful and interest them in the position. Most organizations use both internal and external recruiting.

Internal Recruiting

internal recruiting
posting or advertising a job within the organization and encouraging qualified employees to apply for it

external recruiting
posting or advertising a job with sources outside the organization

Most companies post positions within the company and encourage qualified employees to apply for them. Many organizations provide career paths to guide employees on ways to move up in the hierarchy. **Internal recruiting** builds employee commitment and loyalty.

Many companies also encourage current employees to refer people they know who may be qualified for the position. Posting may consist of placing information about the job on bulletin boards or the company intranet. Companies may also send the information to various departments or individuals that may have an interest.

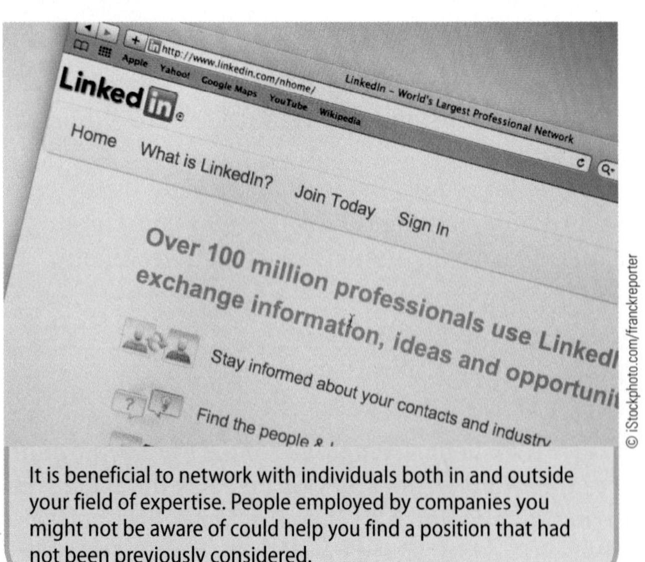

© iStockphoto.com/franckreporter

It is beneficial to network with individuals both in and outside your field of expertise. People employed by companies you might not be aware of could help you find a position that had not been previously considered.

External Recruiting

A wide variety of sources exist for **external recruiting**. Most companies use a number of different sources, both traditional and online. The size of the organization as well as the type or level of job generally determines which sources are most appropriate. Large organizations often recruit for a number of positions at the same time. Usually, recruiting in these organizations is handled by the human resources department or division. Small or medium-size organizations generally recruit for one or a few positions at a time; the appropriate manager or supervisor often handles the recruitment process. Some strategies for external recruiting are discussed on page 145.

1. What would you think if you worked for an organization that had a position open for which you believed you were well qualified and the organization only posted it externally?

____

2. How might you handle the situation?

____

Employment Agencies

Some organizations list jobs with employment agencies. These agencies typically screen candidates to ensure they have the qualifications specified. The organization pays a substantial fee (normally a percentage of the first year's salary) if it hires a candidate recruited and screened by the agency.

Placement Services of Educational Institutions

Most colleges and universities and some high schools provide job placement services for graduating students. Organizations that do not require extensive experience often use these placement services, which are free of charge. Educational institutions also often host job fairs that charge a relatively small fee for setting up a table for candidates to visit.

Print and Online Advertisements

Many employers advertise in traditional print media including newspapers, magazines, and relevant professional journals. Some publications appeal to special groups and enhance the diversity of the pool of applicants. Often print media are linked to online advertising on their own websites and/or on recruiting websites such as Monster or CareerBuilder. Advertising in the print media automatically includes advertising on the online media. Social media websites such as LinkedIn or Facebook are also used for posting advertisements.

Word-of-Mouth Referrals

Word-of-mouth referrals are both effective and inexpensive. In the "Internal Recruiting" section, you learned companies often encourage their employees to recommend open positions to individuals they know who might be good candidates. Many companies provide rewards to employees who refer candidates who are hired. Often university and college faculty provide good sources for referrals for alumni as well as students. Clients and customers also are good sources for referrals.

Recruiting for Diversity

As Martha Scott Smith pointed out in the chapter opening interview, "a diverse workforce allows a company to attract and retain the best and brightest in order to develop the most innovative products and services needed to meet the competitive demands of the marketplace." One of the challenges is creating an applicant pool that is demographically representative of the population at large if diversity is to be achieved. A casual review of recruiting ads reveals abundant evidence of corporate diversity initiatives. For example, Motorola has formed alliances with organizations such as Career Opportunities for Students with Disabilities and the National Urban League for assistance in recruiting and retaining a diverse pool of talented employees.[11]

Preventing job discrimination is a major responsibility of managers and supervisions.

Preventing job discrimination is a major responsibility of managers and supervisors. Chapter 10 covers issues relating to job discrimination and employment laws.

Do you think it is necessary and appropriate for companies to form alliances and partnerships with diversity organizations as a key strategy to enhance diversity recruiting? Why or why not?

Realistic Job Preview

For a number of years, research has shown the benefits of giving job applicants a **realistic job preview**: information or experience regarding what a job really involves on a day-to-day basis. To be realistic, the preview should include both the positive and the negative aspects of the job. Realistic job previews impact:

- Job acceptance. The rate of job acceptance may be higher or lower depending on the type of job and how the negatives are perceived.
- Turnover rate. Realistic job previews tend to reduce turnover. Turnover is often high in the first year because the job may not match what the employee expected.
- Job satisfaction after employment. If the job does not match expectations, the employee is not likely to be satisfied.[12]

Realistic job previews can be provided in a number of ways. Some companies post videos on their websites. Others have applicants meet with current jobholders who discuss the positive and negative aspects of their jobs. Some companies bring in potential employees as interns. If both the intern and the company are satisfied, the intern is hired as a regular employee.

realistic job preview
information or experience on what a job really involves on a day-to-day basis

Best Strategies

The ultimate goal of recruiting is to generate a pool of qualified applicants for new and existing jobs. Recruiting advertisements direct potential candidates on how to submit a résumé or application for employment. In some cases, a company may need to take additional steps to assemble an adequate pool of qualified applicants. Others, such as Google or Facebook, are typically overwhelmed by hundreds of applications for one job.

A substantial portion of positions—in a recent study, 41 percent—are filled through internal transfers and promotions. Recent surveys have found that referrals and networking consistently account for the highest percentage of external hires. Social media such as LinkedIn, Facebook, and Twitter play an important role in networking and, according to staffing leaders in one survey, in influencing job candidates. Other top sources of external hires are job boards, company career sites, and recruiter-initiated contacts.[13]

applicant tracking systems
software used to manage the hiring process

LEVERAGING TECHNOLOGY

APPLICANT TRACKING SYSTEMS

A wide range of software is available to automate a high percentage of the services provided by a human resources department. Usually, large organizations use complete systems to help their human resources employees be more efficient and effective. Small and medium-size organizations are more likely to use **applicant tracking systems** to manage the hiring process. The software varies widely depending on the size of the business and level of sophistication desired. Capabilities of applicant tracking systems include the following:

- Posting notices internally and on the company website
- Allowing applicants to search for jobs
- Designing and accepting online job applications
- Providing job-specific prescreening questions
- Matching applicant skills to job requirements
- Flagging qualified applicants for further review
- Tracking and reporting data

The software generally tracks applicants by using keywords to match information provided in the application with information in the job description and specification. Systems can be used to send out form letters notifying applicants that their application has been declined if certain criteria are not matched. Some organizations prefer that an employee review the information before sending out any communication.

From your perspective as a student, it is important to understand how applicant tracking systems work to enhance your career opportunities. Reading the job requirements carefully and documenting that you meet those standards in your application are essential.

The Selection Process

Human resources experts commonly compare the selection process to a hurdle race. It can become quite complex and drawn out, particularly at companies such as Google, where rapid growth means steady hiring:

> A team of nearly 50 recruiters divided by specialty combs through résumés, which applicants must submit online, and then dumps them into a program that routes those selected for interviews to the proper hiring committee and throws the rest in the electronic trash. Interviewing for a job is a grueling process that can take months. Every opening has a hiring committee of seven to nine Googlers who must meet you. Engineers may be asked to write software or debug a program on the spot. Marketers are often required to take a writing test. No matter how long you have been out of school, Google requires that you submit your transcripts to be considered. The rigorous process is important partly for the obvious reason that in high tech, as on Wall Street, being the smartest and the cleverest at what you do is a critical business advantage.[14]

As noted earlier, the selection process in large organizations is handled by a team of human resources professionals with input from the departments or units hiring. In small and medium-size organizations, the selection is often handled by the office or unit manager. In this chapter, the focus is on small and medium-size organizations.

Equal employment opportunity legislation in the United States and elsewhere attempts to ensure fair and unprejudiced consideration for all job applicants. The first two steps are résumé screening and reference checking; both are very important because false information is found in 49 percent of résumés.[15] Frequently, once supervisors decide whom they want to hire, they want to move as quickly as possible; however, references must always be checked before making an offer.

The ability to make good decisions regarding people represents one of the last reliable sources of competitive advantage, since very few organizations are very good at it.

— Peter Drucker, management expert, consultant, and author

Source: Ira Blank, "Selecting Employees Based on Emotional Intelligence Competencies: Reap the Rewards and Minimize the Risk," *Employee Relations Law Journal* 4, no. 3 (Winter 2008): 77.

Criteria for Decision Making

The criteria for making a hiring decision must be set early in the process, before collecting data and choosing the best-qualified candidate. Most companies use one of two selection strategies: the *multiple-hurdle* or the *compensatory approach*.

- With a multiple-hurdle approach, the applicant must pass a series of procedures or hurdles that apply to a specific job and that must be cleared in order; that is, the applicant must clear one hurdle before progressing to the next. For example, if a certification, license, or specific amount of experience or education is required, candidates would be dropped from the applicant pool if they did not have any of these qualifications. An important requirement is that all hurdles be job-related.
- With a compensatory approach, the applicant can progress through all the procedures or hurdles without being screened out and is evaluated using a composite score. For example, an applicant may have two years of experience rather than the required three years, but may have a four-year college degree rather than the two-year degree required. The extra education may compensate for the lack of experience. A low score in one area can be offset by a high score in another.[16]

Figure 7.2 on page 150 is a sample matrix that can be used to rate a candidate for a specific job. For example, if you were an office manager assessing several candidates for a position as an executive assistant, you might use a form like this with the criteria based on the job description and specification.

Data Collection

The job analysis, description, and specification you created earlier (and have on file for handy reference) provide the criteria for selecting the best-qualified applicants. Many of the items can be observed and/or evaluated during the interview process. Others, such as honesty, may require additional research, such as checking references or administering an integrity test. You are now ready to collect data about the candidates and to begin analyzing the data.

Résumé and/or Application

Data can be collected by creating an application form, requesting a résumé with a letter of application, or doing both. With an application form, you select the type of data you want candidates to provide. With the résumé and cover letter, candidates select and present the information they believe portrays them in the most favorable light. The résumé and letter give candidates a better opportunity to demonstrate their communication skills and creativity.

Pre-employment Testing

Employers may require job candidates to take several different types of tests. Checks of technical skills, personality assessments, drug tests, criminal

FIGURE 7.2
Selection criteria decision matrix

***Candidate: ____________________ Position: Executive Assistant**

Selection Criteria	Rating	X Weight	Total Points
Experience		12	
Education		12	
Professional (dress, appearance, poise, self-confidence)		12	
Communication skills (nonverbal, verbal, written, listening)		12	
Microsoft Office skills (based on work samples, tests, or certification)		9	
Organization and time management skills		9	
Overall impression of candidate's performance		9	
Overall job knowledge and skills		9	
Meeting management skills		6	
Self-management skills		6	
Emotional intelligence		3	
Weighted Total Score			

*Only applicants who meet experience and education criteria are considered as candidates for this job. Ratings should be based on all sources of information collected, such as résumé, application letter, application form, references, testing, work samples, and interviews. Separate forms may be used for recording results of interviews, testing, or other areas. This selection form is a sample only. Many other criteria may be listed based on the job description and specification.

Rating on Selection Criteria	Weight of Selection Criteria
Substantially exceeds standard = 4	Critical = 12
Exceeds standard = 3	Essential = 9
Meets standard = 2	Significant = 6
Improvement required = 1	Desirable = 3

background checks, and psychological tests are examples. Often, employers administer pre-employment tests because they are required to by law or union rules. In other instances, they do so because they have found the results help predict the candidate's future success.

Pre-employment tests may be job-specific and technical. For example, a fiber optics company requires candidates to take a vision test to rule out color blindness because recognizing colors is an essential skill for the job. Other tests assess behavior, thought processes, and analytical skills. In fact, 2,500 cognitive and personality tests are available to employers.[17] Combining relevant industry research with assessments often yields more reliable and useful results. The following story provides a good example:

From a consultant's extensive research, a trucking company learned that truck drivers with multiple delivery sites in a day are more successful if they are social and interact well with people. In contrast, truck drivers who have long distances to travel with limited social interaction typically fare better if they are more introverted and quiet. The company now uses pre-employment assessment tests for social skills to place drivers in appropriate positions. The outcome has been outstanding: driver turnover has fallen to 22 percent, compared with the industry average of 116 percent.[18]

Before deciding to use any pre-employment test or assessment, be sure it is legal. Usually, the safest type of test is one that tests the specific skills the person will have to use on the job. For example, if you are hiring an office assistant who will be responsible for preparing budgets using *Excel* worksheets, a good test would be to have the person prepare a budget using an *Excel* worksheet. Different states and local jurisdictions have different rules and laws regarding pre-employment screening. Choose evaluation tools that match your corporate culture and are appropriate for the position. Candidates may perceive some types of screening as invasive and personally offensive (drug testing, for example), which may lead to well-qualified candidates' withdrawing their applications.

Work Samples or Portfolios

Work samples or portfolios can also provide useful information about capabilities. For example, an executive assistant may use a portfolio of work prepared in an academic setting or for another organization to demonstrate the quality of work he or she is capable of producing and the effective use of software applications.

Interviewing

Interviewing can be a time-consuming process. Since it is usually the final hurdle in the selection process, normally only the most qualified applicants are interviewed. Effective prescreening should eliminate those who are not likely to be successful on the job. It is not unusual for more than a hundred people to apply for a position and only five or six to be interviewed.

If you are reasonably certain that all the final applicants have the knowledge and skills to do the job effectively, you can devote the interview to trying to find the individual whose qualifications best match the position requirements. Often soft skills are the major determinants of whether the person will fit in with the corporate culture, current employees, and the work environment.

Interviews can be conducted in person, on the telephone, and virtually using Internet technology tools such as Skype. Generally, in-person interviews are far more effective than telephone or virtual interviews. A **panel interview**, in which two or more people interview a candidate at the same time, is proving to be a useful and efficient tool in predicting job performance.[19]

Many human resource professionals recommend that at least 50 percent of the questions asked in an interview be behavioral questions. A **behavioral interview** typically involves providing scenarios and asking the individual how he or she handled such situations in the past or would handle them in the future. Several examples follow:

- Have you ever had to deal with two angry employees who report to you and who are having a dispute in the office? How did you handle the situation?
- How would you handle an important customer who comes in without an appointment and demands to speak with the executive you assist if the executive is in a meeting with another customer at the time?
- You prepared a report and gave it to your manager, and now you realize one section contained some inaccurate information. What would you do?

panel interview
a type of interview in which two or more people interview a candidate at the same time

behavioral interview
an interview in which the interviewer provides scenarios and asks how the candidate handled such situations in the past or would handle them in the future

Minimize the number of questions that can be answered with a simple yes or no. Instead, try to develop open-ended questions to get the candidate talking. It is important to ensure all questions you plan to ask are legal and job-related. If you are not sure about a question, ask a human resources specialist to avoid costly lawsuits. Chapter 10, "Legal and Ethical Challenges," provides additional guidance on interview questions and conduct.

© Marcin Balcerzak/Shutterstock.com

Be prepared in an interview with relevant behavioral questions to learn how each candidate would react in different situations. Additional follow-up questions may be needed to probe further.

During the interview, pay careful attention to both verbal and nonverbal communication. One essential element is the first impression. Is the candidate professionally dressed and well groomed? Does he or she greet you with a smile and a firm handshake and otherwise convey an attitude of confidence? As the interview proceeds, continue to be alert to the candidate's poise and nonverbal communication. Listen carefully to answers. Did the candidate answer the question that you asked? How good are the person's verbal skills? Take careful notes, and write them up as soon as the interview is concluded.

SUMMARY

1. Many factors are involved in determining the number and types of employees needed to do a job effectively. First-line or office managers are often in the best position to determine the needs of their units.
2. Recruitment focuses on finding qualified employees who will be successful and will remain with the company for a long time.
3. A job analysis, job description, and job specification must be completed before recruiting.
4. Internal recruiting provides employees with career paths and builds commitment and loyalty. A number of sources can be used for external recruiting.
5. Most companies use either a multiple-hurdle or a compensatory approach in determining the criteria for making selection decisions. Key data sources are the résumé and/or application, pre-employment testing, work samples or portfolios, and interviewing.

Terms

applicant tracking system, 147
behavioral interview, 152
employee turnover, 138
external recruiting, 144
internal recruiting, 144
job analysis, 139
job description, 139
job specification, 139
panel interview, 152
realistic job preview, 146
recruitment, 138
retention, 138
staffing, 137

Study Tools

CourseMate

Located at www.cengagebrain.com

- Chapter Outlines
- Flashcards
- Interactive Quizzes
- Tech Tools
- Video Segments

and More!

Questions for Reflection

1. Why is effective recruitment and selection important?
2. Describe how you would complete the following:
   a. Job analysis
   b. Job description
   c. Job specification
3. Describe how you would do the following types of recruiting:
   a. Internal
   b. External
4. Why should you give both positive and negative information in a job preview?
5. Why is recruiting for diversity important?
6. What criteria would you use for selection if you were hiring for the job you now have or would like to have?
7. Why are those criteria important?

Hands-On Activities

These activities may be completed in teams or individually.

Job Description

Select a job description from your place of employment, or locate one on an employment website such as CareerBuilder or Monster. Choose a job you are familiar with, and critique the job description.

1. What important components does it include?
2. What, if any, components are missing?
3. If you noted any missing items, draft content for them.

Best Hiring Practices

An important skill for administrative managers is learning to make effective hiring decisions. Think about how you would handle the hiring process if you were in a management position and routinely hired employees. Use the following questions to begin building a list of best hiring practices.

1. Which recruiting strategies/advertising tools would be most effective for attracting a diverse candidate pool?
2. Would you use any pre-employment tests? If so, which type(s) would you use?
3. How would you assess a candidate's professionalism, reliability, honesty, and integrity?
4. Whom would you involve in your company (by position name) in the interviewing process?
5. What is one question you would ask every applicant, regardless of the position?
6. What are some examples of questions you would ask to learn more about a candidate's behavior patterns?
7. What other screening or evaluation would you do?

Interview Questions

1. Write a list of questions you would ask if you were hiring for the position described in the previous section.
2. Evaluate your questions as follows:
   a. Are they all job-related?
   b. Have you included a number of behavioral questions?
   c. If you answered no to either a or b, revise your questions appropriately.

You Decide | Case Study

Improving Diversity

Jessica is the new human resources manager of a nonprofit organization in Columbia, Maryland. The organization has 26 employees with very little diversity in race, age, and gender. She has discussed the situation with the president and CEO of the organization, who share her concerns about the lack of diversity.

The president told Jessica that two new positions had been authorized and two vacancies had not been filled. The president suggested she use these four positions and vacancies to improve the organization's diversity.

Questions

1. What could Jessica do to enhance diversity recruiting?
2. What should she do about current employees who may be interested in the new and vacant positions?

MANAGER'S TOOLKIT

Create the following for a job of your choice. It may be the job you currently hold or your dream job.

1. Use the questions in Figure 7.1 on page 140 to do a basic job analysis.
2. Write a job description for the job including all the components listed in the "Job Description" section on page 139 of this chapter.
3. Create a basic selection criteria decision matrix similar to the one in Figure 7.2 on page 150. Include the weighted value for each item listed.

Soft Skills for Success

Multicultural or Diversity Skills

Many employers specify on job descriptions that they value diversity and that multicultural or diversity skills are either highly desirable or required for applicants. As noted earlier, diversity may consist of many factors, including differences in attitudes, perspectives, opinions, gender, age, race, ethnic background, language skills, education, work experience, socioeconomic status, religion, sexual orientation, disabilities, and alternative family structures.

A main issue in business is how to interact and communicate effectively with people of different cultures. Many attributes are required for the development of multicultural or diversity skills. A few are listed below:

- Courtesy and respect for others regardless of differences
- Ability to build trust
- Patience, tolerance, and open-mindedness
- Ability to communicate effectively across cultural and language barriers—especially the willingness to listen carefully
- Empathy and cultural sensitivity
- Willingness to learn more about the people with whom you will work and their culture

Put It to Work

Assume you have been asked to serve on a diverse multicultural team. The eight-member team will work on an important project that could have a very positive effect on your career. The team has the following characteristics:

- It consists of three women and five men ages 28 to 64.
- Three people are members of minority groups.
- Five members speak English as a native language, and three speak it as a second language.
- Five members are from the United States, one is from Brazil, one is from Germany, and one is from South Africa.
- Team members are from different functional areas of the company and different levels of management.

Your company will provide the team with contact information and basic professional information about each member.

1. Rate your strengths on the attributes listed above using a scale of 5 (high) to 1 (low).

    ____ Courtesy and respect for others regardless of differences

    ____ Ability to build trust

    ____ Patience, tolerance, and open-mindedness

    ____ Ability to communicate effectively across cultural and language barriers—especially the willingness to listen carefully

    ____ Empathy and cultural sensitivity

    ____ Willingness to learn more about the people with whom you will work and their culture

2. List the steps you can take to strengthen your ratings and to prepare yourself for this assignment.

CHAPTER
8

Setting Up Employees for Success

Learning Outcomes

1. Explain the importance of planning new employee orientation.
2. Describe steps to prepare for the new hire's first day.
3. List topics that should be included in the company and job-specific orientations.
4. Describe key elements of an orientation training plan.
5. Discuss the reasons companies invest in training.
6. Describe the six-step plan to link training to job performance.
7. Discuss strategies for cultivating a productive coaching relationship and developing peak performers.

Straight Talk From the Field

Vickie Sokol Evans is CEO and president of The Red Cape Company, a technology and productivity training company. She is a Microsoft Certified Trainer and launched her technology career in the early 1990s, when colleagues came to her for help on databases and other software applications.

Photo courtesy V. Evans

What is your greatest training challenge?

Time. It is becoming increasingly challenging for business users to get away from their desk or the office to attend training.

When I first began teaching desktop technology classes in 1997, they were full-day sessions. Employees would leave work for an entire day for technology training. That's nearly impossible for business users to do today. Yet, the pace at which technology changes has increased.

Time away from a busy manager's desk means lost revenue opportunities. The assistant to the executive who supports the revenue-generating employee, and who might even support multiple managers, also finds it challenging to get away for training. Time away from the desk means lower productivity for the organization.

One of the many solutions to meet the challenge is by teaching smaller, bite-sized topics that are relevant to the audience. However, motivating employees to take the time to attend the smaller classes is still difficult.

This is why a half-hour tips and tricks session or webinar is effective for bringing many employees through the learning funnel. Business users can immediately see the time-saving tricks, one after the other, in a room filled with their peers. The session also identifies training needs.

How do you handle new-hire training?

To shorten the learning curve, training new employees has to be a process rather than a one-time experience. Additionally, training must include subject matter that experts within the organization have identified as crucial for new hires to know the first day, week, month, or three months of their employment. Training is best when it is phased in over time as opposed to overwhelming new employees with a flood of new information.

On the first day, only teach what is critical to know that day to get started, and then follow up when it is appropriate to do so.

How do you handle the rollout of new technology?

Organizations vary on how they deploy a new version of software, such as Microsoft Office. Some organizations do so with virtually no training. Others might develop a training process. In my experience, the ideal rollout would be a phased approached which is recommended by Microsoft.

1. The first phase begins with an affinity or awareness campaign with brief introductions to what's new and to get employees excited about what is coming. Some enterprise companies offer a home-use program, giving employees an incentive to purchase the new software to use at home so they can get comfortable with it before they use it at work.

2. The second phase is the upgrade and actual roll out of the technology. The company's focus is to make sure downtime is limited. During the upgrade, employees may attend specific training on the essential skills for using the new technology. Support on the day of upgrade may include quick reference cards, help desk support, or floor support—where one or more trainers are available to answer questions and provide help so productivity is not interrupted.
3. The third phase is the productivity phase, which is delayed until employees are comfortable using the more common features of the system. These smaller classes are hands-on sessions or webinars and tend to be "deep dive" topics where you get to more complex new features, such as a pivot table in Excel.

What do companies expect most from training?

It is important for training to roll up to management and business objectives. Training that can positively affect the bottom line and have the greatest return on investment will meet and could potentially exceed an organization's expectations.

> The objective for technology training is to help employees become more productive, thus allowing the organization to truly realize a return on its technology investment.

All classes developed and taught by The Red Cape Company are focused on what matters most to the client. In most cases the objective for technology training is to help employees become more productive, thus allowing the organization to truly realize a return on its technology investment. From a learner perspective, we equally want to create a memorable learning experience to help attendees to retain the information being presented.

What kind of advice do you give to employees who do not have access to company training?

My best advice is to take the initiative to learn the technology yourself. Invest the time and financial resources when you can in order to gain an edge and enhance your career.

If formal training isn't in the budget, then use books, videos, blogs, and podcasts to learn what you need to know. Many free or low-cost resources are available. Start with what Microsoft offers on its office.com website.

Join and contribute to a learning community. You retain 90 percent of what you learn by teaching others. If you have the resources, hire a technology coach and/or consider having a work-flow audit where a technology coach can watch you work for an hour.

Start a study group. I learned SharePoint this way. Several of my colleagues were interested in learning it with me so I set up a study group—much like a book club. I subscribed to an inexpensive SharePoint service and invited my colleagues to join me online every Wednesday at 5:30 p.m. We each took turns taking a task, learning about it, and sharing our experiences. Our employer wasn't in a position to invest in our training, so our only option was to learn it on our own, which we did at minimal cost.

What are the greatest non-monetary rewards you get from training others?

Knowing that I helped someone discover ways to save time, or that I am able to build their confidence in using the technology, is why I do what I do.

Visit *www.cengagebrain.com* to read the complete profile.

Chapter Outline

First impressions are powerful and may have a lasting impact. Creating a comfortable, positive, and exciting impression on an employee's first day on the job is the first step in setting the employee up for success. But setting up employees for success goes far beyond orientation and initial training. The goal is to coach, motivate, and train all employees long after the orientation has been completed to promote long-term success and retention. This chapter focuses on orientation and initial training as well as long-term training and coaching to help ensure productive, rewarding, and successful careers.

Planning and Preparations

A new employee wants to feel warm, comfortable, and welcomed in the company. These feelings tend to reassure the individual that he or she made a wise decision in accepting the job offer and that the company will be a good fit. Proper handling of a new employee's first 90 days (often called **onboarding**) is essential for long-term success.

Effective orientations do not just happen. They must be planned carefully. In large organizations, the human resources department is likely to have a standard company **orientation**. However, the department or unit where the employee will work must plan specifically for each new employee. In small organizations, the department, unit, or office manager may plan the entire orientation.

onboarding
proper handling of a new employee's first 90 days

orientation
an opportunity to introduce and welcome a new hire and begin the transition from new employee to contributing team member

Involve Current Employees

Orientation planning can be a good experience for your current employees. Involving them can give them the satisfaction of making a valuable

Involving your current employees can give them the satisfaction of making a valuable contribution.

contribution. Ultimately, it can lead to a better orientation plan because they may pinpoint details you have overlooked. In addition, they will be better prepared for the arrival of the new employee and will have some time to reflect on how the change will affect them. This chapter suggests several ways current employees can contribute.

Send Forms and Information

As soon as the hiring is official, some of the required routine forms can be sent (typically electronically) to the new employee to complete and bring in the first day. Send only forms that are not likely to generate questions. Other reading materials about the company and products or services may be sent as well. Most new hires will have visited the company website in preparation for the interview. Many will visit it again before the first day of work.

Braithwaite Communications, a marketing and communications firm in Philadelphia, gives new hires an iPod® a couple of weeks before their first day. Included on the iPod are a prerecorded orientation and personal greetings from some of the firm's employees. CEO Hugh Braithwaite believes the practice leads to new hires' arriving with "higher morale and positive energy."[1] However you choose to do it, the idea of letting new hires know you are looking forward to their arrival is a positive step toward a good first impression and a good first day on the job.

Make Preliminary Preparations

A new employee who arrives on the first day and finds the work space set up and basic needs provided for will be impressed. The following items relate to a position in an office setting:

- **Identification badge**. If a photo identification badge is required, let the employee know ahead of time when the photo will be taken. If a photo is not required, you might order the badge in advance, if possible, so it is available on the first day. Another option is to provide a temporary badge until the employee has completed orientation.
- **Business cards**. If the person will be working with customers, vendors, or business partners, consider ordering business cards ahead of time.
- **Work space**. Decide which office or cubicle the person will occupy. Make sure it is clean (including drawers and cabinets). Check for necessary office supplies such as a desk calendar, pens, pencils, paper clips, a tape dispenser, a stapler, scissors, and a notepad. Determine if any furniture should be replaced or added.
- **Telephone**. If the employee will have a personal telephone and/or company cell phone, have it set up ahead of time. Determine features the employee will need, such as caller ID, long-distance calling, speakerphone, hands-free headset, call waiting, and voice mail.

Provide a copy of the telephone user manual and company phone directory. Be sure to add phone usage and company protocol to the training plan.

- **Email.** Have the employee's email account created in advance. Provide any company policies and guidelines for appropriate use of company email.
- **Computer, network, and printer.** Determine if the employee will use an existing computer or will need a new laptop or desktop computer. Identify what printer the person will use. Provide information on how to access, use, and store information on the network. Also decide what software applications and network files the employee will need.

  Coordinate setup and access with the technology person or department in advance, as it may take a couple of weeks for equipment to be ordered and configured. Add hardware, network, and software application training to your training plan if needed.

Orientation

In an office setting, orientation is generally divided into two segments: the company orientation and the department or unit (job-specific) orientation. As noted earlier, in large organizations, the company orientation typically is a standardized process developed by the human resources department. In small organizations, the department, unit, or office manager may be responsible for it. The types of information that need to be presented are basically the same.

In large organizations, the department or unit orientation is handled by the group where the employee will work. In small organizations, the department, unit, or office manager may handle it.

It is important to present the content in an engaging manner that will create excitement about the new experience. All the content does not have to be presented at one time. In fact, information overload may be a significant problem. Present the information with the highest priority and only information the employee needs to know. Schedule additional sessions with the appropriate people to answer questions and fill in details.

Company Orientation

Materials required for the company orientation include an orientation checklist, employee handbook, and orientation program. In a large organization, these materials are professionally prepared. A small organization may not have formal printed documents. You will likely have to collect and organize the information. Some of the materials may be reviewed in detail, whereas others may be highlighted briefly (the employee can read about them in full later). To prepare for the company orientation, consider providing each new employee with a personal folder. See Figure 8.1 for examples of what to include in this folder.

FIGURE 8.1
Checklist for orientation folders

Orientation Folders

Include these items in the folder:

- An agenda for the day
- Names, titles, and contact information for presenters and other participants
- A copy of the organization's vision, mission, and values statements
- A copy of the organizational chart
- An employee handbook
- Benefits information
- A master calendar including company-paid holidays and major events
- Recent press releases
- A copy of the most recent company newsletter
- Handouts from the guest speakers scheduled
- A notepad and pen

Company Background and Overview

One of the best ways to kick off an orientation session is to begin by talking about the organization. It gets everyone focused and energized, and it is helpful for employees to know the history of the organization and its mission, vision, and goals.[2] This is also a good opportunity to share the company's customer service philosophy and quality standards. In addition, you want employees to know the organizational structure and the names and faces of the executives. It is ideal when a top executive presents this overview session in person or via video.[3] Many companies also present information on company branding and specific guides for using the logo, colors, and type style appropriately.

Employee Benefits

Employee benefits include non-salary compensation such as health, life, and disability insurance; vacation and personal leave; and employee stock option and retirement plans. Health insurance has become so complex that it is helpful to explain the options along with the associated fees. If you have a human resources or benefits specialist, ask that person to attend this session. In addition, ask him or her to prepare a document outlining the cost of each benefit to the employee as well as the employer's contribution. Insurance benefits are one of the fastest-growing expenses for companies, and employees tend to recognize and appreciate them more when they know the actual benefits and costs.

Discuss all benefits your organization makes available. In addition to those described above, they may include, for example, retirement plans, child care, employee discounts, and fitness center privileges.

Hours of Operation and Important Dates

Give an overview of the organization's typical business hours. Provide a list of observed holidays as well as other important dates. For example, many manufacturing sites close for a week between Christmas and New Year's Day for inventory and maintenance. Let employees know if they will be required to take leave at this time. List any mandatory company meetings. Also consider providing dates for corporate events such as major sales or promotions.

Inclement Weather

Review the company's inclement weather policy and procedures. If you typically provide updates via television, radio, or the Internet, let new employees know which stations and websites to check. If you follow the protocol of other organizations, supply their names, and explain where to obtain updated information. For example, a nonprofit organization or small business may choose to follow the local city guides. Provide the URL of the city website and contact information for TV or radio stations that publicize closing information.

Emergency Preparedness and Safety

Personal safety for all employees is an overriding goal for most organizations. In fact, safety training has become mandatory for many employers. However, every company has different risks because various jobs create different levels of exposure. The important point is to review safety protocol with all new employees, including precautionary measures such as fire drills and incident reporting procedures. You should review how to handle potential emergencies, such as tornadoes, fires, and robberies as well as individual illness or injury.

employee benefits
non-salary compensation such as health, life, and disability insurance; vacation and personal leave; and employee stock option and retirement plans

Team up with one or two classmates. Select a company or nonprofit organization everyone is familiar with to answer the following:

1. How do you suggest the company notify employees of closings and delays?

   ____

2. What topics should be included in the company's emergency preparedness and safety plan?

   ____

Legal Issues

Employers can be held liable for the actions of their employees. Therefore, it is important to let new hires know how the company defines appropriate and acceptable behavior. Items to include in this discussion include policies regarding sexual harassment, computer use, email and phone use, confidentiality of corporate and customer information, intellectual property rights (discussed in Chapter 10), theft, alcohol and drug use, and other relevant legal topics. In addition, some companies may require employees to sign conflict of interest statements. A conflict of interest statement is designed to prevent a situation in which an employee or immediate family member takes advantage of the employee's position or exploits the company for personal gain.

Employers can be held liable for the actions of their employees.

Job-Specific Orientation

The job-specific orientation covers items that are unique to the specific department or unit and to the position of the new hire. The following are typical items that might be covered. Departments, units, and jobs vary widely, so these topics would need to be adapted.

Tour and Introductions

New employees are typically eager to meet the employees with whom they will be working. Often they are introduced during the interview process, but they may not remember names. The department tour and introductions are a great way to start the job-specific orientation. Coffee or a light breakfast may be set up for department members to meet the new employee on an informal basis. Usually the department manager also takes the new employee to meet any key executives and managers who are available.

During the first few weeks, new employees are challenged with learning new skills and procedures and getting to know people. To make this transition easier, consider preparing two reference documents. You can refer to one of them as "Whom do you call?" This document should list the names, phone numbers, and email addresses of key members of the

This manager is introducing the new employee to all department employees. What a wonderful way to be welcomed into a new organization!

organization, as well as members of the immediate team or department. Include helpful contacts in human resources, benefits, payroll, information technology, purchasing, and security. Be sure to introduce new employees to anyone on this list they have not already met.

The other document can be titled "A day in the life." Ask your current employees to help you prepare a one- or two-page preview of a typical day in your department. This document is a nice way to acquaint newcomers with routine activities, any common problems, and ways they are typically handled.

Department's Mission and Goals

Each department or division serves a primary purpose within an organization. If the department has a formal mission or statement of purpose, review it with new hires, and let them know how it supports the overall mission of the organization. Also, review the department's goals, and share your plan for achieving them. Be sure to emphasize the new employee's important role in achieving the organization's mission and goals.

> Review the department's goals, and share your plan for achieving them.

Job Functions

In most cases, the new hire will have reviewed the job description in the interview process. However, it is a good idea to provide a copy during the first week and to review it with the employee. Go over each item in detail, providing examples of actual tasks associated with the job duties listed.

Policies and Procedures

New employees will probably have received a copy of the company's policies and procedures manual during the company orientation. However, it is the manager's responsibility to make sure they fully understand relevant policies and procedures. Clarify as necessary rules and expectations regarding company vehicles, purchasing cards, and any other company-supplied resources. If you have a dress code, standards for appearance and/or conduct, or rules regarding parking, displaying an employee ID, or other relevant items, communicate these policies as well. Review security and safety items on the first day.

If there are additional policies and procedures for your department, go over them in detail. This is the time to explain the department's policies and expectations for work schedules, overtime, breaks, lunch, vacation and personal day requests, communication regarding absence in the event of illness or emergency, and attendance and punctuality.

Alternative Work Schedules

Many organizations still operate with a traditional five-day workweek and 8 or 9 a.m. to 5 p.m. hours. Many others, however, offer some form of nontraditional scheduling. If your organization is one of them, you will need to work with your new (and current) employees to develop, maintain, and adjust work schedules.

- **Teleworkers** are employees who work from home or another remote location. Employees who are most successful as teleworkers tend to be technically sophisticated, creative, independent, and self-managed. According to a recent study, most teleworkers are college graduates and *knowledge workers*: professionals in various fields who work with information. The study found that some 26.2 million U.S. employees work remotely at least once a month.[4]
- **Job sharing** is an arrangement in which two professionals form a partnership to do one job. It is designed for people who want to balance their professional and personal schedules, not for two people putting together part-time jobs. Job sharing is most commonly used by mothers who do not want to give up their careers.[5]
- Flexible scheduling, or **flextime**, is an arrangement in which an employer permits an employee to work a modified schedule while still achieving the hours necessary to equate to a full workweek. For example, some companies offer a **compressed workweek** whereby an employee works four 10-hour days or works five 9-hour days and then takes a day off every other week. Flextime also includes modified hours, allowing an employee to arrive and leave early or late. These arrangements are often made to accommodate child-care needs, commuting issues, or class schedules for those taking college courses.

Such accommodations can have a very positive effect on employees. For some workers, location and time flexibility are major factors in retention.

teleworkers
employees who work from home or another remote location

job sharing
an arrangement in which two professionals form a partnership to perform one job

flextime
the practice of allowing an employee to work a modified schedule

compressed workweek
a situation in which an employee works longer hours but fewer days

Corporate Culture

Each company has its own unique culture. The **corporate culture** is the collective or shared values, beliefs, traditions, philosophy, and character or personality of the organization. Organizations sometimes are described as having a culture for innovation and creativity, a competitive culture, or a warm, friendly customer service and employee-focused culture.

While it is not generally part of formal orientation policies, most successful companies try to give new employees a feel or sense for the culture from the first day. They spend time talking about the company history, culture, legends, and recognizable brand names to instill pride in the employee for being a part of the organization. They often give the employee items such as a portfolio, coffee mug, or knit shirt with the company logo.

Orientation Training

Training is the use of guided experiences to change employee behavior or attitudes. Orientation training is focused on the specific company or industry skills and knowledge that would not normally be a part of the new employee's previous experience and education. For example, a person without nonprofit experience who has been hired as an office manager for a nonprofit organization may not be familiar with software for managing fundraising efforts or donor funds. The telephone system may be different. A new employee may need special training to learn how to sell the company's products or services.

Buddy System

New employees may need on-the-job training in work processes and procedures. Often the buddy system is used for this type of training. The **buddy system** is the pairing of new hires with a mentor to help set them up for success.[6] The buddy should be carefully selected, and his or her role should be recognized during the annual performance evaluation. The ideal buddy has a positive and enthusiastic attitude, combined with excellent job skills and comprehensive knowledge of the job functions and the organization. You should meet with the buddy before the new hire's start date to review the orientation training plan and to get the buddy's input.

One of the primary roles of a buddy is to be shadowed by a new hire. **Job shadowing** helps new hires learn about their job and the organization through real-time, firsthand observation of an experienced coworker. The buddy also helps new employees learn the unwritten rules of the department and organization. An example of an unwritten rule might be not to ask other employees about their compensation or discuss your own. New employees need to acquire both technical skills and social information as they begin to adapt to their new environment.[7] Understanding

corporate culture
the shared values, beliefs, traditions, philosophy, and character or personality of the organization

training
the use of guided experiences to change employee behavior or attitudes

buddy system
the pairing of new hires with a mentor to help set them up for success

job shadowing
learning about a job and the organization through real-time, firsthand observation of an experienced coworker

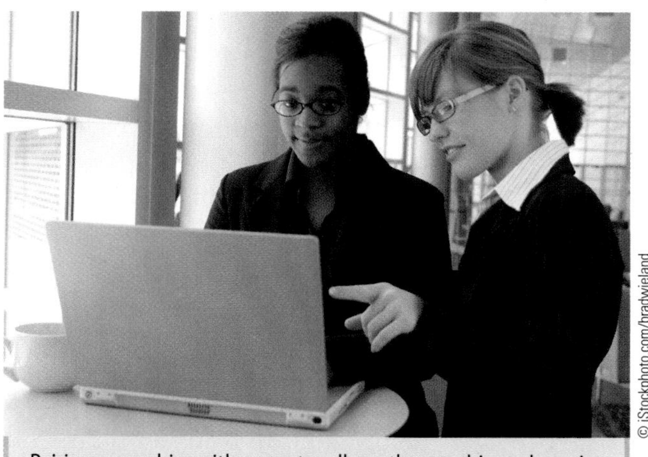

Pairing a new hire with a mentor allows the new hire to learn in real-time about the position and organization. A mentor can also help a new hire establish a network of business contacts.

office politics and how to fit in can have a positive impact on the new hire's decision to stay.

Office politics refers to relationships with people in the office. People tend to focus on the negative side of office politics, such as a certain manager's constantly catering to his or her supervisor and taking actions with the intent of getting something in return. The positive side is developing good relationships with higher-level management as well as peers, such as being willing to do your share and a little more. Offering to help others (not just your immediate supervisors) when you have something special to contribute shows you are invested in the organization, which likely will help your own career.

Another role for the buddy is to help the new person establish a network of relationships with stakeholders, including coworkers, contractors, customers, and vendors. The buddy is usually aware of each person's expertise and interests and can encourage people to share their knowledge, providing opportunities for bonding and team building. Establishing positive relationships with coworkers typically helps with retention when the new hire feels a stronger sense of connection and commitment to the organization.[8]

The key to setting up a productive buddy system is to establish parameters and formal communication channels. The buddy is a newcomer's go-to person when you (the manager) are not available or when the newcomer feels unsure about asking you certain questions. The new hire can ask the buddy anything. But if the question relates to policies or job responsibilities, the newcomer should validate the information with you. In addition, you must be clear with the buddy about his or her role. It is not the buddy's job to supervise the new person. The buddy is there to serve as a resource and constructive role model, to communicate with you regarding how well the new hire is progressing, and to advise you if the newcomer needs additional training or coaching.

Training Plan

Every position is different; therefore, every training plan will need to be tailored to some extent. However, there are some common elements to include as you plan for training your new hires. One item that is difficult to gauge is how long it will take new employees to become independent and productive. One study found that, on average, the time ranges "from eight weeks for clerical jobs to 20 weeks for professionals to more than 26 weeks for executives."[9]

First, identify the detailed list of job functions and tasks each person will be asked to perform. Consider breaking them down into primary and secondary duties. This approach will allow you to focus initial training on primary duties and then expand the employee's responsibilities and training over time. To prepare the list of functions, reference the employee's job description, and invite input from your existing staff. Do not assume that someone with experience in the field does not need training. Every office is unique, with different employee expectations.

Once you have the detailed list of topics for training, identify who will conduct the training, and determine how long it will take. Review the plan with the trainer(s) before each training session. Discuss your expectations, and clarify how you will determine the new employee has been successfully trained. Emphasize good training techniques and consistency. Be sure to connect each training element to the job function and explain how the elements support the mission and goals for the department and organization.

Meet with the new hires to review the orientation training plan, and then meet with everyone involved in the training to clarify expectations. Ask them all to let you know if they feel more or less time is needed for training in a particular area. Give the new employees a master checklist, and explain how you plan to assess their independence in each area. Let them know from the beginning that your approach to training includes the four ingredients of a good training program: goal setting, modeling (or explaining), practice, and feedback.[10] Figure 8.3 in the "Training Methods" section (page 175) illustrates these steps.

I am always ready to learn, although I do not always like being taught.

—Winston Churchill, former British prime minister

Performance Expectations

Many organizations have a probationary period for some types of employees, usually nonmanagerial employees. Regardless of whether a company uses a probationary period, it is important to discuss performance goals and expectations. New employees tend to thrive when they clearly understand what is expected of them. They also tend to be more focused and perform at a higher level when they understand how their performance will be assessed.

Performance appraisal is the process of evaluating individual job performance as a basis for making objective personnel decisions.[11] This definition intentionally excludes occasional coaching, in which a supervisor simply checks an employee's work and gives immediate feedback. Although personal coaching is fundamental to good management and is essential during orientation, formally documented appraisals are needed both to ensure that opportunities and rewards are equitably distributed and to avoid prejudicial treatment.[12]

Formal Performance Appraisals

It is important to discuss with your new employees how and when you plan to evaluate their job performance formally. During the new hire's orientation/probation period, a supervisor may conduct abbreviated performance appraisals after the first three months, six months, and year. These mini-evaluations should be documented and reviewed with the employee.

Give the employee a copy of the appraisal form along with the key indicators, measures, and criteria. Explain how you will measure and/or assess each item on the form. Explain the criteria and what you consider to be key indicators, invite the new employee's input to enhance these items, and make them meaningful for the individual.[13] These steps will reduce the employee's anxiety and the element of surprise that employees often associate with performance evaluations.

Informal Performance Evaluations

Informal performance assessment is part of the manager's coaching role. New employees especially need frequent coaching and positive and constructive feedback. This ongoing evaluation of performance allows employees to make improvements promptly without floundering. Providing new hires with consistent, constructive feedback will help them stay on track to become outstanding team members.

Performance appraisals are discussed in more detail in Chapter 9. Coaching is discussed later in this chapter.

1. Why do you think it is important to clarify performance expectations during a new employee's orientation?

2. What unintended or negative consequences do you think are possible if a manager fails to let employees know how and when their performance will be evaluated?

Training for All Employees

Most organizations offer some form of employee training—in a formal program, informally on the job, or both. Frequently, companies attempt to balance the needs of the organization with the employee's personal goals. Training varies dramatically in small and large organizations and from industry to industry. Typically in large organizations, it is managed by the human resources department. However, in small organizations, the unit manager is responsible. This section provides an overview of employee training in an office setting.

Why Organizations Train

Organizations train for many reasons. Perhaps the main reason is that companies believe training is an investment in one of its most important assets: its employees. When asked about the cost of training, executives often respond that it is expensive but not nearly as expensive as the cost of not training.

Employee development is a continuous process designed to improve an employee's skills, ability, and knowledge. Computer manufacturer Dell explains its philosophy of employee development as follows, and its development model is shown in Figure 8.2.

employee development a continuous process designed to improve an employee's skills, ability, and knowledge

> We aspire to cultivate the confidence, drive and abilities in all of our team members, which empower them to fulfill their potential. Career development at Dell is a collaborative process between individual team members, mentors and the organization at large. Working together, we can balance your aspirations and interests with Dell's strategy and goals, following through with a purposeful plan of action.[14]

FIGURE 8.2
Dell Development Model

The Dell Development Model

At Dell, career development follows a 70/20/10 model, which encompasses personalized development in three distinct categories:

70 Percent On-the-Job Experience

- Discover opportunities to strengthen your skills.
- Grow new strengths through stretch assignments and special projects.
- Develop a personal performance plan.

20 Percent Learning Through Others

- Find a mentor through Dell's Mentor Connect tool.
- Join a Dell Employee Resource Group.

10 Percent Formal Classes or Training

- Take advantage of formal training opportunities.
- Review what you learn with your leader.
- Apply what you've learned to your role.

Source: Dell Career Development, www.dell.com/learn/us/en/uscorp1/learning at dell.

Training is a subset of employee development and differs from employee development in that it is specifically directed to enhancing job performance. An example of an employee development program that is not linked to specific job performance is the college tuition reimbursement many companies offer employees.

Note in the Dell model that 70 percent of employee training consists of on-the-job experience. Many companies use on-the-job experience and training as the primary type of training, and adding mentoring as Dell does is a standard approach in many companies.

Most companies train employees because they want to achieve the following outcomes:

Company/Product Knowledge

Successful companies tend to develop new products and/or services and continue to improve their core offerings. Company-wide training initiatives that introduce employees to new or improved products and services are foundation stones of success. Such training can cover product use, benefits, profiles of the typical buyer, and how the product will be sold, shipped, and serviced.

Performance Improvement

Performance improvement might include cutting costs or improving productivity, quality, customer service, team building, or communication.

Cross-Training

Many organizations, particularly small- to medium-sized businesses, have just one or two individuals who are properly trained to perform key functions or tasks. Organizations invest in cross-training to provide opportunities for employees to grow and also to avoid workflow interruptions if someone is absent. **Cross-training** is the process of learning a new skill or task that is typically the responsibility of a coworker.

Legal Compliance

This type of training is intended to help ensure employees understand and comply with legal requirements. Under this legal umbrella is training related to sexual harassment, discrimination, safe food handling, and accounting and tax regulations.

Safety

The purpose of safety training is to instruct employees on how to protect themselves and others in case of a fire, natural disaster, injury, or illness. The Occupational Safety and Health Administration (OSHA) website provides excellent information on office training. Chapter 10 discusses these legal issues in more detail.

cross-training
the process of learning a new skill or task that is typically the responsibility of a coworker

1. Reflect for a moment on a situation in which you wanted to learn a new skill. What inspired or motivated you to want to learn?

____

2. How can you use this insight and knowledge to be a more effective manager or trainer?

____

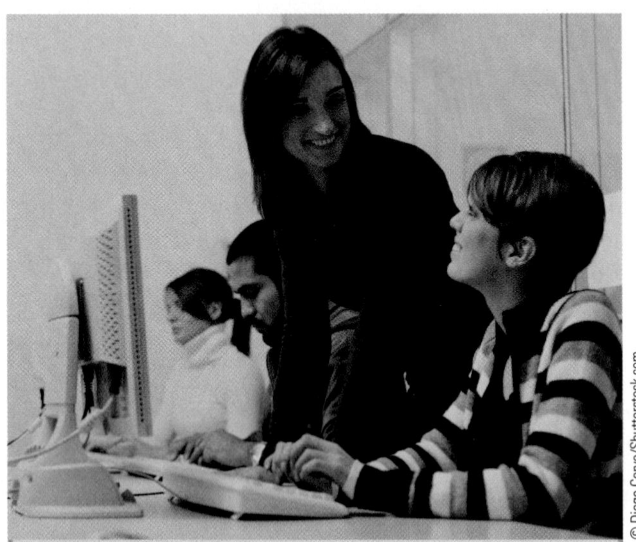
© Diego Cervo/Shutterstock.com

Shhh! Serious teaching and learning in progress. This manager is providing her trainees with a highly effective learning environment that combines personal instruction with hands-on learning and immediate feedback.

Effective Training

For training to be effective, it has to be learning-centered, and employees must be fully engaged in the process. **Learning-centered training** focuses on the individual's specific needs (as opposed to a one-size-fits-all, cookie-cutter approach) and measurable knowledge and skill development. Fully engaged employees take an active, rather than passive, role in learning. For example, in collaborative work, they take responsibility for creating and presenting information, not just absorbing it.

The following six-step training plan is designed to enhance job knowledge or job performance:

1. **Conduct a needs assessment**. Determine what specific knowledge and skills employee(s) need to acquire.
2. **Develop an individual or a group training plan**. Provide training to only those members of the unit who need it.
3. **Select the methods and trainer**. Note that the way factual information is acquired differs from the way skills are developed. However, training frequently involves a combination of factual knowledge and skill building. Budgets often determine who will do the training and how it will be done. (The "Training Methods" section below discusses this topic in greater detail.) Ensure the trainer has the required skills and knowledge and plans to use appropriate methods.
4. **Prepare employees to learn**. Most employees want to be successful. If they believe the training is relevant and will help them succeed in their jobs or develop professionally, they are likely to get the most out of it. Coach your employees individually to ensure they understand its importance, what they can expect to learn, and how it will benefit their careers. If materials must be read or completed before the training, tell employees ahead of time that this preparation is absolutely required to participate.
5. **Conduct the training**. Ensure participants understand the objectives, have prepared appropriately, and are actively engaged in the learning.

learning-centered training
training that focuses on the individual's specific needs

6. **Follow up and evaluate effectiveness**. The best measures are evidence that employees apply what they have learned, that they are better prepared to do their jobs, and that job performance has improved. Note in the Dell model that after formal training, the employee reviews what was learned with the leader and applies it.

Knowledge to
ACTION

In a team, brainstorm to develop a list of methods a manager can use to confirm that the employee he or she is training is successfully learning.

Training Methods

Numerous options exist for training. Many are traditional face-to-face options; others are technology-enabled such as videos, webinars, and online training. Training can be provided by employees or outside consultants with special expertise who conduct training that is custom-designed for your organization. On some topics, such as training for legal compliance or safety, the topic may be generic, so training does not have to be customized. The cost varies widely depending on the option selected. The purpose or specific goals determine the best method to use. A high percentage of training is on-the-job training and coaching by experienced coworkers, supervisors, and managers.

Figure 8.3 illustrates the four essential ingredients for skill-based learning: (1) goal setting, (2) modeling, (3) practice, and (4) feedback.[15]

FIGURE 8.3
Steps for effective skill-based learning

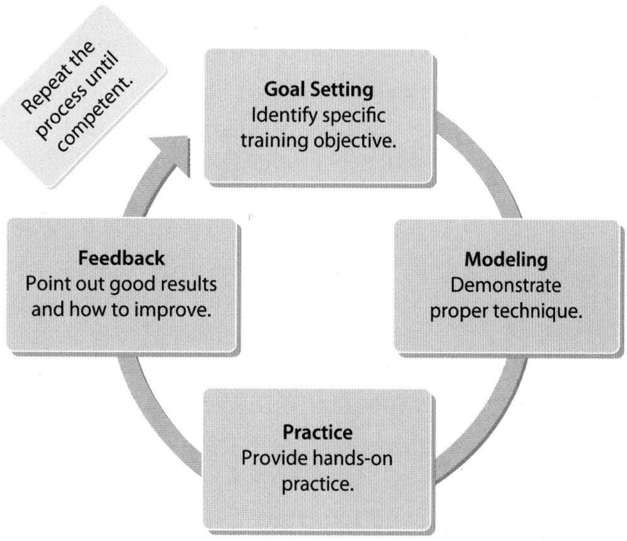
Repeat the process until competent.
Goal Setting
Identify specific training objective.
Modeling
Demonstrate proper technique.
Practice
Provide hands-on practice.
Feedback
Point out good results and how to improve.

Training methods can be divided into three major approaches: face-to-face, technology-enhanced, and a blended or hybrid approach. A blended approach often is most effective to accommodate people with different learning styles. Most of the training methods described below can be blended to provide an effective, interesting, and enjoyable training program.

- **Lectures**. The most effective use of lectures or instructor-led training is to provide factual content. As you know from your own experience in classes, lectures are more effective when illustrations and real-world examples are used and when the audience is actively engaged in the discussion. Having the trainee read materials about the topic before the training session usually enhances the quality of the discussion. Lectures can be presented in a face-to-face setting, by video, or by webinar.
- **Simulations.** You may have had classes that simulate realistic work experience. A simulation gives the trainee an opportunity to learn the task in a safe environment where mistakes will not affect the trainee or customers and clients. An example used in industry is a simulation set up by a bank to train tellers. The setting looks exactly like a branch office, and the trainers with simulated accounts act as customers. The simulation includes a robbery. This type of training is sometimes called *vestibule training*. This example is a blended approach that combines extensive computer simulations with face-to-face training.
- **Case studies.** You have worked with a brief case study at the end of each chapter. In-depth case studies are used in training to develop critical thinking, analytical, and decision-making skills. Case studies can help trainees put newly acquired factual knowledge to work in realistic work situations. An example of a case study is a scenario in which a large retailer opens a store in a town where a small business has operated successfully for 20 years. You (the administrative manager) are part of a team established to do an in-depth study of the impact of the new competition and to propose ways the small business can deal with it effectively.
- **Decision games.** Decision games combine the features of simulations and case studies and are designed to improve analytical and problem-solving skills. They place several participants in a competitive situation that typically involves time pressure and conflict. Each player must choose among alternative strategies for solving a problem or achieving an objective. The winner is often determined not only by the alternatives he or she chose, but by alternatives competitors did not. A common decision game in finance classes is stock market selection in managing a portfolio.

  Many decision games are computer-based. This approach can appeal to trainees who grew up playing computer and online games.
- **Job rotation.** With job rotation, employees spend a few days or weeks on a job and then move to another job. Job rotation is often used for cross-training and conceptual skills training. You learned in Chapter 1 that conceptual skills are the ability to view the organization as a whole and to understand the relationships among its

various components. Rotating to jobs in different departments or divisions is an effective way to develop an understanding of these relationships as well as to establish contacts across the company.

- **Role-playing/behavior modeling.** In this type of training, trainees act out situations that might occur on the job and how they would handle them. Video is often used. An example is learning to interview job candidates. You might first watch a video that demonstrates a poor interview followed by a second video that uses the same setting but demonstrates an effective interview. Then you would be videotaped conducting an interview with someone playing the role of the candidate. The video would be critiqued with appropriate feedback, and the process would be repeated if necessary.
- **Tutorial training**. Tutorial training is usually conducted online. Illustrated, step-by-step procedures are generally used. You probably have had tutorial training to learn software applications.
- **Coaching.** Perhaps one of the most effective types of training is coaching. Many of you have observed coaching in sports or have been coached yourself in an athletic setting. The job of the coach (supervisor, manager, or team leader) is to work effectively with team members or employees to develop them to be the best they can be. Review the chapter opening interview for a good perspective on coaching. The next section of the chapter discusses this topic.

Use methods that actively engage the learner and that vary depending on the learning objective. Use a variety of techniques that involve visual, auditory, and tactile (hands-on) modes, and repeat the material or process to develop competency.

- **Visual tools help everyone.** Using a visual approach helps many people see the "big picture" and how various concepts are related. Visuals can also help you retain information longer and recall it more easily.
- **Use the best approach for the content.** Matching the teaching style to the concepts being learned can be most effective. For example, actively working through a new software program is more helpful than only reading about it.
- **People learn through repetition.** Encountering new information multiple times helps us make sense of the material.[16]

Select a task you can teach a classmate fairly quickly, such as how to create a playlist on an MP5 player, braid hair, frost a cake, or make a paper airplane.

1. What skill are you teaching?

____

2. List each step you will take in teaching this skill. Provide specific examples.

____

LEVERAGING TECHNOLOGY

TRAINING FOR NEW VERSIONS OF SOFTWARE

Most administrative managers and their employees use *Microsoft Office* applications. New versions are released about every three years, with new features usually focused on enhancing productivity. It is not uncommon for managers to discover that employees are not aware of many of these features. In small businesses without training departments, employees often have to learn new features on their own. The following tips provide insight on helping your employees use the free training options at the *Microsoft Office* website:

1. Familiarize yourself with the available materials. Look for options such as "What's New in Office 2013?" or "Make the Switch to Office 2013." The Support menu provides access to a large collection of tutorials on specific applications and tasks.
2. Employees typically use one or two applications intensively and the others much less frequently. Encourage them to start with the application they know best.
3. Provide adequate time for employees to complete the tutorials. They are well designed with step-by-step training videos, practice sessions to apply the skills learned, and a posttest and reference card.
4. Free *PowerPoint*® versions of the training can be downloaded for group training.
5. A series of free e-books that provides information on how to perform basic tasks in each application can also be downloaded.
6. Encourage employees to work together on some of the applications and to share the new features they learn with their associates.

Coaching

coaching
the process of guiding employees when learning a new task, skill, or information and connecting the *how* with the *why*

Managers who *help* their employees tend to encourage weakness, dependence, and passivity. In contrast, managers who *coach* promote strength, self-confidence, and a proactive outlook.[17] **Coaching** involves guiding employees when learning a new task, skill, or information and connecting the *how* with the *why*. By explaining the facts or why something is important and necessary, coaches provide the employee with relevant information. This higher level of understanding encourages the individual to perform a particular task a certain way or to appreciate the value and relevance of achieving a specific goal.

Cultivating a Productive Coaching Relationship

The key is to be genuine in looking for opportunities to set your employees up for success.

Building a trusting relationship takes time, but it creates the foundation for effective coaching. It is a progressive experience that builds on events, interactions, communication, and decisions. Therefore, it is important for managers always to be truthful and follow through on commitments. The key is to be genuine in looking for opportunities to set your employees up for success. Once employees know you have integrity and can be trusted, they are much more likely to respond in a positive manner to your coaching efforts.

Lou Holtz, the Hall of Fame college football coach, has three components to his proven philosophy for success: (1) a winning attitude, (2) a positive self-image, and (3) set a higher standard.[18] Each is relevant to cultivating a productive coaching relationship with your employees.

A Winning Attitude

Holtz believes all people are in control of their attitude and the choices they make:

> You have the power to think, to love, to create, to imagine, to plan. The greatest power you have is the power to choose. Wherever you are today, you're there because you choose to be there. We also choose the attitudes we have.[19]

When people believe in themselves and their ability to attain a goal, they are far more likely to achieve it.[20] A key task of supervisors when coaching is to help people recognize that they have choices and control over their own attitudes and belief system. Whether employees believe they can learn a new task or take on more responsibility depends on their attitude.

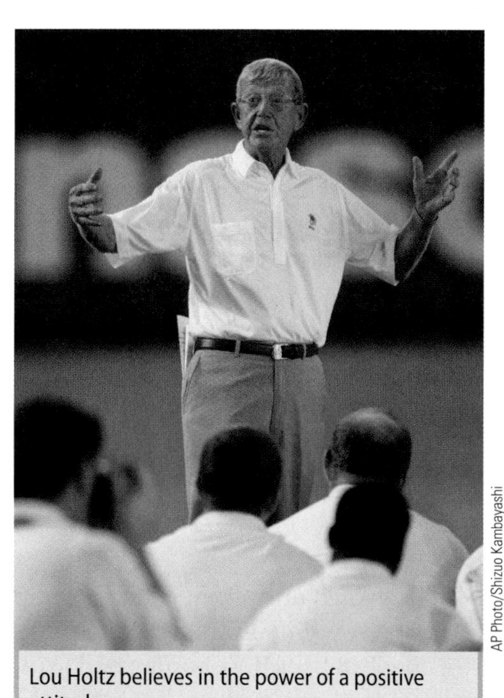

AP Photo/Shizuo Kambayashi

Lou Holtz believes in the power of a positive attitude.

A Positive Self-Image

Another key ingredient for success is a positive self-image. When you feel good about yourself and believe in your abilities, those around you sense this and generally have a positive perception of you. This may lead to more opportunities or, in a coaching situation, greater success as your positive self-image will have a positive impact on your employees.

Clearly, one aspect of developing a positive self-image is to learn from your mistakes and move on. You cannot dwell on the past, nor can you allow your employees to focus on their failures. Instead, celebrate success as often as possible. Rather than dwelling on mistakes, effective coaches refocus people on solving problems, learning from mistakes, and moving ahead. Good coaching helps employees recognize their contributions and how they are vital to organizational success. Encouraging employees to celebrate incremental achievements can contribute to a better self-image. Coaches have to lead by example. If you are sincere in your actions, do the right things for the right reasons, treat people with respect, act with integrity, and work hard, you are likely to get the same in return from your employees.

Set a Higher Standard

Raising the bar brings out the best in people. In fact, research shows people want to use their talents to make a difference and to create new solutions to existing problems.[21] Creating an environment where employees are accountable for their actions, have a sense of autonomy, and feel challenged can lead to excellent results. It is essential that you recognize the achievements of your employees. Give them credit for their contributions. There is nothing worse than having a manager steal your idea or take credit for your work. Give credit where credit is due.

Developing Peak Performers

This section focuses on how to coach your employees effectively in ordinary working conditions (not urgent crisis situations).

Create a Safe Environment

Coaching begins with a conversation. It is essential your employees know you do not expect perfection. You expect their best effort to meet goals, and in return you will give your best. Let them know you realize everyone is human and capable of making mistakes. The key is what happens when a mistake occurs. It is important that employees feel comfortable bringing mistakes to your attention. Dealing constructively with mistakes needs to be focused on the organization's mission and driven into the organization's culture. For instance, this is how Michael Dell, founder of Dell, explains his company's secret to steady growth:

> We all make mistakes. It's not as though at any given time, Dell doesn't have some part of the business that's not working for us as it should. But we have a culture of continuous improvement. We train employees to constantly ask themselves: "How do we grow faster? How do we lower our cost structure? How do we improve service for customers?"[22]

You're going to make mistakes in life. It's what you do afterward that counts.

— Brandi Chastain, World Cup soccer star

Remember, Timing Matters

Supervisors are challenged to balance many roles and manage their time effectively. Some choose to schedule time on their calendars for coaching.

This accomplishes two goals: (1) the coaching session is planned and, typically, objectives and strategies are well thought out, and (2) there is usually less emotion involved, a potential barrier to effective learning.

Another approach to coaching is to take advantage of defining moments, also known as *teachable moments*. These coaching opportunities are spontaneous, unplanned events with one or more of these characteristics:

- **Conflict**. This word often brings to mind a battle or similar uncomfortable situation. However, when handled in a respectful manner, conflict can be a creative and productive experience. The conflict may center on many factors in the workplace. Regardless of its nature, each conflict has at least two sides. This creates an opportunity for supervisors to demonstrate patience, while encouraging exploration of alternative ideas and opinions.
- **Resonance**. **Resonance** is often referred to as the "aha moment" when "the mental lightbulb goes on." These moments are characterized by the employee's learning or realizing something. For example, an office equipment sales supervisor has been emphasizing for months the importance of reading the company's daily email bulletin. One team member does not check the bulletin every day. As a result, she misses an offer to earn a $50 bonus on every order placed that day. After reflecting on her initial anger and disappointment, she remarks to her manager, "Now I know why you kept telling us to check our bulletins every day."
- **Surprise**. Surprises in the workplace are usually not received with joy and enthusiasm. In fact, most people respond to surprises as they do to change. The emotional reaction is often reflected in comments such as "I hate surprises!" or "Why do they always spring things on us at the last minute?"

On the positive side, surprises can turn into wonderful coaching moments. Lexie, a team member, is asked to step in for the team leader and make a presentation to a customer the next day. She knows all about the project, but is not comfortable because she has not made a customer presentation before. As her manager, you could offer to have her practice the presentation with you, which would provide an excellent coaching opportunity.

Communicate Effective Feedback

Providing feedback is a major aspect of coaching. Feedback is typically positive, reinforcing good behavior, or in the form of constructive criticism, redirecting employees to correct their errors. It is important to balance constructive criticism with positive feedback and to focus criticism on the behavior, not the person. A general rule is to praise employees publicly, but never criticize an employee in front of other people.

resonance
the moment when an employee learns or realizes something

1. How important is your manager's feedback to you doing your best on the job?

   ____

2. What experience have you had with positive, inadequate, or inappropriate feedback from your boss (or an instructor, if you are not currently employed)? Explain what happened.

   ____

SUMMARY

1. Planning ahead for a new hire's arrival will help the newcomer feel welcomed and valued, which promotes retention. Three ways to plan ahead are to involve current employees, send forms and information, and make preliminary workplace preparations.
2. Company orientations should include a company background and overview, employee benefits, hours of operation and important dates, inclement weather, emergency preparedness and safety, and legal issues. Job-specific orientations should include a tour and introductions, the department's mission and goals, job functions, policies and procedures, and alternative work schedules.
3. Orientation training is often done by the manager or by using the buddy system. The training plan outlines the specific training, performance expectations, and appraisal criteria. Both formal and informal appraisals may be used.
4. Most companies train for company/product knowledge, performance improvement, cross-training, legal compliance, and safety.
5. A six-step training plan consists of (1) conducting a needs assessment, (2) developing an individual or a group training plan, (3) selecting the methods and trainer, (4) preparing employees to learn, (5) conducting the training, and (6) following up and evaluating effectiveness.
6. A winning attitude, a positive self-image, and setting a higher standard can help in cultivating a productive coaching relationship. Strategies for developing peak performers are creating a safe environment, choosing appropriate times, and communicating effective feedback.

Terms

buddy system, 168
coaching, 178
compressed workweek, 167
corporate culture, 168
cross-training, 173
employee benefits, 164
employee development, 172
flextime, 167
job shadowing, 168
job sharing, 167
learner-centered training, 174
onboarding, 160
orientation, 160
resonance, 181
teleworkers, 167
training, 168

Study Tools

CourseMate
Located at www.cengagebrain.com

- Chapter Outlines
- Flashcards
- Interactive Quizzes
- Tech Tools
- Video Segments

and More!

Questions for Reflection

1. What three steps would you want an employer to take to set you up for success as a new hire?
2. What are three techniques a manager can use to help a new employee feel welcome, valued, and special?
3. Why is employee appraisal important in the orientation period?
4. What are four essential ingredients for skill-based learning?
5. Describe what is involved in developing a productive coaching relationship with your employees.

Hands-On Activities

Employee Development

1. Assume you are a manager in your dream job (or your actual job if you have one). Outline the employee development plan you think would make your employees most successful. Use the Dell model in Figure 8.2 to structure your plan.
2. List the key topics you would like to include for the formal training classes in the program.
3. Select one of the topics and develop the training plan for it.

Employee Orientation

Work in a team of four or five for this activity.

1. Choose a company or nonprofit organization with which your team is familiar.
2. Identify topics that should be included on a recording of the organization's new employee orientation audio file that can be downloaded to an iPod or MP5 player.
3. Plan and outline the information that would be included in the presentation.
4. (Optional) Record the presentation.

Coaching

One way to be successful as a coach is to have a positive relationship with your team members. As you develop your managerial skills, learning how to build long-term relationships of trust with your team is essential.

1. Prepare a document that outlines tips and best practices for building relationships with team members and effective coaching.
2. Identify at least three things you can do to cultivate a positive relationship with your team members.
3. Describe at least three strategies you will use to be an effective coach.

You Decide | Case Study

Orientation Planning

Ken is the supervisor of the Super New Hospital's (SNH) accounting department. He recently hired Maria as a new payroll clerk. She will be starting in two weeks. This is the first time Ken has hired a new employee since joining SNH last year. His previous employer had a very structured employee orientation program, which he relied on to integrate employees into their new positions and acclimate them to the corporate culture. However, SNH does not have any type of orientation plan. Ken would like to create a comprehensive orientation plan for Maria as he believes that investing time and effort in the beginning leads to long-term employee satisfaction and better job performance.

Ken has several dilemmas. He is not sure where to start or what to include. He also does not know how to acquire some of the reference materials and resources he will need. In addition, he is still relatively new in his position, and he does not want to offend anyone or cause any problems.

Questions

1. If you were Ken, what would you do? Would you choose to develop a comprehensive orientation plan? A general company plan? A job-specific plan? Or no orientation plan at all? Explain your rationale.
2. If you chose to develop a plan, who and what would you include?
3. If you chose not to create an orientation plan, how would you set Maria up for success in her new job?

MANAGER'S TOOLKIT

Two strategies for increasing learning are to decrease the stress and anxiety employees have about training and education and to try to make the training interesting and enjoyable. Prepare a document to add to your Manager's Toolkit that outlines methods and best practices for training employees.

1. Using your experiences in classes and what you have learned in this chapter, list steps that could be taken to relieve stress and anxiety before and during training.
2. Using your experiences in classes and what you have learned in this chapter, list tips and methods that could be used to make training sessions more engaging, interactive, and enjoyable.

Soft Skills for Success

Winning Attitude/Positive Self-Image

A winning attitude and a positive self-image are two of the three components Coach Holtz identifies as essential for success. They can also help you cultivate a productive coaching relationship with your employees.

Winning Attitude	Positive Self-Image
• Believe in yourself. • Believe you have the ability to reach your goals. • Have the commitment to reach your goals. • Have the self-discipline to do whatever it takes to reach them.	• Feel good about yourself. • Believe people have a positive perception of you. • Focus on your successes, not your failures. • Accept mistakes and learn from them.

Put It to Work

1. Rate yourself on each attribute of a winning attitude on a scale of 1 to 10 with 10 being *outstanding* and 1 being *poor*.

   ____ Believe in yourself.
   ____ Believe you have the ability to reach your goals.
   ____ Have the commitment to reach your goals.
   ____ Have the self-discipline to do whatever it takes to reach them.

2. Ask a fellow student you trust or a close friend to rate you on each attribute of a winning attitude using the same scale as in #1.

   ____ Believe in yourself.
   ____ Believe you have the ability to reach your goals.
   ____ Have the commitment to reach your goals.
   ____ Have the self-discipline to do whatever it takes to reach them.

3. Coach Holtz believes you have the power to choose your attitude. Prepare a plan listing things you can do to develop a stronger winning attitude.

4. Rate yourself on each attribute of a positive self-image on a scale of 1 to 10 with 10 being *outstanding* and 1 being *poor*.

   ____ Feel good about yourself.
   ____ Believe people have a positive perception of you.
   ____ Focus on your successes, not your failures.
   ____ Accept mistakes and learn from them.

5. Prepare a plan listing things you can do to develop a stronger positive self-image.

CHAPTER
9

Appraising and Rewarding Performance

Learning Outcomes

1. Distinguish formal performance appraisals from employee feedback.
2. Describe at least five appraisal techniques.
3. Explain the criteria that make a performance appraisal legally defensible, and discuss the importance of record keeping and confidentiality.
4. Describe steps that can be taken to make the appraisal system relevant.
5. Explain why performance appraisals should include both quantitative and qualitative measures.
6. Describe factors that influence compensation and the three basic types of decisions for designing a compensation system.
7. Compare individualized and team rewards and provide examples of each.

Photo courtesy of R. VanHuss

Straight Talk From the Field

Rhonda VanHuss is an account management executive for Anthem National Accounts, a WellPoint company in the healthcare products and insurance industry. Over her 25-year career, she has worked in the areas of human resources, provider relations, member services, medical management, account management, project management, communications, training, and strategic and program management.

Printed by permission from Rhonda VanHuss

How have performance appraisals changed?

Performance appraisals in large corporate environments have changed significantly over the last few years, driven in large part by the trimming of management structure and hierarchy. Many supervisory or front-line management positions have been replaced by team leaders who do not have true managerial authority. Therefore, managers and directors currently have many more reports to evaluate. Also, the instrument used for evaluations has been streamlined, aided by technological advances that better support the gathering and reporting of true qualitative metrics to aid in evaluating performance.

Are there other changes to evaluate that go beyond the larger numbers and the sophisticated human resources systems?

Two key changes in the approach to performance appraisals are worthy of mention. The first is the adoption of a common performance appraisal date. Many companies have adjusted the annual evaluation from the specific anniversary date of an employee's employment to a common date for all employees. This practice streamlines everything including the allocation of time by managers and directors for completing evaluations and making payroll adjustments if merit increases are awarded.

While common dates have some advantages, the rush to complete them all at once often negatively affects the thoroughness of the review as it relates to an employee's strengths and weaknesses. The evaluation is often more about meeting or not meeting specific goals and less about employee development. The span of managerial control in large organizations can be daunting, particularly at evaluation time. It is not unusual in a production environment for a manager to have direct span of control for 50 to 100 employees.

The second change is the advent of the self-appraisal. Self-appraisals are helpful to managers in several ways. First, they provide insight into how the employee views him or herself. Second, they highlight common ground upon which the employee and manager agree, which will reduce the amount of time spent preparing the evaluation document. Third, the content of the self-appraisal will help the manager evaluate how well he or she has communicated with the employee throughout the evaluation period about performance. The self-appraisal provides a key building block for the preparation of the evaluation itself, as well as clues to future development of the employee.

Are there things that have remained constant?

One constant in conducting performance appraisals that has not changed, and should not change, is the "no surprises" rule. If employees are being properly managed, performance evaluation is an active, on-going process and not something performed out of necessity quarterly, semi-annually or annually. Performance evaluations should be viewed as the official, documented summary of what the employee already knows about his or her overall performance. This is true for documenting performance over the evaluation period, but is equally as true for future development.

> Performance evaluations should be viewed as the official, documented summary of what the employee already knows about his or her overall performance.

Is the rising cost of benefits of concern to employees and are they discussed in performance appraisals?

The public or government sector has historically done a much better job emphasizing the value of the benefits package. With wages noticeably lower than private sector companies, benefit packages were, and continue to be, a key differentiating factor for attracting and retaining talent in the public sector.

As health care expenses continue to rise at alarming rates, benefits such as retiree medical insurance take on a new significance in the private sector. The value of 401(k) matches, vacation, stock options, and even life insurance and disability benefits are all emphasized far more in the private sector now than in the past. Benefits and their value are still not widely discussed during performance evaluations unless a substitution of stock or another benefit is being provided in place of a merit increase.

On the whole, companies need to do more to educate employees about the value of benefits. Benefits have historically been taken for granted, and not considered part of an overall compensation package. Benefits packages always have been important, but never more so than in our present economic situation.

Visit *www.cengagebrain.com* to read the complete profile.

Chapter Outline

Performance appraisals and rewards are discussed together in this chapter because they are inherently linked. Employees' contributions to the organization are typically measured and rewarded. When performance appraisal systems are administered properly, they can serve as an effective motivational tool and provide measurable indicators for rewards. However, some rewards are not associated with performance appraisals. For instance, rewards can be tied to special projects or incremental goals. Other rewards are public- and team-oriented, as opposed to performance appraisals that are typically confidential and individual in nature.

Performance Appraisal

Without formal measures, assessment criteria, and goals, it is difficult to recognize and reward good performance.

Performance appraisals are such a common part of organizational life that they qualify as a ritual. As with many rituals, the participants repeat the historical pattern without really asking the important questions: "Why?" and "Is there a better way?" Unfortunately, when people hear the term *performance appraisal*, they often experience negative emotions. In many organizations, the consensus is that supervisors do not like giving them, and nobody wants to be on the receiving end. They are too often perceived as a waste of time and often lead to decreased productivity.[1] However, without formal measures, assessment criteria, and goals, it is difficult to recognize and reward good performance. Performance appraisals can be effective and satisfying if systematically developed and implemented.

A **performance appraisal** is the process of evaluating individual job performance as a basis for personnel decisions.[2] It is essentially a communication tool, a formal method for exchanging feedback and instructions between supervisors and their employees.[3] This definition intentionally excludes coaching, a topic discussed in Chapter 8. This chapter focuses on formally documented performance appraisals necessary to ensure opportunities and rewards are equitably distributed.[4] It begins by distinguishing between day-to-day feedback and formal performance appraisals and by examining two important aspects of performance appraisal: (1) commonly used techniques and (2) legal defensibility.

What a performance appraisal requires is for one person to stand in judgment of another. Deep down, it's uncomfortable.

— Dick Grote, author of *How to Be Good at Performance Appraisals*

performance appraisal the process of evaluating individual job performance as a basis for personnel decisions

Feedback Versus Formal Performance Appraisal

It is important to distinguish feedback on day-to-day employee performance from formal performance appraisals. Open communication between a manager or supervisor and employees should occur frequently, and it should include spontaneous feedback on performance. For example, if an employee provides a report on a project, and it shows the project was done well, you should provide positive feedback immediately. If the report raises concerns, you should discuss them immediately and in a constructive manner. Documenting both positive and negative feedback routinely given to employees provides helpful information for formal appraisals.

Communication should include spontaneous feedback on performance.

The *Wall Street Journal* reports that "many younger workers used to instant feedback—from text messages to Facebook and Twitter updates"—want frequent feedback on their work. In response, companies are creating opportunities to deliver feedback more often. At Facebook, for example, "employees are encouraged to solicit and give small nuggets of feedback regularly, after meetings, presentations, and projects."[5]

You don't have to schedule time with someone. It's a 45-second conversation – "How did that go? What could be done better?"

— Lori Goler, vice president of human resources, Facebook

Performance Appraisal Techniques

Just as there are various opinions about the value of performance appraisals, there are also various tools and methods used to evaluate performance. The list of performance appraisal techniques is long and growing. Appraisal software programs are also proliferating. Unfortunately, many appraisal instruments are simplistic, invalid, and unreliable. If an appraisal is overly simplistic, it will not provide managers with a complete assessment of the employee. In general terms, an invalid appraisal instrument does not accurately measure what it is supposed to measure. Unreliable instruments do not measure criteria in a consistent manner. Many other performance appraisal techniques are so complex that they are impractical and burdensome to use.

But armed with a working knowledge of the most popular appraisal techniques, a good manager can distinguish the strong from the weak. The following sections discuss some commonly used techniques. Many companies use a combination of these methods.

Goal Setting (Management by Objectives)

With **management by objectives (MBO)**, performance is typically evaluated in terms of formal goals or objectives set at an earlier date. There is room for assessing accomplishment of individual goals as well as overall department and/or organizational goals. When performance goals are being established, it is helpful to include the employee in the process. In addition, when the individual's goals are linked to the broader mission and goals of the organization, employees tend to develop a higher level of commitment and a greater sense of purpose and value. Typically, achievement of goals is measured in quantifiable terms that relate to performance. However, you

management by objectives (MBO)
an appraisal method in which performance is evaluated in terms of formal goals or objectives

should include a quality component as well. For example, an MBO appraisal at an insurance company might include the following:

> **Objective**: Error-free insurance claim forms processed during prior 3 months = 99%. **Results** = 94%. **Plan for improvement** = ____________________.

The goal-setting technique is a comparatively strong method if desired outcomes are clearly linked to specific behavior. For example, a customer service representative could be measured by the number of customers whose problems were resolved in a timely manner and whose customers rated the interaction as "very satisfactory."

Essays

With the written essay method, supervisors describe the performance of employees in narrative form, sometimes in response to predetermined questions. Evaluators often criticize this technique for consuming too much time. This method is also limited by the fact that some supervisors have difficulty expressing themselves in writing. The essay is not likely to be valid unless it directly relates to specific behaviors describing the employee's performance. Here is a sample item from an essay-based performance appraisal:

> Why (or why not) is this employee a good team player?
>
> ______________________________

Critical Incidents

Critical incidents are specific instances of inferior and superior performance documented by the supervisor when they occur. For instance, using the customer service example described earlier, the supervisor would document incidents in which the employee solved the customer's problem and handled the situation in an exemplary manner and incidents in which the problem was not solved or handled satisfactorily.

An adequate number of critical incidents are needed to evaluate performance objectively. The number varies depending on the severity of the incident—good or bad. A major breach of policy or something like not showing up for an appointment with a customer might require two or three. Something like being late for work may require eight or ten. Somebody that "saved" a major customer from going to a competitor might need just one or two critical incidents to get maximum benefit from it.

The strength of the critical incidents technique is enhanced when evaluators document specific behavior in specific situations and ignore personality traits, as in this sample critical incident for a performance appraisal:[6]

> On 2/5/13, this employee disrupted performance in the office for 20 minutes by starting an argument about who jammed the copier machine.

critical incidents
an appraisal technique in which specific instances of inferior and superior performance are documented when they occur

behaviorally anchored rating scales (BARS)
an appraisal technique that uses performance rating scales divided into increments of observable and measurable job behavior

Behaviorally Anchored Rating Scales (BARS)

Behaviorally anchored rating scales (BARS), performance rating scales divided into increments of observable and measurable job behavior determined through job analysis, are considered one of the strongest performance appraisal techniques. BARS are similar to trait rating scales, which assess personality traits. A trait rating scale might assess an employee on a quality such as initiative, for instance, using a scale from 1 (low) to 5 (high). BARS are more valid than trait rating scales because they rate performance factors rather than personality traits. Figure 9.1 shows a BARS for one dimension of the work performance of a corporate loan assistant: transacting loans.

FIGURE 9.1
BARS for transacting loans (corporate loan assistant)

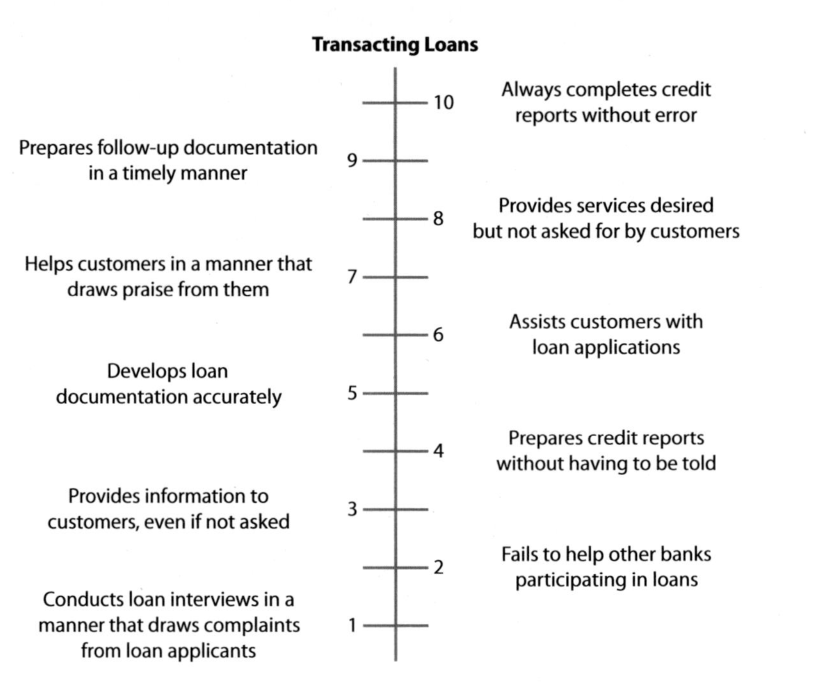
Transacting Loans
10
Always completes credit reports without error
9
Prepares follow-up documentation in a timely manner
8
Provides services desired but not asked for by customers
7
Helps customers in a manner that draws praise from them
6
Assists customers with loan applications
5
Develops loan documentation accurately
4
Prepares credit reports without having to be told
3
Provides information to customers, even if not asked
2
Fails to help other banks participating in loans
1
Conducts loan interviews in a manner that draws complaints from loan applicants

Source: Based on J. P. Campbell et al., "The Development and Evaluation of Behaviorally Based Rating Scales," *Journal of Applied Psychology* 57 (1973): 15–22.

Weighted Checklists

With a **weighted checklist**, evaluators check appropriate adjectives or behavioral descriptions that have predetermined weights. The weights, which gauge the relative importance of the randomly mixed items on the checklist, are usually unknown to the evaluator. Following the evaluation, the weights of the checked items are added or averaged to permit interpersonal comparisons. As with other techniques, the degree of behavioral specificity largely determines the strength of weighted checklists. For example, one item on the checklist may have five specific behavioral requirements described:

weighted checklist
an appraisal method in which evaluators check appropriate adjectives or behavioral descriptions with predetermined weights

1. Treats each customer in a friendly, engaging manner.
   a. Greets with a smile.
   b. Calls the customer by name.
   c. Listens actively to the customer.

d. Confirms that he or she understands exactly what the customer is asking.
e. Offers a solution that meets the customer's needs.

Effective checklists are expensive and time-consuming to develop.

Forced Ranking System

A **forced ranking system** compares or ranks coworkers in a work group in head-to-head fashion according to specified accomplishments or job behavior. This technique points out the best performers in the group; however, it has a major shortcoming, which is that the absolute distance between evaluated employees is unknown. For example, the employee ranked No. 1 may be five times as effective as No. 2, who in turn is only slightly more effective than No. 3. Rankings/comparisons are also criticized for causing resentment among lower-ranked, but adequately performing, coworkers. Figure 9.2 is a sample forced ranking item.

FIGURE 9.2
A forced ranking item

Lowest Performers	Next Lowest	Middle	Next Highest	Highest Performers
10%	20%	40%	20%	10%
(5 employees)	(10 employees)	(20 employees)	(10 employees)	(5 employees)

Multirater Appraisal

This is a general label for a diverse array of appraisal techniques involving more than one rater of the evaluated person's performance. The rationale for multirater appraisals is that two or more heads are less biased than one. One popular approach is the **360-degree review**, in which a supervisor is evaluated by his or her boss, peers, and subordinates. The results are typically pooled and are generally presented anonymously.[7]

Although 360-degree feedback is best suited for use in management development programs, some companies have turned it into a performance appraisal tool for all employees, with mixed results. Some organizations like it; some do not. Many believe that it is not helpful for evaluation purposes, but it is helpful for developmental purposes. The review may include a self-evaluation and assessments from external customers.

forced ranking system
an appraisal method that compares or ranks coworkers in a work group in head-to-head fashion according to specified accomplishments or job behavior

360-degree review
an appraisal technique in which a supervisor is evaluated by his or her boss, peers, and subordinates

continuous improvement review (CIR)
a review process that focuses on customers, the team, and the employee's contribution to system improvements

Continuous Improvement Review (CIR)

A unique approach to performance appraisals is the **continuous improvement review (CIR)**, which "focuses the review process on customers, the team and the employee's contribution to system improvements."[8] CIR identifies employees who have helped improve the organization as a whole. Assessment focuses on productivity, quality measures (quality of product, service, etc.), and customer satisfaction.[9]

LEVERAGING TECHNOLOGY

AUTOMATING PERFORMANCE APPRAISAL RECORDS

Managers often complain about the extensive paperwork required for effective documentation in performance appraisals. Large companies with human resources departments typically have human resources management systems that include customized forms. As Rhonda VanHuss pointed out in the Straight Talk from the Field interview in this chapter, the instrument used for evaluations has been streamlined, aided by technological advances that better support the gathering and reporting of true qualitative metrics. The following tips may be helpful for small organizations:

- Create forms for self-appraisal and for managers or supervisors that can be completed in *Word*. To create forms, add the Developer tab to the Ribbon and then select the forms features.
- Develop BARS by copying the specific requirements from the job analysis or job description so they can be rated.
- Automate the collection of critical incidents feedback from employee interactions with customers.
- Develop a short, easy-to-complete form (survey) to check the quality of the interaction and level of customer satisfaction. Email it to customers immediately after interactions with employees. Ask them to complete it and return it to you.
- Use the Task feature of *Outlook* or other PIM systems to remind you to make performance notes at least once or twice a month for each employee supervised.
- Keep a performance appraisal folder for each employee for the evaluation period.

Making Performance Appraisals Legally Defensible

Lawsuits that challenge the legality of specific performance appraisal systems and the personnel actions that result from them have left scores of human resource managers asking if the organization's performance appraisal system will stand up in court. From the standpoint of limiting legal exposure, it is better to ask this question while you are developing a formal appraisal system rather than after it has been implemented. Supervisors need specific criteria to develop legally defensible performance appraisal systems.

Supervisors need specific criteria to develop legally defensible performance appraisal systems.

Fortunately, researchers have discerned some instructive patterns in court decisions. After studying the verdicts in 66 employment discrimination cases in the United States, one pair of researchers found employers could successfully defend their appraisal systems if they satisfied four criteria:

1. A job analysis was used to develop the performance appraisal system.
2. The appraisal system was behavior-oriented, not trait-oriented.
3. Performance evaluators followed specific written instructions when conducting appraisals.
4. Evaluators reviewed the results of the appraisals with the employees being evaluated.[10]

Each of these conditions has a clear legal rationale. Job analysis, which was discussed in Chapter 7 relative to employee selection, links the appraisal process to specific job duties, not personalities. Behavior-oriented appraisals properly focus the supervisor's attention on how the individual actually performed his or her job.[11] Performance appraisers who follow specific written instructions are less likely to be plagued by vague performance standards and/or personal bias. Finally, by reviewing performance appraisal results with employees personally, supervisors provide feedback to help them learn and improve. Making sure managers and supervisors understand the performance appraisal system and are trained to use it effectively is extremely helpful in establishing credibility with employees. Many organizations provide definitions for the terminology used in appraisals to ensure all managers use the terms the same way.

Record Keeping and Confidentiality

According to the criteria for legally defensible performance appraisals, the evaluator should follow specific written instructions. This means documenting the performance appraisal and any related data such as attendance, productivity, and evidence of superior or inferior work. In large companies, the forms used for performance reviews are generally designed or reviewed by the human resources department. In small organizations, outside consultants or lawyers can review the forms to ensure they are legally defensible.

To prevent errors in evaluation, evaluators should observe performance frequently and regularly throughout the time period covered by the evaluation. Too often, evaluators remember and focus on the most recent items rather than performance during the entire evaluation period.

Individual performance appraisals are a private matter between a supervisor and an employee. **Confidentiality** is essential to maintaining trust. It is important that the performance appraisal, related documents, and subsequent conversations remain confidential. Beyond the supervisor and employee, this information should be shared only with a limited number of individuals in the organization on a need-to-know basis.

confidentiality
the practice of keeping private documents and conversations secret

Mary recently met with her manager, Nancy, for her annual performance appraisal. During the meeting, Mary admitted she had made a few mistakes because she was working too fast. She agreed to slow down and check her work more thoroughly. The following week, one of Mary's coworkers said to her, "I hear you agreed to slow down a little so you'll make fewer mistakes!" Mary is left to assume that Nancy must have discussed their conversation with others.

1. How do you think Mary feels?

   ____

2. What impact do you think this will have on the relationship between Mary and Nancy?

   ____

3. What should Nancy do to resolve the situation?

   ____

Making the Appraisal System Relevant

The best way to make the appraisal system relevant and employees comfortable with it is to do an effective coaching job all year. A manager who gives employees feedback on their job performance throughout the year prepares them for more formalized discussions. Effective coaching helps to identify training needs. The manager can provide on-the-job training or arrange for other formal training to help employees improve their performance. Taking these steps allows the manager to document improvement over the year rather than focusing on deficiencies.

The best way to make the appraisal system relevant is to do an effective coaching job all year.

Tell Employees What to Expect

Planning for a performance appraisal should begin at the time of the last performance appraisal or shortly thereafter. If employees know exactly what factors will be considered in the review and know the performance expectations, they will be better prepared to discuss these issues. Open discussions of the factors used in ratings help prepare employees for discussing job performance. Many managers find it helpful to ask employees several weeks before the scheduled review to provide a written summary of what they thought were their best accomplishments of the year as well as areas in which they were not satisfied, both with specific examples. For areas that were not satisfactory, ask what could be done to improve them and what additional support or training is needed. Also, ask employees to think about their goals for the next year. Some managers provide a self-evaluation form, sometimes the same form the manager will use.

Emphasize Performance Goals

At the beginning of a performance review, it is good to discuss the goals set at the last review or at the beginning of the evaluation period to set the tone for a performance-based discussion. Goals for the next evaluation should be discussed in the performance review or shortly thereafter. Remember that good goals are SMART (specific, measurable, attainable, relevant, and time-bound). Both the manager and the employee should have input on the goals and agree on them. It is also important that the manager and employee discuss the factors that will be used to measure progress and attainment.

Encourage a Productive Discussion

Managers should encourage employees to talk freely during the formal appraisal and should foster a candid discussion of performance. This approach increases the likelihood that employees will be satisfied with the appraisal, will consider it fair, and will improve in meeting future performance goals.[12]

Often managers must discuss deficiencies in employees' work. Remember that criticism should be constructive: it should be specific and focused on the desired behavior and identified performance problems, not personalities. Plan beforehand not only what you are going to say but how you will say it. Be receptive to what the employee has to say. Figure 9.3 on page 198 presents practical tips for effective performance appraisals.

Employees expect to be rewarded for their performance and contributions to the organization. Most companies focus on aligning rewards with performance. However, when compensation is discussed during a performance appraisal, the compensation topic tends to dominate. Most experts recommend that the topics of performance and rewards be discussed in separate meetings.

Performance Measures

performance measures
measures that determine how an employee's performance will be evaluated

quantitative measures
measures focusing on productivity or results that can be counted or measured

qualitative measures
measures focusing on the level of excellence of a product or service

The development of **performance measures** involves defining exactly how employees' performance will be evaluated, including progress toward achieving their goals. Regardless of the techniques or methods you choose for performance appraisals, you still need to define how you will measure progress, when it will be done, and who will be involved in the process.

Quantitative and Qualitative Measures

An effective performance appraisal system includes both quantitative and qualitative measures. **Quantitative measures** focus on productivity or results that can be counted or measured. **Qualitative measures** focus on

FIGURE 9.3
Steps for conducting performance appraisals

Ten Tips for Effective Performance Appraisals

1. Prepare employees for today's appraisal by agreeing on written performance goals at the beginning of the evaluation period.
2. Continue the preparation by discussing progress toward goals in a comfortable coaching setting throughout the evaluation period.
3. Begin today's discussion by indicating you would like it to be similar to the discussions the two of you have had over the past year. This step is designed to make the employee more comfortable and prevent or reduce stress.
4. Briefly talk about the agreed-on goals and earlier discussions of progress toward those goals.
5. Encourage the employee to describe what he or she thinks were his or her most significant accomplishments over the entire evaluation period. Make it obvious you are listening carefully. State your agreement (if you agree), and indicate the employee should take pride in the accomplishments.
6. Discuss the most positive aspects first. Compliment the employee on those items that represent growth and progress.
7. Follow up by discussing items in which some progress was noted, but perhaps not as much as desired.
8. Ask the employee what support, training, or resources are needed, if any, to help achieve these goals at a higher level.
9. Use a problem-solving approach to move toward discussing areas of needed improvement, and ask the employee for suggestions on ways to improve.
10. Summarize key points, again recognizing positive contributions and thanking the employee for them. Express optimism and confidence about the future. Encourage the employee to begin thinking about goals for the next evaluation period.

the level of excellence of a product or service. For example, in an insurance office, an employee might process six claims in an hour, but four of them have inaccurate information. The productivity would be negatively impacted by the poor quality of work, which would likely have to be redone. To assess performance fully and accurately, managers must include both types of measures.

1. Do you agree or disagree with the suggestion that supervisors include a quality component in the performance evaluation to measure quality as well as productivity (quantity)? Explain.

2. What are possible unintended consequences if a supervisor measures only productivity without assessing quality?

3. What would happen if the supervisor evaluated only quality without regard for productivity?

Frequency of Appraisals and Who Conducts Them

Most companies conduct performance reviews semiannually or annually. Annual reviews occur either on the anniversary date of the employee's hiring or at the end of the fiscal year. Semiannual reviews take place either at the midpoint and end of the fiscal year or at the six-month and annual anniversaries. Using anniversary dates enables the manager to spread the appraisals over time rather than having to do them all at once. However, this system makes it more difficult to tie performance to department or company goals set at the beginning of the year.

Generally, the employee's supervisor or manager conducts the appraisal unless a multirater system is used. Usually the supervisor or manager is most familiar with the employee's work and quality of performance.

Compensation

compensation
the financial and nonfinancial awards an employee receives for performing a job

Compensation refers to the financial and nonfinancial awards an employee receives for performing a job. Compensation includes monetary rewards such as wages, salaries, commissions, and bonuses, which are referred to as *direct compensation*. Compensation also includes other types of rewards such as benefits, promotions, and recognition, which are referred to as *indirect compensation*. Many different types of compensation systems exist. Compensation varies widely depending on the industry, level of the employee, and type of position. For example, compensation for factory and sales positions differs substantially from compensation for administrative positions. Compensation for executives usually differs from that of other employees. This discussion will focus on nonexecutive, administrative positions.

Costs

The costs of compensation vary widely. Because of this, national averages are not very helpful in making compensation decisions for specific companies or individuals. The U.S. Bureau of Labor Statistics tracks employer costs for employee compensation monthly. As an example, in a recent month, these costs averaged $28.57 per hour worked. Wages and salaries averaged $20.14 per hour worked and accounted for 70.5 percent of costs, while benefits averaged $8.43 and accounted for the remaining 29.5 percent. For the management, professional, and related group, total compensation averaged $50.23, with salaries and wages averaging $35.05 and benefits $15.18 per hour.[13] Note that benefits were consistent at 30 percent of wages. What is helpful about these statistics is that many employees do not think of the benefits they receive as compensation even though benefits represent almost one-third of their total compensation. Managers should discuss with employees the real value of the benefits they receive.

Factors Influencing Compensation

Compensation is influenced by both external and internal factors.

External Factors

The first thing you will note from the following list is that management cannot control most external factors.

- **Employment laws**—A number of laws have a significant influence on direct compensation, such as minimum wage and equal pay for comparable work. Other laws affect indirect compensation, such as medical leave and accommodations for disabilities.
- **Labor market**—The supply and demand of workers with the required skills for the job influences the level of pay. For example, nurses' salaries have risen significantly over the past few years because, nationally, the demand for nurses far exceeds the number available.
- **Geographic area**—Employees in some geographic areas tend to receive higher pay than in other areas. Also, the pay in large metropolitan cities tends to be higher than in small, rural areas. It should be noted,

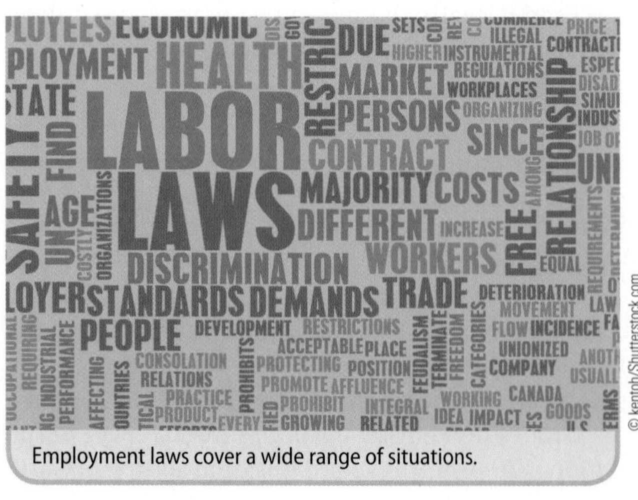

Employment laws cover a wide range of situations.

however, that areas with higher pay levels often have a higher cost of living.

- **Economy**—The health of the economy has a major impact on compensation. When the economy is strong, more money is usually available to reward employees for effective performance. When the economy is weak, less or no money may be available.

Internal Factors

In contrast to external factors, most of the internal factors that influence compensation are under the control of management.

- **Corporate culture and philosophy**—Companies can determine whether they will match the local market rate, pay more, or pay less. Companies that pay less often try to offset the lower rate with other incentives to attract and retain employees, such as making the company a pleasant place to work. Companies not as profitable as their competitors may not be able to afford competitive rates. Often small businesses or startup ventures fit into that category in the early stages of the business. Some companies simply try to minimize costs.

  In the Chapter 2 opening interview (pages 24–25), president and CEO Thomas Suggs describes the compensation philosophy of his insurance company. Read the interview again carefully. Note these points:

  - Employees impact revenue growth by providing quality service, which helps the company attract and retain customers.
  - Revenue growth enables the company to offer higher-than-market pay, an attractive work environment, and other perks.
  - The company culture calls for paying more, but also for expecting more: "We treat them fairly and hold them accountable for reaching goals."

The company culture at Keenan Suggs Insurance Company calls for paying more, but also expecting more: "We treat them fairly and hold them accountable for reaching goals."

- **Performance**—Linking performance to pay is easier in some jobs than others. For example, earning a commission at a specified rate in a sales position is directly linked to compensation. However, you can link compensation to performance of all employees in many jobs.
- **Experience and/or education**—Many organizations believe experience and/or education are important factors in job performance. These organizations often require a specific level of experience or education for certain positions or for promotion to certain positions. Many offer tuition reimbursement for employees who want to advance. A person with an associate's degree may be hired as a manager or supervisor, but he or she would be encouraged to complete a bachelor's degree for promotion. Experience and education often influence pay level as well.
- **Potential**—At the management level, some employees are evaluated based on their potential to move up in the organization. Because of how they handle their jobs and manage employees, some managers

are identified as having the potential to be leaders in certain areas and are compensated accordingly in order to retain them.

In an interview, Anne Mulcahy, former CEO and chairwoman of Xerox Corporation, emphasized two important lessons she had learned relating to compensation. The first was to assess employees accurately and deal with them fairly. Mulcahy prided herself on helping make this approach part of Xerox's company culture. The second was talent development: identifying "high-potential" employees, treating them differently, accelerating their development, and paying them more.[14]

Designing Compensation Systems

Job evaluation is the process used to determine the worth of a job. It focuses strictly on the job and not on the value of the employee performing that job. You are already familiar with the basic process because it begins with a job analysis used to write a job description. Human resources departments or compensation consultants typically perform job evaluations for organizations. Many different methods of job evaluation can be used. Most involve determining compensable factors from the job analysis and then ranking or benchmarking them against other jobs in the organization or against a peer group. **Compensable factors** are common elements of many different jobs that merit compensation.

Three basic types of decisions are involved in designing a compensation system: the salary structure, variability of pay, and level of pay.

job evaluation
the process used to determine the worth of a job

compensable factors
common elements of many different jobs that merit compensation

pay structure
all jobs at the various levels within an organization and total pay, including salaries, bonuses, equity, and benefits

pay variability
types of compensation and the amount of fixed versus variable compensation

level of pay
salary at market, higher than market, or lower than market rate

benchmarking peers
comparing salary structure to that of similar companies

Salary Structure

The salary or **pay structure** consists of all jobs at the various levels within an organization and the total pay, including salaries, bonuses, equity, and all benefits provided. Hourly wages are often considered as a separate pay structure. The structure may be set up in many different ways. It typically includes grades or levels that contain ranges of pay. A qualified applicant would normally be placed at the midpoint of the range and could progress over the years to the top of the range by earning merit raises. Merit raises are generally based on job performance. Many companies no longer give cost-of-living raises.

Pay Variability or Flexibility

Pay variability typically refers to types of compensation and the amount of fixed versus variable compensation. For example, a job may have 90 percent of the total compensation as a fixed salary and up to 10 percent as a bonus for achieving specific goals. Another form of variable compensation is *equity*: a bonus paid in company stock, restricted stock, or options, for example.

Level of Pay

Level of pay relates to paying a salary at market rate, higher than market rate, or lower than market rate. Level of pay is determined by **benchmarking peers**: comparing salary structure to that of similar companies, often competitors or companies with a similar business model.

Benefits

Employee benefits include insurance programs, fully compensated absences (vacations, holidays, sick leave), retirement and stock ownership plans, and employer-provided services such as child care. Some benefits are mandated by law, such as Social Security (retirement benefits), unemployment compensation (payments workers may receive if laid off from their jobs), and workers' compensation (medical and disability benefits to employees who are injured or contract diseases on the job). Others, such as 401(k) retirement accounts and education benefits, are at the option of the employer. Employers choose to pay benefits because they are a major factor in attracting and retaining highly qualified employees. Often employers pay a portion of the cost of optional benefits, and employees contribute a portion.

Not all employees want or need the same benefits. For example, for working parents, child-care support is a significant retention factor, but employees who do not have preschool children do not need that benefit. Therefore, many companies offer flexible or **cafeteria-style benefits**. Employees can select benefits (up to a specific amount) from a range that are available.

cafeteria-style benefits
a range of benefits from which employees can select

extrinsic rewards
payoffs granted to an employee by other people

intrinsic rewards
self-granted and internally experienced payoffs

Extrinsic Rewards

Direct compensation and most of the benefits previously discussed are considered **extrinsic rewards**, or payoffs granted to an employee by other people. Other examples are promotions, company recognition, public praise, and perks such as an expense account or an office with a view.

Intrinsic Rewards

Intrinsic rewards are self-granted and internally experienced payoffs. Examples are pleasure in being recognized for one's work and the feeling of satisfaction gained from a job well done. Usually, on-the-job extrinsic and intrinsic rewards are intermingled. For instance, employees often experience a psychological boost when they complete a big project in addition to reaping material benefits.

1. What extrinsic rewards motivate you to do a better job? Name at least two.

   ____

2. What intrinsic rewards motivate you to do a better job? Name at least two.

   ____

3. Are extrinsic or intrinsic rewards stronger motivators for you? Why do you think this is?

   ____

4. Do you think your peers will respond the same way you did? Why or why not?

   ____

I think a paycheck buys you a baseline level of performance. But one thing that makes a good leader is the ability to offer people intrinsic rewards, the tremendous lift that comes from being aware of one's own talents and wanting to maximize them.

— Abraham Zaleznik, professor emeritus, Harvard Business School

Team Rewards

Team rewards are identical rewards given to team members to recognize team-based goal achievement. The idea of rewarding group performance rather individual performance is sometimes difficult to accept. Perhaps you have worked on team projects in which some people did more or better work, and others did very little. As a manager, you should consider team rewards for high-performance teams. Remember that a common characteristic of these teams is that evaluation and rewards are based on team performance and not on individual performance. Your goal should be to develop mature teams that can be rewarded on a team basis. Many work groups do not meet this goal.

Managers can work with their teams to define measurable goals and objectives. These ultimately become the basis for the team's performance measures. Ideally, a team can agree on rewards that are both appropriate and meaningful. This is not always easy because individuals are motivated by different things, which makes agreement about team rewards difficult. This process may require supervisory guidance. In fact, you may choose to prepare a list ahead of time and let each employee vote on his or her top three.

The reward should be in line with the importance and complexity of the objective or project. For example, an accounting firm set a team goal to reduce the number of extensions it had to file on behalf of its income tax clients by 10 percent. To achieve this goal, employees were required to place additional follow-up phone calls, take messages, research client information for one another, and work extra hours before the tax-filing deadline of April 15. Employees who worked overtime until at least 8 p.m. were provided a dinner brought in from a local restaurant that evening. If they met the team goal, all members were allowed to choose from several rewards:

- An extra paid day off
- A trip to the local amusement park for everyone and their families
- An afternoon off to go to a day spa for massages
- A catered luncheon

team rewards
identical rewards given to team members to recognize team-based goal achievement

individualized rewards
rewards given to individuals to recognize goal attainment unique to the employee

Individualized Rewards: Beyond the Annual Pay Raise

Unlike team rewards, **individualized rewards** are typically unique and of significant value to the employee. However, as is the case with other reward systems, the payoff should be in line with the achievement. You would not want to send an employee on an all-expense-paid vacation for achieving his or her first month's sales goal. If he or she exceeds the sales goal by 20 percent for the entire year, then you may choose a reward of that magnitude. On the other hand, giving that high achiever a company coffee mug could be a real letdown and motivation killer.

The best approach is to ask employees what they value the most. Find out what is meaningful to each individual. The reward will vary depending upon the person and project. Figure 9.4 provides examples of individual rewards supervisors have used in the workplace.

FIGURE 9.4
Individual rewards

Rewarding Your Employees

- **Recognition**—This is one of the most powerful rewards readily available to supervisors, and it doesn't cost a penny. Give credit and recognition often and publicly. Ask your boss to send a personal note specifically recognizing an achievement.
- **Responsibility**—Many employees want to advance. An excellent reward is trusting them to take on more visible assignments and greater responsibility. Most employees want challenging and rewarding work.
- **Flexibility**—Allow employees an alternative work schedule, taking advantage of flextime options or letting them telecommute, perhaps working from home one day a week.
- **Training**—Offer to pay for a class at a local college. Let employees attend a seminar or conference or cross-train with other employees.

  Here are a few other examples of tangible rewards:
  - A gift card to a favorite restaurant or store
  - A gym membership for a year
  - A technology tool that will improve work efficiency, such as a smartphone
  - An afternoon off to go shopping around the holidays

As you can see, the possibilities are limited only by management's imagination. Some rewards are free, while others can be costly. The key is to discover what each employee values. Do not assume that what excites one employee is necessarily going to be a great reward for others.

How supervisors use rewards also makes a difference. Supervisors want employees to know their exceptional efforts and achievements are being recognized. If supervisors give out too many rewards for minimal effort, they could create an environment in which employees always expect something extra. Be thoughtful and strategic in distributing rewards. Sometimes you may choose to identify the "if-then" relationship ahead of time. For example, *if* the employee is successful in achieving a major training milestone, *then* there is a specific reward. However, it is also effective to surprise an employee with an unexpected reward if he or she goes above and beyond. Spontaneous rewards, if made publicly, can have the added benefit of inspiring other employees.

Whatever you choose to do to recognize and reward your employees, make it meaningful to the individual and appropriate for the achievement. Also, ensure rewards are equitable.

What are employees looking for in their careers? Two common answers are to be rewarded financially for good performance and, more and more frequently, to have a balance of work and life. Beyond the traditional category of working parents, Generation X and Y workers are pressing for flexible working hours, and researchers predict baby boomers will soon be demanding them as well.

1. How do you plan to achieve work/life balance in your career?

   ___

2. Which is more important to you, more pay or more leisure time? Explain.

   ___

3. From a manager's perspective, what are the pros and cons of flextime and teleworking?

   ___

Source: Jennifer Ludden, "When Employers Make Room for Work-Life Balance," National Public Radio, March 15, 2010, http://www.npr.org/templates/story/story.php?storyId=124611210.

SUMMARY

1. Employee feedback on performance differs from formal performance appraisals. Open communication and spontaneous feedback should occur frequently.
2. Formal performance appraisal techniques include goal setting, essays, critical incidents, behaviorally anchored rating scales, weighted checklists, forced ranking systems, multirater appraisal, and continuous improvement review. Many companies use a combination of these methods.
3. To be legally defensible, a performance appraisal system should satisfy these criteria: (1) a job analysis was used to develop the system, (2) it is behavior-oriented, (3) evaluators follow specific written instructions during appraisals, and (4) evaluators review the results with the employees being evaluated.
4. The best way to make the appraisal system relevant is to coach effectively all year. Other ways are to tell employees what to expect, emphasize performance goals, and encourage productive discussion during the appraisal.
5. Performance appraisals should include both quantitative (productivity) and qualitative (level of excellence) measures for a full, accurate assessment.
6. Both external and internal factors influence compensation. The three basic types of decisions in designing a compensation system are salary structure, pay variability, and pay level.
7. Team rewards are identical rewards given to team members that recognize team-based goal achievement. Individualized rewards are typically unique and of significant value to the employee.

Study Tools

CourseMate

Located at www.cengagebrain.com

- Chapter Outlines
- Flashcards
- Interactive Quizzes
- Tech Tools
- Video Segments

and More!

Terms

Questions for Reflection

1. Why is assessing job performance necessary?
2. Why is it important to document routine performance feedback provided to employees?
3. Describe a formal method for assessing job performance.
4. In this chapter, you learned about several performance appraisal techniques. Which do you think is best? Explain your answer.
5. List four criteria that should be satisfied for a performance appraisal system to be legally defensible.
6. Many employees and managers have a negative perception of performance appraisals. What suggestions do you have for making this important process a positive, motivational experience?
7. Explain the difference between quantitative and qualitative measures. Provide an example of each.
8. Should performance appraisals be linked to compensation? Explain why or why not.

Hands-On Activities

Performance Appraisal Examples

Work in a team of four or five for this activity.

1. Work with your team to locate a variety of performance appraisal forms, articles about different appraisal techniques, and software applications if available. Each member of the team should locate two of each item. You may bring in your employer's or a local employer's appraisal form.
2. Share your items with the other members.
3. As a team, review all the items, and decide on one the team thinks is most effective.
4. Work collaboratively to prepare a brief explanation of why the team thinks it is effective.

Rewards That Work!

Brainstorm with your classmates to develop a list of additional rewards that have not been mentioned already in the chapter.

1. Identify three rewards that are relatively easy for supervisors to distribute and that have little or no financial cost for the organization.
2. Identify three major rewards that supervisors would distribute on a limited basis because they are likely to cost the company in terms of time and money.

You Decide | Case Study

Evaluating and Rewarding Performance

Margaret is a shift supervisor for Clear Lake Boats, Inc. She has been with the company since it started manufacturing boats more than ten years ago. Margaret worked on the production line until last year, when she was promoted to supervisor. The company started out small, with only 12 employees and one shift working Monday to Friday from 8:30 a.m. to 5:00 p.m. Clear Lake Boats now has more than three hundred employees and runs three shifts a day. Every employee on each shift gets paid the same except for the supervisors, who are paid two dollars more per hour. The night shift employees get paid a dollar more per hour. There is no performance appraisal system or reward structure.

After Margaret was promoted, she asked to take a "Principles of Supervision" class at a local community college to learn proper supervisory skills and coaching techniques. One of the topics discussed in her class was performance appraisals and reward systems. Although the company has grown quickly and has been very successful, she has noticed a decline in employee morale. Production numbers are also down. Margaret thinks the lack of a formal performance appraisal system and the standardized pay structure may be part of the problem.

Margaret is fond of the owners and does not want to offend them. However, she does want to make a difference and contribute to the company's long-term success.

Questions

1. If you were Margaret, what recommendations would you make to the owners regarding performance appraisals?
2. What recommendations would you make regarding employee compensation?
3. What specific recommendations would you make regarding recognition and reward systems?
4. What approach would you suggest for implementing your recommendations so that both the employees and the owners support the new performance appraisal system, compensation plan, and reward program?

MANAGER'S TOOLKIT

Select a job/position of your choice to create a performance appraisal system. The system should include the following:

1. A document that outlines the performance appraisal technique(s) you will use
2. An appraisal form
3. A list of steps you will take to make the appraisal system relevant

Soft Skills for Success

Adaptability and Flexibility

Adaptability and flexibility are high on the list of soft skills desired by most companies when hiring new employees. When she was CEO and chairperson of Xerox, Anne Mulcahy was asked whether she looked for certain qualities in a job candidate more than she had several years before. Her response was as follows:

> Adaptability and flexibility. One of the things that is mind-boggling right now is how much we have to change all the time. For anybody who's into comfort and structure, it gets harder and harder to feel satisfied in the company. It's almost like you have to embrace a lot of ambiguity and be adaptable and not get into the rigidness or expectation-setting that I think there used to be ten years ago, when you could kind of plot it out and define where you were going to go.
>
> I think it's a lot more fluid right now. It has to be. The people who really do the best are those who actually sense it, enjoy it almost, that lack of definition around their roles and what they can contribute.[15]

Adaptability and flexibility are often thought of as being the same, but actually they are different. Adaptability is the ability to adjust to a changed situation or environment. Flexibility is the ability to make changes quickly to meet a special individual or business need, such as changing your schedule to handle an important company issue that arises unexpectedly. From a managerial perspective, two things are clear: (1) If you wish to move up the career ladder, adaptability and flexibility are essential and (2) if you wish to be successful as a manager, you need to be able to coach employees to help them develop these abilities.

Put It to Work

1. Honestly evaluate yourself on how adaptable and flexible you are. Do you resist change, grudgingly accept it, or embrace it? Do you view changed situations as problems or as different situations that may present opportunities?
2. Ask peers and your managers how they rate you on adaptability and flexibility.
3. List five tasks you do routinely. For each task, make notes on how you could improve the way you do it or be more productive in completing it.
4. Make a commitment to do something new every week, such as spend time or work with a person from a different culture or with someone who has very different views than you do.
5. Volunteer to take on a new responsibility.

What should first-line managers know about employment law?

Knowing current employment law is important, but managers do not need to be legal experts. About 95 percent of complying with employment law is exercising good common sense and knowing your company's policies. For example, treating employees the same way, without favoritism, just makes good sense. But when it does not appear this is occurring, many employees begin to believe they are being treated differently based on their race, gender, or other protected classification. If that perception exists, productivity declines and the risk of employment litigation increases.

> About 95 percent of complying with employment law is exercising good common sense and knowing your company's policies.

Managers must be careful not to react in the heat of the moment. When upset or angry, managers often forget to use good common sense and do or say things that are difficult to reverse.

All managers should have a basic understanding of discrimination, harassment, leave laws, etc. They don't need to be experts, but they need to be able to spot the issues. Lawsuits can often be traced to a poor choice not to seek help before the problem spiraled out of control. Unfortunately, we live in a society where the laws change daily. This means it is incumbent on a manager to be self-disciplined enough to stay educated on the laws, so he or she knows when to refer an issue to human resources. If you don't have a human resources department, then get legal advice.

Managers also need to know what their company policies say. Employees expect managers to be able to answer questions about policies, and they expect managers to follow them. When the policies are not followed, mistakes are made that have legal and employee relations implications. Part of good common sense is not guessing. Managers should never guess and need to know when to ask for help. These are the types of mistakes that can reduce a manager's effectiveness and affect a manager's future.

The current trend toward monitoring employee performance electronically and in other ways needs special attention because of the potential legal and employee relations ramifications. If your company has corporate monitoring policies, managers must follow the protocols exactly. Do not initiate a monitoring plan without careful legal review.

Visit *www.cengagebrain.com* to read the complete profile.

Chapter Outline

Highly effective and admired businesses are built with employees—from senior executives to frontline workers—who abide by the law and have high ethical standards. The first-line manager is often responsible for creating a culture where people treat one another with respect. In addition to making sure employment and labor laws are followed, the manager must encourage positive behavior and ethical actions. This chapter provides an overview of legal and ethical topics you will likely encounter at some point during your career. Use this as an opportunity to imagine how you would react if you observed or experienced harassment, discrimination, or unethical conduct. Moreover, think of strategies you can use now and in the future to foster a positive and supportive work environment where people are treated fairly.

Employment and Labor Laws

Managers need to be familiar with many employment-related laws. This is not intended as a comprehensive discussion of these laws, but rather an introduction to key employment and labor laws that are relevant for today's managers. This section provides a brief overview of employment and labor laws related to workplace safety, fair wages, young workers, new employees, and intellectual property. The following section discusses antidiscrimination laws and sexual harassment. The emphasis is on issues primarily related to administrative office management and not other issues in areas such as manufacturing, construction, or technical laboratories.

Workplace Safety

The **Occupational Safety and Health Act (OSHA or OSH Act)** is a federal law passed by Congress in 1970 and amended in 2004. It requires employers to provide a working environment that is safe and free from known hazards that could lead to serious physical harm or death.[1] Importantly, the act holds that occupational safety is the responsibility of both the employer and the employee.

The OSH Act holds that occupational safety is the responsibility of both the employer and the employee.

Occupational hazards, threats, and employee exposure vary by industry. The potential risk of injury or illness for a construction worker is far higher than for someone working in an office. As a result, there are OSH Act guidelines for specific industries, including construction and health care.

An area of interest to administrative employees is potential health problems related to extensive use of computers. Many people attribute carpal tunnel syndrome and other repetitive motion disorders to computer use. The National Institutes of Health provides the following information about carpal tunnel syndrome:

- It occurs when the median nerve, which runs from the forearm into the palm of the hand, becomes pressed or squeezed at the wrist.
- It causes pain, weakness, or numbness in the hand and wrist, radiating up the arm.

Occupational Safety and Health Act (OSHA or OSH Act)
a federal law that requires employers to provide a safe working environment

© Cengage Learning 2015

Proper techniques and posture at the computer minimize strain on your hands and wrists. You should also bend and stretch your wrists periodically and try to alternate tasks.[3]

- Women are three times more likely than men to develop carpal tunnel syndrome, perhaps because the carpal tunnel itself may be smaller in women than in men.
- The risk of developing carpal tunnel syndrome is not confined to people in a single industry or job, but is especially common in those performing assembly-line work: manufacturing, sewing, finishing, cleaning, and meat, poultry, or fish packing. In fact, carpal tunnel syndrome is three times more common among assemblers than among data entry personnel.[2]

Perhaps the best way for organizations to deal with carpal tunnel syndrome and other health issues related to keyboard and computer use is to focus on prevention. Proper techniques and posture are important. Ergonomic chairs and equipment, such as ergonomic keyboards and high-quality monitors, can help reduce or prevent discomfort, fatigue, and pain.

1. As a manager, how would you respond to an employee who complained that working extensively on a computer was jeopardizing his or her health?

____

2. What proactive steps would you propose to prevent problems due to computer use?

____

Fair Wages and Equal Pay

Fair Labor Standards Act (FLSA)
a federal law that establishes minimum wage, overtime pay, record keeping, and child labor standards

Equal Pay Act (EPA) of 1963
a federal law that requires employers to pay male and female employees equal pay for comparable work

Two federal laws that directly impact managers are the Fair Labor Standards Act and the Equal Pay Act of 1963. The **Fair Labor Standards Act (FLSA)** establishes minimum wage, overtime pay, record keeping, and child labor standards. The **Equal Pay Act (EPA) of 1963** requires employers to pay male and female employees equal pay for comparable work.

Minimum Wage

The federal government determines the national minimum wage standards. In 2013, the minimum wage was $7.25 per hour. Figure 10.1 shows the minimum wage for selected years. Some states also have a minimum wage, which may be higher than the federal standard. In those states, employers must pay the higher of the federal or state wage.

FIGURE 10.1
Minimum hourly wage over the years

Federal Minimum Hourly Wage (Selected Years)

1940	$0.30	**1980**	$3.10
1950	$0.75	**1990**	$3.80
1960	$1.00	**2000**	$5.15
1970	$1.60	**2010**	$7.25

Source: "Federal Minimum Wage Rates Under the Fair Labor Standards Act," Department of Labor, www.dol.gov/whd/minwage/chart.pdf.

Overtime Pay

The FLSA requires employers to pay overtime to eligible nonexempt employees. **Nonexempt employees** are typically paid on an hourly basis, as opposed to **exempt employees** who receive a salary. The overtime pay rate is at least 1½ times an employee's regular hourly rate. Employees are entitled to overtime pay if they work more than 40 hours in a workweek (any seven-day period). Some states have additional rules related to overtime pay.

Record Keeping

The FLSA also requires employers to maintain certain records for all nonexempt employees. These records consist of identifying information about the employee, data about the hours worked, and data about the wages earned. Figure 10.2 lists the basic records an employer must maintain.[4]

nonexempt employees
employees who receive an hourly wage

exempt employees
employees who receive a salary

child labor laws
state and federal laws that limit types of work and hours for young employees

Child Labor Standards

Child labor laws limit the types of work young people can do and the hours they can work based on their age. The FLSA sets basic rules, and each state also has its own laws. Where both state and federal laws apply, the employer must follow the standard that affords young workers the most protection.

Exceptions

Certain industries and job classifications are exempt from minimum wage and/or overtime pay requirements. For example, farm workers employed on small farms do not qualify for minimum wage. Also, a number of employment practices are not included in the law such as vacation or sick pay, fringe benefits, and premium pay for holiday work. It is wise to check the U.S. Department of Labor's Compliance Assistance website to ensure you have complete and current information for your situation. A link to the website is provided on the website for this text.

Certain industries and job classifications are exempt from minimum wage and/or overtime pay requirements.

FIGURE 10.2
FLSA record keeping requirements

Basic Records Employers Must Keep

- Employee's full name and Social Security number
- Employee's address, including ZIP Code
- Employee's birth date, if under age 19
- Employee's sex and occupation
- Time and day of week when employee's workweek begins
- Hours worked each day and total hours worked each workweek
- Basis on which employee's wages are paid (e.g., $15 per hour)
- Regular hourly pay rate and total daily or weekly straight-time earnings
- Total overtime earnings for the workweek
- Additions to or deductions from employee's wages
- Total wages paid each pay period
- Date of payment and pay period it covers

Source: "Fact Sheet No. 21," U.S. Department of Labor (note 4 in chapter references).

New Employee Reporting Requirements

Employers are required to report certain types of information when new employees are hired. The U.S. Department of Health and Human Services' Administration for Children and Families requires employers to file a **new hire report** to assist in enforcing child support obligations. According to federal law, employers must file seven data elements on all new employees within 20 days of their start date (submission rules differ slightly for electronic filing). These elements are the employer's full name, address, and federal employer identification number (FEIN); the employee's full name, address, and Social Security number; and the start date. The federal government uses this information to cross-reference various state and national databases to locate parents who have not paid child support.[5] Note that the information is reported to a state agency, and many states have additional requirements.

Every employer must comply with federal income tax withholding and employee eligibility verification.

Every employer, regardless of number of employees or geographic locations, must comply with federal income tax withholding and employee eligibility verification. Each new employee should complete the following forms:

new hire report
a report required by federal law to assist in enforcing child support obligations

- **Form W-4: Employee's Withholding Allowance Certificate**—The employee must complete this form on or before the first day of work.

The employer must submit the form to the Internal Revenue Service and process the employee's payroll following the withholding instructions on the form.

- **Form I-9: Employment Eligibility Verification**—The purpose of this form is to document that each new employee (citizen and noncitizen) hired after November 6, 1986, is authorized to work in the United States. Employers must retain the completed I-9 form for three years after the date of hire or one year after the date the employment ends, whichever is later.[6] To avoid allegations of illegal discrimination, employers should not ask for information other than that required on the form.

Increasingly, employers are using an Internet-based system called **E-Verify** to confirm employment eligibility. The system, which is administered by the U.S. Citizenship and Immigration Services and the Social Security Administration (SSA), compares data from a new employee's Form I-9 with data from the U.S. Department of Homeland Security and SSA. For most businesses, participation is voluntary. However, state or federal law requires some companies to use E-Verify, and it is mandatory for some employers holding federal contracts or subcontracts.[7]

E-Verify
an Internet-based system for confirming employment eligibility

intellectual property (IP)
original or unique items that people create using their imagination and brain power

Intellectual Property

Widespread pirating of music, movies, and printed material and counterfeiting of products have made the misuse and outright theft of copyrighted, trademarked, and patented intellectual property a big issue today. **Intellectual property (IP)** consists of original or unique items that people create using their imagination and brain power. Figure 10.3 provides examples of IP.

FIGURE 10.3
Examples of intellectual property

Intellectual Property

- Textbooks, novels, songs, movies, architectural drawings, and poems
- Art, including paintings, sculptures, pottery, and glass objects
- Computer programs, databases, websites, and computer games
- Logos, brand designs, and symbols
- Products such as toys, cell phones, computers, and cosmetics
- Prepared foods, formulas for beverages, drugs, and medical devices

Protecting IP

An issue that often arises regarding IP is who owns the rights to that item. If you invent a product, write a book or a song, or create computer software on your own time, in your own facilities, and using your own resources, you have the rights to that property and any revenues from its use or sale. If, however, you are an employee or independent contractor paid by a company to do any of these things, the situation is quite different. Generally, if an employee develops IP on company time, using company facilities and resources, the company owns the rights. The ownership of work done by an independent contractor (a person or company who is not an employee but is paid to do a particular job) is usually determined by the agreement between the independent contractor and the hiring company. This type of work is often referred to as work for hire.

Large companies typically have legal departments that establish legal agreements to ensure the company's IP is protected. They provide guides and information for all employees. Small organizations need to protect their IP as well. Many employment attorneys recommend that companies with significant intellectual property to protect have agreements with employees specifying that all intellectual property rights belong to the employer. The agreement should include a statement that the employee assigns all property to the employer. Companies should also use carefully crafted agreements when dealing with independent contractors.

Music Piracy

The music industry provides an example of how harmful not protecting intellectual property can be. The Recording Industry Association of America made the following statement on the issue:

> While downloading one song may not [seem to be] that serious of a crime, the accumulative impact of millions of songs downloaded illegally—and without any compensation to all the people who helped to create that song and bring it to fans [songwriters, recording artists, audio engineers, computer technicians, talent scouts and marketing specialists, producers, publishers and countless others]—is devastating. One credible study by the Institute for Policy Innovation pegs the annual harm at $12.5 billion . . . in losses to the U.S. economy as well as more than 70,000 lost jobs and $2 billion in lost wages to American workers.[8]

It's a campaign to get people thinking about the ethical choices they face when consuming music.

—Stuart Bell, publicist for the Music Matters campaign to fight music piracy

Under federal law, people convicted of music and movie piracy can face severe penalties. For example, the U.S. Supreme Court refused to hear the appeal of a college student who had been fined $675,000 for illegally downloading 31 songs.[9]

© iStockphoto.com/pressureUA

Examples of world-famous corporate logos.

Corporate Brand

The **corporate brand** (logo) establishes the image and identity of a company and is a very valuable asset. It usually consists of the company name, set in a particular type style, color, and size, along with a symbol or other graphic element. The illustration on the left shows several examples of well-known corporate brands. Companies usually register or trademark their corporate brand and pay special attention to its use. One of the most important means of protecting a brand and ensuring it projects the desired image is consistency of use. Its appearance should be consistent in all printed and digital materials. Companies typically provide manuals and guides for the proper use of their brand and require all employees to comply with them.

1. Consider the Starbucks logo with its mermaid image. What negative effects could misuse of the logo by a competitor have for Starbucks?

2. As a manager, how would you attempt to ensure that employees comply with copyright and other intellectual property laws?

Preventing Job Discrimination

Unlawful discrimination is a continuing problem in the workplace. Just look at the front page of a newspaper or check a credible online news source, and you are likely to read about a lawsuit or judgment against an employer because of employment discrimination. Complaints have generally increased over the past 15 years, declining during 6 of those years and increasing during 9. In 2011, a record 99,947 complaints against private-sector employers were recorded in the United States.[10] The most common grounds for complaints were as follows:

- Retaliation 37.4 percent
- Race 35.4 percent
- Sex 28.5 percent
- Disability 25.8 percent
- Age 23.5 percent.*[11]

corporate brand
a logo that establishes the image and identity of a company

* The total exceeds 100 percent because complainants often file charges claiming multiple types of discrimination.

Title VII of the Civil Rights Act of 1964 (Title VII)
a federal law that prohibits employment discrimination based on race, color, religion, sex, or national origin

Age Discrimination in Employment Act of 1967 (ADEA)
a federal law that protects persons age 40 or older against age-based discrimination

Pregnancy and Discrimination Act of 1973
a federal law that makes it illegal to discriminate against a woman because of pregnancy, childbirth, or a related medical condition

Titles I and V of the Americans with Disabilities Act of 1990 (ADA)
federal laws that prohibit discrimination against qualified individuals with mental or physical disabilities who can perform the essential functions of a job

Civil Rights Act of 1991
a federal law that allows monetary damages for intentional discrimination

Family Medical Leave Act of 1993 (FMLA)
a federal law that requires employers to grant employees up to 12 workweeks of unpaid leave

Genetic Information Nondiscrimination Act of 2008 (GINA)
a federal law that prohibits discrimination based on certain types of genetic information

Most allegations of discrimination do not find their way into court. Some are resolved through mediation, and many are found to have no legal basis. Nevertheless, it is in the best interests of both employers and employees to prevent discrimination or the perception of discrimination. Costs for employers include lost productivity, an unpleasant work environment, employee turnover, expense, and a negative public image.

Anti-Discrimination Laws

Several federal laws are in place to prevent employment discrimination based on a variety of personal attributes and characteristics. The U.S. Equal Employment Opportunity Commission (EEOC) is responsible for enforcing most of these laws. The Department of Labor enforces the Family Medical Leave Act of 1993.[12]

- The Equal Pay Act of 1963 was discussed on page 215.
- **Title VII of the Civil Rights Act of 1964 (Title VII)** prohibits employment discrimination based on race, color, religion, gender, or national origin.
- The **Age Discrimination in Employment Act of 1967 (ADEA)** protects persons age 40 or older against discrimination based on age.
- The **Pregnancy and Discrimination Act of 1973** makes it illegal to discriminate against a woman because of pregnancy, childbirth, or a related medical condition.
- **Titles I and V of the Americans with Disabilities Act of 1990 (ADA)** prohibit discrimination against individuals with mental or physical disabilities who can perform the essential functions of a job.
- The **Civil Rights Act of 1991** allows monetary damages in cases of intentional discrimination.
- The **Family Medical Leave Act of 1993 (FMLA)** requires employers to grant employees up to 12 workweeks of unpaid leave during any 12-month period for one or more of these reasons:
  - Birth or care of a newborn child
  - Placement of a child with the employee for adoption or foster care
  - Care for a spouse, child, or parent with a serious health condition
  - Inability to work because of a serious health condition
  - Certain situations arising from a spouse, child, or parent's active-duty military status[13]
- The **Genetic Information Nondiscrimination Act of 2008 (GINA)** prohibits discrimination based on information about genetic tests (for breast cancer risk or Huntington's disease, for example), genetic services (such as genetic counseling), or family history.[14]

All these laws also make it illegal to retaliate against someone who files a discrimination charge or otherwise complains about discrimination.

States and cities have also passed laws prohibiting various types of discrimination. In *Ethics in the Workplace,* Professors Dean Bredeson and Keith Goree note that

> . . . some states and cities go further than the federal government . . . in prohibiting actions and extending protections to additional groups. Local bans on sexual orientation discrimination are fairly common, for example.[15]

As J. Hagood Tighe pointed out in the chapter opening interview, managers should have a basic understanding of employment, labor, and anti-discrimination laws and should stay up-to-date on them. They should be familiar enough with the law to be able to spot issues when they arise. They should also know when to refer an issue to human resources or upper management or seek legal counsel.

Sexual Harassment

The EEOC describes **sexual harassment** as follows:

> It is unlawful to harass a person (an applicant or employee) because of that person's sex. Harassment can include "sexual harassment" or unwelcome sexual advances, requests for sexual favors, and other verbal or physical harassment of a sexual nature."[16]

Illegal sexual harassment can take one of two forms, described in this way by Bredeson and Goree:

- **Quid pro quo** harassment . . . refers to situations in which sexual demands are directly tied to a person's keeping his or her job or receiving a promotion or another job benefit.
- **Hostile work environment** [harassment occurs when] supervisors or coworkers use embarrassment, humiliation, or fear to create a negative climate that interferes with the ability of others to perform their jobs.[17]

sexual harassment
unwanted sexual conduct directed at a job applicant or employee because of that person's sex

quid pro quo
a type of harassment in which sexual demands are directly tied to a person's keeping his or her job or receiving a promotion or another job benefit

hostile work environment
a type of harassment in which supervisors or coworkers use embarrassment, humiliation, or fear to create a negative environment that interferes with the ability of others to perform their jobs

An example of quid pro quo sexual harassment is offering a person a raise or promotion in return for sexual favors. An example of hostile work environment sexual harassment is a situation in which one or more employees frequently display offensive pictures on a computer monitor, tell offensive jokes, or make disparaging or inappropriate comments about a person's body.

It is important to note that sexual harassment is not defined by the accused harasser but by the perceptions of the recipient. A poster of a scantily clad woman posing suggestively on a motorcycle may seem great to the man who brought it to work but offensive to women in the office.

This additional information from the EEOC is relevant for managers:

- The law doesn't prohibit simple teasing, offhand comments, or isolated incidents that are not very serious.

- Harassment does not have to be of a sexual nature . . . and can include offensive remarks about a person's sex. For example, it is illegal to harass a woman by making offensive comments about women in general.
- Both victim and harasser can be either a woman or a man, and the victim and harasser can be the same sex.
- The harasser can be the victim's supervisor, a supervisor in another area, a coworker, or someone who is not an employee of the employer, such as a client or customer.[18]

A great deal of misunderstanding surrounds the topic of sexual harassment because of vague definitions and inconsistent court rulings. Nonetheless, it remains a serious problem in the workplace. To protect themselves against litigation, companies should establish a legitimate sexual harassment policy that encourages complaints to be filed internally and should legitimately investigate all complaints.[19]

The most effective way to deal with sexual harassment is to prevent it from happening.

The most effective way to deal with sexual harassment is to prevent it from happening, an effort in which managers play an essential role. The next section suggests ways of preventing sexual harassment and other forms of discrimination. The EEOC website provides extensive guidance for handling sexual harassment issues. A link to the website is provided on the website for this text.

Manager's Role in Preventing Discrimination

Managers are often the first line of defense in preventing workplace discrimination.

Managers are often the first line of defense in preventing workplace discrimination. Their responsibilities begin with the recruitment and hiring process and continue throughout an employee's tenure.

Job Applicants

Legal protection against employment discrimination extends to job applicants as well as current employees. One area that is particularly important for managers is what should and should not be asked during a job interview. Here are some tips:

- Check with a human resources specialist or your manager to ensure the questions you plan to ask are not discriminatory.
- Focus your questions on job-related skills and work experience. Treat each candidate the same. Be consistent in your demeanor and nonverbal behavior.
- Avoid these topics:
  - Age (including indirect questions that may reveal age, such as "What year did you graduate from high school?"). However, the job description and advertisement need to be clear about age minimum or maximum if there are legitimate age requirements.

- Marital or parenting status
- Medical history or disability
- Race (with online applications and phone interviews, you may not ask for a photo or personal description)
- National origin
- Religion
- Affiliations such as political parties, social groups that identify race, gender, or sexual orientation, or religious organizations
- Military service (for example, you may not ask whether a person was honorably discharged)
- Arrest record (arrests often do not lead to convictions)[20]

Communicate appropriate interview guidelines and their importance to everyone involved in the interview process. If you are also responsible for preparing job applications or advertisements, focus on job-related skills and work experience. Check with a human resources specialist, your manager, or an attorney to ensure questions are not discriminatory. Include a nondiscrimination statement on both types of documents.

Social Networks

Many employers use social networks to verify information about job applicants. A survey conducted by Harris Interactive for CareerBuilder found that nearly half of the 2,667 managers and human resource workers questioned researched potential hires on social networking sites, such as Facebook, LinkedIn, and Twitter. More than a third of employers chose not to hire a candidate because of what they found. The main reasons were provocative photos and references to drinking and drug use.[21] As long as employers do not use the information for discriminatory purposes prohibited by law (for example, to determine from a photograph the race of an applicant), this action is legal.

Many employers use social networks to verify information about job applicants.

Current Employees

Managers cannot control the actions of every person in the organization. But they can certainly take steps to encourage appropriate behavior. The advice provided by J. Hagood Tighe in the chapter opening interview is fundamental. Managers set the tone. They are largely responsible for the work environment, and the climate they should seek to establish is one of respect toward and between employees. As a manager

- Familiarize yourself with the law and behaviors and actions that typically constitute workplace discrimination.
- Know and abide by your company's policies.
- Clearly explain your company's policies and grievance procedures to your employees.

© kycstudio/iStockphoto.com

It has become commonplace to review job applicants' social networking pages. Provocative photos, references to drinking and drug use, and other unprofessional content can legally cost an applicant the job.

- Lead by example in behaving respectfully toward your employees. The Tighe interview describes specific ways of showing respect.
- Lead by example in behaving ethically and with integrity, never inappropriately.
- Do not allow disrespectful or inappropriate behavior by employees.

Some of the qualities of effective leaders discussed in earlier chapters can help you in establishing a positive, pleasant working environment for your employees and in handling any problems that arise. Strive to establish relationships of trust with employees so they have confidence in coming to you with problems. Get to know them, encourage communication, and be a good listener. Be aware of and attuned to what is going on around you. Importantly, courts have held companies liable for sexual harassment that their managers (1) knew about but did not remedy and (2) did not know about but should have through appropriate administrative oversight.

When issues arise, deal with them immediately, either by referring them to the human resources department or by handling them yourself if appropriate. For example, many harassers fail to recognize their conduct is offensive. Simply letting them know may be enough to put an end to the unwelcome behavior.

You are a manager in a small real estate office. You suspect one of your employees, Chris, is sexually harassing another, Alex. A third employee in the department has mentioned the same concern to you. Alex has not filed an official complaint; however, Alex avoids Chris at work and will not work with Chris on projects. Chris is one of your best agents.

1. How would you handle this situation?

   ____

2. Would you involve your manager or another company official? Why or why not?

   ____

3. Note that the names Alex and Chris are interchangeable for both men and women. Would the genders of the employees make any difference in how you handled the situation? Why or why not?

   ____

Ethics

Bredeson and Goree introduce the topic of ethics and distinguish ethical principles from laws in this way: Standards, or norms, are accepted levels of behavior to which people are expected to conform. The **standard of ethics** refers to social expectations of people's moral behavior, whereas the **standard of law** refers to rules of behavior imposed on people by governments. People must follow legal standards, or they will face specific negative consequences. While laws are made valid by authority, ethical principles are made valid by the reasons and arguments supporting them. This is the main difference between laws and ethics.[22] **Business ethics** involves identifying and enforcing socially acceptable standards of conduct in commercial and administrative settings.

In previous chapters, a number of laws and ethical principles have been discussed. Many of the soft skills described in each chapter generally are considered ethical principles. Examples are honesty, integrity, courtesy, trust, respect, and responsibility.

In the discussion of company vision, mission, and values in Chapter 6, values were defined as the core beliefs of an organization and the principles that guide behavior. They are the ethical principles all employees are expected to follow. For example, review the Microsoft values statement on page 115. Some companies describe their ethical principles as a code of business conduct. The ethical principles do not have the power of laws, but the company can insist employees adhere to them. Most companies include the information in an employee handbook, and many also post it on their website.

General Ethical Principles

People's ethical beliefs are shaped by many factors, including family and friends, the media, culture, school, religion, and general life experiences. While some of people's ethical convictions necessarily differ, others are widely shared. For instance, certain actions and behaviors are almost universally considered unethical in the United States (and in most developed countries around the world). These include:

- **Sexism**—treating people unequally (and harmfully) by virtue of their gender.
- **Racism**—treating people unequally (and harmfully) by virtue of their race or ethnicity.
- **Fraud**—intentional deception that causes someone to give up property or some right.
- **Deceit**—representing something as true which one knows to be false in order to gain a selfish end harmful to another.
- **Intimidation**—forcing a person to act against his or her interest or deter from acting in his or her interest by threats or violence.[23]

standard of ethics
social expectations of people's moral behavior

standard of law
rules of behavior imposed on people by governments

business ethics
socially acceptable standards of conduct in commercial and administrative settings

Consider the importance of these general ethical guidelines when facing day-to-day ethical dilemmas. Never take any action that is not:

- Balanced—consider your self-interests with your organization's interests.
- Open, honest, and truthful and that you would not be proud to see reported widely in national newspapers and on television.
- Kind and that does not build a sense of community, a sense of all of us working together for a commonly accepted goal.[24]

1. Which of the preceding general ethical principles appeals most to you in terms of serving as a guide for making important decisions? Why?

   ____

2. As a manager, how can you help your employees adopt one or more of these principles?

   ____

Making Ethical Decisions

The best way to practice applying your ethical principles is to consider a specific ethical question and decide which of these principles should guide your behavior. Sometimes, especially in complex situations, a combination of principles will apply. Begin by gathering all the relevant information. Consider the perspectives of the different stakeholders. See the "You Decide" scenarios at the end of the chapter to practice your ethical reasoning.

© Keith Bell/Shutterstock.com

Ethical Behavior Is Up to *You*

Chapter 5 noted that in a recent survey by the Ethics Resource Center, more than a third of employees reported their direct supervisor does not demonstrate ethical behavior. The same survey found that:

- 45 percent of workers witnessed misconduct on the job.
- 22 percent of those who reported it experienced retaliation.
- 42 percent of companies have weak ethics cultures.[25]

Managers are challenged with raising awareness about unethical actions and fostering a more ethical work environment. The key point is to make employees aware of what the company values and that it expects ethical behavior from all employees at all levels at all times. Review the values and code of ethics that defines the company, and train your employees to ensure they understand the expectations. Remember that employees will look to you to establish ethical values and will take their cue from your behavior. You should be a role model in faithfully abiding by these standards and applying your own high ethical standards to your actions.

In *Ethics in the Workplace*, Bredeson and Goree discuss standards of behavior. You have already learned about two: the standard of law and the standard of ethics. A third is the standard of etiquette: expectations concerning manners and social graces.[26] The "Soft Skills for Success" feature on page 234 discusses business etiquette.

Incivility in the workplace needs to be addressed for what it truly is: a massive time suck that impacts productivity, profits, and employee retention.

—Peter Post, great-grandson of etiquette authority Emily Post, director of the Emily Post Institute, and author of five etiquette books

Employee Monitoring

A major contemporary ethical issue affecting managers, and a source of tension between them and their employees, is employee monitoring. Phone calls, emails, voice mail, and computer use (increasingly, software use) are typical monitoring targets. Many employees resent the practice, particularly the invasion of privacy. Monitoring is stressful for employees, and some fear losing their jobs. Others point to monitoring as evidence of lack of trust and a focus on speed and quantity rather than quality.[27]

A 2011 CareerBuilder survey found that half of U.S. companies monitor their employees' Internet and email use.[28] Since 2001, the American Management Association (AMA) and the ePolicy Institute have surveyed employers periodically about their monitoring activities. Reasons for monitoring include the following:

- Concern about liability with inappropriate websites and emails containing inappropriate language and content
- Identification of training needs and improving employee performance
- Concern about loss of time and impact on productivity
- Concern about security of company data[29]

In other settings, many safety reasons exist for monitoring. Monitoring food safety has had a major impact on detecting problems such as not following rules for processing and packaging, which can lead to food contamination. Many reports point out that hospital employees' not washing their hands properly can lead to potentially fatal staph infections in patients as well as medical personnel.

Few states require employee notification of monitoring. However, most employers do inform their employees. Recent AMA/ePolicy surveys yield the following statistics:

- 14 percent of employees admit to emailing confidential or proprietary information about a firm, its people, products and services to outside parties.
- 14 percent admit to sending third parties potentially embarrassing and confidential company email that is intended strictly for internal readers.
- 89 percent of users admit to using the office system to send jokes, gossip, rumors or disparaging remarks to outsiders.
- 9 percent have used company email to transmit sexual, romantic or pornographic text or images.[30]
- 83 percent of employers have rules and policies in place restricting personal use of company equipment.
- 28 percent of employers have fired workers for email misuse, and of those, 26 percent said it was for "excessive personal use."[31]

In most situations, employers have the legal right to monitor employee telephone calls, emails, voice mail, and computer use and to do video and audio surveillance. As J. Hagood Tighe pointed out in the chapter opening interview, if your company has corporate monitoring policies, you should follow them exactly. The "Leveraging Technology" feature on page 230 provides tips on handling the issue with employees.

1. Suppose you learned the company you were working for was monitoring your work electronically. How would you feel about this situation?

   ____

2. Would you feel more positively if you were told beforehand?

   ____

3. Do you think it would be unethical for your employer to monitor your work without telling you? Why or why not?

   ____

LEVERAGING TECHNOLOGY

BALANCING EMPLOYEE MONITORING ISSUES

Many people would agree that while it is legal, it is not necessarily desirable for an employer to monitor an employee's work electronically. Focusing on rules and risks is a good strategy for reducing resentment among employees.

- Explain the need for any established company policies on personal use of email, computers, telephones, photocopiers, and other equipment.
- If you or the company is in the process of creating policies, involve employees in developing them.
- Provide copies of all policies to employees. Have them acknowledge receipt, and try to ensure they read and understand them.
- Review and update policies regularly.
- Tell your employees if they are being monitored electronically. Ensure they understand what is being monitored and why.
- Distinguish carefully between personal and company emails. Explain you cannot guarantee that a personal email or telephone call will never be monitored, but that the intent is to monitor only company email or telephone calls if that is the case.
- Explain carefully the action that will result from inappropriate content in emails or websites. Emphasize that these activities could offend other employees and create liability issues for the organization. Say they will not be tolerated.
- Focus on the importance of information security and why inappropriate use of personal devices such as smartphones may lead to security problems.
- Provide style guides on how to protect your company's brand and other intellectual property.

SUMMARY

1. All managers should be familiar with the Occupational Safety and Health Act (OSHA or OSH Act), Fair Labor Standards Act (FLSA),Equal Pay Act of 1963 (EPA), relevant intellectual property (IP) laws, and related state and local laws.
2. All managers should be familiar with anti-discrimination laws, including EPA , Title VII of the Civil Rights Act of 1964 (Title VII), the Age Discrimination in Employment Act of 1967 (ADEA), the Pregnancy and Discrimination Act of 1973, Titles I and V of the Americans with Disabilities Act of 1990 (ADA), the Civil Rights Act of 1991, the Family Medical leave Act of 1993 (FMLA), and the Genetic Nondiscrimination Act of 2008 (GINA). They should also be aware of state and city anti-discrimination laws.
3. The manager's role in preventing discrimination includes asking appropriate questions during job interviews, establishing a climate of respect toward and between employees, knowing and abiding by company policies, and leading by example.
4. Five generally acknowledged unethical practices are sexism, racism, fraud, deceit, and intimidation.
5. The process of making ethical decisions involves gathering all the relevant information, considering the perspectives of the different stakeholders, and deciding which of your ethical principles should guide your behavior.

Terms

Age Discrimination in Employment Act, 221
business ethics, 226
child labor laws, 216
Civil Rights Act of 1991, 221
corporate brand, 220
Equal Pay Act of 1963, 215
E-Verify, 218
exempt employees, 216
Fair Labor Standards Act, 215
Family Medical Leave Act, 221
Genetic Information Nondiscrimination Act, 221
hostile work environment, 222
intellectual property (IP), 218
new hire report, 217
nonexempt employees, 216
Occupational Safety and Health Act, 214
Pregnancy and Discrimination Act, 221
quid pro quo, 222
sexual harassment, 222
standard of ethics, 226
standard of law, 226
Titles I and V of the Americans with Disabilities Act of 1990 (ADA), 221
Title VII of the Civil Rights Act of 1964, 221

Study Tools

CourseMate

Located at www.cengagebrain.com

- Chapter Outlines
- Flashcards
- Interactive Quizzes
- Tech Tools
- Video Segments

and More!

Questions for Reflection

1. What laws are in place to provide fair and equitable wages?
2. What three legal obligations does an employer have when hiring a new employee?
3. If an employee is required to develop new products as part of his or her job, does the employee own the intellectual property rights? Explain why or why not.
4. What can a company do to help prevent sexual harassment?
5. If a person's actions are legal, are they ethical? Why or why not? Provide an example that supports your opinion.
6. Your company is developing a code of business conduct that includes ethical principles. What five principles would you recommend be included?
7. If you were a manager being asked to provide input on whether your company should monitor employee work electronically, what would you recommend? Explain why.

Hands-On Activities

Plan a Training Session

Work in a team of four or five for this activity. VanHuss Enterprises is instituting a year-long management development program for its first-line managers, supervisors, and team leaders (approximately thirty people). All of them supervise employees in an administrative office setting where there is a focus on being professional. The executive team has asked your team to outline a one-day training session on business etiquette.

1. Reread Peter Post's quote on incivility on page 228, and read "Soft Skills for Success" on page 234.
2. Think about situations you have experienced where you felt discourtesy, lack of manners, and rudeness created problems in a business or professional setting. How could those situations have been prevented?
3. Each team member should ask one senior manager from a local company what topics should be included in business etiquette training. Alternatively, members can search the Internet to determine topics that should be covered.
4. Each member should prepare a list of the topics he or she thinks is important.
5. The team should review all the topics and determine which should be covered in a one-day training seminar.
6. Work together to prepare an outline for a one-day training session. Include some details under each main topic.
7. Discuss ways the information could be presented. Focus on making sure participants are actively engaged in learning.

Interview Questions

Assume you are a new manager and are in the process of hiring an administrative assistant. You have narrowed the list of candidates whose letters and résumés you received and are ready to begin interviews. You have assembled a list of questions to ask, but you are not sure about questions you are *not* supposed to ask.

1. Do some research on this topic.
2. Make a list of questions you may *never* ask a candidate during an interview.

You Decide | Case Study

Ethical Decision Making

For each ethical scenario, explain how you would handle the situation, and specify which ethical principles apply.

1. You receive too much change from the cashier in a restaurant.
2. You witness a friend at work stealing merchandise.
3. You overhear a supervisor from another department making sexual advances toward one of the employees.
4. Your job requires you to choose a company to supply your business with office supplies. You are given a $200 gift card to a local mall from an office supply company's salesperson who hopes you will decide to purchase from her company.
5. You are traveling on business with a coworker, who tells you how to cheat on your expense report to get reimbursed for money you did not spend.

MANAGER'S TOOLKIT

A goal for managers is to encourage employees to abide by the law and to make ethical decisions. Toward this end, you are preparing an ethics training session for your employees. You decide to provide them with a few reference documents. Select a company that you are familiar with or an industry that interests you. Prepare the following documents to use during your ethics training session:

1. Guidelines for ethical decision making. This document should include a brief explanation of each guideline/principle, along with an example that is relevant for your workplace.
2. A code of ethics or business conduct. You will introduce it to employees as a draft or working document and will encourage their feedback and suggestions for adding, deleting, or modifying items. Your code of ethics or business conduct should include:
   a. An introduction.
   b. The organization's mission, objectives, and values.
   c. Guidance for all stakeholder groups: employees, shareholders, customers, suppliers, and the community, as appropriate.
   d. Expectations about acceptable behavior.

Soft Skills for Success

Business Etiquette

Etiquette is a standard of behavior that applies to good manners and social graces. Most companies include interpersonal skills, courtesy, and good manners in their list of soft skills required when they hire new employees. In the interview process, employers try to determine if applicants will fit in with the culture of the company. First-line managers must be able to lead by example. Employers want employees to make a favorable impression on clients and customers and to help present a positive company image. They want employees to be effective team members. Proper etiquette is an integral part of the skills desired by employers.

Many companies believe that using mentoring and role models is the best way to emphasize the development of good business etiquette. Middle and senior management need to lead by example and serve as good role models for first-line managers. They also need to take an active role in mentoring new managers.

Many companies include business etiquette in employee training programs. Employees who travel internationally for business are often required to take training in appropriate etiquette for the countries being visited. Four topics many companies consider important are the following:

- **Professional dress**. Many companies have dress codes and expect employees to dress professionally. An issue gaining tremendous attention is visible body art and piercings. Many managers say that they look for job candidates with a professional image. They do not consider visible body art and piercings as conveying a professional image. Many managers also indicate that employees with visible body art are less likely to be promoted to higher management positions. Some companies require employees to cover body art, and it has been ruled legal to do so. Company positions about body art may change, however, due to its popularity among young adults.
- **Interpersonal skills**. Some examples of etiquette issues in this area are workplace civility, courtesy, good manners, rudeness, improper language, and the Golden Rule.
- **Dining etiquette**. Many managers participate in business lunches and dinners. The lack of good table manners can create a poor image of an employee and a company. The art and science of business entertaining is especially important for higher-level managers.
- **Responsible use of technology**. Etiquette for email, social media, cell phone usage, voice mail, and interaction with customers and clients is high on the priority list of many companies.

Put It to Work

1. Rate yourself on each of these selected attributes of business etiquette on a scale of 1 to 10 with 10 being *outstanding* and 1 being *very poor.*

   ____ Professional dress (For men, a suit or sport coat, ironed dress shirt, and tie; for women, a business suit with skirt or slacks and a conservative blouse or appropriate dress (no low-cut blouses or very short skirts)

   ____ No visible body art or piercings

   ____ Courtesy and respect toward others

   ____ Appropriate language

   ____ Proper use of silverware, flatware, and glasses at business meals

   ____ Proper behavior at a business meal

   ____ Businesslike and professional email

   ____ Polite voice messages with appropriate information

2. Make a plan for improving those items marked 6 or lower.

CHAPTER

11

Building a Positive, Creative, and Productive Work Environment

Learning Outcomes

1. Explain why corporate culture is important in creating an effective work environment.
2. Describe four steps managers can take to enhance employee motivation.
3. Specify expected behaviors that might be included in an organizational attitude standard.
4. Identify the five core values necessary to support innovation.
5. Discuss the concept of learning to be more creative, and suggest how managers can help employees become more creative.
6. Describe six steps managers can take to help create a positive work environment.
7. Explain how managers can create a productive work environment.

Photo courtesy of S. Cotter

Straight Talk From the Field

Susan K. Cotter is Chief Product Officer for AIG Benefit Solutions. She began her career in sales and marketing with a start-up airline and then was given the opportunity to create a marketing department for an insurance company which led to a variety of opportunities. Her experience includes the property and casualty and the life and health sides of the insurance industry as well as in the carrier and agency sides. She also obtained legislative and regulatory experience by working on Capitol Hill with an insurance trade association.

Printed by permission from Susan K.Cotter

In hiring new employees, do you consciously look for creative people?

Yes, but much depends on the level of the position. I always start with the baseline technical skills and knowledge. Then I look for energy, creativity, problem solving, and the ability to be innovative. A key point is that I don't hire just from within the industry. Some of the best creative ideas come from people outside of a given industry.

What helps people become creative?

Some people have a natural inclination to be creative or to be analytical, but the work environment can have a great influence on creativity. To enable employees to be creative, they have to have the freedom to think, to make suggestions, to make mistakes, and to be bold in the way they approach the business. Management has to create a safe environment to listen to new ideas even though some ideas fail. If ideas are outside the norm, try implementing them in areas that would not involve major risk and that fit within the risk appetite of the organization. You never want to bet the company on new ideas.

To enable employees to be creative, they have to have the freedom to think, to make suggestions, to make mistakes, and to be bold in the way they approach the business.

What practical advice would you give new managers to stimulate creativity?

A couple of things have worked well for me. I always leave time at the end of our regular team meetings to discuss new ideas in a brainstorming, free-flowing environment on things not in our business plan. For example, should we create pet insurance or divorce insurance products—which are products outside our core, but which may present a market opportunity? In department meetings, I ask a team member to present research on something innovative in another industry. The focus is on how that innovation could potentially relate to our industry. It is important for new managers to know that ultimately ideas must be grounded in data. Ideas need to be tested in the marketplace through focus groups and quantitative research. To be successful, ideas have to meet financial metrics.

It is also important to have diversity in your teams and your workforce. Diversity enhances creativity because it brings in different perspectives. Different perspectives help everyone think a little more creatively about the business. You have a diverse population of consumers, and you have to meet their needs.

How do you create a motivating work environment?

I think one of the most important factors is to give employees at all levels a sense of ownership in their jobs. Give them the freedom to make decisions, to be innovative, and to be creative. When employees have pride of ownership in their trade or position, they become engaged, energetic, and really want to go the extra mile for a company.

What really works effectively is strong talent management. You have to recognize high-performing and high-potential talent across the company including in your operational areas. Having strong career paths with programs to develop employees to move both horizontally and vertically helps to build motivation. When individuals see the opportunity to develop, they become much more motivated. Job shadowing and mentoring programs are effective ways to develop employees. Mentors can help guide employees through the development process and really groom them for the desired responsibilities.

Are there other areas that you think are important in building a positive, productive work environment?

Absolutely! Being a good corporate citizen is critical. A company has to be involved in and play a significant role in its community. You live in the community, you hire from the community, and you serve the needs of people in the community. Good corporate citizenship is a value that should be embedded in the company's mission.

Visit *www.cengagebrain.com* to read the complete profile.

Chapter Outline

The culture of an organization is a key factor in setting the tone and feel of the work environment. A strong corporate culture encourages *everyone* in the organization to help create and maintain a positive, creative, and productive workplace.

Instilling Corporate Culture

As you learned in Chapter 8, corporate culture is the collective or shared values, beliefs, traditions, philosophy, and character or personality of the organization. Companies recruit potential employees who they believe will fit in with their culture. Companies expect employees to be a part of their culture and to adhere to its values and traditions. Any employee who expects to be successful must develop a thorough understanding of the culture and demonstrate a passion for being a part of it. Therefore, logic dictates that managers work with the corporate culture in efforts to set up employees for success.

Though the environment in which a successful company operates may change drastically over the years, the values usually remain constant.

Corporate culture is often shaped when a company is founded and provides the guiding principles on which it operates for many years. Though the environment in which a successful company operates may change drastically over time, the values usually remain constant. Keenan Suggs Insurance Company (Chapter 2 opening interview, pages 24–25) provides an example. The company strives to maintain a desirable working environment and to facilitate team building. Suggs says, "We want the workplace to be light, airy, friendly, and viewed by all employees as a comfortable, productive place to work with each other."

Each year, *Fortune* magazine publishes a list of the top 100 companies to work for in the United States. In perusing this list, you will discover corporate culture's positive impact on recruitment and retention.

Corporate culture in successful companies often extends beyond employees, customers, clients, and vendors to include the local community. These companies want employees to be engaged in the community and give back to it.

Motivation

motivation
an employee's desire or drive to achieve

A primary role of managers is to ensure employees perform their jobs efficiently and effectively. Employees generally need to be motivated to achieve personal, team, and organizational goals. **Motivation** involves an employee's desire or drive to achieve. A widely debated question is, Can managers really motivate employees? Those who believe managers cannot motivate employees argue that a manager's job is to create a working environment where people will motivate themselves. According to this line of thinking, motivation comes only

Employee motivation is essential to organizational success.

from within the individual. On the opposite side of this debate are those who believe managers can motivate employees with appropriate words, actions, consequences, and decisions. Regardless of which position you might take, the fact of the matter is that employee motivation is essential to organizational success, and managers need to develop a style that gets results.

1. Do you agree or disagree with the idea that supervisors cannot motivate employees, that people must motivate themselves? Explain.

2. Reflect on a personal experience in which someone was supervising your activities or leading a team. It could be at work, in a volunteer capacity, or in an extracurricular activity. Did the leader's words, actions, rewards, and decisions impact your motivation, and if so, in a positive or negative way? Explain.

Dimensions of Motivation

Motivation factors into many topics already discussed in this textbook. Note from the following quick review how much you have already learned about it. The emphasis in this chapter on fostering a positive work environment will add another dimension to the topic.

- Motivation is a significant component of many of the leadership theories discussed in Chapter 4. For example, on page 76, you learned that path-goal theory is based on the assumption that effective leaders can enhance employee motivation by (1) clarifying the individual's perception of work goals, (2) linking meaningful rewards with goal attainment, and (3) explaining how goals and desired rewards can be achieved.
- Chapter 5 focused on leading, motivating, and empowering teams. The five actions identified by *The Wisdom of Teams* authors Katzenbach and Smith for groups to form themselves into effective teams are (1) shaping a common purpose, (2) agreeing on performance goals, (3) defining a common working approach, (4) developing high levels of complementary skills, and (5) holding themselves mutually accountable for results. All are important elements in motivation.
- Chapter 6 reinforced the key role of goal setting in motivation. You learned about SMART goals and the work of Locke and Latham on motivating employees in the goal-setting process and task performance. You also learned that goals motivate employees by challenging them and by serving as a means of gaining both extrinsic and intrinsic rewards.

- Chapter 9 explained the use of feedback, coaching, fair appraisals, fair compensation, and other extrinsic and intrinsic rewards as motivational tools.
- Many of the soft skills discussed throughout this book, such as self-management, require the ability to motivate oneself. Practicing these soft skills can help employees become more self-motivated.

Practical Advice and Best Practices

Psychologists have studied motivation from a variety of perspectives. Rather than review theories beyond those already discussed in this textbook, the focus in this chapter is on practical business advice that managers can use.

Stop Demotivating Employees

Writing in *Harvard Management Update,* research specialists David Sirota, Louis Mischkind, and Michael Meltzer present an interesting perspective. They think of motivation in terms of enthusiasm about the job. These writers believe companies often demotivate employees rather than motivating them. According to their research, in most companies, motivation tends to be high as employees begin a job. However, it often begins to decline in about six months and continues to fall thereafter. Sirota, Mischkind, and Meltzer make this recommendation:

> To maintain the enthusiasm employees bring to their jobs initially, management must understand the three sets of goals that the great majority of workers seek from their work—and then satisfy those goals:
>
> - Equity: To be respected and to be treated fairly in areas such as pay, benefits, and job security.
> - Achievement: To be proud of one's job, accomplishments, and employer.
> - Camaraderie: To have good, productive relationships with fellow employees.[1]

Promote Model Employees

Human resources consultant Ruth Mayhew suggests that "the best type of employee motivation is promoting an employee who exemplifies the quality and performance expectations of the organization." She proposes these additional methods:

- Reward employees with tasks that challenge their particular skills and abilities.
- Propose them for a committee of the "best and brightest" charged with making important company changes.
- Use job assignments, transfers, promotions, and professional development activities.[2]

Provide Growth Opportunities

A report by management and technology consulting firm Booz Allen Hamilton and the Center for Creative Leadership emphasizes the importance of assisting employees in finding "opportunities that will help them build a career and support the mission." Employees with more access to learning are more committed to the organization's mission. "Researchers have found growth opportunities to be an important motivator for employees to stay at their jobs. These opportunities provide benefits to the organizations, as people learn and master new skills and knowledge."[3]

Provide Support That Enhances Progress

Managers often debate the importance of various workplace factors in employee motivation; however, their views do not always coincide with those of employees. In a recent survey, Teresa Amabile, professor of business administration at Harvard University, and Steven Kramer, an independent researcher, writer, and consultant, asked 669 managers to rank the impact of five workplace factors on employee motivation and emotions. The factors were recognition for good work, incentives, interpersonal support, support for making progress, and clear goals. The majority of managers ranked recognition for good work first.

In a separate study, Amabile and Kramer used daily email surveys to track emotions, motivation levels, and related data for 238 members of different project teams over several months. After analyzing the resulting 12,000 diary entries, the researchers found that for employees, the top motivator for performance was progress—the factor nearly all managers ranked last. "On days when workers have the sense they're making headway in their jobs, or when they receive support that helps them overcome obstacles, their emotions are most positive and their drive to succeed is at its peak," Amabile and Kramer note. They add that the best way for managers to increase their teams' productivity is to:

Employees' top motivator for performance is making progress in their jobs.

- Take actions that directly support their work, such as helping.
- Foster good work in ways such as showing respect or making encouraging comments.
- Remove or prevent obstacles and potentially discouraging or undermining experiences, such as interpersonal conflict.[4]

As you think about motivation, remember that job performance requires both personal motivation and the ability to get the job done. Occasionally, supervisors will say an employee failed because of lack of motivation, when in fact the person was not sufficiently prepared with proper training and experience to be successful. For example, all the motivation in the world will not enable a computer-illiterate person to sit down and create a spreadsheet using a computer. Ability and skills—acquired through education, training, and/or on-the-job experience—are also necessary.

Motivation + Ability = Success

Developing an Organizational Attitude

Supervisors (and customers) frequently comment on their employees' attitude: their viewpoint, perspective, feelings, and disposition (good or bad). Yet attitude is too often ignored during performance evaluations. One way to encourage good behavior and a positive work attitude is to develop an "attitude standard" for your organization and then assess and hold employees accountable for their attitudes.[5]

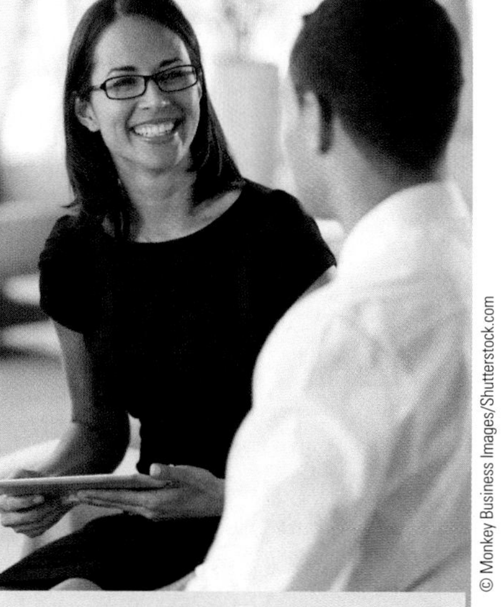

© Monkey Business Images/Shutterstock.com

A positive attitude and a sincere smile make work more enjoyable.

An **attitude standard** is a set of expected employee behaviors for fostering a positive, friendly, creative, and professional corporate culture where employees are civil and pleasant to everyone, including customers, vendors, and each other. Employees' attitudes largely determine their behavior and productivity at work. Both good and bad attitudes are contagious. So it is important to foster a positive environment and quickly address any demonstration of a negative attitude. A good work attitude is essentially a free asset with a positive impact on the organization's bottom line. Conversely, a bad attitude is an expense and has negative impacts.[6]

William Cottringer, a business consultant, sport psychologist, college professor, and author, has identified six personal characteristics that should be included in an organization's attitude standard: (1) friendliness, (2) positivism, (3) teamwork, (4) enthusiasm, (5) responsibility, and (6) professionalism.[7]

Friendliness

Friendliness is a trait exhibited with a simple smile, an act of kindness, good-natured humor, and social pleasantries. Its opposite is found in the employee who frowns, seems always to be angry or defensive, blames others, spreads malicious gossip, and/or is overly serious. Linda Kaplan Thaler and Robin Koval, authors of *The Power of Nice: How to Conquer the Business World with Kindness*, recommend that people "exercise their 'nice' muscles every day for a week, by doing five nice things that yield no personal gain."[8]

Positivism

Positivism is demonstrated by employees with a "can do" attitude who get things accomplished. This sharply contrasts with the negative employee who exhibits cynicism and pessimism, which can drain the creative energy from any team.

attitude standard
a set of expected employee behaviors for fostering a positive, friendly, creative, and professional corporate culture

Teamwork

Teamwork occurs when employees leverage individual strengths and talents and embrace individual differences to work together to achieve organizational goals. Teamwork requires people to get along and to share the credit instead of individuals' doing things their own way and taking full credit. Productive teams ultimately achieve much better long-term results than individuals working independently, especially in today's high-tech global economy.

Enthusiasm

Enthusiasm is exhibited when employees enjoy their work, do not complain or talk negatively, are self-motivated and eager to learn, and see problems as challenges and opportunities rather than obstacles. It can be very contagious.

There is real magic in enthusiasm. It spells the difference between mediocrity and accomplishment.

—Norman Vincent Peale

Responsibility

Employees with a sense of responsibility are committed and hold themselves accountable for their actions. Responsibility is exhibited when employees follow up on their commitments, do what they say they are going to do, have a sense of urgency, and go above and beyond what is expected of them.

Professionalism

Professionalism refers to high standards of performance and quality along with integrity and pride in the work. Employees with professionalism communicate openly and honestly, and they respect themselves and other people. They are persistent in achieving established goals without compromising quality or integrity.[9] Like a great painter or sculptor, they take pride in their craft.

1. If you were asked to create an attitude standard for a team or work group, what elements would you include?

____

2. Pick one of the items listed above, and explain how you would measure or assess your employees to determine if they were meeting the standard.

____

Creativity and Innovation

Some people distinguish between creativity and innovation by defining creativity as generating new ideas, new ways to combine things, or new ways to do things and innovation as using the creative ideas to develop new products and services and to implement new ways of doing things. Some people think of creativity as an internal concept—the process of thinking and generating ideas—and of innovation as an external concept—implementing the creative ideas. This textbook uses the terms interchangeably, and it defines them as **creativity/innovation**: the ability to generate and implement new ideas to support the organization's mission and goals.

Core Values to Support Innovation

Creativity expert Judith Estrin describes five core values of people and organizations that must work in balance to support innovation. In an interview, Estrin said, "Everybody I interviewed [for her book, *Closing the Innovation Gap*], every company I've built or been part of, everybody I've met who is really innovative as a leader or as an individual contributor, has these values." The values are questioning, risk, openness, patience, and trust.[10]

- **Questioning**—Curiosity drives innovation. It typically starts with questions such as, How can I do this better? Why doesn't this work? or Could I think about this differently? Questions should be framed broadly and should not be judgmental.
- **Risk**—Risk is the ability to let yourself be vulnerable and to fail. Failure should be perceived as a lesson to learn from and a step toward success.
- **Openness**—Openness means being ready to imagine, collaborate, and change. It also means being receptive to surprises and others' ideas.
- **Patience**—This is the tenacity to stick with ideas, a process, or a product, especially in the early developmental stages.
- **Trust**—Trust is necessary for people to let themselves be vulnerable or take risks.

Estrin points out that the five core values are intertwined. Having just one or two is not sufficient; they all go together in a comprehensive package.[11]

creativity/innovation
the ability to generate and implement new ideas to support the organization's mission and goals

Igniting a Creative Spark

Often when managers are trying to get employees to think creatively, they challenge them to think outside the box. This is another way of asking people to do something new or different than they are currently doing. A management consultant who specializes in creativity explains as follows:

> Creativity is a function of knowledge, imagination, and evaluation. The greater our knowledge, the more ideas, patterns, or combinations we can achieve. But, merely having knowledge does not guarantee the formation of new patterns; the bits and pieces must be shaken up and interrelated in new ways. Then, the embryonic ideas must be evaluated and developed into usable ideas.[12]

In the opening interview, Susan Cotter emphasizes the influence the work environment has on creativity. To be creative, employees must have the freedom to think, to make suggestions, to make mistakes, and to be bold in their approach.

When people are doing work that they love and they're allowed to deeply engage in it—and when the work itself is valued and recognized—then creativity will flourish.

— Teresa Amabile, professor of business administration at Harvard University

Identifying general types of creativity is easier than explaining the mental process. One pioneering writer on the subject isolated three overlapping domains of creativity: art, discovery, and humor.[13] These have been called the "ah!" reaction, the "aha!" reaction, and the "ha-ha!" reaction, respectively.[14] The discovery ("aha!") domain is most relevant to management. Entirely new products and businesses can spring from creative imagination and innovation.

Workplace Creativity: Myth and Reality

Research has shattered a long-standing myth about creative employees. According to the myth, creative people are eccentric nonconformists. But Alan Robinson's field research paints a very different picture. As reported in *Management Review,* Robinson concluded that "only three out of the 600 [innovators studied] were true nonconformists. The rest were more like your average corporate Joe, much more 'plodding and cautious' than most managers would expect."[15] Thus, creative self-expression through unconventional dress, extreme body art, and strange behavior does not necessarily translate into creative work and marketable products.

Today's managers are challenged to create an organizational culture and climate capable of bringing to the surface the often hidden creative talents of *every* employee. In the Internet age, when intellectual capital is the number-one resource, the emphasis is on having fun in high-energy work environments. For example, as a vice president and general manager at Dell, Theresa Garza sought to generate enthusiasm and encourage employees to invest their creative energy in their work. Garza observed, "It's people who have momentum, who are working hard, and who are excited to be here."[16]

Learning to Be More Creative

Some people seem to be more creative than others. But that does not mean that people cannot develop their creative capacity. It does seem clear that creative ability can be learned, in the sense that our creative energy can be released from the bonds of convention, lack of self-confidence, and narrow thinking. We all have the potential to be more creative.

Creative ability can be learned.

The best place to begin is by trying consciously to overcome what creativity specialist Roger von Oech calls *mental locks*.[17] The following mental locks are attitudes that get us through our daily activities, but tend to stifle our creativity:

1. *Looking for the right answer.* Depending on one's perspective, a given problem may have several right answers.
2. *Always trying to be logical.* Logic does not always prevail, given human emotions and organizational inconsistencies, ambiguity, and contradictions.
3. *Strictly following the rules.* If things are to be improved, arbitrary limits on thinking and behavior need to be questioned.
4. *Insisting on being practical.* Impractical answers to "what-if" questions can become the stepping-stones to creative insights.
5. *Avoiding ambiguity.* Creativity can be stunted by too much objectivity and specificity.
6. *Fearing and avoiding failure.* Fear of failure can paralyze us into not acting on our good ideas. This is unfortunate because we learn many valuable and lasting lessons from our mistakes.[18]
7. *Forgetting how to play.* The playful experimentation of childhood too often disappears by adulthood.
8. *Becoming too specialized.* Cross-fertilization of specialized areas helps to define problems and generate solutions.
9. *Not wanting to look foolish.* Humor can release tensions and unlock creative energies. Seemingly foolish questions can enhance understanding.
10. *Saying, "I'm not creative."* By nurturing small and apparently insignificant ideas, we can convince ourselves that we are indeed creative.[19]

A change in routine can spark creativity. For instance, try reading a different newspaper or magazine.

If you and your employees can conquer these mental locks, then you can encourage the creative process in the workplace. However, the concept of thinking outside the box requires employees to take a step back and look at the big picture first by answering the question, What are the mission and goals?

Then, let the fun begin! By looking at the organization, its customers, challenges, or day-to-day tasks with a different perspective, employees can come up with all kinds of new ideas. Some of these ideas may grow, while others may be considered too outrageous or unrealistic (at least for now). Start by encouraging employees to think outside the box, and give them time to do so.

1. Do you agree or disagree with the assertion that creative ability can be learned? Explain.

____

2. Describe a time when you experienced a mental block or had a difficult time generating ideas. What steps did you take (or should you have taken) to get beyond the block or to generate ideas?

____

Creating a Positive Work Environment

The common wisdom is that job satisfaction results in higher productivity. Yet decades of research show that the correlation of job satisfaction to productivity is very modest. In fact, Lyman W. Porter and Edward E. Lawler, two respected motivation researchers, found that job satisfaction is the result of performance rather than the cause of it.[20] A positive work environment has many benefits—especially with less absenteeism and employee turnover. A **positive work environment** is one in which satisfied employees achieve organizational goals with less turnover and absenteeism.

> Job satisfaction is the result of performance rather than the cause of it.

Managers can do a host of things to create a positive work environment. They can (1) model and promote social responsibility; (2) develop fair and equitable personnel policies and procedures; (3) celebrate achievement; (4) allow employees to have a voice; (5) make learning, creativity, and innovation part of the culture; and (6) make employee and customer satisfaction a way of life. Keep in mind that these steps may not all be feasible or appropriate for your work environment.

positive work environment
an environment in which satisfied employees achieve organizational goals with less turnover and absenteeism

Model and Promote Social Responsibility

When Sirota Survey Intelligence polled 1.6 million workers in a study of corporate social responsibility, they found that 70 percent of respondents believed their organization was socially responsible. Among those employees, 71 percent viewed their senior managers as having high integrity, 75 percent saw their employers as interested in their well-being, and 86 percent experienced high levels of engagement in their jobs. Researchers concluded there is a correlation between employees' satisfaction and their perception of the company's social responsibility.[21]

> There is a correlation between employees' satisfaction and their perception of the company's social responsibility.

Develop Fair and Equitable Personnel Policies and Procedures

Human resources professionals, managers, and supervisors will tell you that employee pay and performance appraisals are confidential. However, the reality is that employees will gossip. Therefore, it is essential to have well-documented personnel policies and procedures that are fair and equitable for all employees. They should include a policy that ties employees' salaries, bonuses, and promotions to performance. These items should also be consistent with the contribution the employee makes to the organization.[22] This approach requires that policies and procedures recognize and reward employees for exceptional performance, while not penalizing those who are good—but not great—workers. Employees' *perceptions* about personnel policies are important. Therefore, it is worth the extra time to meet with employees to explain policies and procedures, invite their input and suggestions, and answer their questions.

Celebrate Achievement

Another way to foster a positive work environment is to celebrate success. You do not have to wait for the organization or your team to achieve a major milestone. As noted in Chapter 6, it is great for team morale to celebrate the completion of an incremental goal, no matter how small. In addition, it is a nice boost to employees' self-esteem and confidence when they are recognized for their contributions and/or for reaching personal goals.

Chapter 9 pointed out that celebrations should be in line with the accomplishment. If the team achieves a reasonable goal, it may be appropriate to provide a team luncheon. How you choose to celebrate will depend on your company, your budget, you, and your employees. What is meaningful and valued as a reward for one person may mean a lot less to another. It is important to learn what motivates each individual employee as you plan to celebrate and reward performance.

It is important to learn what motivates each employee.

Allow Employees to Have a Voice

Listen to your employees. They are the front line of your organization, and they typically have the most contact with your customers. As a result, they understand what your customers like and dislike. In addition, they have great insight into what is efficient and effective about organizational policies and procedures. Yet, managers often feel they need to have all the answers and do not invite those who report to them to share their ideas. By listening to your employees, you will ultimately end up with better ideas that will be implemented with greater success because your employees were part of the process. In addition, your employees will be happier because they will feel they are contributing and making a difference. This increases their sense of worth to the organization and is a source of pride and self-confidence. You want your employees to know you value and respect their opinions.

You may not agree with all your employees' ideas and opinions. However, it is still important to let them share what they are thinking. Even if you disagree, you are giving them the chance to be heard, and they are giving you the chance to explain your decisions. Being open, honest, and up-front with employees will earn their respect. Inviting their input and giving them credit where credit is due will demonstrate your respect for them.

Managers earn respect when they give credit where credit is due.

Listening and responding to suggestions from employees and customers was the key to winning.

—Shelly Reese, *USA Today*, referring to Baldrige Award winner Wainwright Industries

Make Learning, Creativity, and Innovation Part of the Culture

Work specialization usually leads to efficiency and quality, but it can also turn talented employees into bored, unengaged workers. Allowing them to learn new skills or gain new knowledge can keep them interested and challenged. Encouraging creativity and innovation is another way to keep employees interested. In addition, fostering an environment where employees feel safe trying new things will lead to discovery and innovation, but it also may lead to failures because not every new idea actually works. Allowing people to learn from their mistakes in an effort to generate new ideas is a common characteristic of successful and creative organizations.

1. What do you think are the benefits to an organization that permits mistakes?

   ____

2. What do you think are the drawbacks or potential risks to an organization that permits mistakes?

   ____

Make Employee and Customer Satisfaction a Way of Life

Some companies focus on customer satisfaction, while others focus on employee satisfaction. Making both part of the organization's culture increases the odds of having a positive working environment. Organizations focusing on employee satisfaction share the philosophy that a happy workforce will take good care of the customer. In comparison, companies focusing on customer satisfaction believe that if their employees are doing a good job, both customers and employees will be happy. Both approaches are valid and have worked for very successful companies. Still, when you combine them, it creates a powerful force that ultimately can lead to loyal customers and loyal employees.

Creating a Productive Work Environment

Creating a productive work environment involves many factors. Some of the key ones are managing time, meetings, and space and facilities; focusing on health and wellness; managing systems and procedures; and organizing for efficiency and effectiveness. Managers and employees are jointly responsible for many of these factors.

Time Management

Everybody has exactly the same amount of time each day, but some people are more productive than others because they make better use of their time. Each person needs to look at time in a holistic way. People must manage both personal time and work time because invariably one affects the other. The real challenge is to strike a productive and satisfying balance between work and personal time.

Managers should make a concerted effort to encourage and help employees balance work and personal time. Many companies offer alternative work schedules as discussed in Chapter 8, and most will work with employees to vary schedules for special needs. For example, they may allow employees to work at home when a child is sick or to work flexible hours in order to attend a special family or personal event. This approach tends to reduce stress and prevent employees from feeling guilty about missing significant events in their personal lives.

time management
the process of identifying what needs to be done and having a plan to accomplish it within the time allotted

The goal is to be sure the work gets done, while also providing employees with flexibility to manage their lives. In many cases, it does not matter where or what time of day the work gets done, as long as it is high-quality and on time.

Time management is the process of identifying what needs to be done and having a plan to accomplish it within the time allotted. Good time management requires people to be honest with themselves in recognizing their "time wasters" and minimizing these interruptions. Chapter 3 provided a list of time management tips for administrators and supervisors—ways to work efficiently on the job. General keys to effective time management include the following:

- Establish effective goals with clearly defined tasks, timelines, and due dates.
- Schedule time for daily planning. This includes planning for work-related as well as personal goals and activities.
- Prioritize your "to-do" list. Each day brings new challenges, which often require a change in plans. It is important to take time to revisit your original plan and re-prioritize the list.

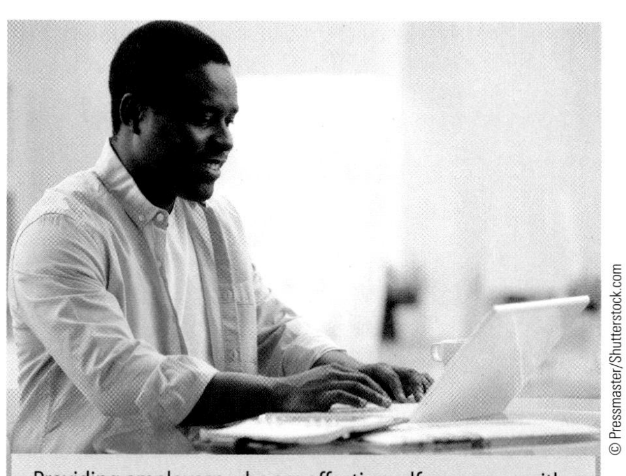

Providing employees who are effective self-managers with the flexibility to work at home or in another remote location often enhances productivity.

- Focus your investment of time on essential and important tasks and activities.
- Eliminate or minimize time wasters such as interruptions and inefficient procedures. Review the tips in Chapter 3 for ideas.
- Get organized! By organizing your office, schedule, activities, and home life, you will become more efficient and feel more in control.

If you never seem to have enough time, keep a time journal for a week. Record what you do throughout each day. The simple act of recording your daily activities will raise your awareness about how you are spending your time. This insight is a key first step toward regaining control of your time and refocusing your priorities and goals.

LEVERAGING TECHNOLOGY

USE TECHNOLOGY WISELY

The latest technology hyped in the media often leads people to purchase and implement gadgets without considering the trade-offs. A goal in reducing stress is to use technology to work more efficiently, but not to let it consume or control you. For example, consider the common wireless devices that serve as a cell phone, media player, and computer. They allow users to text-message, phone, and exchange email from just about anywhere at any time. High-performing employees often feel they cannot turn off these devices because they may miss an important message. (Ask smartphone users if they could live without it for a week.) However, this attitude creates a 24/7 employee who is always on the job. The brain needs a break—and so do your employees. Create policies and procedures that encourage people to turn off their work-related technology unless they are working or are scheduled to be on call or available for a special project.

In addition, evaluate information technology tools to identify solutions that may make your job and/or life easier or more efficient. Before implementing any new technology, consider the positive impacts it will have, and balance them against any negatives.

1. Describe a period in your life when you felt you were in complete control of your time. You had sufficient time for work, school, family, recreation, and other interests. What were the keys to your success in managing your time?

2. What steps can you take today to improve your time management?

Meeting Management

Administrative managers spend a high percentage of their time preparing for meetings, in meetings, and following up on meetings. Both face-to-face and technology-facilitated meetings are often necessary for making decisions, sharing information, coordinating work, solving problems, and other purposes. However, when the same objectives can be accomplished with email or a telephone call, much time and money can be saved by not having a meeting. Managers should schedule meetings only when they are truly needed and should take steps to ensure they are effective. Effective meetings result from careful planning (both logistical and strategic), conducting the meeting effectively, and following up on action items. Figure 11.1 provides an overview of the four phases in the meeting process.

Effective meetings result from planning carefully, conducting the meeting effectively, and following up on action items.

FIGURE 11.1
Overview of meeting process

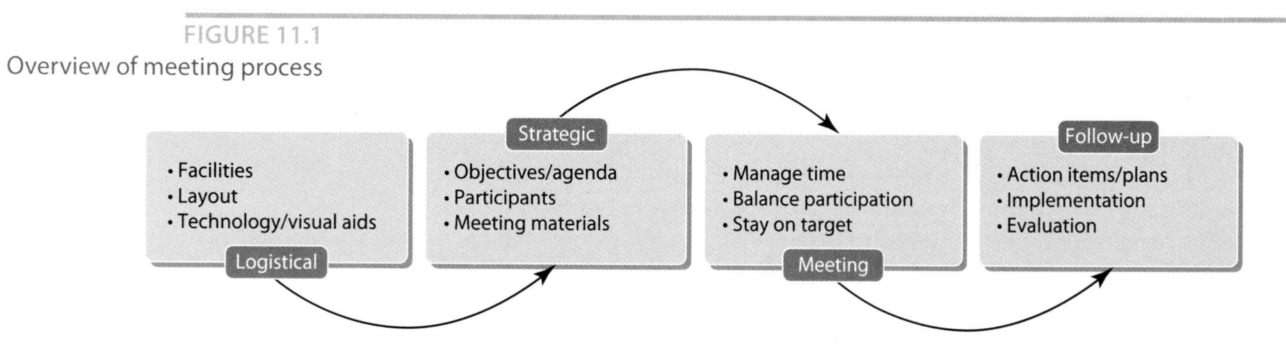

Planning the Meeting: Logistical Phase

Often, the planning phases determine the ultimate success of meetings. Facilities can have a significant influence, particularly on long meetings. Comfort factors include seating, temperature control, and beverages and food if appropriate. The size of the group and purpose of the meeting determine the best room size and layout (Figure 11.2 on page 254).

FIGURE 11.2
Meeting room layouts

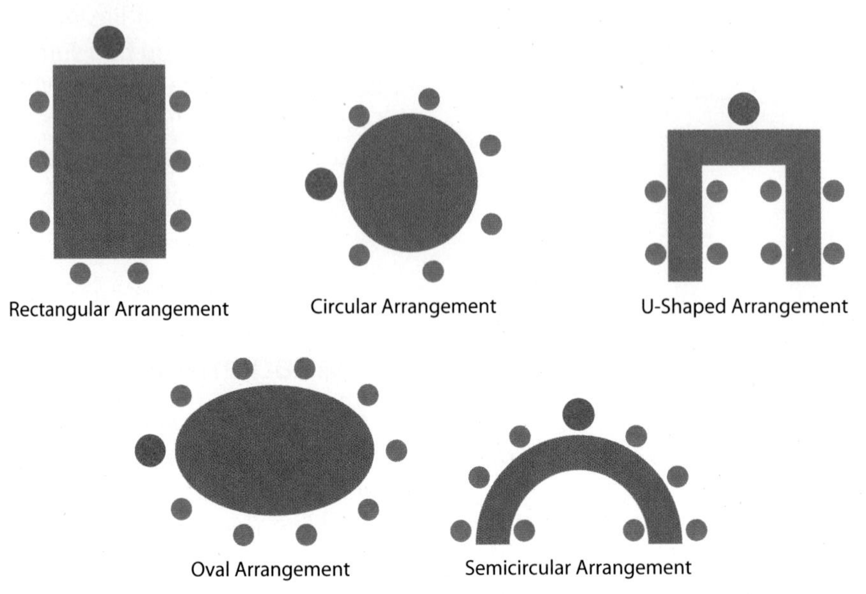

- The rectangular arrangement is a good choice for formal meetings. In this arrangement, the leader sits at the head of the table.
- The circular and oval arrangements work well for relatively informal meetings and discussions in small groups.
- The u-shaped and semicircular arrangements facilitate discussion and the use of visual aids, which can be positioned at the front.

In choosing visual aids (electronic presentations, white boards, flip charts, etc.), the manager should consider the meeting objectives, room size, and setup. All participants must be able to see visual aids clearly.

Planning the Meeting: Strategic Phase

The key to a successful meeting is to determine the specific objectives or outcomes and then set the agenda to accomplish them. The **agenda** provides an outline of the topics to be discussed, the person presenting each topic, and in many companies the amount of time allocated for each topic.

The manager should select participants carefully. A common mistake is not including the individuals who will actually do a particular task or project. Instead, the manager delegates the project to those individuals once plans are finalized. Although they receive a briefing, it does not always include many of the details essential for understanding the project and meeting expectations.

agenda
an outline of the topics to be discussed, the person presenting each topic, and the time allocated for each topic

Advance preparation plays an important role in the effectiveness of meetings and the time required for them. The manager should send participants the agenda and any documents for review several days before the meeting. The cover letter, memo, or email should restate the start and end times and should clarify or remind participants of any work to be completed in preparation.

Conducting the Meeting

The leader's responsibilities are to start and end the meeting on time, keep the discussion focused on the objectives, and ensure all participants are engaged in the discussion. Before the meeting concludes, the leader should review and note all items needing future action, the people responsible, and the relevant timelines. Participants' responsibilities include arriving on time and being prepared to discuss all agenda items. Participants also need to focus on the objectives and should not allow themselves to be distracted by items such as smartphones, side conversations, or topics outside the agenda.

Following Up on Action Items

Action minutes should be prepared and sent to all participants. **Action minutes** are a brief summary of all items needing action, the people responsible, and the timeline. Additional follow-up may be required to ensure all actions have been completed and, if not, to determine what needs to be done to accomplish them. Finally, the manager should take a few minutes after each meeting to evaluate it. Good questions to ask include the following:

- Were the objectives accomplished?
- Did we adhere to the time frame?
- How can future meetings be made more efficient and effective?

Space and Facilities Management

First-line managers rarely have the opportunity to plan and design new facilities, but they are often asked to manage current facilities. Their specific responsibilities depend on the size of the company. Medium- to large-sized companies usually have dedicated facility managers with technical expertise who oversee all aspects of the facility. First-line managers and managers in small companies are often involved in allocating space within a department, deciding how to position work groups to enhance performance, managing furniture and equipment replacements, and handling similar responsibilities. However, it is important for all first-line managers to understand the impact of the physical workplace on communication, productivity, and costs.

The *Wall Street Journal* cited the findings of a 2010 survey by the International Facility Management Association reporting that 68 percent of U.S. offices have an "open plan" or "open seating" design, with desks separated by low or no walls. Frequently, the remaining offices and conference rooms have glass walls. According to employers, these arrangements improve communication and collaboration, encourage teamwork and creativity, reduce real estate and energy costs, and provide more natural light and outdoor views for all employees.[23] However, various studies cite negative aspects of open-plan designs such as lack of privacy, lower productivity, and lower job satisfaction.[24]

action minutes
a brief summary of all items needing action, the people responsible, and the timeline

Many offices have guidelines on what can be displayed on desks or walls of open offices if outsiders frequently visit. Some companies make conference rooms available near the lobby for meetings with customers, clients, and other visitors. It is important for managers to discuss issues that arise from working in an open environment with employees and get their input. If employees can find a workable solution to problems, it is usually better accepted than a management directive.

Health and Wellness

News articles report frequently on the rapidly rising costs of health care and the unhealthful eating and exercise habits of the general population of the United States. Increasingly, employers are supporting and promoting healthful lifestyles and wellness. According to Andy Goldstein of the National Association of State Boards of Accountancy, "Corporate wellness programs are part of a growing trend to fight not only obesity in the U.S., but the skyrocketing cost of medical care and insurance premiums." He cites statistics from the American Institute for Preventative Medicine: 91 percent of organizations offer some type of health promotion program today, versus only 78 percent ten years ago.[25]

Corporate wellness programs are part of a growing trend.

For a number of years, companies viewed workplace wellness programs as a nice, but too costly, benefit for employees. However, current research shows these programs are a good investment. The Wellness Council of America cites the following research results:

- Several scientific reviews indicate that worksite health promotion programs reduce medical costs and absenteeism and produce a positive return on investment.
- The most definitive review of financial impact reported the following:
  - 18 studies indicated that these programs reduce medical costs, and 14 studies indicated that they reduce absenteeism costs.
  - 13 studies calculated benefit/cost ratios and all showed the savings from these programs are much greater than their cost, with medical cost savings averaging $3.48 and the absenteeism savings averaging $5.82 per dollar invested in the programs.[26]

Professors Ann Mirabito and Leonard Berry, and William Baun, manager of a wellness program and a director of the National Wellness Institute and International Association for Worksite Health Promotion, conducted extensive research on workplace wellness programs. They found these programs benefit organizations through lower health care costs, greater productivity, and higher morale, and organizations do not have to spend much money on them. Mirabito and her colleagues identify six elements that will help companies establish a successful wellness program:

1. Encourage leadership at all levels of the company. Managers should model healthful behaviors.

2. Align the program with the organization's core values and priorities.
3. Provide scope, relevance, and quality.
4. Ensure accessibility. Offer services onsite at little or no cost.
5. Create partnerships. Pick up expertise and infrastructure quickly with internal and external partners, such as local gyms.
6. Communicate effectively. Be sensitive and creative in promoting the program.[27]

Wellness programs raise two cautions for managers. First, effective programs are voluntary. Second, health information provided to the company is private and cannot be disclosed to others or used in a discriminatory manner.

1. If your company offered a workplace wellness program, would you participate? Why or why not?

___

2. Would a comprehensive wellness program be a retention factor for you? Why or why not?

___

Systems and Procedures Management

Systems management normally relates to manufacturing and production settings; however, the concept can be applied to an office setting. As noted earlier, a system is a set of parts that work together to accomplish a common purpose or goal. Managers should look for connections between the different parts of an organization to create synergy.[28] For example, if one department is planning a software training program, including other departments with similar needs would save substantial time and money. The same concept applies to creating employee handbooks. As you learned in Chapter 5, synergy is the idea that the whole exceeds the sum of its parts, called the "peanut butter and chocolate effect" by some.

Company policies and procedures are also important in improving quality and increasing productivity. In administrative settings, **standard operating procedures** (SOPs) are used frequently. Standard operating procedures are guides that specify the way an organization wants its employees to do their jobs. In an office setting, SOPs might include a style guide that illustrates document formats and explains rules for use of company branding. High-performing employees usually embrace SOPs because they have to ask fewer questions and have more opportunities to work independently with limited supervision.

standard operating procedures
guides that specify the way an organization wants its employees to do their jobs

Organization for Efficiency and Effectiveness

Efficiency refers to doing a task the most productive way. Many people think of efficiency in terms of speed and time. **Effectiveness** refers to producing good-quality results in a timely fashion. Many people think of effectiveness in terms of working smarter rather than harder.

Managers can encourage effective work organization and provide training or tips for organizing workspaces, data and files, and offices. It is important to focus on organizing both online information and information in hard copy. However, employees have different work styles and preferences for how they function in their work environment. Ultimately, it is up to employees to organize their work and environment so they can be most productive.

efficiency
doing a task the most productive way

effectiveness
producing quality results in a timely fashion

Focusing on priorities and effective time management is closely related to work organization. For example, to save time, employees should handle a document (paper or electronic) only once by reading, responding, or taking appropriate action. Then they should store it. This reduces clutter on desks or in email or electronic document systems. Calendars and planners are excellent organizing tools.

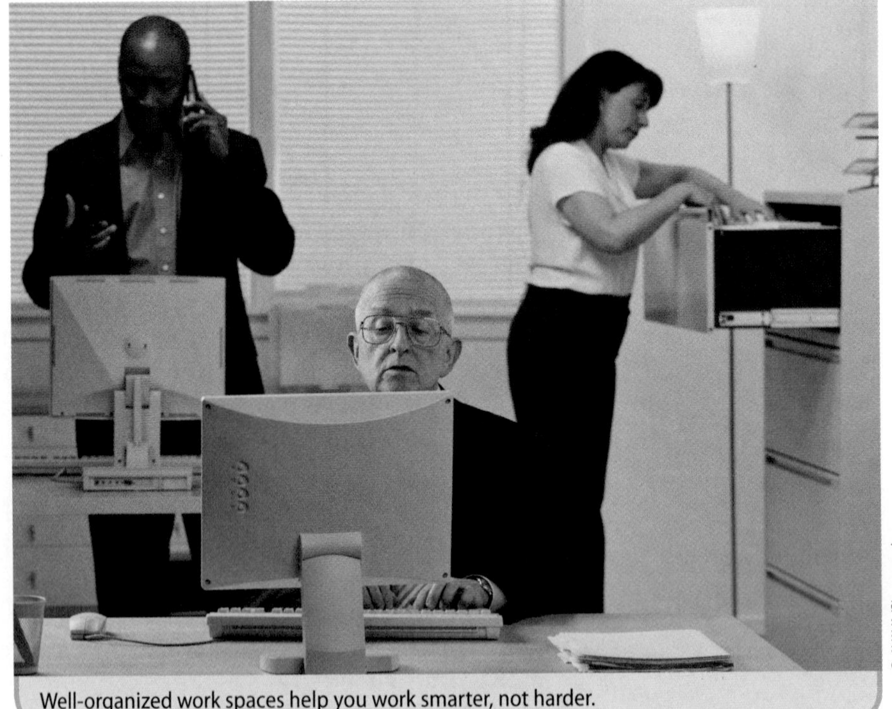

Well-organized work spaces help you work smarter, not harder.

© AVAVA/Shutterstock.com

SUMMARY

1. Corporate culture is a key factor in setting the tone and feel of the work environment.
2. Managers can enhance motivation by (1) understanding and satisfying employee goals of equity, achievement, and camaraderie; (2) promoting model employees; (3) providing growth opportunities; and (4) providing support to enhance progress.
3. An organizational attitude standard might include the characteristics of friendliness, positivism, teamwork, enthusiasm, responsibility, and professionalism.
4. The five core values needed to support innovation are questioning, risk, openness, patience, and trust.
5. Employees can begin learning to be more creative by overcoming mental locks, looking at the big picture (mission and goals), and striving for ideas. Managers can start the process by providing time and encouragement to think outside the box.
6. To create a positive work environment, managers can (1) model and promote social responsibility, (2) develop fair and equitable personnel policies and procedures, (3) celebrate achievement, (4) allow employees to have a voice, (5) make creativity and learning part of the corporate culture, and (6) make employee and customer satisfaction a way of life.
7. Steps that help create a productive work environment include managing time, meetings, space, and facilities; promoting health and wellness; managing systems and procedures; and organizing for efficiency and effectiveness.

Terms

action minutes, 255
agenda, 254
attitude standard, 243
creativity/innovation, 245
effectiveness, 258
efficiency, 258
motivation, 239
positive work environment, 248
standard operating procedures, 257
time management, 251

Study Tools

CourseMate
Located at www.cengagebrain.com

- Chapter Outlines
- Flashcards
- Interactive Quizzes
- Tech Tools
- Video Segments

and More!

Questions for Reflection

1. Why should managers consider corporate culture in setting employees up for success?
2. Do you think it is important for managers to encourage employee engagement in the community and giving back to the community? Why or why not?
3. Why is an attitude standard an important tool for managers to use and include in employee appraisals?
4. Do you think you are a creative person? What could you do to become more creative?
5. A key to creating a positive work environment is to try to balance day-to-day activities with some fun and creativity. If you were a manager, how would you accomplish this?
6. Think about meetings you have attended that were not productive. What would you suggest to make them more productive?
7. What role should managers play in helping employees achieve work/life balance?
8. Do you think it is your job as a manager to help employees develop healthful habits? Why or why not?

Hands-On Activities

Creativity/Innovation

Work in a team of four or five for this activity. Your manager has noticed that your team is exceptionally creative and has asked you to prepare a short presentation for your peers on creativity/innovation:

1. Review the Creativity and Innovation section on pages 245–247.
2. Have each team member read at least one additional article on creativity or innovation.
3. As a team, brainstorm to determine what advice would be the most helpful to share with your peers.
4. As a team, prepare an outline of the presentation.
5. (Optional) As a team, prepare *PowerPoint* slides for the presentation.

Visualization

1. Read the "Soft Skills for Success" feature on page 262.
2. Select an activity you would like to improve. It could be a physical activity, a process at work, or preparation for an interview, presentation, or similar activity. How will you measure your success? In other words, write down your description of what it will look like when you complete this activity successfully.
3. Visualize yourself doing it perfectly from beginning to end, including senses (sight, sound, touch) and feelings. Practice two or three times.
4. Actually do what you visualized.

You Decide | Case Study

Idea Generation

Matt is a supervisor for a regional economic development agency. His job has three main aspects: (1) attract businesses from other states to move to the area, (2) retain and help employers in the area, and (3) support aspiring entrepreneurs who want to start new businesses.

Matt's performance has always been measured based on the number of jobs and total revenue generated by the region's companies. Therefore, he spends most of his time trying to attract large businesses from other areas to move into the region. This strategy has worked for him in the past because large companies are more likely to have more jobs and higher revenue, which reflect nicely in his performance measures.

Recently, Gretchen was hired as the new regional director, and she has added another performance measure for Matt: total number of new businesses started in the region. Matt has never spent much time focusing on helping start-up companies. However, two of his employees, Kelly and Beth, previously worked for small business development councils in other cities. In addition, Matt's new boss, Gretchen, has prior experience working with entrepreneurs. Matt's first task is to prepare a list of possible outreach activities and education programs the agency can offer to help aspiring entrepreneurs successfully launch their businesses.

Questions

1. How would you suggest Matt get started generating ideas for possible outreach activities?
2. What are a few specific techniques Matt can use by himself to spark creative ideas?
3. What are a few specific techniques he can use to involve Kelly, Beth, and perhaps Gretchen?
4. How would you suggest he generate ideas for potential education topics that can help aspiring entrepreneurs?

MANAGER'S TOOLKIT

Fostering a positive work environment and encouraging creativity involve promoting a healthful, productive work environment. As you develop your managerial skills, you will learn how to inspire creativity, reduce stress, and improve team performance. Prepare a few documents to add to your manager's toolkit that outline tips and best practices for promoting health and wellness, reducing stress, and achieving work/life balance.

1. Most managers would like to reduce their employees' stress and absenteeism. One way to accomplish this is by improving their health and safety. Identify at least three ways to promote health and wellness at work.
2. Another factor that contributes to employee stress is balancing work with family/home. What are examples of corporate initiatives you would consider in an effort to help employees strike a balance?

Soft Skills for Success

Visualization

In Chapter 6, you learned about using visualization in setting and achieving goals. Visualization is a technique of focusing mentally on something you want to do or accomplish. By creating a mental picture and "practicing" what you want to do, you help the mind establish a positive view that you can accomplish it.

Sports training programs frequently include visualization as part of the training for an event. For example, a football player who wants to become a better receiver may visualize specific routes he wants to run effectively. He closes his eyes, relaxes, and visualizes the best route he runs—a fade. He visualizes the quarterback calling a fade and dropping back to pass, and he takes off running full-speed down the sideline toward the end zone. He ignores the crowd yelling wildly as the quarterback throws a long pass to him. He feels the presence of the defender right behind him and times a perfect jump to bring down the ball over the defender's outstretched arms. He hears the crowd roaring, watches the referee signal the touchdown, and feels the satisfaction of making a great play. He practices this process many times for his best routes.

The concept is often applied to business activities by visualizing how to improve a work process that is slowing down productivity or how to change a product to enhance it significantly. A person who fears making a presentation might rehearse it mentally from dressing properly all the way through the process to applause from the audience.

Stories abound about a legendary prisoner of war in Vietnam, Major James Nesmeth, who played a perfect mental round of golf each day during his seven-year imprisonment. After he was released, his first round of golf was about 20 strokes better than his average before he was imprisoned. While this account cannot be documented, many motivational speakers and writers have used it.[29] Zig Ziglar, a popular motivational seminar leader, describes the process as "the mind complet[ing] whatever picture we put in it." The example he uses is that if you place a 12-inch plank on the floor, you see yourself easily and safely walking it—your mind completing a positive outcome. But if that 12-inch plank is stretched between two buildings high in the air, you see yourself falling from it—your mind completing the negative outcome.[30]

Put It to Work

1. Think of a professional activity you would like to improve, such as making a presentation, conducting an effective meeting, or demonstrating how to use a new technology.
2. Determine what specific knowledge and skills this objective requires.
3. Describe in detail how you would visualize yourself successfully doing this activity.

CHAPTER

12

Project Management

Learning Outcomes

1. Explain how projects can be created and authorized.
2. Describe what the scope of the project means and how risk is managed.
3. List several factors that determine how project teams are formed.
4. Describe the initial or strategic project plan.
5. Explain why Gantt charts are so useful in project management.
6. Describe how the project operational plan differs from the initial or strategic project plan.
7. Describe the role of ground rules and team communication guides when a project is launched.
8. Describe who is accountable for monitoring and tracking a project from the time it is launched until it is terminated.
9. Describe the key things that must be accomplished to terminate a project successfully.

Straight Talk From the Field

Dan Hoover, PMP, is Chief Operating Officer (COO) of Cyberwoven, a web development company. Dan received formal training in project management while working in the Technology Group of BlueCross BlueShield. As COO of Cyberwoven, he manages 20 to 80 projects a year.

Printed by permission from Dan Hoover

Photo courtesy of D. Hoover

How important is software to managing projects effectively?

Over the years, I have used both general project management software, such as Microsoft Project, and more specialized software in the digital media space, such as Workamajig and Basecamp. However, software only takes you so far in managing a project. It is good for creating standardization and transparency, but the human side of project management is the critical element, and software cannot do that for you.

What are some of your greatest challenges in managing projects?

One of the biggest challenges is managing expectations. Often at the start, everyone seems to have a shared vision of what needs to happen, but over the course of a project two things always happen: The first is that as the project progresses, the vision begins to change and you realize everyone did not have the shared vision. Lack of clarity on vision, mission, and purpose can get a project off track after time and money has been expended. The second thing is managing uncertainty. If you have the luxury of having done the project before, you have an idea that it will follow a certain sequence. If you have not done the project before, questions like *how long will this take* or *what are some of the things we need to be on the lookout for* are a challenge. As a project manager, you have to create some structure around those problems to provide boundaries for the team.

The final major challenge is communication, particularly in keeping decision makers informed. Decision makers are in different categories—those who participate in the decision and those who don't but whose opinion matters. As an example of the latter category, a Board of Directors may not agree with the course a project is taking and decide to withhold the necessary approvals. The key is determining at the beginning who to communicate with, what to communicate, and how to best present the information—written, verbal, in person, or via technology.

How do you form effective teams?

You typically have two different types of teams. In some cases, employees work on a set team and when they finish one project, the same team goes to the next project. However, the majority of my project work has been where team members come together for a temporary assignment, and when the project is over, they go back to their regular work unit. Both can be effective. In the case of an established team, you have an understanding of how the various members work together, which is easier for the team leader. With an ad hoc team, the team dynamics are taking place for the first time on that project. This creates an immense amount of risk because you don't know how members work, their personalities, how they handle stress, their approach to their work, and their ability to estimate unknowns. As a project manager, you need to assess your team carefully and not assume too much.

What is the impact of facilities on teamwork?

We believe that having a more open office setting has a positive impact on teamwork. We actually have a hybrid setting so that all of the cubicles have doors and windows that open to peers to send the message, I am either open or closed for business. The challenge with open offices is that while you can communicate whenever you would like to, when you are focusing on a specific activity, you would prefer not to be interrupted.

The hybrid atmosphere with the open or closed window and door provides an opportunity for you to give visual signals of when you are ready to brainstorm on project ideas or when you are in a software development mode and an interruption might take you 45 minutes to get your mind back to the point where you were. Interruptions in software development can compromise productivity.

How does your company evaluate a team or a project?

I definitely think evaluation needs to occur throughout a project—primarily in the sense of feedback because it gives you the opportunity to change things as you go along. Evaluation at the end of a project is of less value except for future learning. I think the best approach is for the team members to be able to evaluate themselves and each other throughout the project. The team can take care of issues as they arise. It is also important to set expectations for each team member and performance measures at the front end of the project. Team members bring different skill sets and abilities to a project, and the entire team counts on each person performing at their best and on schedule. Lack of performance on the part of one team member can hold all other team members back. The final evaluation of a project is based on total performance. Evaluation is best conducted by team members because they know where the person is in relationship to goals, and peer pressure is much stronger than pressure from a team leader.

How do you develop a high-performance team?

The first thing to look at is whether to allow the team to shape the work versus dictating how the work should be done. Some of the constraints often make it difficult for the team to feel a sense of ownership. To create a high-performance team, you have to bring the project to them at the "why we are doing it" stage. Allowing the team to shape the *what* and giving them space to do what they know how to do creates an engaged team. In terms of performance, have sensitivity to what people like to do and try to align work with passions. When people do what they love and have the baseline competencies needed, the quality of working together is high. When you have a high-performing team you can focus on outputs rather than inputs. It is amazing what can happen when a team is really engaged and doing its best.

> When people do what they love and have the baseline competencies needed, the quality of working together is high.

What advice would you give a new team leader?

The most important thing is to listen first. Listening is critical to success of projects. Start by leading with questions rather than directives. By letting people express themselves, you learn more about what could and should happen than you ever could by leading with directives. The next thing is that the project manager must make sure that he or she understands the boundaries of the project—the scope, the timeline, the resources—and make sure that those are adhered to. Where they go from that point is best learned by listening and asking questions of those who are going to do the work. They are the experts.

Visit *www.cengagebrain.com* to read the complete profile.

Chapter Outline

Project management, a popular topic in industry today, is the sole focus of Chapter 12. A **project** is typically thought of as a defined set of tasks with specific outcomes that form a unit of work to be completed in a specified timeframe with specified resources. The opening interview describes some of the key issues in managing projects effectively. Dan Hoover, COO of Cyberwoven, discusses successful project management and teamwork in a technology environment. Effective project management relies on high-performance teams. It may be helpful to review the section on high-performance teams in Chapter 5 before beginning this chapter. This chapter focuses primarily on projects performed in an administrative setting.

Sources of Projects

In some industries and companies, employees spend almost all of their time working on projects. When they complete one project, they move to another one. Architecture, engineering, and construction firms are typical examples. In other cases, employees may work on several projects at one time. In many administrative management situations, employees may spend only a small part of their time working on an occasional project. For example, a small business may participate in two or three tradeshows a year. Each would be managed as a special project. Administrative employees in a bank or insurance company may work on a variety of projects such as developing a new product or service, creating content and format for a new standardized proposal, or organizing a retreat for the Board of Directors. A team usually handles most projects and is managed by a team leader.

project
a defined set of tasks with specific outcomes that form a unit of work to be completed in a specified timeframe with specified resources

Effective project management relies on high-performance teams.

Authority for Projects

Authority to do a project usually comes in one of two ways—the team or team leader proposes the project or senior management determines that a project needs to be done and assigns it to the appropriate team.

Proposed Projects

In some creative environments, a team may propose a project and get it approved. For example, a team may decide that new software would enhance its work significantly. The team may propose to senior management that it be allowed to investigate various software products available, evaluate the work that could be automated or ways that productivity could be enhanced, and determine the time and cost savings that could be achieved. In other situations, a team may propose a new or improved product or service.

Assigned Projects

Most projects are assigned or delegated to a team to complete. Unfortunately, higher-level managers frequently discuss a project for some period of time, and then after many decisions are made, assign the project to a team to complete. The project would more likely meet expectations if, at a minimum, the team leader has participated in all of the discussions. When the team leader is not involved in the early discussions, often a team will waste time and money considering options that were already discussed and eliminated.

Scope of the Project

The **project scope** is a definition of the objectives, everything that is included in the project, everything that is specifically excluded, and the outcomes that must be produced. The scope is sometimes referred to as the project specifications. The outcomes are often called the **deliverables**. Deliverables are defined, measurable results or tangible things that the customer, client, or your company expects to have at the completion of the project. It is always wise to get confirmation that you clearly understand what is expected from the managers who approved or assigned the project. Experienced project leaders will advise you to present a written, detailed scope of the project to the customer, client, or your managers and ask them to review and sign off on the scope of the project. With external customers or clients, often a formal written agreement is used to make sure that the customer or client and the company clearly understand what to expect. The final deadline for completing the project may or may not be specified at this stage.

project scope
the objectives, everything that is included, everything that is specifically excluded, and the outcomes that must be produced

deliverables
defined, measurable results or tangible things that the customer, client, or your company expects to have at the completion of the project

risk
the possibility of loss, damage, or adverse results

Project Risks

All projects have inherent risks that must be assessed. **Risk** is the possibility of loss, damage, or adverse results. However, when a team proposes and obtains approval for a project, the team should expect to be held to a higher level of accountability.

Assessing Risk

For any project, the first risk assessment may be done by the leader prior to the formation of the final team that will be responsible for the project. However, the entire team shares in the risk of a project and once a team has been formed, the entire team should be included in assessing the risks in the specific project. Team formation is discussed in the next section.

Most of you are familiar with the popular concept of *Murphy's Law*—which assumes that if anything can go wrong, it will and at the most inopportune time (original author unknown). *Murphy's Law* clearly applies to projects because the results are often based on a variety of estimates and assumptions—the estimate of time to complete the project, the estimate of the costs, the estimate of human resources needed, the assumption that other types of resources are available and can be obtained in a timely manner, and the assumption that most things will work as projected. To assess the risk, the best question to ask is what can go wrong with each aspect of the project.

All projects have inherent risks that must be assessed.

Prioritizing Risks

Assessing risk is only the first step. The next step is to think about what will be the adverse impact if something does go wrong. Some things that go wrong may be minor and result in a simple delay that affects only a small portion of the plan. Other things that happen may be major and could impact the entire project negatively. It is important to prioritize the risks inherent in the project. Once the risks have been assessed and prioritized, then the team needs to think about how to deal with the problems, starting with those having the potential for the greatest adverse impact on the project.

Contingency Planning

After prioritizing the risks, the team must think about how to react and develop plans for those things that do not go according to the original plan. As you learned in earlier chapters, these are called **contingency plans**. It is also important to consider ways that you might be able to prevent things from happening. If you are conscious of the risk in certain situations, precautionary steps may be taken to try to keep things from going wrong such as building more time into certain phases of the project, planning for cost overruns, and ordering inventory or supplies earlier than normal.

Forming the Team

A project team consists of a leader and a number of members. The team leader is generally appointed and must possess strong leadership and communication skills as well as the technical expertise required for the project. The team leader frequently has input in the selection of team members. An effective team leader is critical to the success of a project.

contingency plans
plans for those things that do not go according to the original plan

Team Size

Team size usually depends on the scope and complexity of the project. A general rule of thumb is that a large team working on a collaborative project is more challenging to manage than a small team working on the same project. In some cases, the team members are a leadership group that has the responsibility for getting things done through the staff that report to them.

Type of Team

The type of team also varies with the type of project. For example, a project designed to improve work processes within a department would have members selected from that department. Projects that affect different areas of an organization may require a **cross-functional team**—that is, a team that represents different functional areas because they add a different perspective. For example, a team working on a new product or service or improving a current product or service may consist of members from senior management, finance, legal, marketing or sales, and production as well as members with the technical expertise required. An example of an administrative project might be planning a three-day retreat for the Board of Directors for a small company such as a community bank. The project leader may be a manager from human resources, but the team would consist of representatives of the executive team and the strategic functions of the bank.

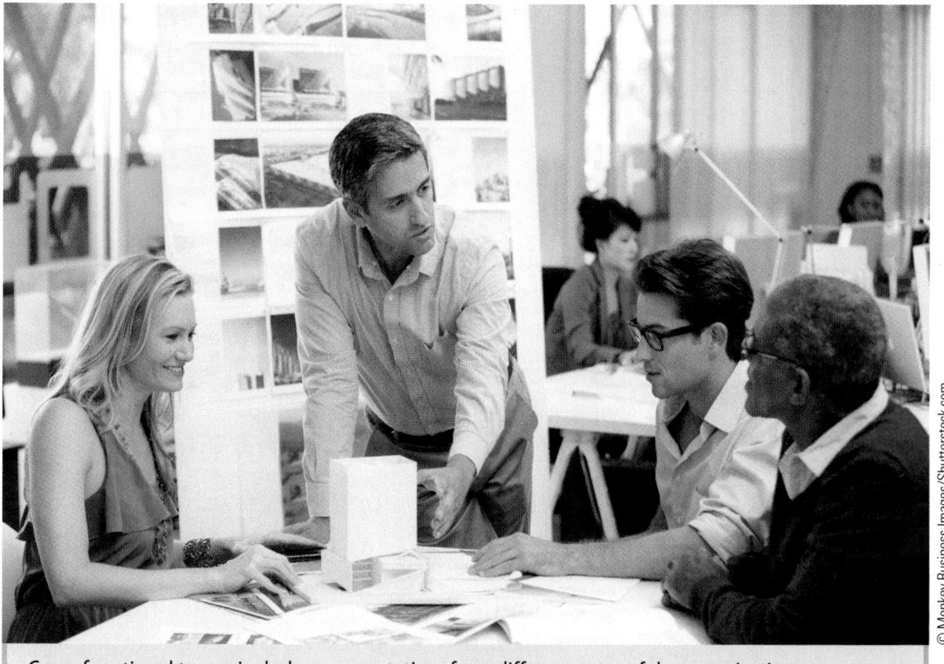

© Monkey Business Images/Shutterstock.com

Cross-functional teams include representatives from different areas of the organization.

cross-functional team
a team that represents different functional areas

For some projects, technical expertise and cognitive ability may be critical diversity factors that are required.

Previous chapters of this textbook have emphasized the importance of diversity on teams. Project teams need diversity based on a number of factors. As Martha Scott Smith pointed out in the "Straight Talk from the Field" interview in Chapter 7, diversity is far broader than race and gender. For some projects, technical expertise and cognitive ability may be critical diversity factors that are required.

Another factor to consider in forming a project team is whether the project is an internal project or an external project. At the conclusion of an external project, the deliverables of the project are presented to the client or customer for final approval. Once final approval is given, the project is completed. The situation is often different with internal projects. For example, if a team completes a project involving the development of new work processes and management approves the final work, the real challenge begins with implementing and integrating the new processes throughout a department or division. Therefore, it is important to include team members who will be responsible for the implementation and integration once the project has been completed.[1]

Once a team has been formed, the leader should involve the entire team in planning and making decisions about the project. All team members must be involved if they are to be held accountable for the final results.

1. If you were asked to lead a project team, would you prefer to have a team from your own department or a cross-functional team that represents the whole division or company? Explain the reasons for your selection.

   ____

2. What are your main strengths that would make you a good team leader?

   ____

Project Plan

The best way to think about the initial plan is to think of it as the strategic plan for the project. The team should review the scope of the project which defined the objectives and the deliverables of the project before proceeding with the planning and make sure the entire team understands what is expected.

Major Activities and Tasks

The next step in the plan should be to determine the major components (activities or tasks) and an estimate of the time required for each activity that must be completed to meet the objectives. If the final deadline was identified in the scope, the best approach may be to start at the final deadline and work backwards to determine the time available and whether the time estimates for doing each of the major components will fit in the time available for the total project.

Resources Required

The project components and the time estimates provide the information needed to determine the types and kinds of resources needed. Resources include the people (generally employees but consultants may also be used) needed to complete the project, the budget or financial resources, and, depending on the type of project, technology or equipment needed. Some team members may be located in other geographic areas, and technology-facilitated communications may be necessary. For projects completed within the department or work unit, both human and financial resources are easier to manage and control than for cross-functional projects which are controlled by other areas. The timeline may also affect the resources needed. If the time is compressed, more employees may be required to complete the project in a timely manner. Scheduling can become complicated. Some tasks can be done simultaneously but some need to be scheduled consecutively because they are dependent on other tasks being completed first.[2]

A Gantt chart is a good tool for monitoring a project.

Large or complicated projects can be quite a task to plan, schedule, and monitor. Gantt charts are frequently used to show graphically the order in which tasks need to be scheduled and the progress made toward completing a task. Resources—including human resources—can also be included in a Gantt chart, which is helpful in balancing team members' workload. A Gantt chart is also a good tool for monitoring a project.[3]

Figure 12.1 provides an example of a Gantt chart that illustrates the scheduling of a software development project.

FIGURE 12.1
Gantt Chart

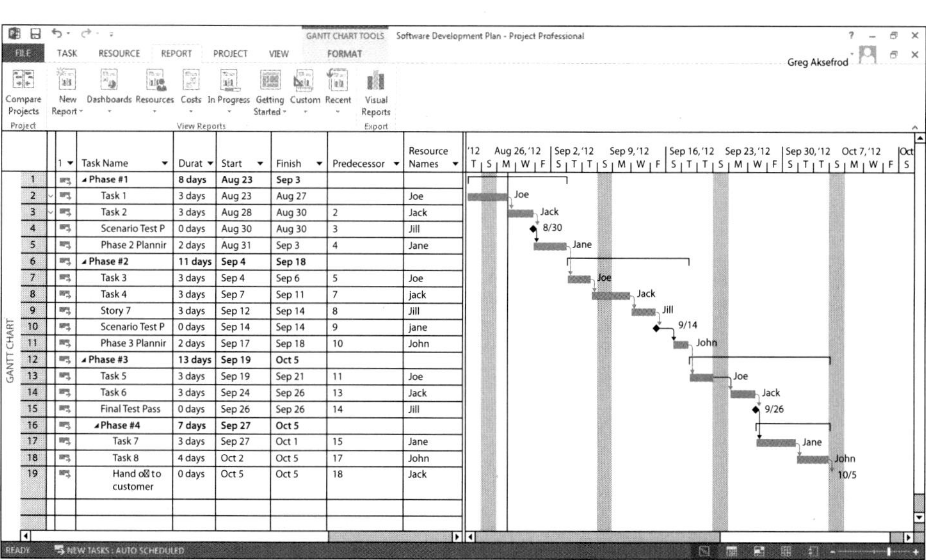

	Task Name	Duration	Start	Finish	Predecessor	Resource Names
1	Phase #1	8 days	Aug 23	Sep 3		
2	Task 1	3 days	Aug 23	Aug 27		Joe
3	Task 2	3 days	Aug 28	Aug 30	2	Jack
4	Scenario Test P	0 days	Aug 30	Aug 30	3	Jill
5	Phase 2 Plannir	2 days	Aug 31	Sep 3	4	Jane
6	Phase #2	11 days	Sep 4	Sep 18		
7	Task 3	3 days	Sep 4	Sep 6	5	Joe
8	Task 4	3 days	Sep 7	Sep 11	7	jack
9	Story 7	3 days	Sep 12	Sep 14	8	Jill
10	Scenario Test P	0 days	Sep 14	Sep 14	9	jane
11	Phase 3 Plannir	2 days	Sep 17	Sep 18	10	John
12	Phase #3	13 days	Sep 19	Oct 5		
13	Task 5	3 days	Sep 19	Sep 21	11	Joe
14	Task 6	3 days	Sep 24	Sep 26	13	Jack
15	Final Test Pass	0 days	Sep 26	Sep 26	14	Jill
16	Phase #4	7 days	Sep 27	Oct 5		
17	Task 7	3 days	Sep 27	Oct 1	15	Jane
18	Task 8	4 days	Oct 2	Oct 5	17	John
19	Hand off to customer	0 days	Oct 5	Oct 5	18	Jack

Source: Microsoft, Project Professional are either registered trademarks or trademarks of Microsoft Corporation in the United States and/or other countries.

The critical path is simply the series of tasks that controls the start and finish date of the project. When the last task in the critical path is complete, the project is also complete.

— Sonia Atchison, Technical Writer, Microsoft

Source: "Back to Basics: Let's talk about the critical path," Microsoft 2010 Project Blogs, July 9, 2009.

Another function of a Gantt chart or of project software is to show what is called the **critical path**. The critical path refers to mapping the tasks that impact the completion date of a project. In calculating the critical path you consider the time required to complete the tasks and the resources you have to monitor to ensure they stay on schedule. Calculating the critical path can be automated with project software. Sonia Atchison, Technical Writer at Microsoft, simplified the concept as shown in her quote above.

Figure 12.2 shows work and tasks completed and the remaining work and tasks to be completed.

FIGURE 12.2
Burndown Chart

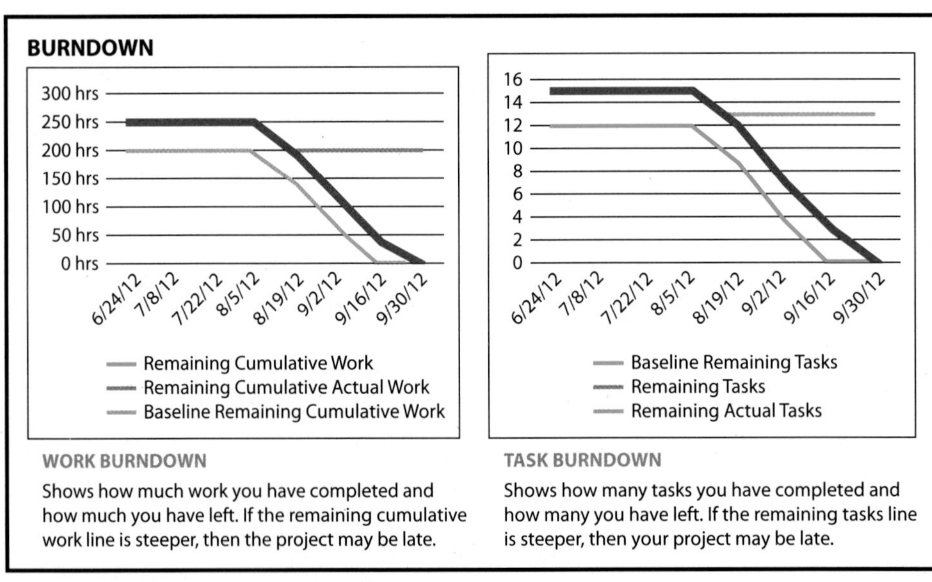

Source: Microsoft, Project Professional are either registered trademarks or trademarks of Microsoft Corporation in the United States and/or other countries.

This view shows at a glance the work and the number of tasks that have been completed and those that still need to be completed. It helps to project whether the project is on schedule or if it is likely to be late.

critical path
mapping the tasks that impact the completion date of a project

Figure 12.3 illustrates using a digital notebook to manage a small project for a client. This illustration using OneNote software, which is part of the Microsoft Office suite, shows the tabs used to plan and manage a trade

FIGURE 12.3
Digital Notebook

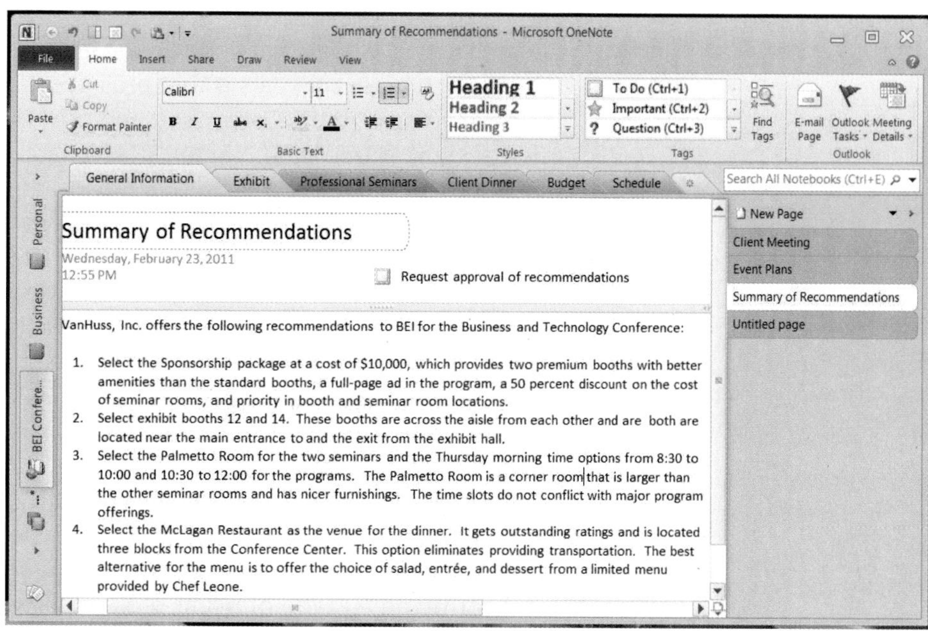

Source: Microsoft, OneNote are either registered trademarks or trademarks of Microsoft Corporation in the United States and/or other countries.

show project for a client. A team of six people will plan the project and be on site to coordinate and manage all activities. The notebook can be shared using a server or cloud-based services so that the team members and the client can access it whenever information is needed.

Project Operational Plan

Once the high-level or strategic plan for the project has been completed, it is wise to present it to management (or in the case of an external plan, to the client). This will ensure that all key components are included and the resources required are available as needed. The next step is to prepare a project operational plan. In preparing this plan, team members break down the key components to include all the tasks that have to be performed, the timing and sequence of the tasks, and a confirmation that resources are available to complete the project.

Again, it is critical that the entire team participate in developing the operational plan and in reevaluating the risk assessment and contingency plans. A diverse team is more likely to discover things that may have been missed in the earlier plan and to evaluate both the human and financial resources needed to be effective. It is better to detect problems at this stage than to start the plan and find out much later that major adjustments need to be made. If significant changes in the plan are needed, they should be brought to the attention to the appropriate stakeholders before launching the project.

LEVERAGING TECHNOLOGY

PROJECT SOFTWARE

Gantt charts have been used for many years to simplify project scheduling. What has changed in recent years is that project software automates and simplifies the development of the Gantt chart and provides many other tools for project management. Numerous commercial software packages are available to plan, schedule, and monitor projects. Some packages are customized for particular industries such as construction or specific types of projects. The complexity of the software and the cost vary significantly. The *Microsoft Project* software was selected for illustration because it is part of the Microsoft Office software application suite. It is basic software that works well for small businesses and many types of projects in office situations. Most people in the administrative area are already familiar with using products in that suite such as *Excel* and *PowerPoint*. *Project* uses the same Fluent interface and many of the same commands that the other applications use.

The *OneNote* illustration was selected because many administrative managers already have the software but may not be aware of its value for projects. *OneNote* is a part of the Microsoft Office Professional suite.

Another advantage of using project software is that graphic representations of plans and status of completion that can easily be shared helps to enhance communication among team members. It also aids the preparation of status reports to management.

Launching the Project

It may seem that an inordinate amount of time is spent on the planning stages. The actual amount of time will depend on the size and complexity of the project. Regardless of the amount of time spent on planning, it will probably be one of the best investments made during the entire project.

By involving the team members in the planning stages, each one has ownership of the project and is responsible for contributing to its successful completion. A number of things need to be accomplished at the time the project is launched.

Ground Rules

It is important to set the expectation that a high-performance team is critical to complete the project successfully. **Project ground rules** are often described as the behavior expected of each member as the members interact as a team. Each member must understand the team goals as well as the specific, individual goals for which each member will be held accountable. Each team member is expected to do his or her own fair share of work. This also means that each member must be empowered and controls his or her own responsibilities.

1. Describe some of the ground rules you think are important to establish.

   ____

2. Should team members participate in establishing the ground rules? Why or why not?

   ____

Team Communication

In the planning stages, team members generally meet to brainstorm ideas and to discuss the issues related to the project. Once the actual work of the project begins, team members often work on their own or with employees who are designated to do the actual work. Regularly scheduled team meetings (face-to-face or virtual, if necessary) are the best way to involve everybody in the project. Team meetings are critical to discuss ideas, share experiences, and ensure that the various components of the project fit together as expected.

Timothy R. Barry, a trainer and consultant for ESI International, reported that ESI maintains a list of the top-ten qualities that project managers feel are required for effective project management. Communication was the second most important quality.[4]

Project leadership calls for clear communication about goals, responsibility, performance, expectations, and feedback.

— Response from project leaders on Top 10 Qualities of a Project Manager

Source: As quoted by Timothy R. Barry, a trainer and consultant for ESI International.

Monitoring the Project

While the team leader has primary responsibility for monitoring or tracking the progress of each team member on the project, the entire team needs to be kept abreast of the progress. The work of one team member may affect the work of other members. Careful monitoring gives the team leader and members an opportunity to detect needed changes in the project and make those changes in a timely manner. The critical path is a helpful way to track the progress made and the impact when problems are incurred. The team should review and approve each phase of a project regardless of who was responsible for that phase.

project ground rules
the behavior expected of each member as the members interact as a team

The team should review and approve each phase of a project regardless of who was responsible for that phase.

Team members may hit a snag in the work or face an obstacle that was not anticipated in the operational plan or in the contingency plans. Some things simply do not work out as expected. In those cases, the entire team can brainstorm and try to develop ways to work around the issues. On the positive side, as the team hits milestones set in the project, the successes should be celebrated. As discussed in Chapter 11, it is important to create an environment that celebrates achievement.

Project monitoring usually involves documentation. The team leader is expected to keep management or clients informed periodically of the status of the project, any changes made, and the reasons for making the changes, and obtain approval for the changes. When a client has a formal agreement for a project, generally written change agreements are used to ensure that both parties agree to the changes, and then they are added to the original agreement.

Project Termination

The first step in completing a project is to ensure that all of the deliverables have been met and meet quality standards. The second step is to prepare a report that documents the project. The process of completing a project often depends on whether the project was an external or an internal project.

External Projects

If the project is an external one, normally a formal or written document defining the scope of the project and the deliverables was prepared, agreed upon, and signed by the client or customer. Changes during the project that affected the agreement are usually noted in writing and are agreed upon by both parties.

Quality assessment is a critical component of ensuring that deliverables meet—and preferably exceed—expectations.

The agreement with the client or customer should be reviewed carefully and each outcome or deliverable should be analyzed carefully to ensure that it met all specifications in the original agreement as well as any change agreements added that were agreed upon during the project.

Quality assessment is a critical component of ensuring that deliverables meet—and preferably exceed—expectations. Exceeding expectations frequently generates additional business.

1. What do you think are the main advantages of having frequent team meetings?

2. What pitfalls do you see to having frequent team meetings?

3. What could you do to make meetings more effective to minimize any pitfalls?

Internal Projects

With internal projects, formal agreements often do not exist. Typically, internal projects are discussed in one or more meetings before being assigned to a team. Action minutes may or may not exist. That is why it is important to provide extensive feedback to management to ensure that the scope of the project, as the team defined it, was accurate and that expectations are being met. Feedback provided by management during the project should be carefully noted so that it can be reviewed to ensure that suggestions were implemented.

The same type of analysis used in external projects to ensure that all deliverables have been met and the quality meets or exceeds expectations should be used for internal projects as well. Meeting and exceeding expectations can enhance careers—both of the team leader and the team members—significantly.

Final Report

Typically at the end of the project, a written report is prepared. While the leader has primary responsibility for the project report, input is required from all team members and all project members should read and approve the final document. The written report documents that all aspects of the project were completed and met all quality and quantity specifications. The written report is also very useful in planning and preparing for future projects. The report usually includes the names of all team members as authors.

In both internal and external situations, an oral presentation is frequently used to present the findings and summary of the projects, to answer questions, and to provide suggestions for implementation when appropriate. Again, the team leader may take the primary responsibility for developing and delivering the presentation. However, all team members should participate in the process. Often multiple team members will participate in the presentation. With large teams, it may not be feasible to have all team members participate, or even possible for all members to be in attendance. However, it should be clear that the presenters are making the presentation on behalf of the entire team.

It is important to keep in mind that evaluation and rewards at the conclusion of either an internal or external project are based totally on team performance and not on individual performance. Clients, customers, and senior managers are not going to judge a project on who did what and how much each person contributed. They expect all members to do their fair share to ensure that the project is completed on time and to insist on high standards of quality at every stage of the project. With external projects, the client may sign the project agreement accepting it as meeting all of the requirements of the agreement. With internal projects, senior managers often celebrate the success of the team on the project or may provide resources for the team to celebrate the success of the project.

Evaluation and rewards at the conclusion of either an internal or external project are based totally on team performance and not individual performance.

Terms

contingency plans, 268
critical path, 272
cross-functional team, 269
deliverables, 267
project, 266
project ground rules, 275
project scope, 267
risk, 267

SUMMARY

1. Projects may be part time or full time and proposed by senior management or a team or team leader.
2. The scope of the project defines what is included in the project, what is excluded, and the specific outcomes or deliverables that must be met.
3. Teams include a leader and members. The size and type of team varies with its type, size, and complexity.
4. At the project's initial, strategic, planning stage, the major parts of the plan are determined and the amount of time to complete each component is estimated.
5. Gantt charts show graphically the order in which tasks need to be scheduled and map the project's critical path.
6. The operational plan breaks down the key components into specific tasks to perform, the timing and sequence of tasks, and a confirmation that needed resources are available.
7. Once planning has been completed, the project is launched and rules and guidelines for communication established.
8. The leader monitors and tracks the team's progress, but the entire team should review and approve each phase of the project as soon as it is completed.
9. The process of completing a project is to ensure that deliverables are met and meet or exceed quality standards.

Study Tools

CourseMate

Located at www.cengagebrain.com

- Chapter Outlines
- Flashcards
- Interactive Quizzes
- Tech Tools
- Video Segments

and More!

Questions for Reflection

1. In projects that you have worked on in college or at work, what were the things that were done well and produced good results?
2. What were the things that were done poorly? What caused the poor performance?
3. With the information you now have, how would you suggest improving projects that you have worked on?
4. What five personal qualities do you think are the most important qualities needed to be an effective project leader?
5. Organizations rarely evaluate projects on an individual team member basis. The whole team has the same evaluation—the project was either effective or not. Do you agree with this type of evaluation? Why or why not?

Hands-On Activities

Explore Project Software—Individual or Team Activity

Learn more about project management software. Search the Internet using "project management software" as the search term. You may complete the following activities as an individual, or you can review and discuss the software with the members of your team.

1. Find a commercial software package that includes a free demo of the product online. Watch the demo. Then answer the following questions:
   a. Was the software general so that it could be used for any type of project or was it customized for a particular industry?
   b. Did the demo illustrate the use of a Gantt chart?
   c. Did the demo illustrate the use of a critical path?
   d. What were the key advantages to using the project software?
   e. If the answer to b or c was no, find another project management software package demo that includes an illustration of both a Gantt chart and a critical path and watch it. Then answer questions a through d.
2. If you have Microsoft Office software that includes the OneNote application or if you use Microsoft Web Apps, open the OneNote application and set up tabs to organize a project you have been assigned or to organize one of the courses you are now taking. If you can't access the OneNote software, find a demo of it on the Internet and watch it.

You Decide | Case Study

Leading a Cross-functional Team

Laura Brooks has been asked to be the team leader for a cross-functional project that is designed to improve customer service in her company. Laura is a manager in the customer service department and is highly respected, but this is her first experience as a team leader. The team consists of 12 members from marketing, sales, customer service, and accounting. Team members were appointed by their department managers. The team has met at least once a week for the past month and has completed the planning for the project.

On the quarterly surveys administered over the past five years, customers have rated overall customer satisfaction between 8.0 and 9.5 on a 10-point scale except for the past three quarters. The rating for the past three quarters was 7.8, 7.7, and 7.5 for the last quarter. The team has been tasked with developing a plan to increase the rating in the next year to a minimum of 8.5. The plan will be implemented in the departments represented because they have primary responsibility for working with customers.

Laura is especially concerned about Drew, a team member from the marketing department, who does not seem to be engaged in the project. Drew attended all of the meetings except one. He had been asked to present information about how marketing handled a number of situations with customers. He called another team member from marketing and asked her to present the information saying he did not feel well and would not be in that day. He did not have anything prepared to give to her. He told her she worked with those kinds of situations as much as he did and could just talk about them. Drew usually did not make comments in team meetings unless someone specifically asked him a question. Then he answered as briefly as possible. He always agreed with whatever the team said or decided. Most of the team members were very active when tasks were assigned—Drew was not. He simply said okay when others suggested that he should be responsible for a particular task.

The project is now being launched and each team member will assume his or her responsibilities and work independently. The team will meet weekly to report progress and discuss issues. Laura is very concerned about Drew's participation.

Questions

What would you advise Laura to do at this stage?

1. Should Laura wait until she sees how Drew performs working independently before she does anything?
2. Should Laura talk with Drew's manager about the situation now? Why or why not?
3. If not, should she talk with Drew about the situation? If so, should she talk with Drew before talking to his manager, at the same time, or after talking to his manager? Explain why you selected this approach.
4. Should she talk with the other team members from marketing individually about Drew? Why or why not?

MANAGER'S TOOLKIT

Prepare documents to help you develop as an effective leader of a high-performance project team. Review the information in Chapter 5 and in this chapter if necessary to prepare the documents.

1. Describe the steps that are required to plan a project effectively.
2. Assume you have the responsibility of selecting the team members for a team you will lead. Describe the criteria that you will use for selecting the team members.
3. Describe the ways you would go about trying to engage all members of the team and ensure that each will be accountable personally and to the team.
4. Earlier you were asked to reflect on the five top qualities required to be an effective team leader. Refine that list and expand it to the ten top qualities.

Soft Skills for Success

Accountability

The topic of accountability has been discussed several times in this textbook. However, there is no better place to learn the value of accountability and how to become accountable than in a project management setting. In project management, accountability is a core value, and the culture of a high-performance project team is based on accountability. Accountability can be thought of in terms of either personal accountability or workplace accountability as described below:

1. Accountability begins with the individual being willing to accept responsibility for his or her commitments, behavior, successes, and failures. With personal accountability, each individual is responsible for taking ownership of his or her areas of responsibility and meeting his or her commitments. Individuals, in effect, must police themselves rather than rely on others to police them. When an individual accepts responsibility for the situation and sets about to find the best way to correct it and move on to achieve results, he or she empowers himself or herself.
2. Employees who are not willing to be personally accountable create many of the workplace accountability problems, which are extremely costly to industry. Using external control or discipline is not the way to establish a culture of accountability. Discipline only works when you observe something wrong and take action. What happens when you are not there to observe the situation? Too often, slackers and non-productive people thrive while contributing very little, and productive team members have to do their own share of the work plus that of the slackers.

Put It to Work

As manager of a department with several teams, you want to develop a project management tool entitled: *Guide for Creating a Culture of Accountability*. Use the information in this chapter (including the Straight Talk from the Field interview) and in Chapters 5 and 6 to prepare the guide.

After the title, write a short paragraph of three or four sentences explaining that for projects to be successful, each team member (not just the team leader) is responsible and accountable for the successful completion of a project on time, within budget, and meeting quality standards. The guide will consist of the following three principles. Use the information shown in parentheses after each of the three guides to write a paragraph expanding on the principle. Edit your document carefully.

1. Specify outcomes (or goals) carefully; divide the goals into tasks listing the team member responsible for each task and the timeframe for achieving the results. Include information about the importance of all members participating in this process to develop ownership of it.

2. Develop appropriate charts (such as a Gantt chart) to communicate visually all tasks, the person responsible, and the progress or lack of progress toward completion. Explain why it is important for all team members to be aware of team progress and also to be able to monitor the quality.

3. Meet frequently as a team to review the progress and quality of each phase and to approve each phase as it is completed. Explain why this is important. Point out the value of team problem solving when needed.

CHAPTER

13

Effective Workplace Communication

Learning Outcomes

1. Describe the levels and types of communication required in organizations.
2. Describe how technology can be used to remove time and distance communication barriers.
3. Explain several ways in which culture affects managerial communication.
4. Explain what is meant by media richness and how managers can use it to decide on the media to be used in communicating.
5. List four or five things you can do or avoid doing to enhance listening.
6. Describe three or four techniques for asking effective questions.
7. Explain what is meant by nonverbal communication and how it affects workplace communication.
8. Describe two or three things you can do to improve writing in the workplace.

Straight Talk From the Field

Sandra Dillon-Anderson was communications manager for the Bay Shore Group of Comcast, the country's largest provider of cable services and one of the world's leading communications companies. She currently serves as director of communications for Hospice of the Chesapeake.

Photo courtesy of S. Anderson

What were your responsibilities as communications manager for Comcast's Bay Shore Group?

As the communications manager for the Bay Shore Group, I was responsible for communicating with close to 900 Comcast employees serving customers in Delaware and Maryland. Comcast has an incredibly diverse workforce for a variety of reasons, most importantly because of each person's unique perspective and job responsibilities. The Bay Shore region includes business operations people such as accountants, programmers, and warehouse personnel. It also has an administrative group that is responsible for human resources management, government relations, and community affairs. However, its largest group of employees, approximately 85 percent, work on the front lines as account executives handling customer phone calls and as technicians working in the field. One of my challenges at Comcast was to ensure that all of these employees receive important company information, consistently, and without interrupting the customer experience.

What is Comcast's approach to communicating with a diverse workforce?

As an industry leader in communication technology, Comcast uses video, Web links, and other forms of technology to communicate with employees and customers. I found personal communication to be the most effective way to communicate with the workforce. Comcast empowers managers and front-line supervisors to deliver information to their teams and provide two-way communication between the staff and upper management. Supervisors also conduct one-on-one connection meetings with each of their employees. During these meetings, they encourage individuals to share their ideas, comments, and suggestions for improvement. Supervisors use these meetings to discuss each person's career path. In addition, they take time to share information about the company, their division, and their team.

How did you adapt your message for your audience?

I worked with managers and supervisors to develop a consistent message that is also relevant for their particular areas. One message for the entire company does not work. Instead, I designed three or four versions of the same basic message. Each version was adapted for the intended recipients. The message must be relevant to the workforce. I took time to identify how the information would impact them personally. I prepared messages that highlight how the new information will make their jobs easier, benefit their customers, or provide opportunities for growth.

How do you typically deliver your messages to employees?

All key messaging points are clear, concise, and direct. One of my goals is to "remove the noise" from the message and simply focus on the key points. In a perfect world, all supervisors and managers would deliver the message consistently. However, people have unique perspectives and filter the information based on their role and expertise. As a result, I spent time with company leaders providing coaching and feedback in an effort to ensure all corporate communication is consistent, clear, concise, direct, and appropriate for the intended audience.

How does Comcast solicit feedback from employees?

Comcast holds large group meetings for employees twice a year. Prior to each of these meetings the company asks employees, "What's on your mind?" It invites employees to submit questions, comments, and suggestions in advance. This provides the opportunity to address the topics that are of interest to the workforce. It also allows the opportunity to dispel rumors and keep everyone informed and up-to-date on our new products and services.

To learn more about what employees are thinking, the company also sends out an annual electronic survey with approximately twenty categories. Effective communication is one of the categories the company evaluates. This is another way it gathers information to determine what is working and what needs improvement. Comcast strives to encourage effective two-way communication throughout the organization. However, everything it does is within the context of customer service.

Visit *www.cengagebrain.com* to read the complete profile.

Chapter Outline

communication
the exchange of information

Virtually every managerial function involves some form of communication. Communication can be defined in many ways. In the workplace, **communication** is the exchange of information. Note that information in the workplace can take many forms and be exchanged in many ways. Few skills are more important for managers to develop than communication skills. Most business students aspiring to careers in management or work in administrative positions complete a course in business communication. If the program you are enrolled in does not require a business communication course, you should enroll in one as an elective course. This chapter assumes that you have already taken or will take a course in business communication. Therefore, it does not include basic communication theory or processes. Much of the information on levels and types of communication and on required communication skills provided in this chapter is based on the experience of one of the authors.[1] The focus is on understanding the type of communication that is effective at the various levels of communication in the workplace. It also covers intercultural communication and applies basic communication skills—nonverbal, listening, speaking, reading, and writing—to effective workplace communication.

Effective Workplace Communication

The important thing to remember is that developing effective communication skills will enhance significantly your management effectiveness and ultimately your management career. To help you develop effective workplace communication skills, a wide range of communication skills have been embedded throughout this textbook. This chapter provides a conceptual or big-picture view of how many of the elements discussed throughout the book fit together and affect employees and managers at every level of the organization.

Master the message. You can have the greatest idea in the world, but if you can't communicate your ideas, it doesn't matter.

— Steve Jobs, former CEO of Apple

Source: From "Steve Jobs and the Seven Rules of Success," by Carmine Gallo, www.entrepreneur.com/article/220515?utm_medium=twitter&utm_source=twitterfeed.

Levels of Communication

The level of communication applies to both internal and external communication. Many differences exist in the way you communicate internally and externally. However, it is critical that you recognize that internal communications are just as important as external communications—especially to your own career. Do you want your managers and your peers to evaluate your communication skills as inadequate because you do not bother to pay careful attention to the quality of internal documents? People often make the mistake of thinking that it is not necessary to edit and proofread internal documents carefully only to find out later that they were passed over for promotions because their communication skills were not appropriate for the job. Internal communication—the documents, emails, text messages, conversations, and presentations you make within the organization—generally form the basis for evaluating your communication skills. Also remember that documents are frequently

Internal communications are just as important as external communications—especially to your own career.

shared with other people. A report you think you are preparing just for your manager may be sent to his or her manager or even outside of the organization.

Internal Communication

The levels of internal communication and their complexity depend on the size of the organization, the dispersion of employees, and the industry. **Internal communication** refers to communication with employees of your organization. Types of communication appropriate for each level are discussed in a later section. As you review the following levels, think about how the size of the organization and the industry might impact the way you would communicate at each level. Keep in mind that message consistency is important in internal communications as indicated by Sandra Dillon-Anderson in the opening interview.

1. **Communication with the Entire Organization.** Compare how you might communicate with all employees at one time in a consulting firm that had 40 employees in one location to how you might communicate with all employees in an organization that had 10,000 employees in 50 states and 10 countries. Face-to-face communication is much easier to accomplish in a small organization than in a large organization. In Chapter 4, the Leveraging Technology section focused on ways you can use technology to enhance large-group communication and to remove some of the barriers to effective communication.

   Content designed to be appropriate for an entire organization differs from that used in a department or team whose members are typically focusing on the same type of goals, work, and issues. Communicating content to an entire organization occurs less frequently than communicating to departments and teams. Content for the entire organization typically is focused on big-picture issues, such as vision messages, changes in organizational direction, major accomplishments, announcements of new products, services, mergers or acquisitions, and changes that directly affect all employees in areas such as benefits. Typically, senior executives are responsible for communication with the entire organization.

2. **Communication within a Division or Department.** Divisions are typically used in large organizations and are usually subdivided into departments. Small and mid-size organizations may only have departments. The size and geographic disbursement of divisions present many of the same challenges that exist in communicating with an entire organization. The primary differences are that communication within a division usually occurs more frequently and focuses on the same general type of goals, work, and issues. Departments generally are smaller than divisions and they focus on more specific goals, work, and issues. Communication occurs much more frequently in departments than in divisions. Communication with the entire group at the

internal communication
communication with employees of your organization

same time is usually initiated by division or department managers. Communication within the group may be initiated by any member of the division or department.

3. **Communication with a Team or Work Group.** Teams and work groups are small, closely knit groups that must communicate frequently to be effective. They are focused on the same goals and do the same type of work. In many cases, the work is in the form of a project. In Chapter 5, communication with team members was emphasized and the Leveraging Technology section focused on tools to facilitate web-based communication when team members were dispersed geographically and time zones varied. Reviewing that information may be helpful at this time. Communication within a team should be free flowing and may be initiated by the team leader or any member of the team.
4. **One-on-One Communication.** Communication between two individuals is usually specific and focused. It may occur frequently in an informal daily work setting such as discussing work issues and receiving assistance or coaching. It might also be more personal and occurs less frequently in a more formal, private setting, such as discipline or negative feedback.

1. Think about the four levels of internal communication. At which level do you think it is most difficult to communicate with employees? Explain why.

   ____

2. At which level do you think it is easiest to communicate with employees? Explain why.

   ____

External Communication

Employees of an organization often communicate with customers, clients, partners, vendors, other stakeholders, and the general public. **External communication** refers to communication with individuals or groups who are not employees of your organization. Levels of external communication exist but the types of communication are not as easy to place in categories.

1. **Large-Group Communication.** Typically, when an organization communicates externally to a large group, it is related to product or service promotions or advertising, news about the company and its employees, or communications to groups of stakeholders, such as analysts from companies that have invested in the company. Normally, large-group communications are handled by senior executives or by the Marketing and Public Relations Departments. Communication directed to the general public is usually referred to as **mass communication**. Mass communication is generally in the form of an annual report, a news release, or advertisements.

external communication
communication with individuals or groups who are not employees of your organization

mass communication
communication directed to the general public

2. **Small-Group Communication.** One of the most common types of external small-group communication relates to a project that a team or work group handles for a client or customer. Occasionally, joint ventures or work with partners will utilize small groups for communication. In addition, one employee from a company may work with several employees from a client or customer organization.
3. **One-on-One Communication.** One-on-one communication occurs frequently when an employee of an organization works with an employee of a client or customer organization. A sales representative may have a primary contact with a customer or client. A customer service, claims representative, or an accountant may work with an employee of a customer or client.

1. Think about the ways you communicate internally and externally. In a one-on-one situation such as solving a work-related problem, how would communicating with one of your employees be similar to communicating with a client or customer's employee?

___

2. How would communicating with one of your own employees be different from communicating with a client or customer's employee?

___

Types of Communication

The types of communication can be viewed from many different perspectives. Three common approaches are (1) formal vs. informal communication, (2) upward and downward communication, and (3) oral, written, and technology-enhanced communication.

Formal vs. Informal Communication

Both formal and informal communications are used internally and externally and at every level of communication. **Formal communication** is often referred to as communication that has a defined structure or format, uses proper language, and meets specific standards. A proposal used to obtain business from a customer would probably be designed and presented as a formal communication. Formality is sometimes defined by the recipient or by the perceived importance of the content. You would probably prepare a letter accepting a job offer or a letter to the president of the company as a formal communication. **Informal communication** is often referred to as casual or relaxed communication. In terms of quantity or frequency of communication, informal communication predominates. Emails, text messages, memos, face-to-face conversations, and telephone calls to fellow employees or clients are generally informal types of communication. Perhaps the best way to think about formality is on a continuum with very formal at one extreme and very informal at the other extreme. Figure 13.1 illustrates this formality continuum.

formal communication
communication that has a defined structure or format, uses proper language, and meets specific standards

informal communication
casual or relaxed communication

FIGURE 13.1
Formality Continuum

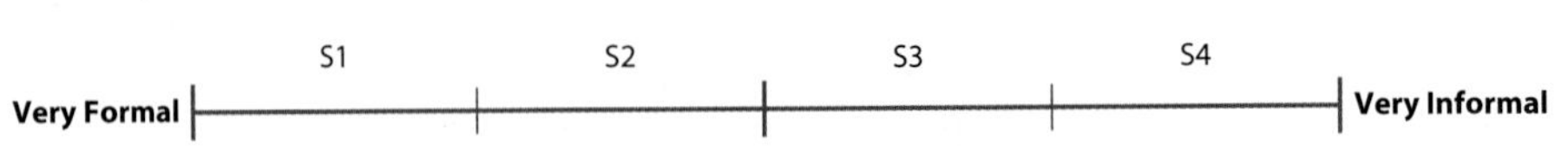

Note that the continuum is divided into four sections. The center line is at the midpoint and the lighter lines mark the half-way points between the extreme left or right and the center point. Think of the four sections as S1, S2, S3, and S4 beginning from the left. Very formal documents such as legal documents, annual reports, important letters, and reports would be in S1. Most written documents and presentations supported by visuals would be in S2. Very informal documents such as text messages with slang, colloquialisms, and abbreviations would be in S4. The "grapevine" is a good example of informal oral communication. The **grapevine** usually consists of gossip, rumors, and unverified or unannounced information about the organization or employees. Sometimes the information is accurate, and sometimes it is not. Telephone calls and face-to-face conversations with colleagues on the same team or work unit are usually in S3. Any document that is saved in the organization's record or data system should have a level of formality that matches S1 or S2. Most businesses prefer that workplace communication be in S1, S2, or S3 and they limit S4 to personal communication.

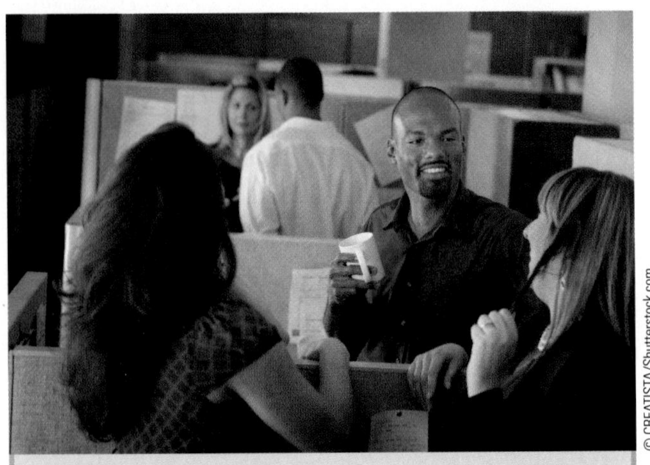
Communication via an office grapevine takes place informally.

1. Why do you think most businesses prefer that very informal communication (S4) be limited to personal communication? Do you agree or disagree with this? Why or why not?

___

2. Why is it important that communications stored in the records or data system should be limited to S1 or S2?

___

grapevine
gossip, rumors, and unverified or unannounced information about the organization or various employees

upward communication
information shared by a subordinate to a manager

Upward, Downward, and Horizontal Communication

Workplace communication may be upward, downward, and horizontal. **Upward communication** refers to information shared by a subordinate to a manager. **Downward communication** refers to information shared by a manager to a subordinate. **Horizontal communication** refers to information shared among peers. Communication among peers tends to be more informal than upward or downward communication. However, as individuals at a variety of levels work closely with each other and share information frequently, the communication lines between managers and subordinates are often blurred. Meetings, coaching, and feedback are critical parts of upward and downward communication as you learned in Chapters 8 and 11. Standard operating procedures are an example of written upward and downward communication. Specifying the way a task should be done provides the necessary information that supervisors would otherwise have to communicate orally and enables employees to work without having to ask as many questions and to work more independently. Most employees like standard operating procedures because they tend to minimize frequent over-the-shoulder supervision.

Oral, Written, and Technology-Enhanced Communication

downward communication
information shared by a manager to a subordinate

horizontal communication
information shared among peers

oral communication
conversations, discussions, or presentations

written communication
reading and writing paper-based documents and documents transmitted electronically including email

technology-enhanced communication
communication through technological options such as media sites, telepresence, webinars, websites, blogs, and webcasts

telepresence
making people in remote environments feel as though they were all present in the same location

culture
the shared values, beliefs, traditions, philosophy, and character or personality of the country or region

As mentioned in previous sections, the terminology used for these types or forms of communication varies widely, and they are often subdivided into other categories. In today's workplace, these categories are often used together—for example, a meeting might include discussion while drafting or reviewing written content and with some participants contributing through the use of technology.

Oral communication in workplace terms generally refers to conversations, discussions, or presentations. Oral communication consists of speaking, listening, and visual (nonverbal) components. These components are discussed in detail in the basic communication skills section. **Written communication** refers both to reading and writing paper-based documents and documents transmitted electronically including email and text messages. Written communication may also include visual representations such as charts, graphs, and pictures.

Technology-enhanced communication refers to communication through technological options such as social media sites, **telepresence**, webinars, websites, blogs, and webcasts. Social media sites were initially used for personal communication, but they have grown and matured to the point that they are now considered an integral part of workplace communication. Some organizations ban their use except for employees who use the sites for marketing purposes. This eliminates employees' use of work time for extensive social communication on the sites.[2]

Intercultural Communication

In previous chapters, we focused on corporate culture. In Chapter 8, corporate culture was defined as the shared values, beliefs, traditions, philosophy, and character or personality of the organization. In this chapter, the emphasis is on communicating effectively with individuals from different cultures from a global perspective. From a global perspective, **culture** refers to the shared values, beliefs, traditions, philosophy, and character or personality of the country or region. Cultures vary widely from one country or region of the world to other countries or regions. Intercultural communication is important because people from other countries probably live in the same neighborhoods and work in the same companies that you do. Even small, entrepreneurial companies conduct business in other countries.

The Internet, cloud-based computing, and telepresence systems make it easy to communicate and work with individuals all over the world. If you have traveled internationally, think about the ways you may have conducted business or communicated internationally on the trip. From a personal perspective, here are a few of many examples that were very easy to accomplish:

- Used online banking from the North China Sea.
- Purchased and downloaded books from Amazon while visiting countries in Europe, Africa, and the United Kingdom, and posted high-resolution digital pictures for use in projects.

LEVERAGING TECHNOLOGY

TELEPRESENCE

Sophisticated telepresence systems are gaining wide acceptance in the workplace, especially in large companies that have employees located in many states and countries. These systems provide effective two-way communication by utilizing high-resolution cameras, effective lighting, high-quality audio, microphones, high-resolution visual display monitors, and a physical setting that simulates a boardroom or training room.

Telepresence refers to making people in remote environments feel as though they are all present in the same location. The telepresence system illustrated in the photograph is a Cisco system that is called an "immersive experience." It is easy to sense how participants from the remote locations would have the feeling that they are in the same boardroom as the participants in the host room. Cisco TelePresence systems are voice activated, so that whichever room's speaker is active, that room will appear on screen.

High-resolution cameras, sound, monitors, and appropriate lighting enable participants to pay attention to nonverbal communication and interpret it appropriately. This element is often missing in video-based collaboration. Although high-quality telepresence systems are expensive, organizations believe that they are less expensive than traveling and that they save a significant amount of time for remote participants.

Cisco Systems, Inc

- Wrote manuscript using both cloud-based and materials on laptop for a textbook while in Bangkok and posted it from a ship in the Gulf of Thailand to an FTP site.
- Participated in a webinar and in a board meeting by audio conference from a foreign country.
- Taught short courses in Vienna, Austria, and followed up by critiquing papers and helping Vienna IMBA students prepare presentations through technology-enhanced communications from South Carolina. Also conducted training programs in Canada and the Dominican Republic with one country adhering to very precise time schedules and the other adhering to extremely flexible time schedules.
- Communicated with a tailor in Hong Kong from the United States to ensure that items met specifications and noted that the measurement systems were different.
- Received College World Series baseball scores every half inning through a Twitter feed on a smartphone at 3 a.m. Copenhagen time.

One challenge was not being able to transmit information easily. A bigger challenge was making sure that the information was communicated effectively to individuals from different cultures. Although English is generally considered to be the language of business, both language and culture can have a major impact on communication with individuals from different cultures.

We didn't all come over on the same ship, but we're all in the same boat.

— Bernard Baruch, A well-known South Carolinian who became an American financier and an international statesman

Source: "Cross Culture Communication," www.mindtools.com/CommSkll/Cross-Cultural-communication.htm.

Dimensions of Culture from the GLOBE Project

The GLOBE (Global Leadership and Organizational Behavior Effectiveness) project was conceived by Robert J. House, a researcher from the Wharton School of Management at the University of Pennsylvania. It is an ongoing cross-cultural study of leadership and national culture. The GLOBE team used data from 825 organizations in 62 countries to identify nine dimensions on which cultures differ. Note that some of the original work completed from 1993 and published in 2004 has been updated.

Understanding how cultures differ helps to to determine how to communicate with individuals from different cultures. Again it is useful to think of each dimension on a continuum (from one extreme to another) in the same way that formality was analyzed on page 290 of this chapter. The high end of the scale would relate to things that the culture rewards and values; the low end of the scale would be the opposite extreme—things that the culture does not reward and value. A common approach is to list two or three countries that score on the high end and on the low end of the continuum for each dimension. That approach may be adequate for illustration purposes, but a more targeted approach is critical for the workplace. Learning specific information about the culture of a hundred countries is not feasible. However, if you are going to work with individuals from Mexico, Germany, or Singapore, it is not only feasible, but also very important that you obtain in-depth information about the culture of those specific countries. The nine dimensions used to describe cultural differences are listed below.

1. Assertiveness—the high end of the continuum relates to being aggressive, confrontational, and even dominant; competitive would be somewhat lower; the low end of the continuum would be non-assertive, passive, and less demanding.
2. Future orientation—the high end of the scale rewards planning and saving for the future, focusing on long-term goals; the low end of the scale focuses on short-term goals and instant gratification.
3. Gender equality—the high end of the scale relates to equal status or treatment of men and women; the low end of the scale would indicate that men have higher status economically, educationally, and in organizations.
4. Humane orientation—the high end of the scale refers to treating people in a kind, generous, fair, and helpful manner; the low end of the scale corresponds to letting people take care of themselves and rewards self-enhancement over enhancement of others.
5. Individual collectivism—the high end of the scale focuses on the extent to which the individual takes pride in and has loyalty to family, the team, or organization; the low end relates to loyalty to societal institutions over family and close-knit groups.
6. Performance orientation—the high end of the scale relates to rewarding and emphasizing high performance, improvement, and excellence; the low end of the scale places less emphasis on individual performance and more on loyalty.
7. Power distance—the high end of the scale gives leaders power over others; the low end of the scale shares power among the people.
8. Societal collectivism—on the high end of the scale more emphasis is placed on loyalty to society and institutions such as schools, businesses, and other organizations; the low end of the scale places emphasis on the individual and loyalty to family, the team, and small groups.

Digital Vision/Photodisc/Getty Images

Understanding the culture of a person's country is critical to effective communication with that person.

9. Uncertainty avoidance—the high end of the scale uses social norms and rules to reduce ambiguity and uncertainty; the low end of the scale is more comfortable with and tolerant of ambiguity and uncertainty.[3]

Other Sources of Cultural Diversity

There are no right or wrong elements of cultural diversity, only cross-cultural differences.

There are no right or wrong elements of cultural diversity, only cross-cultural differences. The goal is for managers to understand these differences and how they affect communication and relationship building.

Individualism vs. Collectivism

This distinction between "me" and "we" cultures deserves closer attention because it encompasses two of the nine GLOBE cultural dimensions. People in individualistic cultures focus primarily on individual rights, roles, and achievements.[4] The United States and Canada are highly individualistic cultures. Meanwhile, people in collectivist cultures—such as Egypt, Mexico, India, and Japan—rank duty and loyalty to family, friends, organization, and country above self-interests. Group goals and shared achievements are paramount to collectivists: personal goals and desires are suppressed. Individualism and collectivism are extreme ends of a continuum, along which people and cultures are variously distributed and mixed. For example, in the United States, one can find pockets of collectivism among Native Americans and immigrants from Latin America and Asia. This helps explain why a top-notch engineer born in China might be reluctant to attend an American-style recognition dinner where individual award recipients are asked to stand up for a round of applause.

Time

Time has been referred to as a silent language of culture.[5] Specifically, **monochronic time** refers to perceiving time as a one-dimensional straight line divided into standard units such as seconds, minutes, hours, and days. In monochronic cultures, including North America and northern Europe, everyone is assumed to be on the same clock and time is treated as money. The general rule is to use time efficiently, be on time, and above all, do not waste time. In contrast, **polychronic time** involves the perception that time is flexible, elastic, and multidimensional.[6] Latin American, Mediterranean, and Arab cultures are polychronic. Managers in polychronic cultures such as rural Mexico see no problem with loosely scheduled, overlapping office visits. For example, a monochronic American arriving 10 minutes early for an appointment with a regional Mexican official could resent having to wait another 15 minutes. The American perceives the Mexican official as slow and insensitive. The Mexican official believes the American is self-centered and impatient.[7] Different perceptions of time are responsible for this collision of cultures.

monochronic time
the perception that time is divided into standard units

polychronic time
the perception that time is flexible, elastic, and multidimensional

Interpersonal Space

People in a number of cultures, including Arab and Asian cultures, prefer to stand close when conversing. However, an interpersonal distance of only six inches is very disturbing to a northern European or an American, accustomed to conversing at arm's length. Cross-cultural gatherings in the Middle East often involve an awkward dance as Arab hosts strive to get closer while their American and northern European guests back away to maintain what they consider to be a proper distance.

Language

Foreign language skills are the gateway to true cross-cultural understanding. Human translators generally are not available, and there often is not time for computer software translations. However accomplished, translations are not an adequate substitute for conversational ability in the local language.[8] As the immigrant population continues to grow in the United States, a manager likely will have at least one employee who comes from a country where English is not the primary language.

> Foreign language skills are the gateway to true cross-cultural understanding.

Religion

Awareness of a business colleague's religious traditions is essential for building a lasting relationship. Those traditions may dictate dietary restrictions, religious holidays, and worship schedules, which are important to the devout and represent cultural minefields for the uninformed. From a scheduling perspective, particularly if you are conducting business with employees located in different countries, it is helpful to know their scheduling traditions. For example, the official day of rest in Iran is Thursday; in Kuwait and Pakistan it is Friday.[9] In Israel, the official day off is Saturday.

> Religious traditions may dictate dietary restrictions, religious holidays, and worship schedules.

1. Assume you were given the opportunity to work in a major company in a country of your choice for a one-semester internship. What are some of the things you would like to know about the culture of that country before you arrive?

   ___

2. How do you think you could go about gaining the needed information?

   ___

Barriers to Effective Workplace Communication

Being aware of barriers that prevent effective communication is the first step to improving workplace communication. Many of the barriers have already been discussed in this and other chapters. As you review the following examples of barriers, the important thing to keep in mind is that

Virtually all barriers to effective communication can be removed or at least minimized if you make an effort to do so.

virtually all barriers to effective communication can be removed or minimized if you make an effort to do so.

- Physical barriers—working with individuals in different locations, time zones, or other things that prevent access to individuals. Technology-enhanced communication provides one way to remove physical barriers; however, in some cases it is not as effective as face-to-face communication.
- Cultural barriers—cultural differences in addition to the nine dimensions of culture were discussed earlier in this chapter. Understanding how the culture of the individuals with whom you work differs from yours enables you to communicate in a courteous, sensitive way that enhances trust and improves results.
- Semantic or linguistic barriers—language, vocabulary, word choices, and information overload often lead to misunderstandings even when individuals speak the same language. When individuals communicate in a second language, the likelihood of miscommunication is much higher. Avoiding slang or colloquialisms and using simple, clear language helps to overcome some of the semantic barriers.
- Attitudinal or emotional barriers—a person's state of mind can be a major barrier to communication. Biases, anger, mood, fear, and a host of other factors can make communication with others uncomfortable. Learning to be open and to control attitudinal and emotional barriers enhances communication and is important to developing good working relationships.
- Competence barriers—lack of expertise, technical knowledge, or confidence in one's ability often creates problems communicating effectively with a team. Careful selection of team members helps to avoid putting team members in uncomfortable positions.

1. Think about situations in which you have had to interact with individuals in class or at work and the interaction did not go well. Which of the barriers to communication do you think may have contributed to the situation?

   ____

2. How could you minimize or reduce those barriers to improve the situation?

   ____

Communicating for Workplace Success

Some of the basic communication skills that are often taken for granted have a major impact on communicating successfully in the workplace. Those skills include listening, understanding and using nonverbal communication, speaking, reading, and writing. The way you transmit your message is also very important.

Media Richness

Communication media refers to the form of transmission used such as text messaging, face-to-face, email, or telephone calls. Some media are richer or more robust than others. **Media richness** refers to the effectiveness of a given medium in conveying information and promoting learning. Research by Lengel and Daft identified characteristics that enhanced media richness.[10] Media can be analyzed for richness by using a continuum in the same way that formality and culture dimensions were analyzed. The media richness continuum is illustrated in Figure 13.2. Media at the high end of the richness scale would convey multiple information cues at one time, be personal, and facilitate immediate feedback. Media at the low end of the richness scale would convey a limited number of information cues at one time, be impersonal, and require more time for feedback. Think about some of the media you use to transmit information. Using the same type of scale you used for formality, where would you position the media?

communication media
the form of transmission used such as text messaging, face-to-face, email, or telephone calls

media richness
the effectiveness of a given medium in conveying information and promoting learning

FIGURE 13.2
Media Richness Continuum

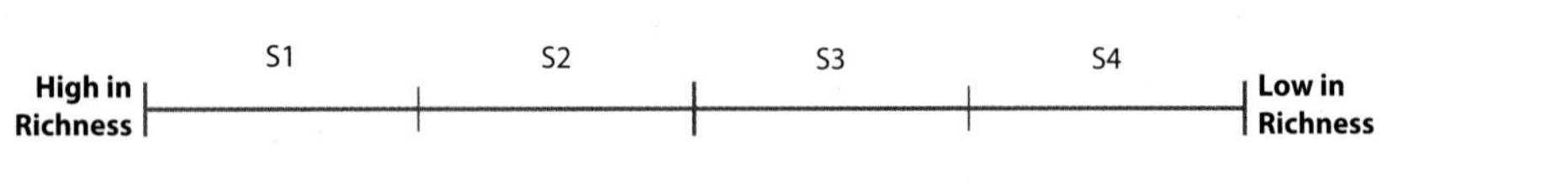

Face-to-face communication is very high in richness because it includes all of the characteristics required—it provides multiple information cues such as message content, tone, and body language; it facilitates immediate feedback; and it is very personal. Posting something on a website would

Complete the following by matching the message with the communication transmission media you think is most appropriate for the type of message being sent.

Choose the Best Match

Type of Message	**Transmission Media**
Performance counseling and/or appraisal.	a. Email
Plans to lay off 50 employees by the end of the year.	b. Face-to-face, one-on-one in person
Last-minute change in plans, the meeting will start at 3:00, not 1:00 as originally scheduled.	c. Face-to-face, group meeting in person
Announcing plans for the company's annual holiday party.	d. Company website posting
Promotional notice advertising new product.	e. Phone call

See end of chapter for correct answers.

be on the opposite end of the scale because it is limited in information cues, it is impersonal, and it does not facilitate immediate feedback. A telephone call may be in S2 whereas a text message may be in S3. You can enhance communication by matching the type of message you wish to convey with the appropriate media you use to convey it.

The Art of Listening

Larry King, host of the long-running show *Larry King Live*, has conducted more than 50,000 interviews during his broadcasting career spanning more than 50 years. He has been called the "master interviewer."[11]

Here is what King says about his success:

> To be a good speaker, you must be a good listener. This is more than just a matter of showing interest. Careful listening makes you better able to respond when it's your turn. Good follow-up questions are a mark of a good conversationalist.
>
> Don't ask "yes or no" questions. Ask "what-if" questions, especially those that require a moral or philosophical response. And ask "why?" It's the greatest question ever asked and will keep a conversation lively and interesting.[12]

Of course, King was referring to his career in broadcasting and the need to generate interesting dialogue as a television talk show host. However, his comments are relevant for managers as well. Extract his key points:

- Listen carefully.
- Ask good follow-up questions.
- Don't ask "yes or no" questions.
- Ask "what-if" questions.
- Ask "why?"

© Pressmaster/Shutterstock.com

Active listening is essential to effective communication.

If you follow these recommendations, you will gain a better understanding of your customers and employees. Additionally, you will reinforce your commitment to developing and sustaining mutually beneficial relationships that embrace open and honest communication.

Almost all training in oral communication in high school, college, and management development programs is focused on effective speaking. But what about listening, the other half of the communication equation? Listening is the forgotten component in communication skills training. This is unfortunate, because even the most profound oration is a waste of time if it is not heard.

We can hear and process information more quickly than we can talk. According to researchers, our average rate of speaking is about 125 words per minute, whereas we are able to listen to about 400 to 600 words per minute.[13] Thus, listeners have a considerable amount of slack time during which they can daydream or alternatively analyze information and plan a response. Active listeners know how to put that slack time to good use. However, unlike math or science, there is no exact formula for listening. Most people are not born great listeners, so it takes practice and a commitment to improve. Note: Some researchers question whether the specific rates between speaking and listening are accurate. Most researchers, however, confirm that a significant gap exists between the rates of speaking and listening and using that gap helps you to become an active listener.

Impact of Nonverbal Language on Listening

Most researchers agree that nonverbal language (often called body language) conveys a significant part of the meaning of a message. Some researchers have estimated that 55 to 93 percent of communication is conveyed through nonverbal signals. The high percentages are from very specific situations that do not represent general communication, and trying to determine percentages is not important. What is important is understanding that nonverbal communication represents an important component of effective workplace communication.

How does body language impact listening? Think about the richness of media discussion in the previous section. Face-to-face communication is very high on the media richness continuum. The primary reason is that multiple information cues are used, feedback is immediate, and the communication is personal. Nonverbal communication is what positions face-to-face communication on the high end of the media richness continuum. Nonverbal communication provides numerous information cues as described in the next paragraph, gives instant feedback, and it is between two individuals which makes it personal. Silence combined with eye contact also can deliver a strong message. For example, if an instructor asks a question and you do not respond in a reasonably short amount of time, an inexperienced instructor is likely to supply the answer to the question for you or move on to someone else. An experienced instructor is likely to make direct eye contact with you and remain silent until you answer the question. Even though you do not know the answer to the question, you are likely to be uncomfortable with the silence and come up with some type of response even if it is something to the effect that you did not have time to read the chapter. On the other hand, a way to emphasize a particular point is to pause after a statement you want to emphasize and give people time to think about it and then repeat the point.

nonverbal communication facial expressions, eye contact, gestures, posture, proximity or closeness to others, and tone or quality of voice

Nonverbal communication consists of facial expressions, eye contact, gestures, posture, proximity or closeness to others, and tone or quality of voice among other factors, such as professional dress or a warm, firm handshake. For example, a smile, nod of the head, leaning forward, and relaxed eye contact would be interpreted in a positive way whereas a frown, a glare, arms crossed, and leaning backward would be interpreted in a negative way. From a workplace perspective, it is very important that body language agrees with and confirms or supports the message being communicated. For example, if the message to be communicated is negative, such as a person being laid off from a job, body language that normally accompanies a positive message would not be received well. Conversely, if the message is intended to praise an employee for a job well done, negative body language would be inappropriate.

Do's and Don'ts of Effective Listening

The way you listen depends on the circumstances, and especially on the richness of the medium. Listening occurs in a variety of situations, including one-on-one conversations, small face-to-face meetings, live presentations to large groups, telephone calls, podcasts, and recorded messages. Good listeners are active—not passive listeners. Figure 13.3 presents a number of do's and don'ts of active listening and incorporates many differences between active and passive listeners.

FIGURE 13.3
Do's and Don'ts of Active Listening

Do's of Active Listening	Don'ts of Active Listening
Do remain active; try to process everything that is being said	Don't be passive or waste the time between listening and speaking
Do keep an open mind and try to be objective about the message	Don't have preconceived assumptions, thoughts, and expectations
Do ask good, clarifying, open-ended questions	Don't be defensive
Do try to read and interpret the nonverbal language of the speaker	Don't let your nonverbal language indicate that you are not paying attention
Do demonstrate nonverbally that you are listening and provide nonverbal feedback—use eye contact, smile, nod in agreement when appropriate	Don't be distracted by checking for text messages or email, talking to others, or reading other materials
Do be patient and let the speaker complete his or her thoughts	Don't interrupt the speaker while he or she is trying to make a point
Do paraphrase what the speaker said to confirm that you heard the intended message accurately	Don't be combative if you do not agree with what you heard
Do think about what has not been said that you expected to be said and ask tactful questions	Don't ignore sensitive topics that need to be discussed

Oral Communication

Speaking is the other part of listening. As noted earlier, speaking occurs in one-on-one conversations, team or small-group meetings, telephone calls, or presentations. One of the key things to remember is that effective listening and nonverbal language support oral communication. Good command of the language is also very important. Most organizations try to screen employees for good communication skills during the interviewing and selection process. However, managers need to follow up and provide additional communication training for employees when it is needed. The training may be presented in the form of customer service training, team building, or a basic communication skills review. Training on how to give presentations also may be given. Managers need to follow up on the implementation of the training on the job. Managers may also need to enhance their own communication skills. Coaching employees requires the ability to interact and communicate effectively with employees. Asking effective questions is the heart of obtaining information comfortably in a work setting.

Tips for Asking Effective Questions

1. Ask questions in a nonthreatening manner. If an employee is relating a problem, try these approaches:
   a. Tell me more about this…
   b. What do you think might be causing or influencing this…?
   c. What do you think would help to…?
2. Be courteous in the way you ask questions:
   a. Would you please describe the circumstances...?
   b. How may I help you to…?
   c. This is an interesting idea…tell me more about it.
3. Paraphrase what the person is saying and ask for confirmation or clarification:
   a. Do I understand you correctly that…?
   b. You indicated that the new process needs to be refined…in what ways would you suggest…?
   c. If we were to do…, would this solve the problem?
4. Match your question to your objective. If you want specific information, ask a specific question. If you want general information, ask an open-ended question:
   a. What is the earliest date you can have this project completed?
   b. What if we provided additional resources, such as…could you complete the project in one week?
5. Ask your question, maintain eye contact, and wait silently for an answer; do not interrupt the person answering the question.
6. Don't make assumptions with your questions, let the person provide the information:
   a. You have mentioned three factors that…are there other things that should be considered?
   b. You mentioned several changes that would improve…why would these changes be better than the current process?

Proactive vs. Reactive Language

In Chapter 11, you learned about fostering a creative and positive working environment. Effective communication is central to achieving a high-performance workplace. One of the keys is to shift your perspective from being reactive to proactive. This requires using proactive language rather than reactive language.

In Stephen Covey's book, *The 7 Habits of Highly Effective People*, he chose being proactive as the first habit. He follows the same philosophy of many other writers over the years who have emphasized the importance of having a positive attitude and understanding what has become to be known as the self-fulfilling prophecy. The **self-fulfilling prophecy** enforces the belief that if you think you can do something, you are very likely to do it. If you do not think you can do it, you are not likely to do it. Covey places emphasis on reactive and proactive language becoming a self-fulfilling prophecy. Reactive language tends to be negative and transfers responsibility from the individual to someone else. Examples of reactive language include:

- I can't do anything about that.
- It's not my problem.
- Let them worry about it.

Proactive language accepts responsibility and focuses on what the individual can do rather than cannot do. Examples of proactive language include:

- This may be a challenge, but the outcome is worth it.
- I can do this, and it will make a difference.
- Let's come up with an alternative that will work.

Proactive people take control of their lives and jobs whereas reactive people focus on what they cannot do or control.[14]

Reading in the Workplace

Special attention needs to be paid to reading and writing because written media is not as rich as face-to-face communication. You do not have as many information cues or the opportunity to get immediate feedback. Anyone preparing for a management career would be expected to have reasonably good reading skills. However, reading for business purposes is very different from reading for general information or personal enjoyment, and much of it is done on-screen. Think about the types of documents you have to read in a business office and the reasons why you are reading them. Consider the following examples:

- Reading for editing and proofreading. Read each external and internal document (email, letter, memo, report, or other document) that you write at least twice. The first time you read the document is for the purpose of editing the content. You need to ensure that the content is correct and that all information that is needed is contained in the document. The second time you read the document is to ensure that the document is free of grammar, punctuation, spelling, and keying errors.

self-fulfilling prophecy
the belief that if you think you can do something, you are very likely to do it. If you do not think you can do it, you are not likely to do it.

© Otna Ydur/Shutterstock.com

Many documents are read on-screen in the workplace.

- Reading a request, claim, complaint, or information from a customer, client, or vendor. You may need to read the document several times to ensure that you understand exactly what is being requested and to evaluate the situation to see if the information presented matches your assessment of the situation. This process may involve checking records to see if the request, claim, or complaint is valid. You may even have to read between the lines to try to determine the writer's motive and mindset. Is the writer being logical or emotional?
- Reading specifications for products, services, projects, or other requirements that must be met. This type of document must be analyzed carefully to ensure that the specifications can be met and that they are appropriate for the work that will have to be done. Policies, procedures, agreements, medical reports, and legal documents may also fit in this category. They need to be read carefully so that you can adhere to them.
- Reading to locate information that will be useful for a report or project. You may skim many reports or articles to see if they contain useful information. You can then read carefully the articles that appear to have useful information.
- Reading professional literature for your own career growth. This type of literature includes specialized newspapers, magazines, or books that relate to your career. However, you may want to bookmark or highlight information that you think is particularly valuable for future review.

Writing in the Workplace

Regardless of the career you choose, the ability to write effectively is likely to enhance your opportunities for success. Writing in the workplace incorporates many subskills, such as planning, organizing, analyzing, evaluating, and decision making. This section focuses on two areas of writing—basic guides for workplace writing and strategies for effective team writing. These two sections incorporate many of the subskills described and are of particular importance to administrative managers who are often held responsible for ensuring that documents enhance the company brand and image.

Guides for Workplace Writing

The ten guides presented below emphasize the content, structure, and image of the final document that represents your organization.

1. Plan messages carefully. Many people skip the planning part of writing and just begin writing. Planning is a mental process that requires you to determine the specific purpose of writing and make decisions about the best way to meet both the reader and the writer's objectives.

2. Write for the reader. You are writing to communicate to the reader; therefore, using empathy is the best way to meet the needs of the reader. Most readers expect a message to be logical, helpful, sincere, and courteous. Writing in a fair, unbiased, and culturally sensitive manner represents both you and your organization in a positive way. Even negative messages can meet these expectations.
3. Present ideas positively. The power of positive thinking has been emphasized throughout this text. In the workplace, conditions require you to present both positive and negative information. Use an honest—but positive—writing style. Think of it as being able to disagree without being disagreeable.
4. Write in a clear, readable style. Clarity means being clear. A message written with clarity cannot be misinterpreted. Clarity is required to get your message across in a multicultural environment. Graphs, charts, and illustrations are ways to get the message across in technical writing.
5. Check for completeness. A complete message is one that contains all the information necessary to meet your objectives and those of the reader. Anticipate questions and be careful with assumptions. Assuming what the reader knows or does not know is a difficult judgment. It is better to assume too little and provide more information than to assume too much and leave out needed information.
6. Use an efficient, action-oriented style. Writing in an efficient style means saying everything that needs to be said and nothing more. Busy people consider conciseness a virtue; however, do not confuse an efficient style with a blunt or curt style. Building goodwill should be a part of all communication in the workplace.
7. Use concrete language. Concrete language is very specific language that conveys precise meaning. General ideas can often be interpreted in different ways. If someone says, "I will finish the report as soon as possible," when can you expect it to be complete? Specific language takes the guesswork out of reading.
8. Use sentence and paragraph structure strategically. A simple sentence presents an idea clearly and emphatically. Place things that you want to emphasize in simple sentences. Complex sentences should be used to present ideas of unequal importance whereas compound sentences should be used to present ideas of equal importance. Note the differences below.
   a. Modifying the proposal as presented saves you $5,000. (simple and emphatic)
   b. Although the meeting took two hours, it was a great investment of time. (time was not as important as the value)
   c. The proposal was revised as requested, and all of the objectives were met. (ideas of equal value)

Unity, coherence, and emphasis are key concepts in developing paragraphs. Unity means that all sentences relate to one topic. A coherent paragraph contains ideas that are linked logically to each other. Using emphasis means stressing important ideas and de-emphasizing less important ideas.

9. Format documents effectively. The key reasons for focusing on format are company image and readability. Most organizations provide style guides so that documents produced are consistent with the company branding and make a good impression. Effective document format adds structure and increases readability.
10. Edit and proofread documents carefully. Documents with errors or missing information create a poor impression and may create doubt in the mind of the reader about your competence or the quality of your work overall.[15]

Team Writing

Project teams generally are required to prepare a report at the end of a project. Writing as a team presents a special challenge because the report is normally written by several people and should read as though it was written by one person. The content and appearance of a team report should be consistent. The following strategies are useful in developing a project report:

1. Prepare a detailed outline, specifying content to be included and who will cover each section.
2. Discuss what content should be emphasized and what should be minimized. The level of detail should be decided before writing begins.
3. Insist that all writers agree to use a specific writing style determined by the team, such as direct, action-oriented, concise style.
4. Ensure that sections of the report fit together and flow smoothly. An effective way to ensure coherence is to begin each section with a brief overview statement of what is included in the section and close each section with a brief summary statement.
5. Use a consistent pattern to present charts, graphs, tables, and other visuals.
6. Make the entire team responsible for editing the report carefully.[16]

SUMMARY

1. Both internal and external communication is required at all levels of an organization, including mass communication, small-group communication, and one-on-one communication.
2. Cultural differences have an impact on communication.
3. Barriers to effective communication include physical, cultural, semantic, attitude, and competence barriers.
4. Managers can enhance communication by matching the type of message they wish to convey with the right media.
5. Effective listeners are active listeners and understand nonverbal communication.
6. Oral communication consists of speaking in one-on-one discussions, to a team or small-group meeting, telephone calls, and presentations.
7. Proactive language focuses on what can be done. Reactive language tends to be negative and transfers responsibility to someone else.
8. Reading in the workplace is different from reading for personal use.
9. Writing is a critical career skill. Team writing requires special attention because the final product must read as though it was written by one person.

Terms

communication, 285
communication media, 298
culture, 291
downward communication, 291
external communication, 288
formal communication, 289
grapevine, 290
horizontal communication, 291
informal communication, 289
internal communication, 287
mass communication, 288
media richness, 298
monochronic time, 295
nonverbal communication, 300
oral communication, 291
polychronic time, 295
self-fulfilling prophecy, 303
technology-enhanced communication, 291
telepresence, 291
upward communication, 290
written communication, 291

Study Tools

CourseMate
Located at www.cengagebrain.com

- Chapter Outlines
- Flashcards
- Interactive Quizzes
- Tech Tools
- Video Segments

and More!

Questions for Reflection

1. Why must internal communication be as effective as external communication?
2. How does the global economy and workforce diversity impact communication on the job?
3. List four barriers to effective workplace communication and identify a strategy to overcome each.
4. Describe five techniques you can use to become a more active listener.
5. List four types of nonverbal communication and explain how each could be used in the workplace.
6. Explain how proactive language can be used to improve the relationship between managers and employees.

Answers to Knowledge to Action Exercise (page 298)

Type of Message	Choose the Best Match	Transmission Media
Performance counseling and/or appraisal.	**b**	a. Email
Plans to lay off 50 employees by the end of the year.	**c**	b. Face-to-face, one-on-one in person
Last-minute change in plans, the meeting will start at 3:00, not 1:00 as originally scheduled.	**e**	c. Face-to-face, group meeting in person
Announcing plans for the company's annual holiday party.	**a**	d. Company website posting
Promotional notice advertising new product.	**d**	e. Phone call

Hands-On Activities

Media Richness

1. Explain the concept of media richness.
2. List four or five specific transmission media.
   a. For each method, provide an example from your personal experience. Describe the nature of the message content.
   b. Indicate the section (S1, S2, S3, or S4) that each medium would be related to on the continuum of media richness on page 298.
   c. Describe how the message was conveyed and analyze whether or not you think the appropriate method was selected for the situation. If the method was appropriate, explain why. If the method was not appropriate, what would have been a better medium for the situation?

You Decide | Case Study

Recognizing and Overcoming Communication Barriers

Cari Lyn has worked for Springbreak Scooters for three years. She started out on the manufacturing floor while taking college courses at the local university. She graduated last May with a bachelor's degree in business management. She was planning to start looking for another job when she received a notice that Brad, one of the section managers, was leaving and the company was accepting applications for the position.

Although she had no formal managerial experience, Cari Lyn believed that working as a section leader provided her with hands-on experience leading people and accomplishing goals. In addition, she was familiar with the team, which included a balanced mixed of age, gender, and ethnic diversity. Their education levels varied as well: three had associates degrees, one had a bachelor's degree, and the rest had a high school diploma or equivalent.

During the interview process, Rich (the day-shift floor manager) and Daphne (the plant manager) asked fairly typical questions. Then they surprised Cari Lyn by sharing that productivity on first shift had been declining over the last year, primarily because the previous manager's communication style was defensive. He would frequently say, "There's nothing I can do to increase productivity." Daphne also shared that she had met with Brad's team after he left to get a better understanding of their concerns. Everyone agreed that Brad, who had a Ph.D. in engineering, always used technical terms when it was not necessary and seemed to talk down to people. He never listened and would always blame others for his mistakes. Daphne concluded the interview by requesting that Cari Lyn prepare a communication strategy report that included a list of potential barriers to communication as well as Cari Lyn's suggestions for improving communication and her overall strategy for improving productivity.

Questions

1. How would you suggest Cari Lyn begin?
2. What are a few specific communication barriers that Daphne mentioned when referring to the previous supervisor?
3. How should Cari Lyn avoid these barriers?
4. What other suggestions do you think Cari Lyn should make for improving communication?
5. What should her strategy be for communicating effectively with her new team?

MANAGER'S TOOLKIT

Most people would agree that there is always room for improvement with our communication skills. Managers are not only striving to improve their personal communication skills but are also teaching their employees these same skills. Prepare a couple of documents that outline tips and best practices for effective communication related to the following situation.

Assume you are coaching an employee who consistently demonstrates negative communication and uses reactive language. Identify three communication techniques to help shift his or her communication style to be more effective and at the same time help shift his or her attitude to be more positive and proactive.

Soft Skills for Success

Personal Presentation

This topic focuses on you rather than on making an oral presentation. You might refer to it as personal branding or making a personal impact. Obviously the topic could be in any type of setting—social or business. For the purposes of this exercise, the focus will be in a business setting. Organizations focus on presenting a carefully crafted, consistent image—often called corporate identity or branding. Have you thought about how you can present a carefully crafted, consistent image—call it your personal identity or branding if you wish to do so? Personal presentation is not only making a good first impression, but also a good lasting impression. A good way to think about this topic is to ask yourself a few questions.

- How do you think you present yourself to others?
- How do you think others view you?
- How would you like others to view you?
- What words would you like them to use in describing you?

Put It to Work

Take a look at the list of characteristics listed below. Which ones would be on your list? More importantly would any of these characteristics **not** be on your list?

professional appearance	tolerant and respectful to all
self-confident	responsible
positive, winning attitude	accountable
high energy	flexible, adaptable
self-disciplined	self-managed
enthusiastic	trustworthy, credible
always do your share	sensitive to others
honest, strong integrity	courteous, good manners
makes good decisions	assertive
critical thinker	good communicator
engaging	

Perhaps by now you have recognized that the characteristics listed are the soft skills expected by businesses and that you have been working on developing in the previous chapters. What you may not have thought about is how you can use those soft skills to present yourself to others so that you will make both a good first impression and a good lasting impression. In the Soft Skills activity in Chapter 11, you learned how to use the visualization technique. Your task now is to select one or two of the characteristics that you would like to develop to a higher level. Using the technique you learned, visualize yourself projecting the personal identity that you want others to have of you. Practice until you become comfortable with the image you project.

CHAPTER 14

Managing Workplace Challenges

Learning Outcomes

1. Describe the six-step process that can be used to get underachievers on track.
2. Explain what is meant by progressive discipline and the steps taken to implement a progressive discipline plan.
3. Explain why it is important to handle termination effectively and provide several tips to do so.
4. Identify and describe five styles to resolve workplace conflict.
5. Describe two difficult situations to manage and give helpful suggestions on how to manage them.

Straight Talk From the Field

JoAnn Turnquist is President & CEO of the Central Carolina Community Foundation, a nonprofit organization. She also has extensive experience managing sales teams and administrative assistants in major corporations—including serving as Vice President of Sales–Corporate Accounts, JohnsonDiversey, and Vice President of Sales for the Clorox Company.

Printed by permission from JoAnn Turnquist

Photo courtesy of J. Turnquist

How does managing workplace challenges in for-profit and nonprofit organizations differ?

Both types of organizations address workplace challenges in a similar fashion. The key difference to me has been in the size of the organization. Size adds complexity and additional regulations when dealing with human resources issues. Managing staff effectively, particularly underachieving staff, is the greatest challenge in both types of organizations.

How do you deal with employees who are underachieving?

The first step is to implement a rigorous bi-annual review process that focuses on specifics and takes subjectivity out of the assessment. As you analyze the results of the review, it is important to ask first what you, as a manager, can do to improve that person's performance. What aspects of training have not been met? What tools and resources have you provided or failed to provide that would allow your employee to be more successful? If you find that you have not fulfilled your organization's obligation to the person, then you must revise your management approach or provide the resources needed to help the employee become successful.

Once this has been done, if poor performance continues and progress has not been made in meeting job requirements, then the next step is to place the employee in a performance improvement plan (PIP). To initiate the PIP, you must provide a thorough review of the employee's performance that clearly illustrates how the performance does not meet requirements and why the person is being placed in a PIP. It is important to ensure that there is total clarity on both your side and the employee's side as to why you initiated the PIP.

In the PIP, two or three key areas that need improvement should be identified. The plan should focus on the most critical skills or aspects of the job. The specific activities and results that must be accomplished in a defined period of time—usually 90 days—are listed. Specific, measurable goals are agreed upon and both the manager and the employee must sign the plan. The goals must be realistic and achievable, but they should be enough of a stretch to ensure that the person will be successful after the PIP has been completed.

How do you know if the employee is on target to meet the goals in 90 days?

During the PIP period, the manager and employee must meet weekly for the employee to update the manager on his or her progress. As a manager, your job is to recognize improvement, if progress has been made, or to coach the employee if his or her performance and results are not on target. In every meeting, the employee should be reminded that performance must improve before the end of the PIP in order to retain his or her employment with the organization. The goal of the PIP is to convert underachieving employees into productive employees, but not every employee will have the capacity, capability, or will to achieve their PIP goals. You must ensure that an employee who does not meet the requirements of the PIP will be terminated. At the end of the PIP, performance is evaluated. If the employee has met the goals, he or she is taken off the PIP. Notification is given that if performance lapses, termination will occur. If the employee's position or area of responsibility changes, a second PIP with new objectives should be implemented.

The goal of the PIP is to convert underachieving employees into productive employees, but not every employee will have the capacity, capability, or will to achieve their PIP goals.

How difficult is it to terminate an employee?

It is a nightmare, especially if the manager hired that employee and so has a vested interest in the employee doing well and meeting company expectations. Effective managers must focus on the well-being of the entire company and understand that high levels of performance are expected of everyone. An employee who does not perform well in the PIP will likely never progress nor meet his or her own career expectations. It is better to not prolong the termination process so that the employee can move on to a career in which he or she is more suited. Critical to managing poor-performing employees is recordkeeping and documentation. Oftentimes, the poor-performing employee is alerted to the subpar performance through conversation or email. However it is very important, whether dealing with a poor-performing employee or any employee, that you maintain consistent and comprehensive documentation. With high-performing employees, those records will enable you to justify promotion and increased compensation. For average-performing employees, your records will help you create an effective training and development plan. For poor-performing employees at risk of termination, your records will provide the legal backup that is required to support your actions.

Visit *www.cengagebrain.com* to read the complete profile.

Chapter Outline

The terms *discipline, conflict, poor performance*, and *termination* tend to be associated with powerful negative emotions. Most supervisors do not enjoy handling difficult situations and will often avoid addressing them. But most problems do not just go away. In this chapter, you will learn how to work with underachieving employees in an effort to help them reach their potential. We will also discuss specific remedial techniques such as progressive discipline and action plans. Unfortunately, there are times when these strategies are not effective and the best decision is to terminate an employee.

Prior to taking any major personnel action, you should consult with your manager and/or human resources department. It is wise to seek their guidance in resolving difficult employee situations. If you are unsure, your company should request input from an attorney, preferably one with expertise in employment law. If your company employs union members, familiarize yourself with the specific terms of the labor contract.

Getting Underachievers on Track

Most supervisors have great expectations when they hire new employees. During the interview process, new hires do or say something to make themselves stand out from the other applicants. This may involve their knowledge, experience, communication skills, or a combination of these variables. A disappointing day in the life of a manager is when she or he realizes that a new hire is not living up to expectations. In all fairness, the first step in addressing poor performance is to openly and honestly assess the situation with the individual. This process involves discussing the following topics with the employee: (1) expectations, (2) performance measures, (3) resources, (4) training, (5) obstacles, and (6) action plan.

The first step in addressing poor performance is to openly and honestly assess the situation with the individual.

Expectations

One of the keys to setting employees up for success is clarifying expectations. When you feel an employee is not reaching her or his potential, take the time to discuss and clarify expectations. Making sure the employee understands the job expectations is the first step. A good way to do this is to have the employee tell you what he or she thinks the expectations are. This provides valuable insight into the employee's view of the job and engages her or him.

If you both agree on the expectations, then you are ready to move on to a discussion about performance measures. If your expectations are different from those the employee just described, then you need to review the employee's job description with her or him and reiterate your expectations. It is also helpful to provide the employee with this information in writing so it can be referenced later.

Performance Measures

Companies use both subjective and objective performance measures. **Subjective performance measures** are based primarily on perception and judgment because some areas that are important to organizations are hard to quantify, such as contributions to building culture or professionalism. **Objective performance measures** are based on quantifiable data. Clearly, objective metrics are preferred because employees perceive them to be fair and equitable. In many cases, organizations use a blend of both objective and subjective metrics. The blended approach uses objective metrics primarily and, at the same time, makes employees aware of the importance of the subjective areas to the success of the organization.

When objective measures are used exclusively, employees may perceive falsely that quantity is more important than quality. Objective measures can and should be designed so that it is clear that quality is an important part of the metrics. For example, in a claims-processing unit, quantitative metrics are likely to include the number of claims processed in an hour and are weighted by the complexity of the claims. Complexity may be specified by a quantifiable metric that lists criteria for ranking claims as Levels 1, 2, or 3. Qualitative metrics may include the number of claims that had to be reprocessed or were appealed by the client and overturned.

subjective performance measures
measures based primarily on perception and judgment

objective performance measures
measures based on quantifiable data

resources
things needed to get the job done successfully

With few exceptions, objective metrics can be devised for jobs in almost all industries. Employees must understand what metrics will be used to measure their productivity and work quality. Just as expectations needed to be clarified, performance metrics must also be clarified. Asking employees to describe the metrics that are used to evaluate performance is a way to ensure that they know how they are being evaluated. If they do not describe the measurement system appropriately, you have an opportunity to clarify how they are evaluated and get employee buy-in on the metrics.[1]

1. One way to set employees up for success is to minimize the use of subjective performance measures, clarify expectations, and establish mutually agreed-upon objective measures. Provide two examples of subjective measures.

   ____

2. Provide two examples of objective performance (quantifiable) measures.

   ____

Resources

Managers often assume that their employees have the necessary resources to be successful. **Resources** are things employees need to get their jobs done successfully, such as access to information, people, and technology. As JoAnn Turnquist pointed out in the opening interview, managers are responsible for providing the resources and training needed for an employee's success. Employees, particularly new ones, may be uncomfortable asking for additional resources. For example, the employee may want a new version of the software used or project software to expedite the completion of projects. Getting access to needed information in a timely manner may be causing work delays. Asking employees what resources would make completing work assignments more efficient or effective may provide valuable information for increasing productivity.[2]

Training

Chapter 8 provided an in-depth discussion of orientation and training. Even though the company conducted orientation and training, managers cannot assume that employees have retained the information or that they can transfer what they learned to specific job applications. Underachievers may need additional on-the-job coaching and training. In some cases, you may determine that the initial training was not adequate and needs to be enhanced.

Obstacles

Workplace or personal **obstacles** may hinder employees from doing their jobs effectively. Asking employees about barriers to doing their jobs effectively must be done in a sensitive manner and in a private setting. One approach might be to ask about distractions or interruptions that may be causing workplace issues. Keep in mind that an employee may not be comfortable discussing personal problems or sharing information about problems with others—including you as the manager. Trust is a prerequisite for honest feedback on sensitive issues.

obstacles
challenges that hinder an employee's ability to do the job effectively

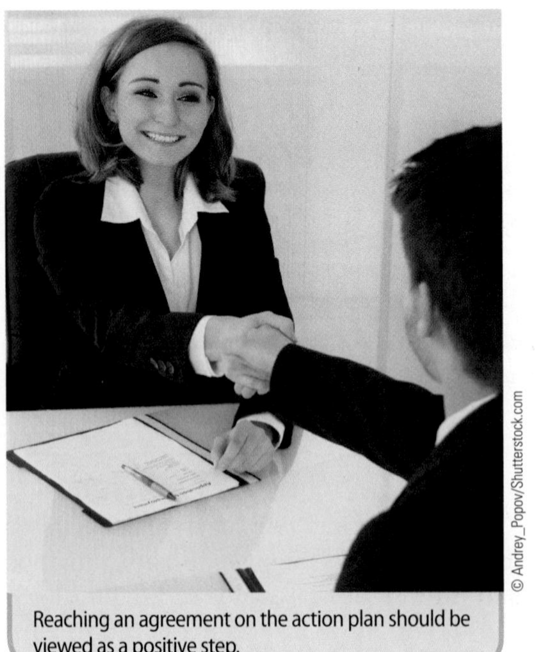

© Andrey_Popov/Shutterstock.com

Reaching an agreement on the action plan should be viewed as a positive step.

Action Plan

The five topics discussed so far focused on collecting information and determining why an employee is an underachiever and what can be done to change the status from underachieving to performing effectively. The idea of an action plan is to provide the employee with specific written guidance on actions needed to improve performance or to meet expected standards of behavior. For example, an employee may have the ability and skills to do the job effectively, but the performance is affected by behavior issues, such as chronic lateness or excessive unauthorized absences. These behaviors may not significantly affect performance of some employees, but making an exception for some may create problems with others who adhere to the company policies on tardiness and attendance.

The action plan describes the task or behavior that needs attention; what specific, objective measure of improvement is expected; and the timeframe in which the objective must be met. The action plan is viewed positively as a way to avoid discipline. Discipline typically is viewed negatively. To some, discipline refers to mandatory compliance with bureaucratic rules or dictates from a supervisor or manager to correct behavior.

Perhaps a better way to think of the action plan for underachievers is that it is a prescription for self-discipline. With self-discipline, the individual employee assumes the responsibility for meeting job expectations. Others may define discipline in a way that avoids corrective behavior language.

Discipline, in essence, is consistency of action—consistency with values, consistency with long-term goals, consistency with performance standards, consistency of method, consistency over time.

— Jim Collins and Morten T. Hansen describing what they believe to be true discipline

Source: Jim Collins and Morten T. Hansen, *Great by Choice*, (New York: HarperBusiness, 2011), p. 21.

Progressive Discipline

Most large companies and many small companies have a **progressive** (or graduated) **discipline** policy that is shared with employees through the employee handbook, on the company website, or directly from the human resources department. Legal review is always advised for a progressive discipline policy that leads to termination.

progressive discipline
a graduated process of disciplinary action leading toward termination

The steps described in the previous section are often the preparatory steps used prior to initiating a progressive discipline plan. The goal of these preparatory steps is to avoid having to initiate a progressive discipline plan, sometimes called a performance improvement plan. It is far more desirable and cost effective to detect the problems and to work with the employee to correct the situation. Making sure the employee understands the expectations, knows the performance metrics and behavior standards, has adequate resources, has been coached and trained, and does not face obstacles often creates the desired results. A critical factor that should be documented is that the employee has been engaged in each of these preliminary steps. The steps also provide an opportunity for the manager to determine the severity of the problems. Companies use a progressive discipline policy so that managers throughout the company consistently treat employees fairly. Usually four steps follow these preliminary activities.

1. Counseling. The manager meets with the employee in a private, formal setting and explains the purpose of the meeting, reviews the former conversations including descriptions of specific problems, and asks the employee about the problems. Then they mutually discuss the action plan for solving the problems. Managers should document the meeting date, time, and the specifics of the action plan agreed upon.

2. Written notification given to the employee. If the problem has not been corrected in the time designated in the action plan, then the

manager should meet with the employee and provide written notice describing exactly what has already occurred and what the employee must do in a specified timeframe to avoid more serious consequences, such as being suspended without pay for a certain amount of time. The employee is again engaged in discussions of ways to correct the situation.

3. Written warning including suspension or other consequences specified in the previous step. The purpose of a suspension is to give employees time to reflect on their actions with the expectation that performance will improve when they return to work. This is similar to detention or suspension for school children. Again the

The purpose of a suspension is to give employees time to reflect on their actions with the expectation that performance will improve.

LEVERAGING TECHNOLOGY

AUTOMATING HUMAN RESOURCES RECORDS

The importance of automating record keeping for human resource functions for businesses of all sizes has been emphasized throughout this text. Comprehensive human resources information systems used in medium to large businesses have the ability to track and manage all of the documentation required for progressive discipline. The following tips are helpful to small businesses:

- Make sure the following electronic records are stored for easy access for managers needing the information for their areas of responsibility
  - Job analysis and job description—used to clarify expectations and set objective performance measures
  - Company policies that affect employee conduct
  - Performance appraisal records
- Keep employee attendance records online
- Set up a template or develop a form to record supervisory notes that includes all information needed for documentation. Examples include:
  - Employee name
  - Date of meeting or discussion with employee
  - Key areas covered
  - Employee responses
  - Actions required
  - Schedule for completing action and next meeting

employee is engaged in the discussion, and the warning is placed in the employee's personnel file. The suspension or other consequences specified are implemented if the problem is not corrected. Notice is given the employee that termination will result if the specified improvement is not reached by the new time specified.

4. Termination. The employee is fired. Ways to handle termination effectively are discussed in the next section.[3]

Employee Termination

Termination is the involuntary release of an employee. Terminating an employee is never easy, but it is important to handle it properly. Typically, termination occurs at the conclusion of a progressive discipline action. However, on occasion an employee may be fired with no advance notice whatsoever. Usually, it is for an egregious action, such as illegal drug use, intoxication on the job, theft, sexual misconduct with another employee, or violence.

Termination occurs for cause (usually preceded by progressive discipline or egregious action), because of workforce reductions, or for no cause (employment at will). The principle of **employment at will**, recognized by most states, means an employer can terminate an employee at any time without explanation or cause as long as discrimination or **whistle blowing** is not involved. It also means that the employee can quit at any time without notice. Whistle blowing refers to an employee's reporting of corporate fraud or other illegal and unethical behavior. This information is usually contained in the employee handbook, and, in many cases, it is contained in the offer letter that both the employer and employee sign at the time of hiring. Jobs also may be eliminated because the job is no longer needed by the organization for a variety of economic reasons, such as loss of business, closing of an office, outdated or automated job, or a company merger with or acquisition by another organization.

termination
the involuntary release of an employee

employment at will
an employer can terminate an employee at any time without explanation or cause

whistle blowing
an employee's reporting of corporate fraud or other illegal and unethical behavior

Tips for Terminating Employees

As you read in the previous section, using a progressive discipline approach prepares the employee for the termination and takes away the common grounds used for lawsuits. In the opening interview of Chapter 10, Hagood Tighe, an employment lawyer, emphasized the importance of following the Golden Rule and treating employees with respect and dignity. This is especially true in termination situations. The following recommendations for terminating employees will minimize the likelihood of the employee suing the organization.

1. Treat employee termination as a business decision and follow company policies exactly as they are written. Remember that policies are designed to ensure fair treatment of employees and to protect the company and its proprietary information.

2. Plan the termination meeting carefully, including the setting and the timing. The setting should be very private either in a conference room or in the direct supervisor's office. Opinions differ on the timing—originally Friday afternoons were recommended, but current thought is that an early weekday (Monday or Tuesday) in the midafternoon is preferable. This gives the person time to take care of other business, such as signing up for unemployment. The meeting should be short and to the point—usually 15 minutes or less.

Treat employee termination as a business decision and follow company policies exactly.

3. Arrange for the employee's access to computers, the network, or company data to be cut off during the meeting. Protecting company data is a priority.
4. Determine exactly how you will present the information and anticipate the questions that will be asked and how they will be answered. Get advice from your manager and the human resources department or legal representative (if available). The information should be presented in the past tense—a fact already accomplished, effective immediately.
5. The employee's direct supervisor should be the one to inform the employee of the termination. A second person from the organization should sit in the meeting and take notes. Usually, a human resources employee is selected.
6. Set the tone immediately and present the information as a business decision. Do not engage in small talk—especially avoid asking about family or personal situations. The way that the message is stated depends on the reason the employee is terminated. If it is for cause, remind the employee of the previous conversations and indicate that, unfortunately, the person's skills and performance do not meet the company's requirements. If the reason is that the job has been eliminated, point out that the reason for the termination is due to economic conditions or changes in business conditions. If the company uses the employment-at-will agreement as the reason for termination, simply state that the company has decided to exercise its right to terminate the person's employment.
7. Give the employee an opportunity to respond and to ask questions. Listen carefully and empathetically, but do not argue or debate the situation with the employee. If necessary, state that the decision is final. Stay in control of the meeting.
8. Provide the employee with a letter of termination and written information about benefits, unpaid leave, and anything else the company provides employees who have been terminated.
9. Arrange for the return of all company property—laptops, cell phones, and company documents that the employee may have. Be prepared to have someone help the person pack up personal belongings or offer to have them packed and sent to the individual. Escort the person to the parking area.
10. Thank the employee for the contributions made to the company and wish him or her well in future endeavors.

Separation Agreements

Many organizations find it to their advantage to offer employees severance pay and benefits for a specified period of time in consideration for giving up certain rights, such as filing complaints or legal action against the organization. Typically, a separation agreement includes disparagement provisions that apply to both the employee and the organization. They typically specify that neither the company nor the employee will demean or make negative comments about each other. Often they include the specific language the company will use to respond if someone contacts them about a reference for the employee. Separation agreements must be accepted in a purely voluntary manner. Employees should be advised to have an attorney review the document and be given adequate time to make the decision to accept or reject the offer and return the signed agreement if desired.

Separation agreements are complex documents and should be prepared by an employment attorney to ensure that employees are treated fairly and that all provisions are enforceable. Getting good legal advice is well worth the investment.

Put yourself in the position of a person who is being terminated for cause. The organization followed all of the recommendations and handled the interview professionally. Read each of the following reactions and comment on why it represents or does not represent the way you would react. You would:

1. Think that the way the interview was handled positively impacted how you feel about being terminated.

   ____

2. Be upset, get angry, blame your manager, and vow to get even with the manager or the company.

   ____

3. Recognize that you simply were in the wrong job and make sure that the next job fits your capabilities and work style, and will not require you to change.

   ____

4. Recognize that you can learn from this experience and begin with a self-analysis to develop a plan for your future employment.

   ____

Resolving Workplace Conflict

Conflict in the workplace is inevitable and, to be successful, managers must develop conflict resolution skills. Conflict, in itself, is not bad. It is bad only if it is not resolved effectively and becomes negative and destructive. For example, think about a team of 15 people working on an innovative project. Bright people interacting and trying to develop new concepts or products are going to have different ideas on the best way to approach the project. Competing ideas generally will have some similarities and differences but, in some cases, they will be diametrically opposed to each other (often referred to as a win/lose situation). The conflict issue is whose ideas will win and how the team members will go about resolving the differences. The ideal resolution is often called a win/win situation. In this scenario, the winning ideas end up being satisfactory to everybody on the team.

Conflict Resolution Styles

Researchers have worked on conflict resolution theories for many years. Some of the best-known research focuses on the style that people use to deal with conflict situations. In the early 1970s, Kenneth W. Thomas and Ralph H. Kilmann identified two major dimensions of behavior and five styles that people use to handle conflict. The two dimensions were assertiveness and cooperativeness. The five styles were competing, accommodating, avoiding, collaborating, and compromising. Thomas and Kilmann developed the TKI, an instrument to assess an individual's mode of handling conflict. The TKI is still used extensively.[4]

This theory has similarities to the Blake/Mouton Leadership grid that was discussed in Chapter 4. The different leadership styles had two dimensions—concern for people and concern for production. In this case, the two dimensions are related to concern for others and to concern for the best ideas or approach to reaching a successful outcome. Think about how the 15 members of the team described at the beginning of this section might handle conflict. A team of 15 could easily have members whose preferred mode of handling conflict represented all of the five styles Thomas and Kilmann identified. It is highly unlikely that they would all have the same style preference. Let's take a look at each style that a team member might prefer.

1. **Competing**. People who are competitive want to win even though someone else loses in the process. The team members who want to win will be very assertive with their ideas and are not likely to cooperative or give in easily to other members' ideas.
2. **Collaborating**. In Chapter 5, collaboration was listed as a key attribute of high-performing teams and often included conflict, but to be effective the conflict had to be well managed. People who are willing to collaborate are assertive with their ideas, but they also respect the ideas of other team members.
3. **Compromising**. Most people would define a compromise as both sides having to give up something in order to gain something. Therefore, people who prefer a compromising style are not likely to fight for their ideas or assert themselves strongly in order to win, but they are willing to cooperate with others to get some of their ideas implemented. Often with a compromise, neither side is happy with the results.

4. **Avoiding**. Some team members are not going to put forth strong ideas that they are willing to fight for; neither are they going to try to block ideas that they think may not be very good. They avoid the situation and let other team members determine which ideas are accepted.
5. **Accommodating**. A team member who accommodates others who have stronger ideas may sacrifice his or her own ideas to support the more competitive member. They cooperate with others rather than assert themselves and their ideas.

Just as no one leadership style is best for all situations; no one mode of resolving conflict fits all situations. In the situation described with a team working on an innovative project, one style would clearly be better. If the team is to be a high-performance team with successful results, the synergistic or collaborative approach would be the best way to resolve conflict.

Guides for Managers

In many cases, conflict in the workplace is not based on cognitive issues, such as who has the best idea for a project. Conflict may be based on emotions, personalities, politics, miscommunication, and a host of other causes. In those situations, a different style may be needed to resolve the problem. Managers are usually responsible for resolving workplace conflict. In a few cases, avoiding the situation may give the individuals time to work out their differences without a manager intervening. However, in most cases, avoiding a conflict situation will not make it disappear. Normally, the best way for a manager to resolve conflict is to follow a few basic steps.

© Warren Goldswain/Shutterstock.com

It is important for a manager to understand the source of an employee's frustration.

1. Collect as much information about the problem as you can. Remain neutral in the data-collection process.
2. Discuss the issues separately with each individual. Try to determine what each wants to achieve and what each thinks is the source of the problem. Often perceptions people have of situations are just wrong, or people may interpret what someone said very differently from what was actually said. Try to identify the real causes and solutions that might work.
3. Get the individuals together to discuss the situation in a non-emotional, logical way. Try to point out ways to work out the situation to satisfy both sides.
4. Give people time to work the issues out. However, not all conflict can be resolved.
5. Establish guides of what is expected from each person to ensure that the work unit or organization is not negatively impacted. If necessary, use appropriate discipline.

Dealing with Difficult Situations

Most organizations have policies for dealing with many types of difficult situations, especially if safety or legal issues are involved. Experienced managers will verify that a wide range of difficult situations—many totally unexpected—will arise during your managerial career. Learning how to handle difficult situations effectively is a skill that will enhance your potential for higher managerial positions. This section includes six categories of difficult situations: workplace violence, personal hygiene and body art, behavior/attitude, theft, substance abuse, and harassment. Any of these situations can have a major impact on organizations, including lost productivity, fearful employees, absenteeism, and legal action.

Workplace Violence

Workplace violence includes threats, verbal abuse, and physical abuse. The U.S. Department of Labor's Occupational Safety and Health Administration (OSHA) reports that nearly two million incidents of workplace violence are reported annually, and many more incidents go unreported. In 2010, 506 workplace homicides occurred.[5] Employees in certain occupations are more at risk than others. They include those who: work in late-night retail establishments, work in high-crime areas, handle money, work with unstable people (healthcare and social workers), and work in customer service. However, no occupation is free from risk of workplace violence.

Workplace violence often starts with small incidents and threats and then escalates. The perpetuators of violence usually are employees, vendors, customers, or clients, but some may be spouses, other individuals who have a relationship with an employee, or random outsiders. Employers must make reasonable efforts to protect their employees regardless of the source of the violence. A number of government publications are available to help employees recognize and prevent situations which could lead to physical violence. Employers can take a number of steps to prevent or minimize workplace violence, including the following:

1. Establish a zero-tolerance policy for violence in your workplace, publicize it, and enforce it. OSHA and many security experts point out that this is one of the best deterrents to workplace violence.[6]
2. Provide appropriate security for the workplace.
3. Train employees to recognize potential situations that could lead to violence and to report them immediately. Often workplace violence is triggered by workplace actions such as firing, demotion, or promoting someone else to a job the offender wanted.
4. Screen potential employees carefully to determine if they have a record of past violence.
5. Take hostile behavior and any threats, especially threats by disgruntled employees, seriously.

Establish a zero-tolerance policy for violence in your workplace, publicize it, and enforce it.

workplace violence
threats, verbal abuse, and physical abuse

Personal Hygiene and Body Art

Personal hygiene is one of those areas that most supervisors avoid discussing with employees unless there is a complaint by a customer or other employees. You can save an employee from continued embarrassment by talking with the individual in private. Talking with an employee about personal cleanliness, including appearance and body odor, can be awkward. This is particularly true in cross-cultural situations. If handled improperly, the person can be deeply offended and emotionally defensive. Therefore, it is important to approach the conversation in a sensitive manner. Remember the Golden Rule and try to imagine how you would feel if you were in the employee's place. It is very helpful to have the support of a written policy regarding general appearance and cleanliness, as well as stated limitations on facial hair, piercings, tattoos, and use of colognes.

Companies have a right to ban visible body art as part of their professional dress policies as long as they do not unlawfully discriminate against employees. This topic will continue to be a major point of discussion in future years. Body art has moved toward the mainstream of society and is prevalent in young adults under 40, but it is still considered a negative in business organizations that tend to be more conservative than society in general. Many companies include policies on professional appearance, and the display of body art and piercings (with the exception of earrings) are often addressed in those policies. Many human resources professionals indicate that body art often creates a negative first impression in an interview.

1. If you have an employee who has body odor or is using heavy perfume or cologne that is offensive to coworkers and customers, what would you do?

   ____

2. Your organization has a professional dress policy which prohibits visible body art. An employee who is scheduled to participate in a meeting with customers comes to work that day with a dirty, wrinkled short-sleeve shirt that does not cover body art on his arms. What would you do?

   ____

Behavior and Attitude

Inevitably, some employees will display a bad attitude. They may be rude or disrespectful to customers or coworkers and insubordinate to their managers. The good news is that managers do not have to accept this behavior. It is helpful to create an "attitude standard" (see Chapter 11). An attitude standard establishes a baseline of expectations for employee conduct. In the absence of a documented attitude standard, you can still describe to all of your employees the characteristics of a positive attitude. If an employee consistently demonstrates a bad attitude, it is futile to sit back and hope it goes away. As difficult as it may be, you need to address the situation before the individual's negativity contaminates the entire workplace. Remember, attitudes are contagious—both good and bad.

Initiate this change by meeting privately with the employee to explain that you have concerns about his or her negative behavior and attitude. Share a few examples of when a bad attitude was displayed and the negative impacts this behavior had on coworkers and productivity. Clarify your expectations and provide examples of how he or she can demonstrate a positive attitude. Although the employee's bad attitude may be obvious to everyone else, individuals who are confronted with the information are generally surprised. They often are completely unaware of how they are perceived by others. In these cases, put your coaching hat on and work with your employee to improve. Agree on an action plan for a better attitude. A good idea is to include a gesture or code word you can use to signal the employee when he or she begins to display a negative demeanor. This secret code will help avoid embarrassment in front of others while nipping the problem in the bud. The action plan should also include time lines for incremental improvement along with consequences if the negative behavior does not change. Consequences may include reassignment of duties or disciplinary action.

Theft

Generally, managers and small business owners trust employees and perceive a low risk of theft or other fraudulent behavior. If they discover a loss of inventory, money, or other valuables, managers tend to believe it is a result of thieves from outside the company. But, in many cases, the culprit is an employee. The ease with which theft can be accomplished in many companies makes it tempting.

I can resist anything . . . except temptation

— Oscar Wilde

Source: The play, *Lady Windermere's Fan.*

Minor thefts include pilfering of supplies, using equipment for personal use, and using work time for personal use. Most employees would not even think of these minor misuses of company assets as stealing, and the percentage of employees who occasionally do these things is high. Over time and a number of employees, however, these losses can add up to a substantial amount. Most employers tend to be more concerned about theft of money, inventory, and equipment, which involves fewer employees but higher dollar losses per incident.

In retail establishments, inventory theft accounts for most of the losses. Many employers find it difficult to believe that their own employees steal more from their companies than shoplifters and organized crime.

However, these national statistics have been consistent for many years.[7] In office settings, embezzlement by accounting and financial people account for major losses. Surprisingly to some, many embezzlers are female.

Employees steal more from their companies than shoplifters and organized crime.

A small percentage of employees account for the bulk of these types of employee theft, but the total amount of theft is massive. Recently, in the FDIC process of closing a failed bank that had been well-respected in a Georgia community for many years, investigators determined that millions of dollars of fraud by several bank employees had occurred causing the bank failure. In fact, many companies have been bankrupted by employee embezzlement and fraud.

Employee theft is neither easy to prevent nor detect, particularly in office settings. Some of the steps employers can take include the following:

1. Prevention starts with hiring employees. Always check references thoroughly and do comprehensive background checks.
2. Create systems of checks and balances. Separate job duties so that different employees handle receipt of cash, checks, and credit transactions; accounting; verifying; reconciling bank statements and financial documents; and financial reporting.
3. Make employees aware that they can report any suspicious behavior involving theft without fear of retaliation, and make it easy to do so.
4. Check expense records carefully.
5. Be aware of employees who obviously are living a lifestyle that is not affordable given their level of compensation.
6. Make sure that any investigation and action is legally defensible. Taking action and prosecuting employees who are caught stealing or embezzling sends a strong message throughout the organization.

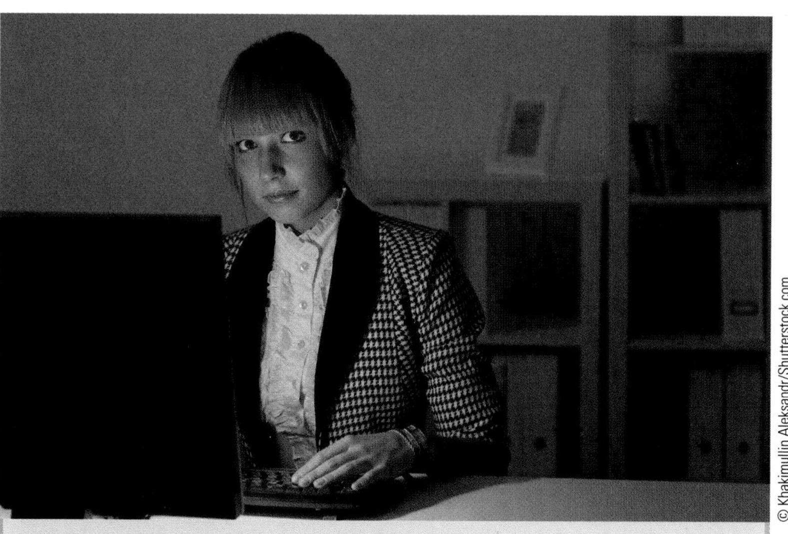

Embezzlement by employees who work in finance or accounting may result in major losses to businesses.

Substance Abuse

Alcohol and illegal drug abuse have a major negative and costly impact on the workplace. Managers frequently have to deal with a variety of problems—absenteeism, injuries, poor productivity, poor quality, morale problems, and disruptive behavior—caused by substance abuse. As a result, many organizations implement a comprehensive program to promote a drug-free workplace. Key components of the program include employee education, **employee assistance programs (EAPs)**, and drug testing. EAPs consist of company-paid services to assist employees with personal problems including substance abuse.

employee assistance programs (EAPs)
company-paid services to assist employees with personal problems including substance abuse

Harassment

Harassment as a form of discrimination was discussed in Chapter 10. People often think of harassment only as sexual harassment, but it also can apply to race, age, lifestyle, or any other type of discrimination that creates a hostile work environment. If an employee is suspected of harassment, your role as manager is not to analyze or interpret his or her behavior as a therapist. Instead, you should gather facts and observe the employee's actions. Importantly, focus on his or her performance and the job. For example, rather than spending a lot of time and energy analyzing the reasons for a harassment claim, discuss specific performance issues such as uncooperative behavior. Be careful not to attack the individual's personality. Remind him or her of the overall goals for the organization and how vital his or her role is in achieving those goals. Explain the importance of teamwork and cooperation.

Your plan for correcting the problem should emphasize the desired behavior. Rather than saying, "Don't be a troublemaker," describe the preferred outcome, "Be a good team player." Remember, you cannot control other people's behavior or emotions, but you can control your own actions, emotions, and decisions. Remain calm, be aware of the entire situation, and focus on the facts when dealing with challenging and difficult situations. Visualize the outcome you desire and then work with your team to achieve it.

You cannot control other people's behavior or emotions, but you can control your own actions, emotions, and decisions.

SUMMARY

1. Putting underachievers back on track involves clarifying expectations, ensuring understanding of performance measures, ensuring adequate resources are available, providing training, removing obstacles, and establishing an action plan to improve performance.
2. Progressive discipline involves four graduated steps—counseling, written notification, written warning including consequences such as suspension, and termination.
3. Employee termination is the involuntary release of an employee—normally the culminating step in progressive discipline. It should be handled following the Golden Rule and treating employees with dignity and respect.
4. Resolving workplace conflict is an important managerial role that must be handled effectively recognizing different conflict-resolution styles and being a neutral convener of conflicting parties to work out the differences.
5. Some of the difficult situations managers must be able to handle effectively are workplace violence, personal hygiene problems and body art, behavior and attitude problems, theft, substance abuse, and harassment.

Terms

employee assistance programs (EAPs), 328
employment at will, 319
objective performance measures, 315
obstacles, 316
progressive discipline, 317
resources, 315
subjective performance measures, 315
termination, 319
whistle blowing, 319
workplace violence, 324

Study Tools

CourseMate

Located at www.cengagebrain.com

- Chapter Outlines
- Flashcards
- Interactive Quizzes
- Tech Tools
- Video Segments

and More!

Questions for Reflection

1. Explain the difference between subjective and objective performance measures. Which of these is generally more effective for managers to use with their employees? Why?
2. What is an action plan? When would you consider using one?
3. Describe the preliminary planning you would do if you had to terminate an employee.
4. Describe your understanding of the employment-at-will concept.
5. If you were being terminated because the job was eliminated due to economic conditions, would you consider signing a separation agreement? Explain.
6. Which of the five styles or modes of resolving conflict do you prefer? Explain.
7. If you had reasonably strong evidence that a fellow manager (on the same level as you) was stealing from your company, what would you do? Explain.
8. Explain whistle blowing. Do you think employers should be permitted to fire a person for this? Why or why not?

Hands-On Activities

Conflict Resolution

1. If you were the manager of the 15-member team described in the Conflict Resolution Styles section, would you expect to have problems resolving conflict due to so many members having different conflict resolution style preferences? Why or why not?
2. You believe your team is a high-performing team, and it would be important to set ground rules for the way the team will operate to ensure that team members will approach conflict issues in a constructive manner. You may want to review the section on developing effective teams in Chapter 5 on page 93. Prepare the list of ground rules that you would like to discuss with team members and get their support for establishing operational ground rules.

Theft

1. Select a business with which you are familiar. Provide a brief description of the business. Indicate if you think the business fits the high-risk category for theft, and explain why.
2. What three steps would you recommend to the manager to prevent or minimize theft?
3. Explain how you would implement the three steps.

You Decide | Case Study

Making Difficult Decisions at Work

Lorena has been a police officer with the Pleasanton Police force for eleven years. Until last year, she was primarily assigned to foot patrol in the downtown business and shopping district. Merchants and other locals knew her by name and commented on her firm yet fair approach to maintaining a safe place for people to work, live, and shop. The safety rating in her jurisdiction was always rated as excellent, with fewer than ten violent crimes per year and fewer than five robberies per year.

Last year, one of the patrol officers retired and the sergeant asked Lorena to change assignments from foot patrol downtown in the commercial district to car patrol in one of the outlying neighborhoods. Lorena was ready for a change, so she agreed. She even offered to walk the downtown patrol with her replacement to introduce him to local merchants. Derek, a relatively new member of the police force, was selected to take over the downtown foot patrol. Lorena spent a half day with him showing him around the commercial district.

At first, everything seemed to be going along fine. Lorena was enjoying her new assignment, and Derek reported to her that criminal activity in the commercial district was down. However, after six months the sergeant called Lorena into his office to discuss a confidential matter. He noticed in his quarterly report that violent crimes and robberies were on the rise in the downtown area. He expressed concern and asked Lorena for her opinion. She offered to go chat with some of the downtown merchants to see if they had any observations or information to share. What she learned was shocking. The merchants told her that Derek was involved with an illegal gambling operation. Instead of patrolling the streets, he was focusing his time on collecting gambling debts.

Questions

1. If you were Lorena, would you report Derek? Why or why not?
2. If you were Derek's supervisor, how would you handle this situation once you found out about the illegal gambling operation?

MANAGER'S TOOLKIT

You want to develop the ability to handle difficult situations effectively. Therefore, this is an area on which you want to focus.

1. Select two of the following difficult situations: workplace violence, personal hygiene and body art, behavior and attitude, theft, substance abuse, or harassment. Write an introductory paragraph or two providing information about the topics.
2. For each area, prepare a document that includes tips for preventing the situation from occurring and describe the steps you would take to manage the situation if it occurs.

Soft Skills for Success

Influencing Skills

Persuading, negotiating, and influencing others are skills that managers need to be effective in today's work environment. Influencing outcomes means that you make things happen with an end result that satisfies everyone.

In previous chapters, you have already learned many of the skills for influencing others—building credibility, trust, and integrity. You have also developed critical and logical thinking skills. Therefore, you can persuade others because you can present information logically and in a believable manner and because you are trusted and have credibility and integrity. To negotiate effectively, you have to go a step further. What is missing is making sure you understand the needs and style of others. Listening and empathy are critical skills for understanding others. The ability to listen carefully helps you determine what is really important to others. Empathy means that you put yourself in their position and adapt to their style.

The actions you should not take when trying to influence others are sometimes more important than the actions you should take. For example:

1. Don't try to coerce people to do something.
2. Don't bully or try to intimidate others.
3. Don't oversell ideas.
4. Don't manipulate others.
5. Don't use politics or other people's power to try to accomplish what you want.
6. Don't have preconceived notions about the only way to do something.
7. Don't assume you know what others are thinking or need.
8. Don't assume that you have all the answers.

Put It to Work

The five-member cross-functional team that you lead has been asked to develop a plan to improve employee morale in your company, which is a small business with 40 employees in one location. Company executives are concerned about negativity in the company and some employees have a poor attitude. None of the team members report to you or to anyone in your work unit. By design, they represent the other five major work units, which means that you have no direct authority over any of them. As a leader, you have to influence the team to produce the desired outcomes.

1. You are preparing for the first team meeting. The president has asked you to report back with the plan within 30 days. List the items you wish to accomplish at this first meeting.
2. Describe several things that you will do in the meeting to influence team members to take the project seriously and to commit the necessary time and efforts to develop a comprehensive plan that will meet the executive team's objectives.

CHAPTER
15

Enhancing Your Management Career Potential

Learning Outcomes

1. Explain what is meant by self-awareness and describe its value.
2. Describe how you can adapt a SWOT analysis to your career planning.
3. Explain how you can use self-assessment tools for personal discovery.
4. Explain how managers should use assessment tools to make personnel decisions.
5. Describe how managers and current or potential employees can use skills inventory tools.
6. Explain what is meant by emotional intelligence and why it is important.
7. Describe how you can leverage your strengths in the workplace.

Straight Talk From the Field

Saminda Wijegunawardena, P.M.P., currently is Sr. Manager, Technical Program Management, at Box, which offers clients a flexible content-sharing platform. Prior to working at Box, he held management positions at Pixar Animation and Golden Gate University.

As you have progressed in your career, have you changed your views on managing effectively?

My view of the most important skills for a manager has evolved significantly through my career. Fundamentally, it reflects the transition from my sense of being a supervisor whose focus was managing work to a manager whose goal is leading a team. In the latter, quality work emerges as a byproduct of a high-functioning team, but in the former, while you may initially produce good work, you are not cultivating the interpersonal relationships of a healthy team.

As you can imagine, varied instances of interpersonal conflict, both passive and active, emerge in the workplace and can corrode an otherwise healthy and skilled team. Detecting the root causes of these systemic issues may be difficult because of individual attitudes toward power or entitlement within the workplace that can cloud perception.

What are the most essential skills for a successful management career?

I feel emotional intelligence (including emotional awareness) can be the most valuable skill a manager can possess in resolving problems. The abilities to effectively organize, cast/delegate, monitor, and coordinate work are of course important core skills. But the ability to function with emotional intelligence in all these aspects is the distinguishing factor from simply getting things done to building a fertile team that continues to perform well in changing, challenging environments.

Work is done by people and people do not stop having feelings because they are at work. For me, emotional intelligence is simply knowing who you are. If you do your best in this pursuit, you are able to interact genuinely and rationally with your team by removing your own personal projections from those interactions. You are then able to listen more openly and objectively to your team members, encouraging them to do the same. You can then reflect and take proactive steps to strengthen those relationships and employ skills in motivating and coaching your team members in this aim.

How do the employees you manage now differ from those when you started your career?

As my career has progressed, I have been fortunate to manage more and more skilled, talented people. The only thing that has remained consistent is the types of relationship issues that arise. Developing an emotional intelligence quotient (increasing emotional awareness) has become for me, an integral step in developing into a strong manager and leader.

Visit *www.cengagebrain.com* to read the complete profile.

Chapter Outline

Understanding self-awareness and emotional intelligence and being aware of the tools available to assist you with these areas are the first steps in enhancing your management career potential. The same steps can be used to help the employees you supervise develop their potential as well. Numerous self-assessment and professionally administered tools are available that evaluate a range of topics, including personality, learning styles, communication style, and conflict resolution style. Although these tools are helpful, they need to be used with caution because no tool is a perfectly valid and reliable predictor of actual job performance. One of the keys to personal improvement and professional growth is accurate assessment of your strengths and limitations.

One of the keys to personal improvement and professional growth is an accurate assessment of your strengths and limitations.

Self-Awareness

Self-awareness is a measure of how well you know yourself—your strengths and weaknesses, and your impact on others. Your emotions play a major role in how you react to actions of others and how they react to you. In the opening interview of this chapter, Saminda Wijegunawardena points out how emotional intelligence affected his career development. Emotional intelligence is discussed in the Soft Skills section on page 349. Some of the factors that should be considered in gaining a better self-awareness, include your interests, likes, dislikes, cognitive abilities, physical abilities, energy level, skills, values, personality, life style preferences, work style preferences, learning styles, communication styles, conflict resolution styles, fears, and desires.[1]

self-awareness
knowing your own strengths and weaknesses, and your impact on others

Self-awareness enables us to stand apart and examine even the way we "see" ourselves—our self-paradigm, the most fundamental paradigm of effectiveness. It applies not only to our attitude and behaviors, but also how we see other people.

— Stephen R. Covey

Source: Stephen R. Covey, *The 7 Habits of Highly Effective People* (New York: Free Press, 2004), 66–67.

Physical fitness and health are areas that are often overlooked in a self-assessment even though they can have a significant influence on your energy level, attendance, and productivity. As noted in Chapter 11, the trend among employers to support and promote healthy lifestyles and wellness is increasing significantly. Employers are creating comprehensive wellness programs to fight obesity and accompanying health issues, enhance quality of life, and reduce medical costs and absenteeism. Leadership at every level of the organization is a key to creating a successful wellness program. Managers are expected to lead both by example and by encouraging employees to participate in the voluntary wellness program.

A key value of self-assessment is to ensure that you have a positive self-concept. In the "Soft Skills for Success" activity at the end of Chapter 8, you completed an analysis of your self-image and prepared a list of things that would help you develop a stronger, positive self-image. Lists for self-improvement are often in the same category as "New Year's resolutions." Each year many people with very good intentions set a number of resolutions to accomplish in the next year. However, before the end of January, most of the resolutions have disappeared from their personal radar screens.

1. Review your list of things to help you develop a stronger, positive self-image that you prepared in the activity at the end of Chapter 8. Describe the action you have taken on one or two of the items and the results.

   ____

2. If you cannot find your list or did not take action on it, complete steps 3 and 4 of the activity in Chapter 8 and then prepare an action plan to begin working on one or two of the items.

   ____

Often people get in the habit of saying negative things about themselves. For example, you may do something that was not what you intended or that did not produce the expected results, and then say something to yourself like: "Dummy, that wasn't the way to do that." The way to counteract each negative statement is to monitor your "self-talk" or your "inner voice" until you have done at least four or five things with good results. Force yourself to say something positive about yourself each time to create the habit of positive self-talk. Note that you need to be very objective about yourself. You should not say something good just to be saying it. The time to say something good about yourself is when you actually do something well or something that produces good results. Remember that habits are formed by doing things multiple times. Create positive habits rather than negative ones by conscientiously paying attention to what you say about yourself. Generally, people are far more critical of themselves than they are of others. You can influence your own success by focusing intentionally on what you do well rather than on what you do not do well.

SWOT Analysis

Managers involved in strategic planning often use a tool or process called a **SWOT analysis**. The letters represent **S**trengths, **W**eaknesses, **O**pportunities, and **T**hreats. Managers start by analyzing the strengths and weaknesses of the organization. These are the internal factors that they can influence or improve. Then they look at the opportunities they can use to their advantage. Managers also consider any threats that might harm the organization. These are external factors and managers may try to minimize their negative impact or use them to their advantage.

This managerial planning tool can be adapted easily to a personal career assessment tool that could apply to those who are in college preparing for a management career or to those who are already in the workforce planning for advancement to a higher position. The next four sections provide suggestions for doing a career-based SWOT analysis. A SWOT analysis is valuable only if you are objective about your strengths, weaknesses, opportunities, and threats.[2]

An effective way to adapt a SWOT analysis to your career is to use the three types of expertise and skills described in Chapter 1—technical skills, soft skills, and conceptual skills—as the basis for the analysis. Two factors you also must consider are education and experience. They are generally key requirements for managerial positions, and the managerial level dictates the types of skills and expertise needed. Another effective approach is to search the Internet and find several job descriptions for the specific position to which you aspire. You will note that the descriptions contain many common requirements. You can then use the common requirements as a basis for conducting your SWOT analysis.

Strengths Assessment

The strengths assessment is the most critical and perhaps the most difficult part of your SWOT analysis. You can influence your own success by focusing intentionally on what you do well rather than on what you do not do well. As you identify your strengths, think about having comparative benchmarks. Should you compare yourself to others or should you compare yourself to fixed standards or both? The best answer is that it depends on the situation. If you are in a position and you know that the position you desire is available and will be filled internally, the answer is clearly both. In addition to thinking about your own strengths, it would be helpful

SWOT analysis
a tool for analyzing strengths, weaknesses, opportunities, and threats

to think about other employees who would likely apply for the position. How do your strengths compare to those individuals? Look for areas in which you are superior to those individuals.

Use the following questions as a sample to start identifying your strengths:

- Do I have the education degree that is preferred or required for the job level I am seeking? Do my major and GPA give me an advantage? Does the currency of my education give me an advantage over people who received a degree five or ten years ago?
- Do I have the amount of experience that is preferred or required for the job level I am seeking? Is the experience relevant to the position? Can I show results of my experience? What did I learn from the experience that could give me an advantage in the desired position?
- What specific technical skills and expertise do I have that are required for the job? Computer skills? Financial knowledge? Organizational skills? Work habits? Refer to the Skills Inventory section starting on page 342.
- What soft skills have I developed that give me a competitive advantage? Critical thinking skills? Communication skills? Good team player? Excellent interpersonal skills? Integrity and ethics? Strong work ethic? Refer to the Skills Inventory section starting on page 342.
- Do I understand how my role fits in the big picture of the company? Do I understand why my manager makes the kind of decisions he or she makes? Do I look at things from the perspective of what is best for the entire team or department rather than just from my perspective?
- What are the things I think I do best? What do others, including my instructors or supervisor, tell me are areas where I excel?

1. Make a list of three of your strengths.

   ____

2. Select one of your strengths and make a list of reasons why this is a value to your current employer or will be a value to a future employer.

   ____

Weaknesses

As you asked yourself questions to identify your strengths, you probably identified a number of things that you did not consider to be strengths or things that might give you a competitive advantage. Ask the same types of questions to come up with a list of things that you could improve.

- Is my current level of education, my major, and my GPA appropriate for the desired position? Will I be at a competitive disadvantage?
- Is my current experience appropriate for the desired position? Will I be at a competitive disadvantage?

- Which of my technical skills are weakest and are likely to hold me back?
- Which of my soft skills are weakest and are likely to hold me back?
- What are the things I have difficulty doing? What do others, including my instructors or supervisor, tell me are things that I do not do well or that I need to improve?
- Do I have difficulty packaging my skills and marketing myself to a company?

1. Make a list of three of your weaknesses.

   ____

2. How can you turn these weaknesses into strengths?

   ____

Opportunities

The previous two sections focus on things that you can control or at least influence. You can build on your strengths and work to improve your weaknesses. Opportunities are different in that you do not control them, but you may be able to take advantage of them to build strengths in needed areas. The following are just a few of the many types of opportunities that might be useful:

- If you are still in college, could you schedule additional elective courses that would add to your technical skills? Are jobs available in your area that provide management development programs for new employees?
- Could you get a part-time job in your field to gain experience? Could you enroll in an internship or simulated work experience program to compensate for your lack of experience?
- If you are employed, are training programs available that would add to your technical skills? Are management development programs available that would prepare you for upward mobility? Does your company have a college tuition program that could be used to work toward a higher degree?
- Can you network and find a mentor who will coach you and open doors that might enhance your career opportunities? Are you taking advantage of professional development opportunities in your area?
- Do opportunities for advancement exist in your current field and company? Demonstrating excellent performance, being a good team member, and working well with others may position you for promotion.
- Are you willing to move to a new location to enhance job opportunities?

Threats

Threats are similar to opportunities in that you do not control them. The best you can do is to minimize or avoid them. The following questions help you identify threats you face. Once you identify threats, then you need to focus on ways to overcome or minimize them.

- Is unemployment in your area so high that experienced workers are competing for entry-level jobs that are normally filled by community college graduates?
- Are jobs in your field declining? Are your skills becoming outdated within a year or two of graduation because of changing technology?
- Are jobs in your field being outsourced?
- Are you competing with classmates or fellow employees who are better qualified for the position you desire than you are?
- Is there limited opportunity for advancement in your field?

A SWOT analysis simply provides you with valuable information about yourself. It is up to you to do something with that information. The best place to start is to build on your strengths. You can also turn a weakness into a strength by doing something about it.

Self-Assessment Tools

Self-assessment tools are tests, questionnaires, inventories, surveys, or other instruments designed primarily to measure various aspects of personality, motivation, or competence. Thousands of assessment tools are available—some are free, but most are available for a fee. College placement offices often provide free or inexpensive assessment tools to students to help them prepare for careers. Human resources departments also generally provide a number of assessment tools for employees.

Managers may use assessment tools to make personnel decisions and employees may use them to learn more about themselves. Assessment tools, whether they are self-administered or handled by an expert in the field, need to be viewed as just one step in the journey to becoming more self-aware. No assessment tool, even a professionally administered one, is 100 percent accurate. Many survey-style tools rely on subjective questions and answers that change depending on the person's mood or status at work.

No assessment tool is 100 percent accurate.

Managerial Use of Self-Assessment Tools

Managers may use assessment tools on their own incorrectly to make human resources decisions. But, when used properly, evaluation tools can provide an excellent baseline for discussion and improving overall self-awareness. In fact, the results of personal assessments are just the start.

The ideal scenario for completing the self-assessment process involves:

- Completing the assessment
- Evaluating the results
- Reflecting on your personal goals

self-assessment tools
tests, questionnaires, inventories, surveys, or other instruments designed to measure aspects of personality, motivation, or competence

- Reflecting on organizational goals
- Meeting with your supervisor
- Preparing an action plan—this should incorporate feedback and insight from assessments to leverage your strengths and identify steps to improve areas you deem appropriate for personal improvement
- Discussing plans with your supervisor for follow-up and receiving ongoing feedback

Supervisors need to follow this process with each of their employees. It is essential that everyone understand that the assessment tools will not be used in a negative manner. The reason for participating is to identify strengths and styles, and to look for opportunities to benefit both the individual and the organization.

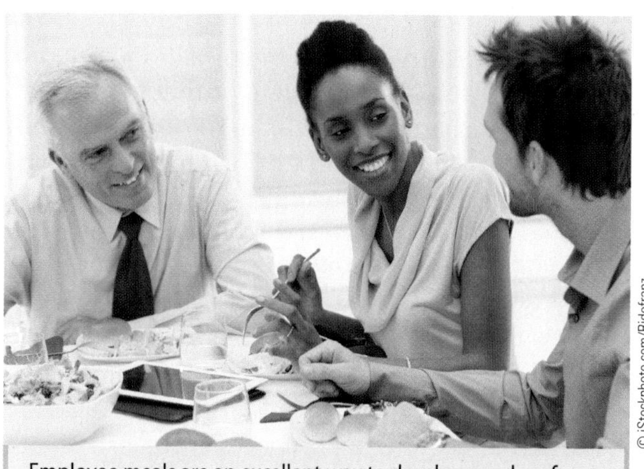

© iStockphoto.com/Ridofranz

Employee meals are an excellent way to develop good professional relationships.

Companies frequently have their employees do assessments in groups and teams. These types of assessments are often designed to enhance teamwork. Thomas E. Suggs in his interview for Chapter 2 provided an example of how his company used a professional survey that measures employee engagement and best predicts employee and workgroup performance. One of the survey questions on which his company scored low was "I have a best friend at work." To correct the problem, the company offers a quarterly company-paid dinner for any employee who wants to attend without any managers present. It provides an excellent way for employees to get to know and develop friendships and relationships with other employees.

Use of Assessment Tools for Personal Discovery

Throughout this textbook, many of the Knowledge to Action segments and the end-of-chapter activities help you discover your talents that are in demand in most administrative management positions. They also give you an opportunity to address weaknesses and to develop additional technical, soft, and conceptual skills needed for administrative management careers. The skills inventory tools in the next section demonstrate how to conduct a comprehensive, in-depth analysis of your value to an organization.

We believe that employee engagement with accountability is one of the reasons that we have been so successful.

— Thomas E. Suggs, President and CEO, Keenan Suggs Insurance

Source: Interview, Columbia, South Carolina, October 28, 2011

Skills Inventory Tools

Assessing your strengths in a SWOT analysis and preparing a skills inventory have some similarities and overlap, but the focus is different. The SWOT analysis is broad-based and focuses on career development or enhancing potential for a job category, such as management. A skills inventory is usually focused on a specific position, such as an administrative manager in a medical or public relations organization or an office manager for a consulting organization.

Many people think of a skills inventory as a listing of technical skills; however, today the emphasis on soft skills is so great that most people use a two-part skills inventory. The first part inventories technical skills, sometimes called tangible skills, and the second part inventories soft skills, sometimes called intangible skills, needed for a specific position.

Skills inventories can be looked at from different perspectives—the organization's perspective or your perspective. Some organizations prepare skills inventories that employees are asked to complete or that job seekers complete as part of the job application process. Skills inventories also are used by managers to evaluate employees' skills and to develop training programs. Some inventories are just long, detailed checklists that you check as having or not having the specific skills listed. Most also include a qualitative ranking, consistency ranking, or a mastery/effectiveness level. When companies prepare the skills inventory, they typically use the results of the job analysis to list all of the skills that are needed for the job.

From your perspective, developing and completing a skills inventory for a specific position helps you to compare your skills to the skills required for the position. While you may not have the results of a job analysis, you can obtain comprehensive job descriptions from different companies that include the skills required for the type of position you seek. You can also search the Internet for some skills inventories that serve as a guide for developing your skills inventory. An important concept to remember is that many skills are transferable to other positions. For example, if you can develop effective PowerPoint presentations, you will be able to use those skills in preparing a presentation for employees in a training program or for a variety of other situations.

Sample Skills Inventory

The following sample skills inventory is one small segment of a skills inventory that includes both technical and soft skills for a position as an administrative manager in a consulting firm. The job description has many technical skills requirements including this statement: "Requires strong computing skills, including in-depth knowledge of at least two applications in the latest version of Microsoft Office and a working knowledge of all other applications in the suite." The job description also has many soft skills requirements including critical thinking, communication, collaboration, team building, and creativity and innovation skills.

Technical Skills Inventory

The position description states that for in-depth knowledge of an application, an overall mastery level rating of 3 is required. For working knowledge, an overall mastery level of 2 is required. See Figure 15.1, below.

Soft Skills Inventory

The position description indicated that consistency is important in the application of soft skills. For example, "critical thinking skills should be used regularly for decision making." As the employee becomes more effective with a soft skill, the consistency level should increase as well. See a sample soft skills inventory for "critical thinking skills" in Figure 15.2 on page 344.

FIGURE 15.1
Technical Skills Inventory

Detailed list of major technical skills required.
Knowledge of Microsoft Office
In-depth Knowledge: Excel and Word
Working Knowledge: PowerPoint, Publisher, OneNote, Access, and Outlook
Level 0 No knowledge of the skill
Level 1 Essential—applies basic, frequently used commands to tasks; may need assistance
Level 2 Working knowledge—applies commands to average difficulty tasks independently
Level 3 In-depth knowledge—applies commands to solve complex tasks independently
Level 4 Expert—uses the application to solve highly complex problems; trains others
Comments: Provide additional information such as currently enrolled in training, not covered yet; certified at the essential level; course scheduled; or other explanation.

Skills/Tasks	Comments	Level
Create worksheets for various business documents		
Enter and manipulate data		
Add and rename tabs		
Edit worksheets		
Merge and center cells		
Insert/delete rows, columns, and cells		
Format cells and numbers		
Create formulas and insert functions		
Format and print worksheets with headers and footers		
Create, edit, and format charts		
Sort and filter data		
Create and filter PivotTables		
Use "what if" scenarios to solve basic business problems		
Use "what if" scenarios to solve complex business problems		

FIGURE 15.2
Soft Skills Inventory

Detailed list of major soft skills required.
Critical thinking skills
Consistency (C)

Level 1	Rarely	Level 3	Often
Level 2	Sometimes	Level 4	Most of the time

Effectiveness (E)

Level 1	Rarely achieves desired outcome	Level 3	Often achieves desired outcome
Level 2	Sometimes achieves desired outcome	Level 4	Most of the time achieves desired outcome

Comments: Provide information demonstrating success, special training, or specific examples

Soft Skills	**Comments**	**C Level**	**E Level**
Applies inductive (from specific to general) and deductive (from general to specific) logic			
Uses research from credible sources to collect information			
Thinks objectively			
Separates opinions from facts			
Recognizes biases			
Avoids emotional appeals and faulty logic			
Seeks alternative explanations			
Asks questions to clarify information			
Challenges the validity of statements including his or her own			
Understands historical context—what may have been true in past may not be true now			
Questions generalizations from facts to ensure they are accurate			

Leveraging Strengths in the Workplace

Knowing as much as possible about yourself is important, but leveraging what you know about yourself can empower you. You can create a personal growth and development plan that will enable you to reach your potential. Leveraging can best be accomplished by focusing on your strengths. Approach your limitations or weaknesses from the perspective of how you can make them a strength.

Completing a skills inventory is an excellent way to prepare a résumé and for an interview. If you are realistic and make an effort to understand what the organization seeks and how you measure up against the organization's expectations, you will be able to show the potential employer how your skills match the organization's expectations. Working with current employees to complete a skills inventory is also an excellent way for managers to map future training opportunities to meet specific employee development needs.

1. What are two of your most valuable technical skills that are beneficial in your current job or are relevant in the career you plan to pursue? Explain why.

---

2. What are two of your most valuable soft skills that are beneficial in your current job or are relevant in the career you plan to pursue? Explain why.

LEVERAGING TECHNOLOGY

INFORMATION QUALITY

For most people, the Internet is a very easy and convenient way to access information needed. In fact, so much information is posted on virtually any topic you research that it would take days to sort through it all. Much of the information, however, does not meet basic quality standards. The following tips may be helpful in evaluating information that you obtain from the Internet.

- Determine who is responsible for the Internet site. Is the provider a responsible, reputable source of information about the topic? Education, government, and some organization sites generally take responsibility for the quality of the content on their sites. What is the purpose of the website?
- Is the author qualified to provide credible information on the topic? Is information, including contact information provided about the author? What is the author's motive in providing the information?
- Is the information well-written, logical, accurate, and complete?
- Are sources, references, and other appropriate documentation provided?
- Is the information consistent with information from sites that you know to be reputable?
- Is the date of publishing and most recent update provided? Is the information current and not outdated?
- Are distinctions made between opinions and facts? Is the information balanced and objective?

SUMMARY

1. Self-awareness is a measure of how well you know yourself—your strengths and weaknesses, and your impact on others.
2. A SWOT (strengths, weaknesses, opportunities, and threats) analysis can be used as a personal career assessment tool. It provides the foundation for building on your strengths.
3. Other self-assessment tools can be used by managers to help develop employees and by individuals for personal discovery.
4. Skills inventory tools should include both technical and soft skills. Skills inventories should include a qualitative rating, a consistency rating, or a mastery/effectiveness rating.
5. Knowing as much as possible about yourself is important, but leveraging what you know about yourself can empower you to reach your potential.

Terms

self-assessment tools, 340
self-awareness, 335
SWOT Analysis, 337

Study Tools

CourseMate

Located at www.cengagebrain.com

- Chapter Outlines
- Flashcards
- Interactive Quizzes
- Tech Tools
- Video Segments

and More!

Questions for Reflection

1. Why is it beneficial for all employees to increase their self-awareness?
2. In the Knowledge to Action sections after the SWOT Analysis discussion, you reflected on your strengths and weaknesses. Identify two opportunities and explain how you could take advantage of them.
3. Identify two threats and explain how you could minimize or avoid them.
4. Assume you are in an administrative management position. How would you use assessment tools to make personnel decisions?
5. How would you use self-assessment tools for personal discovery?
6. Use the skills inventories in Figures 15.1 and 15.2 to rate yourself on skills with using an Excel spreadsheet and with critical thinking. What level do you think would be your overall rating for each of these skills? Explain why.

Hands-On Activities

SWOT Analysis

1. Use the Internet, your institution's career center, local companies, or your company if you are employed to locate a job advertisement and job description for a position that you would like to have.
2. Use a complete SWOT analysis to determine how your skills match the requirements of the position.
3. Make a list of things you could do for personal development in the next few months to prepare yourself for the position.

Self-Assessment

1. Locate one or more free online self-assessment tools and complete the assessment.
2. What results were consistent with your self-perception and expectations?
3. Were there any surprises? Anything you were not aware of or did not expect?
4. How can you use the results of the survey and your increased self-awareness to improve performance and/or to plan your career?

You Decide | Case Study

Employee Assessment

A small real estate company recently hired Frances to be its administrative manager. The owners recruited Frances from another real estate company because of her successful experience with the expansion and opening of new locations. One of her first objectives is to learn as much as possible about her current employees. She wants to quickly select a few top performers to be part of a team dedicated to opening new stores. Frances needs people who are not only technically good at their jobs but who also have excellent communication and problem-solving skills.

Frances is trying to decide the most efficient method for learning about the current employees to decide who she wants to recruit for her team. One approach she is considering is to shadow each person for a day. Another idea is to use one or more assessment tools. However, Frances has never used an assessment tool, so she is not sure what to use and how to get started.

Questions

1. How do you think Frances should proceed?
2. What are the benefits of shadowing a person?
3. What are the downsides to shadowing (observing) someone all day?
4. What assessment tool(s) would you recommend? Explain why and how she should use the results.

MANAGER'S TOOLKIT

In this chapter, you have discovered a few tools for learning about yourself and your employees. Working with your team, prepare a list of resources available to managers that may be helpful in increasing their own personal self-awareness as well as that of their employees. You may use the Internet or personal interviews with supervisors, friends, and family to discover what tools individuals and companies are using in this area. Your goal is to gain an understanding of tools and techniques available in an effort to develop your own strategy for encouraging self-awareness.

Soft Skills for Success

Emotional Intelligence

Emotional intelligence relates to being aware of and understanding your emotions and those of others. Often interpreting body language of others is the key to helping you understand and influence the emotions of others. The ability to assess, manage, and control your own emotions is necessary to handle the stress and pressures that occur in the workplace and to develop good professional relationships at work. While you cannot control the emotions of others, if you understand their emotions you may be able to influence them. If you observe body language and listen carefully, you can detect when a person expresses emotion, such as being happy, frustrated, concerned, or angry. Then you can act based on the information you have. Emotional intelligence is a composite of many competencies that are featured in the soft skills and other sections of each chapter, including:

• Self-management, trustworthy, honesty, integrity, and credibility; willing to embrace change and deal with stress and competing pressures; self-motivation; self-control • Critical thinking/problem solving • Empathy and cultural sensitivity • Ability to communicate effectively, especially willing to listen carefully	• Positive self-image, self-confidence • Adaptability and flexibility in handling change • Accept responsibility for commitments • Influencing skills • Collaboration and cooperation • Conflict resolution

Put It to Work

As a new manager, you want to learn more about your own emotional intelligence and to improve it. Use the following steps to begin the process.

1. Take an EQ test. Use the keywords *free EQ test* to locate and take a free EQ test online. You will be provided with your results as soon as you complete the test.
2. If your score indicates that you did not get a high rating on the EQ test, review the soft skills section including the activities at the end of each chapter in this book. Pay particular attention to the competencies listed above.
3. Then find another free EQ test and test your skills again. Emotional intelligence is developed over time, so do not expect dramatic improvements immediately.

References

CHAPTER 1

1. Robert L. Katz, "Skills of an Effective Administrator," *Harvard Business Review* 33, no. 1 (1955): 33–42.
2. "Framework for 21st Century Learning," Partnership for 21st Century Skills, www.p21.org/overview/skills-framework.
3. "Skills and Tasks for Jobs: A SCANS Report for America 2000," The Secretary's Commission on Achieving Necessary Skills, U.S. Department of Labor, iii–iv; "What Work Requires of Schools: A SCANS Report for America 2000," The Secretary's Commission on Achieving Necessary Skills, U.S. Department of Labor, June 1991, i.
4. "AMA 2010 Critical Skills Survey," American Management Association, April 15, 2010, http://www.amanet.org/organizations/2010-critcal-skills-survey.aspx.

CHAPTER 2

1. "Management Functions," *Encyclopedia of Management*, 5th ed. (Farmington Hills, CT: Gale, 2006), www.enotes.com/management-functions-reference/management-functions.
2. Doris Christopher, *The Pampered Chef* (New York: Doubleday, 2005), 2–3.
3. Chuck Williams, *Effective Management: A Multimedia Approach*, 5th ed. (Mason, OH: Cengage Learning, 2012), 9–10.
4. Richard Daft, *Management*, 10th ed. (Mason, OH: Cengage Learning, 2012), 36.
5. "Frederick Taylor and Scientific Management," NetMBA Business Knowledge Center, www.netmba.com/mgmt/scientific/.
6. Frederick Winslow Taylor, *The Principles of Scientific Management* (New York: W.W. Norton, 1911), 36–38.
7. Chuck Williams, *MGMT*, 4th ed. (Mason, OH: Cengage Learning, 2012), 25–26.
8. Ibid., 28.
9. Daft, *Management,* 42.
10. Warren Plunkett, Gemmy Allen, and Raymond Attner, *Management: Meeting and Exceeding Customer Expectations*, 10th ed. Mason, OH: Cengage Learning, 2013), 48.
11. Williams, *Effective Management: A Multimedia Approach*, 411–412.

CHAPTER 3

1. National Labor Relations Act, 29 U.S.C. § 152 (1935), Office of the Law Revision Counsel, in effect January 7, 2011, 143.231.180.80/.
2. Doris Christopher, *The Pampered Chef* (New York: Doubleday, 2005), 3.
3. Daniel Goleman, *Working with Emotional Intelligence* (New York: Bantam, 1998), 7.
4. "An Interview with Harvard Professor and Best-selling Leadership Author John Kotter," *Leadership Guide Magazine*, August 2011, www.leadershipdevelopment.com/html/magazine2.php?page_id=5&sub_id=190.
5. Robert Lussier, *Management Fundamentals: Concepts, Applications, Skill Development*, 5th ed. (Mason, OH: Cengage Learning, 2012), 222–223.
6. Mitra Toossi, "Labor Force Projections to 2020: A More Slowly Growing Workforce," *Monthly Labor Review* 135, no. 1 (January 2012): 43.
7. Ibid., 56.
8. Ibid., 57.

CHAPTER 4

1. Inspired by the definition in Andrew J. DuBrin, *Leadership: Research Findings, Practice, and Skills*, 7th ed. (Mason, OH: Cengage, 2013), 2. Also see Francis J. Yammarino, Fred Dansereau, and Christina J. Kennedy, "A Multiple-Level Multidimensional Approach to Leadership: Viewing Leadership Through an Elephant's Eye," *Organizational Dynamics* 29, no. 3 (Winter 2001): 149–163.
2. Warren Bennis and Joan Goldsmith, *Learning to Lead: A Workbook on Becoming a Leader* (Cambridge, MA: Basic Books, 2003), 8.
3. U.K. Department of Trade and Industry (now Department for Business Enterprise and Regulatory Reform), "Inspired Leadership: Insights Into People Who Inspire Exceptional Performance" (London: Department of Trade and Industry, 2004), 5.
4. Based on a content suggestion from David L. Batts, Ed.D., Associate Professor, East Carolina University, Greenville, NC.
5. Shelley A. Kirkpatrick and Edwin A. Locke, "Leadership: Do Traits Matter?" *Academy of Management Executive* 5, no. 2 (May 1991): 49–55.
6. Ibid., 56.

7. Bill Repp, "Leadership Flexibility Gets Results," *The Capital* (Annapolis, MD), August 28, 2007, B4–B5.
8. Michael G. Aamodt, *Industrial/Organizational Psychology: An Applied Approach*, 7th ed. (Belmont, CA: Wadsworth/Cengage, 2012), 443.
9. Kenneth H. Blanchard and Paul Hersey, "Great Ideas Revisited," *Training & Development* 50, no. 1 (January 1996): 44.
10. Ibid., 45.
11. Fred E. Fiedler, "Job Engineering for Effective Leadership: A New Approach," *Management Review* 66, no. 9 (September 1977): 29.
12. Fred. E. Fiedler and Martin M. Chemers, *Leadership and Effective Management* (Glenview, IL: Scott, Foresman, 1974), 91.
13. Robert J. House and Terence R. Mitchell, "Path-Goal Theory of Leadership," *Journal of Contemporary Business* 3, no. 4 (Autumn 1974): 85. An updated path-goal model is presented in Robert J. House, "Path-Goal Theory of Leadership: Lessons, Legacy, and a Reformulated Theory," *Leadership Quarterly* 7, no. 3 (Autumn 1996): 323–352.
14. Adapted from Chuck Williams, *MGMT,* 4th ed. (Mason, OH: Cengage Learning, 2012), 270.
15. Adapted from House and Mitchell, "Path-Goal Theory of Leadership," 83.
16. James MacGregor Burns, *Transforming Leadership* (New York: Grove Press, 2004), 24–28; Bernard M. Bass and Ronald E. Reggio, *Transformational Leadership*, 2nd ed. (Mahwah, NJ: Lawrence Erlbaum Associates, 2006), 3–15.
17. Ibid., Bernard M. Bass and Ronald E. Reggio, *Transformational Leadership.*
18. Robert K. Greenleaf and Larry Spears, *Servant Leadership: A Journey into the Nature of Legitimate Power and Greatness* (Mahwah, NJ: Paulist Press, 2002), 21–26, 147–150.
19. Carol Smith, *Servant Leadership: The Leadership Theory of Robert K. Greenleaf*, December 4, 2005, www.carolsmith.us/downloads/640greenleaf.pdf, 3–15.

CHAPTER 5

1. Jon R. Katzenbach and Douglas K. Smith, *The Wisdom of Teams: Creating the High-Performance Organization* (New York: HarperBusiness, 2003), 21.
2. Ibid., 14–15.
3. Ibid., 119–128.
4. For more information on the work of Tuckman and Jensen, see Bruce W. Tuckman, "Developmental Sequence in Small Groups," *Psychological Bulletin* 63, no. 6 (1965): 384–399; and Bruce W. Tuckman and Mary Ann C. Jensen, "Stages of Small-Group Development Revisited," *Group & Organizational Studies* 2, no. 4 (1977): 419–427.
5. The descriptions of using the Tuckman group stages were developed from the Tuckman and Jensen materials cited in note 4 and from "Form, Storm, Norm, Perform," *ChangingMinds*.org., http://changingminds.org/explanations/groups/form_storm_norm_perform.htm.
6. J. Richard Hackman, "Six Common Misperceptions about Teamwork," HBR Blog Network, June 7, 2011, blogs.hbr.org/cs/2011/06/six_common_misperceptions_abou.html.
7. Ibid.
8. Ethics Resource Center, "2011 National Business Ethics Survey: Workplace Ethics in Transition," 2011, www.ethics.org/nbes/files/FinalNBES-web.pdf, 21.
9. Joyce A. Thompsen, "Leading Virtual Teams: Five Essential Skills Will Help You Lead Any Project—No Matter How Distant," *Quality Digest*, September 2000, www.qualitydigest.com/sept00/html/teams.html.
10. Steve Bates, "Unique Strategies Urged to Keep 'Emerging Leaders,'" *HR Magazine* 47, no. 9 (September 2002): 14; and Carol Hymowitz, "The Confident Boss Doesn't Micromanage or Delegate Too Much," *Wall Street Journal*, March 11, 2003, B1.
11. Warren Plunkett, Gemmy Allen, and Raymond Attner, *Management: Meeting and Exceeding Customer Expectations*, 10th ed. Mason, OH: Cengage Learning, 2013), 146, 213.
12. Tom Davis and Michael J. Landa, "Developing Trust," *CMA Management* 73, no. 8 (October 1999): 48.
13. Martin Tillman, "Help! My Team Won't Accept Empowerment!" *Defense AT&L* 33, no. 3 (May–June 2004): 33.
14. Larry Bossidy, "The Job No CEO Should Delegate," *Harvard Business Review* 79, no. 3 (March 2001): 46–49; and Sharon Gazda, "The Art of Delegating: Effective Delegation Enhances Employee Morale, Manager Productivity and Organizational Success," *HR Magazine* 47, no. 1 (January 2002): 75–78.
15. Gazda, "The Art of Delegating."
16. Donald Mosley and Paul Pietri, *Supervisory Management,* 9th ed. (Mason, OH: Cengage Learning, 2014), 149.
17. Google, "Global Diversity & Talent Inclusion: 2010 Annual Report," http://static.googleusercontent.com/external_content/untrusted_dlcp/www.google.com/en/us/diversity/Google-2010-Report-on-Global-Diversity-and-Inclusion.pdf, 9.
18. Diversity@Google: A Place to Be You," Google, http://www.google.com/diversity/.
19. J. Richard Hackman, "Six Common Misperceptions."

CHAPTER 6

1. "Vision—Corporate Profile—About Samsung," http://www.samsung.com/us/aboutsamsung/corporateprofile/vision.html.

2. R. Duane Ireland and Michael A. Hitt, "Mission Statements: Importance, Challenge, and Recommendations for Development," *Business Horizons* 35, no. 3 (May–June 1992): 34–42; and Barbara Bartkus, Myron Glassman, and R. Bruce McAfee, "Mission Statements: Are They Smoke and Mirrors?" *Business Horizons* 43, no. 6 (November–December 2000): 23–28.
3. Chuck Williams, *Effective Management: A Multimedia Approach*, 5th ed. (Mason, OH: Cengage Learning, 2012), 114–115.
4. Linda Nacif, "The Secret to Setting and Achieving Your Goals," *Supervision* 68, no. 8 (August 2007): 18–20; Guy Kawasaki, "The Art of Execution," *Entrepreneur* 35, no. 9 (September 2007): 26; Amy Jones, "Get Ready, Get Set, Go!" *Get Motivated Workbook* (Tampa, FL: Get Motivated Seminars, 2006): 46–47; Bryan S. Schaffer, "The Nature of Goal Congruence in Organizations," *Supervision* 68, no. 8 (August 2007): 13–17; and Cynthia Kersey, "Become Unstoppable," *Success from Home* 3 (April 2007): 50–53.
5. Edwin A. Locke and Gary P. Latham, "Building a Practically Useful Theory of Goal Setting and Task Motivation: A 35-Year Odyssey," *American Psychologist* 57, no. 9 (September 2002): 705–717; Gary P. Latham, "Motivate Employee Performance Through Goal Setting," in *Handbook of Principles of Organizational Behavior: Indispensable Knowledge for Evidence-Based Management*, 2nd ed., ed. Edwin A. Locke (Chichester, UK: John Wiley & Sons, 2009), 161–178; Don Hellriegel and John Slocum, *Organizational Behavior*, 13th ed. (Mason, OH: Cengage Learning, 2011), 194–199; Edwin A. Locke and Gary P. Latham, *A Theory of Goal Setting and Task Performance* (Englewood Cliffs, NJ: Prentice-Hall, 1990), 260, 268.
6. Marion E. Haynes, *Project Management—Get from the Idea to the Implementation Successfully*, 4th ed. (Fairport, NY: Axzo Press, 2010), 45–46.
7. "Best Practices: Developing Budgets," *Inc.*, www.inc.com/articles/2000/01/16379.html.
8. Tom Peters, "What Gets Measured Gets Done," Tom Peters Company, April 28, 1986, www.tompeters.com/printer_friendly.php? print=1¬e=columns/005143.

CHAPTER 7

1. "Calculating the High Cost of Employee Turnover," *Thinking Leaders* (blog), April 21, 2011, www.thinkingleaders.com/archives/1253.
2. "Job Analysis: Asking Questions," Department for Business Innovation & Skills (UK), http://www.bis.gov.uk/policies/higher-education/access-to-professions/prg/recruitment-step-by-step/defining-the-job/job-analysis-questions; David Ngo, "Job Analysis Interview Questions," *HumanResources.Hrvinet.com* (blog), March 30, 2010, http://www.humanresources.hrvinet.com/job-analysis-interview-questions/; "Job Analysis: Overview," HR Guide to the Internet.
3. Chuck Williams, *Effective Management: A Multimedia Approach*, 5th ed. (Mason, OH: Cengage Learning, 2012), 588.
4. Entrepreneur Press, *Start Your Own Business*, 5th ed. (Irvine, CA: Entrepreneur Media, 2010), 354.
5. Wendell Williams, "How to Leave the Interviewing Stone Age," ERE.net, July 18, 2006, http://www.ere.net/2006/07/18/how-to-leave-the-interviewing-stone-age/.
6. Entrepreneur Press, Start Your Own Business, 356–357; John C. Kelly, "What Will He or She Do on a Daily Basis?" *Chamber News* 9 (February 2007): 5.
7. John C. Kelly, "What Will He or She Do," 5.
8. Ibid.
9. Jim Collins, *Good to Great: Why Some Companies Make the Leap . . . and Others Don't* (New York: HarperBusiness, 2001); and Jim Collins, "Good to Great," *Fast Company* 51 (October 2001): 90–104.
10. PWC, "Delivering Results: Growth and Value in a Volatile World," 15th Annual Global Survey 2012, www.pwc.com/gx/en/ceo-survey/pdf/15th-global-pwc-ceo-survey.pdf, 3, 7, 20.
11. Motorola, "Diversity and Inclusion," www.responsibility.motorola.com/index.php/employees/diversityinclusion/.
12. Information summarized from Bruce M. Meglino, Angelo S. DeNisi, Stuart A. Youngblood, and Kevin J. Williams, "Effects of Realistic Job Previews: A Comparison Using an Enhancement and a Reduction Preview," *Journal of Applied Psychology* 73, no. 2 (May 1988): 259–266; Bruce M. Meglino, Elizabeth C. Ravlin, and Angelo S. DeNisi, "When Does It Hurt to Tell the Truth? The Effect of Realistic Job Reviews on Employee Recruiting," *Public Personnel Management* 26, no. 3 (Fall 1997), 413–422; Paula Popovich and John P. Wanous, "The Realistic Job Preview as a Persuasive Communication," *Academy of Management Review* 7, no. 4 (October 1982): 570–578; CPS Human Resource Services, "Realistic Job Preview: A Review of the Literature and Recommendations," February 2006, http://www.cps.ca.gov/workforceplanning/documents/06.02_realistic_job_preview.pdf.
13. CareerXroads, "2012 Sources of Hire: Channels That Influence," http://www.careerxroads.com/news/slide-shows.asp; Susan Adams, "Networking Is Still the Best Way to Find a Job, Survey Says," *Forbes*, June 7, 2011, www.forbes.com/sites/susanadams/2011/06/07/networking-is-still-the-best-way-to-find-a-job-survey-says/.
14. Fred Vogelstein and Doris Burke, "Google @ $165: Are These Guys for Real?" *Fortune* 150, no. 12 (December 13, 2004): 106, 108.
15. CareerBuilder.com, "Nearly Half of Employers Have Caught a Lie on a Résumé, CareerBuilder.com Survey

Shows," July 30, 2008, www.careerbuilder.com/share/aboutus/pressreleasesdetail.aspx?id=pr448&sd=7%2f30%2f2008&ed=12%2f31%2f2008&siteid=cbpr&sc_cmp1=cb_pr448_.

16. James Lindner and Chris Zoller, "Selecting Employees for Small Businesses: Doing It Right the First Time," Small Business Series, Ohio State University Fact Sheet, Ohio State University Extension, ohioline.osu.edu/cd-fact/1383.html.
17. Stephanie Clifford, "The New Science of Hiring," *Inc. Magazine* 28, no. 8 (August 2006): 90–98.
18. Ibid.
19. Philip L. Roth and James E. Campion, "An Analysis of the Predictive Power of the Panel Interview and Pre-employment Tests," *Journal of Occupational & Organizational Psychology* 65, no. 1 (March 1992): 51–60.

CHAPTER 8

1. Mark Henricks, "You Know the Drill . . . or Do You? The Latest Training Tools Might Surprise You," *Entrepreneur* 35, no. 4 (April 2007): 24.
2. Marilyn Moats Kennedy, "Is Your Orientation Program an Adhesive or a Solvent?," *Physician Executive* 27, no. 1 (January/February 2001): 64–66.
3. Pamela F. Weber, "Getting a Grip on Employee Growth," *Training & Development* 53, no. 5 (May 1999): 87–94.
4. "Telework 2011: A WorldatWork Special Report," the Dieringer Research Group Inc. and WorldatWork, www.worldatwork.org/waw/adimLink?id=53034.
5. Ellen Weinreb, "How Job Sharing May be the Secret to Work-Life Balance," *Forbes*, October 24, 2011, www.forbes.com/sites/work-in-progress/2011/10/24/how-job-sharing-may-be-the-secret-to-work-life-balance.
6. Kennedy, "Is Your Orientation Program an Adhesive or a Solvent?," 64–66; and "Hire the BEST!" *Get Motivated Workbook* (Tampa, FL: Get Motivated Seminars, 2007): 67.
7. Zandy B. Leibowitz, Nancy K. Schlossberg, and Jane E. Shore, "Stopping the Revolving Door," *Training & Development* 45, no. 2 (February 1991): 43–50.
8. Keith Rollag, Salvatore Parise, and Rob Cross, "Getting New Hires Up to Speed Quickly," *MIT Sloan Management Review* 46, no. 2 (Winter 2005): 35–41.
9. These numbers are for external hires. Internal transfers get up to speed about twice as fast. See R. Williams, "Mellon Learning Curve Research Study" (New York: Mellon Corp., 2003); and Rollag, Parise, and Cross, "Getting New Hires," 35–41.
10. Kenneth N. Wexley and Gary P. Latham, *Developing and Training Human Resources in Organizations* (Glenview, IL: Scott, Foresman, 1981).
11. Karen McKirchy, *Powerful Performance Appraisals: How to Set Expectations and Work Together to Improve Performance* (Franklin Lakes, NJ: Career Press, 1998); and Carla Joinson, "Making Sure Employees Measure Up," *HR Magazine* 46, no. 3 (March 2001): 36–41.
12. William S. Swan and Philip Margulies, *How to Do a Superior Performance Appraisal* (New York: John Wiley & Sons, 1991).
13. "Getting Your Talent in Shape," *HC* Online, October 17, 2006, www.hcamag.com/resources/HR-Strategy/getting-your-talent-in-shape/113180/.
14. "Learning at Dell," content.dell.com/us/en/corp/learning-at-dell.
15. Wexley and Latham, *Developing and Training*. Also see Diana Hird, "What Makes a Training Program Good?" *Training* 37, no. 6 (June 2000): 48–52; and Natalie Shope Griffin, "Personalize Your Management Development," *Harvard Business Review* 81, no. 3 (March 2003): 113–119.
16. A source for some of these concepts is Derek Bruff, "Learning Styles: Fact and Fiction—A Conference Report" (blog), http://cft.vanderbilt.edu/2011/01/learning-styles-fact-and-fiction-a-conference-report/.
17. Special thanks to Professor Charles Wyckoff at Riverside Community College, California, for suggesting this perspective.
18. Lou Holtz, "Setting a Higher Standard," *Get Motivated Workbook* (Tampa, FL: Get Motivated Seminars, 2006): 22.
19. Ibid., 35, 443.
20. Ibid., 36, 443.
21. "USA Today Snapshots®," *USA Today*, February 6, 2007: B1 (source: Ace Hardware survey of 1,059 adults 18 and older conducted by Impulse Research). See also, for example, Quint Studer, *Results That Last: Hardwiring Behaviors That Will Take Your Company to the Top* (Hoboken, NJ: John Wiley & Sons, 2008), 55; and "Recognition Gone Wrong: OfficeTeam Survey and Video Bloopers Highlight Importance of Employee Recognition," OfficeTeam, http://officeteam.rhi.mediaroom.com/recognition_gone_wrong.
22. As quoted in Thomas A. Stewart and Louise O'Brien, "Execution Without Excuses," *Harvard Business Review* 83, no. 3 (March 2005): 106.

CHAPTER 9

1. Mary K. Pratt, "No More Job Reviews: Subtle Changes in Focus Can Transform the Dreaded Performance Review Into an Opportunity to Build Better IT Employees, Teams and Organizations," *Computerworld* 41, no. 14, April 2, 2007: 29; Tom Davis and Michael Landa, "Pat or Slap? Do Appraisals Work?" *CMA Management* 73, no. 2 (March 1999): 24–27; W. Timothy Weaver, "Linking Performance Reviews to Productivity and Quality," *HR Magazine* 41, no. 11 (November 1996): 93–99; and John C. Kelly, "Be a Manager and Leader, Not a Scorekeeper," *Chamber News* 9 (May 2, 2007): 5.

2. Lori Ashcraft and William A. Anthony, "Turn Evaluations into Mentoring Sessions: Performance Evaluations Don't Have to Be Dreadful," *Behavioral Healthcare* 27, no. 4 (April 2007): 8–10; Karen McKirchy, *Powerful Performance Appraisals: How to Set Expectations and Work Together to Improve Performance* (Franklin Lakes, NJ: Career Press, 1998); and Carla Joinson, "Making Sure Employees Measure Up," *HR Magazine 46* (March 2001): 36–41.
3. Kelly, "Be a Manager and Leader"; and Ashcraft and Anthony, "Turn Evaluations into Mentoring Sessions."
4. For Equal Employment Opportunity Commission guidelines during performance appraisal, see William S. Swan and Philip Margulies, *How to Do a Superior Performance Appraisal* (New York: John Wiley & Sons, 1991); see also Equal Employment Opportunity Commission, "Meeting of May 16, 2007, on Employee Testing and Screening: Statement of Lawrence Ashe, Ashe, Rafuse & Hill, LLP," www.eeoc.gov/eeoc/meetings/archive/5-16-07/ashe.html.
5. Rachel E. Silverman, "Yearly Reviews? Try Weekly," *Wall Street Journal*, September 6, 2011, B6.
6. For related research, see Todd J. Maurer, Jerry K. Palmer, and Donna K. Ashe, "Diaries, Checklists, Evaluations, and Contrast Effects in Measurement of Behavior," *Journal of Applied Psychology* 78, no. 2 (April 1993): 226–231.
7. Jai Ghorpade, "Managing Five Paradoxes of 360-Degree Feedback," *Academy of Management Executive* 14, no. 1 (February 2000): 140–150; Angelo S. DeNisi and Avraham N. Kluger, "Feedback Effectiveness: Can 360-Degree Appraisals Be Improved?" *Academy of Management Executive* 14, no. 1 (February 2000): 129–139; John Day, "Simple, Strong Team Ratings," *HR Magazine* 45, no. 9 (September 2000): 159–161; and Susanne G. Scott and Walter O. Einstein, "Strategic Performance Appraisal in Team-Based Organizations: One Size Does Not Fit All," *Academy of Management Executive* 15, no. 2 (May 2001): 107–116.
8. Weaver, "Linking Performance Reviews to Productivity and Quality."
9. Ibid.
10. Hubert S. Feild and William H. Holley, "The Relationship of Performance Appraisal System Characteristics to Verdicts in Selected Employment Discrimination Cases," *Academy of Management Journal* 25, no. 2 (June 1982): 392–406. A later analysis of 51 cases that derived similar criteria can be found in Gerald V. Barrett and Mary C. Kernan, "Performance Appraisal and Terminations: A Review of Court Decisions Since *Brito v. Zia* with Implications for Personnel Practices," *Personnel Psychology* 40, no. 3 (Autumn 1987): 489–503.
11. For more information, see Ashcraft and Anthony, "Turn Evaluations into Mentoring Sessions"; Dick Grote, "Painless Performance Appraisals Focus on Results, Behaviors," *HR Magazine* 43, no. 11 (October 1998): 52–58; and Peter Gwynne, "How Consistent Are Performance Review Criteria?" *MIT Sloan Management Review* 43, no. 4 (Summer 2002): 15.
12. "Appraisal Methods," Archer North & Associates, www.performance-appraisal.com/methods.htm.
13. "Employer Costs for Employee Compensation—December 2011," Bureau of Labor Statistics, U.S. Department of Labor, March 14, 2012, www.bls.gov/news.release/ecec.nr0.htm.
14. "The Keeper of That Tapping Pen," *New York Times*, March 21, 2009, http://www.nytimes.com/2009/03/22/business/22corner.html.
15. Ibid.

CHAPTER 10

1. Occupational Safety and Health Act, 29 U.S.C. § 654 (1970), Office of the Law Revision Counsel, in effect January 3, 2012, 143.231.180.80/.
2. "Carpal Tunnel Syndrome Fact Sheet," National Institutes of Health, November 2002, www.ninds.nih.gov/disorders/carpal_tunnel/detail_carpal_tunnel.htm.
3. "Carpal Tunnel Syndrome: Prevention," Mayo Clinic, February 22, 2011, www.mayoclinic.com/health/carpal-tunnel-syndrome/DS00326/DSECTION=prevention.
4. "Fact Sheet #21: Recordkeeping Requirements Under the Fair Labor Standards Act (FLSA)," U.S. Department of Labor, last revised July 2008, www.dol.gov/whd/regs/compliance/whdfs21.htm.
5. "New Hire Reporting," U.S. Department of Health and Human Services Administration for Children and Families, www.acf.hhs.gov/programs/cse/newhire/employer/private/newhire.htm.
6. "Form I-9, Employment Eligibility Verification," Department of Homeland Security, revised August 7, 2009, http://www.uscis.gov/i-9.
7. "What Is E-Verify?" U.S. Citizenship and Immigration Services, last updated September 15, 2011, www.uscis.gov/portal/site/uscis/menuitem.eb1d4c2a3e5b9ac8-9243c6a7543f6d1a/?vgnextoid=e94888e60a405110VgnVCM1000004718190aRCRD&vgnextchannel=e94888e60a405110VgnVCM1000004718190aRCRD; and "100,000 Employers Use E-Verify Program," U.S. Citizenship and Immigration Services, January 8, 2009, http://www.uscis.gov/portal/site/uscis/menuitem.5af9bb95919f35e66f614176543f6d1a/?vgnextoid=6d92c4b7e3b17210VgnVCM100000b92ca60aRCRD&vgnextchannel=de779589cdb76210VgnVCM100000b92ca60aRCRD.
8. "Who Music Theft Hurts," Recording Industry Association of America (RIAA), www.riaa.com/physicalpiracy.php?content_selector=piracy_details_online.

9. O'Ryan Johnson, "Supreme Court Won't Listen to Music Piracy Case," *Boston Herald*, May 22, 2012, news.bostonherald.com/news/regional /view/20220522supreme_court_wont_listen_to _music_piracy_case/srvc=home&position=also.
10. "Charge Statistics: FY 1997 Through FY 2011," Equal Employment Opportunity Commission, www.eeoc .gov/eeoc/statistics/enforcement/charges.cfm; and "Private Sector Bias Charges Hit All-Time High," Equal Employment Opportunity Commission, January 25, 2012, www.eeoc.gov/eeoc/newsroom /release/1-24-12a.cfm.
11. "Charge Statistics," Equal Employment Opportunity Commission.
12. "Laws Enforced by EEOC," Equal Employment Opportunity Commission, www.eeoc.gov/laws/statutes /index.cfm.
13. "Fact Sheet #28: The Family and Medical Leave Act of 1993," U.S. Department of Labor, www.dol.gov /whd/regs/compliance/whdfs28.pdf.
14. Genetic Information Nondiscrimination Act of 2008, Office of the Law Revision Counsel, in effect January 3, 2012, 143.231.180.80/; and "Frequently Asked Questions," Genetics & Public Policy Center, www.dnapolicy.org/gina/faqs.html#general6.
15. Dean A. Bredeson and Keith Goree, *Ethics in the Workplace*, 3rd ed. (Mason, OH: Cengage Learning, 2012), 103.
16. "Sexual Harassment," U.S. Equal Employment Opportunity Commission, www.eeoc.gov/laws/types /sexual_harassment.cfm.
17. Bredeson and Goree, *Ethics in the Workplace*, 106.
18. "Sexual Harassment," U.S. Equal Employment Opportunity Commission.
19. Bredeson and Goree, *Ethics in the Workplace*, 106.
20. John H. Dise, Jr., "Avoiding Liability in Employee Selection: Risk of Discrimination Lawsuits," *School and College* 33 (June 1994): 32–33; Laura M. Litvan, "Thorny Issues in Hiring," *Nation's Business*, April 1996: 34–35; Denise Dubie, "Asking the Right Questions," *Network World* 16, no. 45 (November 8, 1999): 54; John Durso, "Interviewing Techniques Must Be Proper," *McKnight's Long-Term Care News* 23 (September 13, 2002): 39; John Durso, "Legal Issues: Don't Ask These Things When Hiring," *McKnight's Long-Term Care News* 23 (October 4, 2002): 14; and George D. Fagan, "Workplace Discrimination: Be Crystal Clear on Antidiscrimination Policies and Procedures So That Managers and Employees Know Exactly Where You—and They—Stand," *Pool & Spa News* 43 (September 3, 2004): 34.
21. Jenna Wortham, "More Employers Use Social Networks to Check Out Applicants," *Bits* (blog), August 20, 2009, bits.blogs.nytimes.com/2009/08/20 /more-employers-use-social-networks-to-check-out -applicants/.
22. Bredeson and Goree, *Ethics in the Workplace*, 6, 7.
23. Richard Paul and Linda Elder, *The Miniature Guide to Understanding the Foundations of Ethical Reasoning* (Tomalas, CA: Foundation for Critical Thinking, 2006), 12.
24. LaRue Tone Hosmer, *Moral Leadership in Business* (Burr Ridge, IL: Richard D. Irwin, 1995): 39–41.
25. Ethics Resource Center, "2011 National Business Ethics Survey: Workplace Ethics in Transition," 2011, www.ethics.org/nbes/files/FinalNBES-web.pdf, 12.
26. Bredeson and Goree, *Ethics in the Workplace*, 6.
27. Reshlen, "Electronic Monitoring: The Employee's Point of View," April 11, 2010, www.macemployee -monitoring.com/?p=123.
28. "Half of American Workers Will Shop Online This Holiday Season, According to CareerBuilder 'Cyber Monday' Usage Survey," CareerBuilder, November 27, 2011, www.careerbuilder.com/share/aboutus /pressreleasesdetail.aspx?id=pr670&sd=11/28/2011 &ed=11/28/2011.
29. List compiled from a number of sources including Laura Petrecca, "More Employers Use Tech to Track Workers," *USA Today*, March 17, 2010, www .usatoday.com/money/workplace/2010-03-17-work -placeprivacy15_CV_N.htm; and Eve Tahmincioglu, "Sexting Case Raises Workplace Privacy Issues," April 27, 2010, msn.careerbuilder.com/Article/MSN-2256-Workplace-Issues-Sexting-Case-Raises-Workplace -Privacy-Issues/.
30. Laura Petrecca, "More Employers Use Tech."
31. Eve Tahmincioglu, "Sexting Case."

CHAPTER 11

1. David Sirota, Louis A. Mischkind, and Michael Irwin Meltzer, "Stop Demotivating Your Employees!" *Harvard Management Update* 11, no. 1 (January 2006): 3.
2. Ruth Mayhew, "Manager Limitations to Motivate Employees," eHow, www.ehow.com/info_8009067 _manager-limitations-motivate-employees.html.
3. Jeffrey L. Herman et al., "Motivated by the Organization's Mission or Their Career? Implications for Leaders in Turbulent Times," Center for Creative Leadership and Booz Allen Hamilton, March 2011, www.boozallen.com/media/file/Motivated_by _Mission_or_Career.pdf, 5.
4. Teresa M. Amabile and Steven J. Kramer, "The Power of Small Wins," *Harvard Business Review* 89, no. 5 (May 2001): 71–80; and Teresa M. Amabile et al., "Breakthrough Ideas for 2010," *Harvard Business Review* 88, no. 1/2 (January/February 2010): 41–57.
5. William Cottringer, "The Right Work Attitude," *Supervision* 64, no. 5 (May 2003): 6–8.

6. Ibid.
7. Ibid.
8. Daniel Gross, "Nice Work: In the Corporate Culture, A Little Kindness Won't Hurt You," *US Airways Magazine* (February 2007): 51–53.
9. Jon Reinfurt, "Back Page: Selling for Success," *Small Business Success* (2006): 443.
10. "Judith Estrin: Closing the Innovation Gap," interview by Jeff Ubois, reported in *Jeff Ubois* (blog), posted January 30, 2009, www.fondazionebassetti.org/en/ubois/2009/01/judith_estrin_closing_the_inno.html.
11. Ibid.
12. Sidney J. Parnes, "Learning Creative Behavior," *The Futurist* 18, no. 4 (August 1984): 30–31; Liz Simpson, "Fostering Creativity," *Training* 38, no. 12 (December 2001): 54–57; and Polly LaBarre, "Weird Ideas That Work," *Fast Company* 54 (January 2002): 68–73.
13. Arthur Koestler, *The Act of Creation* (London: Hutchinson, 1969), 27.
14. James L. Adams, *Conceptual Blockbusting* (San Francisco: Freeman, 1974), 35; Dean Foust, "Getting to "Aha!" *BusinessWeek*, issue 3999 (September 4, 2006): 100; and Siri Schubert, "A Duffer's Dream," *Business 2.0* 7, no. 10 (November 2006): 56.
15. Minda Zetlin, "Nurturing Nonconformists," *Management Review* 88, no. 9 (October 1999): 30; Diane L. Coutu, "Genius at Work," *Harvard Business Review* 79, no. 9 (October 2001): 63–68; Ryan Mathews and Watts Wacker, "Deviants, Inc.," *Fast Company*, no. 56 (March 2002): 70–80; and Robin Hanson, "The Myth of Creativity," *BusinessWeek*, issue 3991 (July 3, 2006): 134.
16. John Byrne, Andy Reinhart, and Robert D. Hof, "The Search for the Young and Gifted," *BusinessWeek*, issue 3649 (October 4, 1999): 108. Also see Thomas H. Davenport, Laurence Prusak, and H. James Wilson, "Who's Bringing You Hot Ideas, and How Are You Responding?" *Harvard Business Review* 81, no. 2 (February 2003): 58–64.
17. Roger van Oech, *A Whack on the Side of the Head: How You Can Be More Creative*, 25th ed. (New York: Hachette, 2008), 22.
18. Ian Wylie, "Failure is Glorious," *Fast Company*, no. 51 (October 2001): 35–38; and Jena McGregor et al., "How Failure Breeds Success," *BusinessWeek*, issue 3992 (July 10, 2006): 42–52.
19. List adapted from Roger von Oech, *A Whack on the Side of the Head* (New York: Warner Books, 1983). Reprinted with permission.
20. Lyman W. Porter and Edward E. Lawler, III, *Managerial Attitudes and Performance* (Homewood, IL: Irwin, 1968), 165.
21. "Corporate Social Responsibility: A Sirota Initiative," Sirota Survey Intelligence, June 2007, www.sirota.com/pdfs/Corporate_Social_Responsibility_June_2007.pdf, 14, 15; and "Engaging Employees Through Social Responsibility," *Leader to Leader* 46 (Fall 2007), www.sirota.com/pdfs/Engaging_Employees_through_Social_Responsibility.pdf.
22. T. L. Stanley, "Generate a Positive Corporate Culture," *Supervision* 68, no. 9 (September 2007): 5–7.
23. Sue Shellenbarger, "Indecent Exposure: The Downsides of Working in a Glass Office," *Wall Street Journal*, January 4, 2012, D1–D2.
24. See, for example, V. G. Oommen, M. Knowles, and I. Zhao, "Should Health Service Managers Embrace Open Plan Work Environments? A Review," *Asia Pacific Journal of Health Management* 3, no. 2 (2008): 37–43.
25. Andy Goldstein, "Wellness Programs Benefit Employees and Companies," National Association of State Boards of Accountancy, January 11, 2012, www.nasba.org/features/wellness-programs-benefit-employees-and-companies/.
26. David Hunnicutt and Madeline Jahn, "Making the Case for Workplace Wellness Programs," 2011, http://www.hccnetwork.org/files/MakingtheCase.pdf.
27. Ann M. Mirabito, William B. Baun, and Leonard L. Berry, "Using Workplace Wellness to Strengthen Your Sales Organization," Keller Center Research Report, September 2011, www.baylor.edu/content/services/document.php/148982.pdf; and Leonard L. Berry, Ann M. Mirabito, and Willam B. Baun, "What's the Hard Return on Employee Wellness Programs?" *Harvard Business Review* 88, no. 12 (December 2010): 104–112.
28. Chuck Williams, *MGMT*, 4th ed. (Mason, OH: Cengage Learning, 2012), 38.
29. "Legend in His Own Mind," Snopes.com, last updated May 9, 2010, http://www.snopes.com/sports/golf/innergolf.asp.
30. Zig Ziglar, *See You at the Top,* 25th anniversary ed. (Gretna, LA: Pelican, 2005), 54.

CHAPTER 12

1. Susan M. Heathfield, "How to Manage the Perfect Project," November 19, 2003, http://humanresources.about.com/b/2003/11/19/how-to-manage-the-perfect-project-2.htm.
2. For more information on planning and managing projects, see F. John Rey, "How to Manage a Project," management.about.com/od/projectmanagement/ht/ProjMgtSteps.htm, and "Be an Effective Project Manager," www.ehow.com/how_2054731_be-effective-project-manager.html.
3. For more information about Gantt charts, see "About Gantt Charts" and "Evolution of the Gantt Charts," www.ganttchart.com, KIDASA Software.

4. Timothy R. Barry, "Top Ten Qualities of a Project Manager," www.projectsmart.co.uk/top-10-qualities-project-manager.html.

CHAPTER 13

1. Information on types and levels of communication is based on training experience in customer service; effective presentations; memo, letter, and report writing; assertiveness; management development; and other training programs by Susie H. VanHuss in a wide variety of companies and industries over a number of years. While the terminology and descriptions in industry vary significantly, the concepts are aligned with those in research-based articles.
2. For additional reading on the levels and types of communication, refer to Aarti R., "Four Types of Communication," December 9, 2011, www.buzzle.com/articles/four-types-of-communication.html; "Types of Communication," 2012, www.typesofcommunication.org/communication.
3. Rao, V.S. Rama, "Socio Cultural Environment," December 12, 2010, www.citeman.com/12747-socio-cultural-environment.html. Rao, V.S. Rama, "What Effect Does Globalization Have on Managers?" November 3, 2009, www.citeman.com/7518-what-effect-does-globalization-have-on-managers.html. "Globe Frame Work in Assessing Cultures," June 10, 2007, http://www.citeman.com/1879-globe-frame-work-in-assessing-cultures.html. Rao, V.S. Rama, "Globe Project Value Dimensions," December 14, 2010, http://www.citeman.com/12794-globe-project-value-dimensions.html. For additional reading on the Globe Project, refer to *Culture, Leadership, and Organizations: The GLOBE Study of 62 Societies*, Robert J. House, editor, (Thousand Oaks, CA: Sage, 2004).
4. John Schaubroeck and Simon S. K. Lam, "How Similarity to Peers and Supervisors Influences Organizational Advancement in Different Cultures," *Academy of Management Journal* 45 (December 2002): 1120–1136.
5. Allen C. Bluedorn, Carol Felker Kaufman, and Paul M. Lane, "How Many Things Do You Like to Do at Once? An Introduction to Monochronic and Polychronic Time," *Academy of Management Executive* 6 (November 1992): 17–26; and Allen C. Bluedorn and Rhetta L. Standifer, "Time and the Temporal Imagination," *Academy of Management Learning and Education* 5 (June 2006): 196–206.
6. Alison Overholt, "The Art of Multitasking," *Fast Company*, 63 (October 2002): 118–125.
7. Gregory K. Stephens and Charles R. Greer, "Doing Business in Mexico: Understanding Cultural Differences," *Organizational Dynamics* 24 (Summer 1995): 39–55; Mike Johnson, "Untapped Latin America," *Management Review* 85 (July 1996): 31–34; and Yongsun Paik and J. H. Derick Sohn, "Confucius in Mexico: Korean MNCs and the Maquiladoras." *Business Horizons* 41 (November–December 1998): 25–33; Laura Petrecca, "Stores, Banks Go Speedy to Win Harried Customers," *USA Today*, December 1, 2006: 1B.
8. Karl Albrecht, "Lost in the Translation," *Training* 33 (June 1996): 66–70; Daniel Pianko, "Smooth Translations," *Management Review* 85 (July 1996): 20; and Rebecca Ganzel, "Universal Translator? Not Quite," *Training* 36 (April 1999): 22, 24.
9. Based on Figure 2 in Gary Bonvillian and William A. Nowlin, "Cultural Awareness: An Essential Element of Doing Business Abroad," *Business Horizons* 37 (November–December 1994): 44–50.
10. Robert H. Lengel and Richard L. Daft, "The Selection of Communication Media As an Executive Skill," *Academy of Management Executive* 2 (August 1988): 225–232; John R. Carlson and Robert W. Zmud, "Channel Expansion Theory and the Experiential Nature of Media Richness Perceptions," *Academy of Management Journal* 42 (April 1999): 153–170.
11. CNN website, http://www.cnn.com/ALLPOLITICS/1996/analysis/bios/frames/cnn/king.html?iref=allsearch.
12. Larry King, "Communicating for Success," *Get Motivated Workbook* (2006): 12–13.
13. Data from Cynthia Hamilton and Brian H. Kleiner, "Steps to Better Listening," *Personnel Journal* 66 (February 1987): 20–21. Also see Madelyn Burley-Allen, "Listen Up," *HR Magazine* 46 (November 2001): 115–120.
14. Stephen Covey, *Seven Habits of Highly Effective People* (New York: Free Press, 2004): 79.
15. Susie H. VanHuss, *Basic Letter & Memo Writing*, 5th ed. (Cincinnati: Thomson/South-Western, 2005): 21–55.
16. Ibid., 165–167.

CHAPTER 14

1. Jason Gillikin, "Subjective vs. Objective Performance Evaluations," Small Business Chron.com, http://small business.chron.com/objective-vs-subjective-performance-evaluations-4848.html.
2. "How to Help an Underachieving Employee," eHow, http://www.ehow.com/how_2058226_help-under-achieving-employee.html, February 22, 2011.
3. For additional reading, see Patricia Lotich, "Progressive Discipline – 4 Steps to Successful Employee Progressive Discipline," April 22, 2011, http://thethrivingsmallbusiness.com/articles/progressive-discipline-4-steps-to-employee-progressive-discipline; and Lisa Guerin, "What is Progressive Discipline for Employees?" http://www.nolo.com/legal-encyclopedia/employee-progressive-discipline

-basics-30242.html and "Using Progressive Discipline" NOLO Law for All, http://www.nolo.com/legal-encyclopedia/using-progressive-discipline-employees-29983.html.
4. Thomas, K. W., & Kilmann, R. H. (1974, 2007). Thomas-Kilmann Conflict Mode Instrument (Mountain View, CA: Xicom, a subsidiary of CPP, Inc.): 8–9.
5. U.S. Department of Labor, OSHA, "Workplace Violence," http://www.osha.gov/SLTC/workplaceviolence/.
6. Ibid.
7. Jimmy Sailors, "Employee Theft Costs Employers More Than Shoplifting, Organized Crime," *Dothan Eagle*, February 25, 2012.

CHAPTER 15

1. Woehler, Ashley, "Self-awareness and Career Success," http://www.careerpath360.com/index.php/self-awareness-and-career-success-15258/, July 13, 2009.
2. Hansen, Randall S. and Katharine Hansen, "Using A SWOT Analysis in your career planning," http://www.quintcareers.com/SWOT_Analysis.html.

Glossary

A

achievement-oriented leadership style a leadership style in which managers set challenging goals, emphasize excellence, and seek continuous improvement

action minutes a brief summary of a meeting that includes all items needing action, the people responsible, and the timeline

administrative management an approach to management that emphasizes managers' ability to lead and to use effective management practices in accomplishing the organization's goals

Age Discrimination in Employment Act (ADEA) a federal law that protects persons age 40 or older against age-based discrimination

agenda an outline of the topics to be discussed, the person presenting each topic, and the time allocated for each topic

applicant tracking system software used to manage the hiring process

attitude standard a set of expected employee behaviors for fostering a positive, friendly, creative, and professional corporate culture

authoritarian leader one who retains all authority and responsibility

B

behavioral interview an interview in which the interviewer provides scenarios and asks how the candidate handled such situations in the past or would handle them in the future

behavioral leadership styles patterns of leadership behavior

behaviorally anchored rating scales (BARS) an appraisal technique that uses performance rating scales divided into increments of observable and measurable job behavior

benchmarking peers comparing salary structure to that of similar companies

best practices broad standards, policies, procedures, and guides used by the most successful businesses and nonprofit organizations

Blanchard and Hersey's situational leadership model a model based on four different leadership styles or characteristics: directing, coaching, supporting, and delegating

buddy system the pairing of new hires with a mentor to help set them up for success

budget a systematic method of allocating financial, physical, and human resources to achieve strategic goals

bureaucracy the exercise of control on the basis of knowledge, expertise, or experience

business ethics socially acceptable standards of conduct in commercial and administrative settings

C

cafeteria-style benefits a range of benefits from which employees can select

child labor laws state and federal laws that limit types of work and hours for young employees

Civil Rights Act of 1991 a federal law that allows monetary damages for intentional discrimination

coach a person who guides employees with instruction, feedback, and encouragement

coaching the process of guiding employees when learning a new task, skill, or information and connecting the *how* with the *why*

communication the exchange of information

communication media the form of transmission used such as text messaging, face-to-face, email, or telephone calls

compensable factors common elements of many different jobs that merit compensation

compensation the financial and nonfinancial awards an employee receives for performing a job

compressed workweek a situation in which an employee works longer hours but fewer days

conceptual skills the ability to view the organization as a whole and to understand the relationships among its components

confidentiality the practice of keeping private documents and conversations secret

contingency plan a backup plan prepared in case a situation does not go according to the original plan

continuous improvement review (CIR) a review process that focuses on customers, the team, and the employee's contribution to system improvements

controller a person who measures quality and performance

controlling ensuring performance does not deviate from standards and meets the goals of the organization

corporate brand a logo that establishes the image and identity of a company

corporate culture the shared values, beliefs, traditions, philosophy, and character or personality of the organization

creativity/innovation the ability to generate and implement new ideas to support the organization's mission and goals

credibility the quality of being believable and worthy of trust

crisis management plan a plan that outlines steps the company should take if a crisis causes a serious threat to or disruption of business

critical incidents an appraisal technique in which specific instances of inferior and superior performance are documented when they occur

critical path mapping the tasks that impact the completion date of a project

critical thinking the use of logical thinking, reasoning, and evidence to question assumptions and evaluate ideas before determining an outcome or reaching a conclusion

cross-functional team a team consisting of employees from different functional areas of the organization

cross-training the process of learning a new skill or task that is typically the responsibility of a coworker

culture the shared values, beliefs, traditions, philosophy, and character or personality of the country or region

D

delegation the process of assigning duties and responsibilities to others

deliverables defined, measurable results or tangible things that the customer, client, or your company expects to have at the completion of the project

democratic leader one who delegates authority while retaining ultimate responsibility

directive leadership style a leadership style in which managers tell people what is expected of them and provide specific guidance, schedules, rules, regulations, and standards

diversity a wide range of individual characteristics

downward communication information shared by a manager to a subordinate

E

effectiveness producing quality results in a timely fashion

efficiency doing a task the most productive way

emotional intelligence the ability to manage feelings so they are expressed appropriately and effectively, enabling people to work together smoothly toward common goals

employee assistance programs (EAPs) company-paid services to assist employees with personal problems including substance abuse

employee benefits non-salary compensation such as health, life, and disability insurance; vacation and personal leave; and employee stock option and retirement plans

employee development a continuous process designed to improve an employee's skills, ability, and knowledge

employee turnover the process of employees' leaving a company voluntarily or because they were asked to leave

employment at will an employer can terminate an employee at any time without explanation or cause

empowerment the process of making employees full partners in decision making and giving them the necessary tools and rewards

entrepreneurial venture a new or emerging start-up business

Equal Pay Act (EPA) a federal law that requires employers to pay male and female employees equal pay for comparable work

E-Verify an Internet-based system for confirming employment eligibility

executives the senior leadership team that takes the lead in casting the organization's vision and strategic mission

exempt employees employees who receive a salary

external communication communication with individuals or groups who are not employees of your organization

external recruiting posting or advertising a job with sources outside the organization

extrinsic rewards payoffs granted to an employee by other people

F

Fair Labor Standards Act (FLSA) a federal law that establishes minimum wage, overtime pay, record keeping, and child labor standards

Family Medical Leave Act (FMLA) a federal law that requires employers to grant employees up to 12 workweeks of unpaid leave

Fiedler's contingency theory a model based on the notion that a leader's performance depends on the likelihood that he or she can successfully accomplish the job and the leader's basic motivation

first-line management the operational team that manages day-to-day operations and ensures goals and objectives are achieved

flextime the practice of allowing an employee to work a modified schedule

forced ranking system an appraisal method that compares or ranks coworkers in a work group in head-to-head fashion according to specified accomplishments or job behavior

formal communication communication that has a defined structure or format, uses proper language, and meets specific standards

G

Genetic Information Nondiscrimination Act (GINA) a federal law that prohibits discrimination based on certain types of genetic information

goal a specific commitment to achieve a measurable result within a given time frame

grapevine gossip, rumors, and unverified or unannounced information about the organization or various employees

H

high-performance team a team that consistently outperforms competent individuals in the organization

horizontal communication information shared among peers

horizontal specialization the various divisions of labor across an organization

hostile work environment a type of harassment in which supervisors or coworkers use embarrassment, humiliation, or fear to create a negative environment that interferes with the ability of others to perform their jobs

I

individualized rewards rewards given to individuals to recognize goal attainment unique to the employee

informal communication casual or relaxed communication

intellectual property (IP) original or unique items that people create using their imagination and brain power

internal communication communication with employees of your organization

internal recruiting posting or advertising a job within the organization and encouraging qualified employees to apply for it

intrinsic rewards self-granted and internally experienced payoffs

J

jargon informal terminology unique to a business or industry, often not understood by new employees, customers, and other people outside the organization

job analysis the process of identifying the task and skill requirements for a specific job, determined by studying superior performers in related jobs

job description a document that outlines expectations, tasks, responsibilities, education, and skill requirements for a specific job

job evaluation the process used to determine the worth of a job

job shadowing learning about a job and the organization through real-time, firsthand observation of an experienced coworker

job sharing an arrangement in which two professionals form a partnership to perform one job

job specification a written summary of the qualifications needed to successfully perform a particular job

L

laissez-faire leader one who grants responsibility and authority to a group of individuals, who are told to work problems out themselves

leader one who sets the tone for the organization, creates the vision, and inspires other to achieve

leadership the process of inspiring, influencing, directing, and guiding others to participate in a common effort

leading inspiring and motivating others to achieve organizational goals

learning-centered training training that focuses on the individual's specific needs

level of pay salary at market, higher than market, or lower than market rate

M

management the process of leading and working with people to accomplish organizational goals and objectives using available resources efficiently and effectively

management by objectives (MBO) an appraisal method in which performance is evaluated in terms of formal goals or objectives

management functions general administrative duties that need to be carried out in virtually all productive organizations

mass communication communication directed to the general public

media richness the effectiveness of a given medium in conveying information and promoting learning

middle management the management team that translates strategies into operational plans and oversees first-line management

mission a formal statement of the core purpose of an organization that defines its objectives and focus

monochronic time the perception that time is divided into standard units

motion study the process of breaking each task or job into separate motions and then eliminating those that are unnecessary or repetitive

motivation an employee's desire or drive to achieve

motivator a person who inspires people to perform at their best and achieve a common goal

N

new hire report a report required by federal law to assist in enforcing child support obligations

nonexempt employees employees who receive an hourly wage

nonverbal communication facial expressions, eye contact, gestures, posture, proximity or closeness to others, and tone or quality of voice

O

objective performance measures measures based on quantifiable data

obstacles challenges that hinder an employee's ability to do the job effectively

Occupational Safety and Health Act (OSHA or OSH Act) a federal law that requires employers to provide a safe working environment

off-shoring the outsourcing of business activities and processes to foreign countries

onboarding proper handling of a new employee's first 90 days

operational plan a plan specifying how the work will be done to accomplish a work unit's objectives over a 30-day to six-month period

oral communication conversations, discussions, or presentations

organization Any type of business (small, large, entrepreneurial, or professional), nonprofit entity, or governmental office

organization chart a diagram of an organization's official positions and formal lines of authority

organizing creating the structure of an organization

orientation an opportunity to introduce and welcome a new hire and begin the transition from new employee to contributing team member

outsourcing the use of outside organizations to complete work that was previously done internally

P

panel interview a type of interview in which two or more people interview a candidate at the same time

participative leadership style a leadership style in which managers consult with employees to seek their suggestions and then seriously consider those suggestions when making decisions

path-goal theory a model that suggests leaders motivate their followers by providing clear goals and meaningful incentives for reaching them

pay structure all jobs at the various levels within an organization and total pay, including salaries, bonuses, equity, and benefits

pay variability types of compensation and the amount of fixed versus variable compensation

performance appraisal the process of evaluating individual job performance as a basis for personnel decisions

performance measures measures that determine how an employee's performance will be evaluated

plan a goal and one or more action statements

planner a person who evaluates goals, objectives, and future needs to prepare plans that provide the necessary resources and action items to achieve success

planning the process of determining the mission and goals of an organization and specifying what it will take to achieve the goals

polychronic time the perception that time is flexible, elastic, and multidimensional

positive work environment an environment in which satisfied employees achieve organizational goals with less turnover and absenteeism

Pregnancy and Discrimination Act a federal law that makes it illegal to discriminate against a woman because of pregnancy, childbirth, or a related medical condition

progressive discipline a graduated process of disciplinary action leading toward termination

project a defined set of tasks with specific outcomes that form a unit of work to be completed in a specified timeframe with specified resources

project ground rules the behavior expected of each member as the members interact as a team

project scope the objectives, everything that is included, everything that is specifically excluded, and the outcomes that must be produced

project team a team that works on a specific project until it is completed

Q

qualitative measures measures focusing on the level of excellence of a product or service

quantitative measures measures focusing on productivity or results that can be counted or measured

quid pro quo a type of harassment in which sexual demands are directly tied to a person's keeping his or her job or receiving a promotion or another job benefit

R

realistic job preview information or experience on what a job really involves on a day-to-day basis

recruiter one who assists in identifying potential job candidates

recruitment efforts by an organization to find and hire qualified employees

resonance the moment when an employee learns or realizes something

resources things needed to get the job done successfully

retention efforts by an organization to keep employees; the opposite of turnover

risk the possibility of loss, damage, or adverse results

S

scheduler a person who prepares the schedule to ensure proper staffing and resources are available to meet production or customer needs

scientific management an approach to management that emphasizes scientifically determined jobs and management practices as the way to improve efficiency and labor productivity

self-assessment tools tests, questionnaires, inventories, surveys, or other instruments designed to measure aspects of personality, motivation, or competence

self-awareness knowing your own strengths and weaknesses, and your impact on others

self-fulfilling prophecy the belief that if you think you can do something, you are very likely to do it. If you do not think you can do it, you are not likely to do it.

servant leadership ethical leadership that focuses on employees and meeting their needs first rather than the organization's needs

sexual harassment unwanted sexual conduct directed at a job applicant or employee because of that person's sex

situational leadership the concept that successful leadership occurs when the leader's style matches the situation

soft skills skills that relate to how you interact and work with others

staffing the process of recruiting, selecting, hiring, orienting, training, and retaining employees

stakeholder anyone who has a vested interest in the success of an organization

standard of ethics social expectations of people's moral behavior

standard of law rules of behavior imposed on people by governments

standard operating procedures guides that specify the way an organization wants its employees to do their jobs

strategic plan a document that specifies the overall direction, long-term goals, and decision-making process for resource allocation and describes how the organization will position itself to achieve its goals

subjective performance measures measures based primarily on perception and judgment

supervisor an individual who typically has the authority to hire, direct, promote, discharge, assign, reward, or discipline other employees

supportive leadership style a leadership style in which managers treat employees as equals in a friendly manner while striving to improve their well-being

SWOT analysis a tool for analyzing strengths, weaknesses, opportunities, and threats

synergy the idea that the whole exceeds the sum of the parts; the increased effectiveness that results from combined action or cooperation

system a set of parts that work together to accomplish a common purpose or goal

systems management theory an approach to management that focuses on managing all parts of a system to ensure that they are working together and that synergies occur

T

tactical plan a plan that specifies how the company will use resources, budgets, and people over the next six months to two years to accomplish specific goals within its mission

team a small group of people with complementary skills committed to a common purpose and specific performance goals

team rewards identical rewards given to team members to recognize team-based goal achievement

technical skills the knowledge, expertise, and ability required to do the job

technology-enhanced communication communication through technological options such as media sites, telepresence, webinars, websites, blogs, and webcasts

telepresence using technology to make people in remote environments feel as though they were all present in the same location

teleworkers employees who work from home or another remote location

termination the involuntary release of an employee

360-degree review an appraisal technique in which a supervisor is evaluated by his or her boss, peers, and subordinates

time management the process of identifying what needs to be done and having a plan to accomplish it within the time allotted

Titles I and V of the Americans with Disabilities Act of 1990 (ADA) federal laws that prohibit discrimination against qualified individuals with mental or physical disabilities who can perform the essential functions of a job

Title VII of the Civil Rights Act of 1964 a federal law that prohibits employment discrimination based on race, color, religion, sex, or national origin

trainer a person who teaches employees and coworkers new information and skills

training the use of guided experiences to change employee behavior or attitudes

trait theory a leadership theory that contends effective leaders have similar personality or behavioral characteristics that ineffective leaders lack

transformational change change that affects an entire organization

transformational leadership leadership that inspires followers to share a vision, motivates and empowers them to achieve the vision, and provides coaching and support to develop their potential

trust a belief in the integrity, character, or ability of others

U

upward communication information shared by a subordinate to a manager

V

values the core beliefs of the organization and the principles that guide behavior

vertical hierarchy chain of command

virtual team a team of employees who use electronic technology for their primary interactions

vision the future direction of the organization; what it wants to become

W

weighted checklist an appraisal method in which evaluators check appropriate adjectives or behavioral descriptions with predetermined weights

whistle blowing an employee's reporting of corporate fraud or other illegal and unethical behavior

work ethic the willingness and ability to get things done effectively and efficiently

work group two or more employees who work together to complete a task or achieve a common goal

workplace violence threats, verbal abuse, and physical abuse

written communication reading and writing paper-based documents and documents transmitted electronically including email

Index

D

E

F

O

P

W

Z